ANDREA PALLADIO
The Four Books of Architecture

ANDREA PALLADIO
The Four Books of Architecture

with a new introduction by
ADOLF K. PLACZEK
Avery Library, Columbia University

Dover Publications, Inc., New York

Published in Canada by General Publishing Company, Ltd.
30 Lesmill Road, Don Mills, Toronto, Ontario

Published in the United Kingdom by Constable and Company, Ltd.
10 Orange Street, London, WC2H 7EG.

This Dover edition, first published in 1965, is an unabridged and unaltered republication of the work originally published by Isaac Ware in 1738, to which has been added a new Introduction written especially for this edition by Adolf K. Placzek.

DOVER *Pictorial Archive* SERIES

This book belongs to the Dover Pictorial Archive Series. You may use the designs and illustrations for graphics and crafts applications, free and without special permission, provided that you include no more than ten in the same publication or project. (For permission for additional use, please write to Dover Publications, Inc., 31 East 2nd Street, Mineola, N.Y. 11501.)

However, republication or reproduction of any illustration by any other graphic service whether it be in a book or in any other design resource is strictly prohibited.

International Standard Book Number: 0-486-21308-0
Library of Congress Catalog Card Number: 64-18862

Manufactured in the United States of America

DOVER PUBLICATIONS, INC.
31 East 2nd Street
Mineola, N.Y. 11501

Introduction to Dover Edition

It can be safely said that Andrea Palladio ranks not only among the most famous, but also among the most influential architects of all time. However, when we turn to his life and to his person, we find that very little of either the man or of his life is known. He was born in Padua in 1508, of humble family, but grew up in Vicenza. He was originally trained as a sculptor (a not unusual thing for Renaissance architects) and as a stone mason. In Count Giangiorgio Trissino he found a generous patron, who took him to Rome in 1541. It was there that his eyes were opened to the full glory of classic architecture and that he turned to the study of ancient buildings. He traveled widely in Italy, but—with the possible exception of Nîmes—never outside. He returned to Rome several times, but he did not become connected with the greatest architectural task of his age, the rebuilding of Saint Peter's. Most of his life he spent in Vicenza, where he died in 1580. Palladio was a superb architect, but he was not an innovator like Brunelleschi or Michelangelo. He built churches, town and country houses, public buildings and bridges in Venice and on the Venetian mainland and in and around Vicenza. Many of these buildings were built of cheap material (brick faced with stucco instead of stone for which the designs would have called) and are therefore now in rather poor condition. Among his main works are the churches of S. Giorgio Maggiore and of Il Redentore in Venice, the Villa Capra near Vicenza, the Palazzi Valmarana, Chiericati and Thiene, and the exterior of the Basilica (Town Hall), all in Vicenza. His last great work was the Teatro Olimpico in Vicenza, which his pupil Vincenzo Scamozzi finished after his death. It contains a permanent stage built in perspective—a most remarkable creation.

The question immediately arises: why this enormous fame and influence? For it was not only his buildings that were imitated again and again, both in their pure plans and elevations and in their details; also his writings, above all the *Four Books of Architecture*, have had the most profound and widespread impact. This book has been translated into every major European language, issued and reissued time after time and has remained a basic book for every architectural library. Why this fame and influence? The answer, in all likelihood, lies in the fact that Andrea Palladio was more than an interpreter of a particular style or a skillful publicist for his own works; that he was— and remains—the spokesman for the belief in valid rules, in immutable canons, for the belief that there is a correct, a right way to design. One can go even further and call him a spokesman for absolute standards. He is the only architect after whom an architectural idiom is named: Palladianism. Nobody speaks of Brunelleschism, Bramantism, or, in more recent examples, of Wright-ism or Le Corbusier-ism. "Miesian" would be a possible term, and in a way for the same reason—because of the striving for a perfect, a valid form inherent in it. In this sense, Mies van der Rohe himself could be labeled a Neo-Palladian.

Palladianism is the conviction, first of all, that a universally applicable vocabulary of architectural forms is both desirable and possible; secondly, that such a vocabulary had been developed by the ancient Romans (Palladio's knowledge of Greek architecture was scant), and thirdly, that a careful study and judicious use of these forms will result in Beauty. This Beauty, according to the Palladians, is therefore not only derived from ideal forms and their harmony; it is also rooted in historical correctness; and it includes the most practical, reasonable solution of the specific problem on hand.   Much of Palladio's thought is based on Leon Battista Alberti's *De Re Aedificatoria*, the first of the great architectural treatises of the Renaissance (published in 1485), but even more closely on the writings of a Roman architect of the Augustan age, Vitruvius, which were issued in print for the first time in 1486.   This is the only architectural book preserved from the Roman and Greek world, and was, as such, for Palladio and his contemporaries the authoritative voice of Antiquity. Of course Palladio was deeply impressed by the Roman remains themselves.   He studied them thoroughly and even published the first scholarly guide book to classical Rome (*Le Antichità di Roma*, 1554), a little volume much used in the next two centuries.

Palladio's main work, however, and the one on which much of his fame and of the durability of Palladianism rests, is *I Quattro Libri dell' Architettura*, as the *Four Books of Architecture* are called in the original.   It was first published in Venice in 1570, and proved immediately to be a book of the greatest importance.   A second edition followed in 1581, a year after the author's death, another in 1601, and so on in remarkable succession.   The effect of this book on the major European countries—France, the Netherlands and Germany above all—where the Renaissance developed more slowly, was equally profound.   In England it was the great Inigo Jones (1573–1652) who first imported Palladianism.   During his visit to Italy in 1614 he not only acquired a number of original drawings by Palladio from the latter's pupil Scamozzi, but also a copy of the *Quattro Libri*, which he studied most carefully and richly annotated.   This annotated copy is preserved at Worcester College, Oxford, and it can be called a book in which literally two civilizations meet.   The Banqueting House at Whitehall (1619–1622), the Queen's House in Greenwich (1616–1635) and other buildings are the result of this meeting; with them the Italian High Renaissance finally reached England.

The first complete English translation of *I Quattro Libri* was not published until 1715, by an enterprising Venetian architect, Giacomo Leoni, who had settled in London.   In the following years Palladianism became the ruling style in England.   The hegemony of one style or taste at a given time is of course the result of concurring factors; but if a single individual can be credited (or blamed, as the position may be), then Richard Boyle, third Earl of Burlington (1695–1753) is the man to whom England owes the long rule of strict Palladianism in the eighteenth century—and, more indirectly, America its own brand of the same style.   An art patron of vast influence and wealth, he was also an architect in his own right, and a precise and demanding scholar.   The engravings in Leoni's edition of Palladio had not been faithful to the original: there had been decorative embellishments in the Baroque spirit, additions, and even misinterpretations of the original design intent.   This, most probably on Burlington's suggestion, was to be remedied by a faithful and accurate reproduction of the original plates, and an exact translation of the text.   The man to accomplish this was Isaac Ware (birthdate unknown, d. 1766), who was himself an architectural writer, a fairly prominent architect of his day, and a follower of Burlington.   The edition came out in 1738 and can certainly be considered a successful accomplishment.   Indeed the accuracy of the reproductions is amazing.   In spite of this, it has remained the less accessible of the two variants, partly because Leoni was first on the scene, was more ambitious in his publishing ventures and persisted through two more English editions.   In fact, Ware's faithful edition became somewhat of a rarity; and it is for this reason, too, that the present reissue is of the greatest value.   It will make a work available to the general public which has long been elusive and inaccessible, yet can still be considered essential to the study of architectural forms.   And while the short and factual text is obviously of less importance than the plates, the good English translation deserves a special mention.   To those who do not read Italian, it will convey something of the clarity and restraint of Palladio's own style, besides containing the necessary key to the structures and forms he chose to illustrate.

The work, as is evident from the title, is divided into four parts ("books"):

The *First Book* is concerned with building materials, building techniques, and most of all with that great preoccupation of the Renaissance architect, the five orders of architecture (Tuscan, Doric, Ionic, Corinthian, Composite), as they are expressed in columns, pilasters and the architraves resting on them.   Palladio then turns briefly to the other parts of a classic building (stairs, chimneys, roofs, etc.).

The *Second Book* treats of private houses on a grand scale.   Apart from a few Roman reconstructions, this book shows Palladio's own designs—the many villas on the Venetian mainland and in and around Vicenza, among them the most famous of all, the Villa Capra ("La Rotonda" as it is sometimes called; plate 13).

The *Third Book* deals with streets, piazzas, bridges and basilicas (a basilica was originally not a religious building, but a Roman hall of justice).   Again, Palladio reproduces Roman works, including a reconstruction of Julius Caesar's Rhine bridge, and then turns to his own designs. Plate 19 shows the famous arcades of the Basilica in Vicenza, from which the much imitated "Palladian motif" derives.

The *Fourth Book* deals with Roman temples; particularly noteworthy are the beautiful drawings of the Pantheon (plates 51–60). Plates 44–45 show Bramante's Tempietto in S. Pietro Montorio. This is the only building in the book which is not either by Palladio himself or of Roman origin. The remarks on p. 97 (chapter XVII) throw a bright light on Palladio's position towards his Renaissance precursors and contemporaries.

A modern biography of Palladio in English is still lacking. For the most illuminating analysis of Palladio's design ideas, particularly his use of mathematical proportions, the reader is referred to *Architectural Principles in the Age of Humanism* (3rd rev. ed., 1962) by Rudolf Wittkower, to whom we are indebted for much of our present knowledge of sixteenth-century as well as eighteenth-century Palladianism.

1964

ADOLF K. PLACZEK
Avery Library
Columbia University

REGINA VIRTUS

THE FOUR BOOKS
OF
ANDREA PALLADIO's
ARCHITECTURE:
WHEREIN,
After a ſhort Treatiſe of the Five ORDERS,
Thoſe Obſervations that are moſt neceſſary in
BUILDING,
PRIVATE HOUSES, STREETS, BRIDGES, PIAZZAS,
XISTI, and TEMPLES are treated of.

LONDON,
Publiſhed by
ISAAC WARE,
Anno MDCCXXXVIII.

To the Right Honourable

R I C H A R D

Earl of Burlington, &c.

My Lord,

 OUR giving me free accefs to Your ftudy, wherein many of the original drawings of PALLADIO, befides thofe which compofe this work, are preferved, and taking upon You the trouble of revifing the tranflation, and correcting it with Your own hands, are fuch inftances of Your love to arts, and of Your friendfhip to me, that I cannot too publickly return YOUR LORDSHIP thanks for favours that furpafs all acknowledgment.

YOUR LORDSHIP need not be informed of what importance it is to fuch who make architecture their ftudy to have the works of our excellent author put into their hands truly genuine. Nor can I doubt but this performance will be acceptable to the publick, fince it has had the good fortune to meet with YOUR LORDSHIP's approbation: To obtain which, will always be the chief ambition of

YOUR LORDSHIP's

Moft Obedient Humble Servant,

Ifaac Ware.

THE
NAMES
OF THE
SUBSCRIBERS.

A

RIGHT Honourable the Earl of Albemarle.
    Honourable Richard Arundell, *Esq;*
Richard Aymor, *Esq;*
John Aisleby, *Esq;*
William Prichard Ashurst, *Esq;*
John Armstrong, *Esq;*
William Archer, *Esq;*
Mr. William Armstrong.
Mr. Nathanael Adams.
Mr. Thomas Allison.
Mr. John Andrews.

B

Right Honourable the Earl of Burlington.
Right Honourable Lord Viscount Boyne.
Sir Henry Bedingfield.
Honourable Benjamin Bathurst, *Esq;*
Hugh Bethel, *Esq;*
William Burton, *Esq;*
George Bowes, *Esq;*
Edmund Brampston, *Esq;*
William Bristow, *Esq;*
Thomas Bryan, *Esq;*
———— Bateman, *Esq;*
Richard Barlow, *Esq;*
The Reverend Dr. Bland, *Dean of* Durham.
Mr. William Blakesley.
Mr. John Barnard.
Mr. ——— Burrat.
Mr. Matthew Brettingham.
Mr. John Bosson.
Mr. John Barlow.
Mr. Edward Baylis.
Mr. Holden Bowker.
Mr. Edward Bilcliffe.
Mr. Samuel Breach.
Mr. John Burrough.
Mr. William Bates.
Mr. Robert Brown.

C

Right Honourable the Earl of Carlisle.
Right Honourable the Earl of Cardigan.
Right Honourable the Earl of Chesterfield.
Right Honourable Earl Cowper.
Right Honourable Earl Cholmondeley
Right Honourable Lord Cornwallis.
Right Honourable Lord Chewton
Sir Thomas Chudley, *Bart.*
Sir Robert Corbet, *Bart.*
Thomas Cowslad, *Esq;*
Anthony Chute, *Esq;*
———— Coke, *Esq;*
John Campbell, *Esq;*
Richard Chandler, *Esq.*
Richard Cliffe, *Esq;*
James Caltorpe, *Esq;*
Martin Clare, *M. A. and F. R. S.*
Mrs. Chandler.
Mr. Cavendish.
Mr. Thomas Carter.
Mr. Abraham Curtis.
Mr. Charles Carne
Mr. John Collyer.
Mr. ———Cushnie.
Mr. George Chamberlaine.
Mr. Charles Clay.
Mr. Thomas Clark.

D

Right Honourable Earl of Derby.
Right Honourable Earl of Dysert.
Right Honourable Sir Conyers Darcy.
Honourable General James Dormer.
Mr. George Devall.
Mr. John Davis.
Mr. William Davis.
Mr. George Dalby.

The SUBSCRIBERS Names.

E

Sir John Evelyn, *Bart.*
Honourable Richard Edgcumbe, *Efq;*
Robert Eyre, *Efq;*
James Eckerfall, *Efq;*
Mr. George Evans.
Mr. ------- Eifler.
Mr. Thomas Elkins.
Mr. Thomas Edwards.
Mr. Richard Edwards.

F

Right Honourable the Earl Fitzwilliams.
Right Honourable the Lord Vifcount Fau-
    conberg.
Honourable Sir Thomas Frankland.
Honourable Sir Andrew Fountaine.
Honourable Henry Fox, *Efq;*
Charles Fleetwood, *Efq;*
Mr. Henry Flitcroft.
Mr. Thomas Fuller.
Mr. Elias Ferris.
Mr. Richard Ford.
Mr. Edward Fitzwater.
Mr. Devereux Fox.
Mr. Richard Fortnam.
Mr. John Ford.

G

Right Honourable Lord Vifcount Gallway.
Sir John Goodrick.
Philips Glower, *Efq;*
Roger Gale, *Efq;*
George Gray, *Efq;*
Weftby Gill, *Efq;*
Mr. John Goodchild.
Mr. Robert Goodchild.
Mr. William Gray.
Mr. Thomas Gray.
Mr. Edward Gray.
Mr. James Gume.
Mr. Thomas Gladwin.
Mr. ------ Gough.
Mr. John Green.

H

Right Honourable Lord Harrington.
Honourable Charles Hamilton, *Efq;*
Hugh Howard, *Efq;*
Edward Hody, *M. D. and F. R. S.*
Benjamin Hays, *Efq;*
Mr. William Hogarth.
Mr. Francis Hayman.
Mr. Thomas Howlet.
Mr. Thomas Heath.
Mr. -------- Hundefhagen.
Mr. John Hooper.
Mr. Francis Hilliard.

Mr. Jofeph Hutchinfon.
Mr. James Holmes.
Mr. ------- Hawkins.
Mr. John Harriffon.

I

Charles Jervies, *Efq;*
------- Jefferys, *Efq;*
Mr. Henry Joynes.
Mr. Andrews Jelfe.
Mr. John Jenner.
Mr. Samuel Johnfon.
Mr. William Jones.
Mr. ------- Jolife.

K

Right Honourable the Lord Killmurry.
Ralph Knight, *Efq;*
William Kent, *Efq;*
Mr. Thomas Kenyfton.
Mr. Thomas Kincy.

L

Sir Henry Lyddell, *Bart.*
Sir William Leman, *Bart.*
Matthew Lamb, *Efq;*
Robert Long, *Efq;*
Mr. John Lane.
Mr. George Lucas.
Mr. Richard Lawrence.
Mr. Luke Lightfoot.

M

His Grace the Duke of Montagu.
Right Honourable Earl Macclesfield.
Right Honourable Earl Malton.
Charles Mordaunt, *Efq;*
George Medcalfe, *Efq;*
William Manley, *Efq;*
Bacon Maurice, *Efq;*
Peter Mainwaring, *M. D.*
Governour Morris.
Mr. Henry Mills.
Mr. Roger Morris.
Mr. Galfrydus Mann.
Mr. Richard Marfh.
Mr. Thomas Malie.
Mr. George Mercer.
Mr. John Mayhew.
Mr. John Marfden.
Mr. George Murry.
Mr. John Millan.

N

His Grace the Duke of Norfolk.
Sir Roger Nudigate.

Mr.

The SUBSCRIBERS Names.

Mr. Joseph Norton.
Mr. ------- Nivelon.

O

Right Honourable the Earl of Orrery.
Right Honourable Arthur Onslow, *Esq;*
Sir Danvers Osborne.
William Osbaldeston, *Esq;*
Mr. Richard Osterfield.

P

Right Honourable the Earl of Pembroke.
Honourable Henry Pelham, *Esq;*
Thomas Prowse, *Esq;*
Thomas Pullien, *Esq;*
John Pollen, *Esq;*
Mr. Leonard Phillipps.
Mr. John Phillips.
Mr. Thomas Phillips.
Mr. Joseph Pattison.
Mr. Robert Pollard.
Mr. Pickford.
Mr. John Pine.

Q

His Grace the Duke of Queensberry.
Sir William St. Quintin, *Bart.*

R

Honourable Sir Thomas Robinson, *Bart.*
Thomas Ripley, *Esq;*
Thomas Robinson, *Esq;*
John Rivett, *Esq;*
Mathew Ridley, *Esq;*
Daniel Rich, *Esq;*
Mr. Alexander Rouchead.
Mr. James Richards.
Mr. William Robinson.
Mr. William Reading.
Mr. Thomas Reeves.

S

Right Honourable the Earl of Scarborough.
Right Honourable Earl Stanhope.
Honourable Sir Hugh Smithson, *Bart.*
Honourable Sir Miles Stapylton, *Bart.*
Honourable Sir William Stanhope.
John Stanhope, *Esq;*
Richard Shuttleworth, *Esq;*
Samuel Sandys, *Esq;*
Thomas Boothby Skrymsher, *Esq;*
Henry Streatfield, *Esq;*
John Strowbridge, *Esq;*
Edward Shepard, *Esq;*
Colonel ------- Steward.
Colonel ------- Skelton.
William Saunders, *M. D.*
Mr. John Simmonds.
Mr. Samuel Smith.

Mr. John Saunderson.
Mr. Joseph Saunderson.
Mr. James Simmons.
Mr. John Spinnage.
Mr. Henry Stenton.
Mr. Richard Stenton.
Mr. Jonathan Sisson.
Mr. Thomas Shirley.
Mr. ------- Skemaker.
Mr. ------- Strawne.

T

Right Honourable the Lord Viscount Town-
shend.
Right Honourable Lord Torrington.
Right Honourable Lord Talbot.
George Tash, *Esq;*
Stephen Thompson, *Esq;*
John Thornhill, *Esq;*
Mr. Thomas Townshend.
Mr. Kellom Tomlinson.
Mr. Richard Trowbridge.
Mr. William Thompson.
Mr. James Terry.
Mr. Richard Twist,

V

Honourable Henry Vane, *Esq;*
William Vaughan, *Esq;*
James Vernon, *Esq;*
George Venables Vernon, *Esq;*
Mr. Umplebee.
Mr. John Vardy.

W

Lord Viscount Windsor.
Right Honourable Sir Robert Walpole.
Sir Marmaduke Wyvil, *Bart.*
Honourable Thomas Walker, *Esq;*
Honourable Edward Walpole, *Esq;*
Captain William Wickham.
Mr. ------ Wills.
Mr. James Wilkie.
Mr. John Wood.
Mr. Robert West.
Mr. Stephen Wright.
Mr. Fryer Walker.
Mr. Thomas Wagg.
Mr. Henry Wynn.
Mr. Samuel Watson.
Mr. Westfield Webb.
Mr. George Warren.
Mr. George Weston.
Mr. John Wilton.
Mr. Thomas Weston.
Mr. Thomas Webb.
Mr. Charles Wale.
Mr. Thomas Woodroffe.
Mr. William Winarles.
Mr. ------- Williams.

REFERENCES to such Places of the AUTHOR, where his Terms of Art are by himself best explained, alphabetically disposed.

A

ABACO, page 14. plate 10.
Aeroteria, p. 93. pl. 30.
Alato a torno, v. Peripteros.
Amphiprostilos, pl. 83.
Anti, p. 45.
Antis, p. 82.
Annelli, Annulets, or Gradetti, p. 18. pl. 15.
Architrave, p. 15. pl. 11. and p. 18. pl. 15.
Areostilos, p. 84.
Astragal, or Tondino, p. 14. pl. 10.
Atrio, or Porch, p. 42. pl. 18.

B

Base, p. 17. pl. 14.
Basilica, p. 73. pl. 13. and p. 75. pl. 17.
Bastoncino, p. 93.
Bastone, or Torus, p. 14. pl. 10.
Benda, or Tenia, p. 18. pl. 15.
Bronze, bellmetal, pl. 5.

C

Campana, the body of the Corinthian capital.
Cancellarie, libraries, p. 44 and 45. pl. 29.
Cartelli, or Cartocci, a kind of scroll, p. 26.
Cavetto, p. 15. pl. 11.
Cauriola, p. 88. pl. 10.
Caulicola, stem of the leaf in the Corinthian capital.
Cimacio of capital, p. 15. pl. 11.
Cimacia of pedestal, p. 17. p. 14.
Cima recta, or Gola diritta, p. 15. pl. 11.
Cima or Gola reversa, p. 18. pl. 15.
Cimbia, Fillet, or Cincture, p. 14. pl. 10.
Ciziceni, p. 45. pl. 29.
Colonelli, p. 63. pl. 3.
Collarino, p. 14. pl. 10.
Correnti, p. 67. pl. 6.
Corridors, balconies, p. 40. pl. 7.
Cortile, little court, p. 44. p. 24.
Corona, or Gocciolatoio, the drip, p. 15. pl. 11.
Curia, p. 73. pl. 30.

D

Dado, the dye of a pedestal, p. 17. pl. 14.
Dentelli, or Dentels, p. 22. pl. 24.
Diastilos, p. 84.
Dipteros, double winged with columns, p. 83.

E

Eustilos, columns placed at reasonable and convenient intervals, p. 84.

F

Fascia, p. 18. pl. 15.
Fluting or Flutes, the chanellings of a column.

Fregio or Frize, p. 15. pl. 11.
Fusarolo, p. 24.
Fust, shaft of a column.

G

Goccie, p. 18. pl. 15.
Gocciolatoio, or Corona, p. 15. pl. 11. and p. 18. pl. 15.
Gola diritta, or Cima recta, p. 15. pl. 11.
Gola, or Cima reversa, p. 18. pl. 15.
Gradetto, Gradetti, or Annuli, p. 18. pl. 15.
Gronda, or Drip, p. 14.
Guttæ, or Drops, p. 18.

I.

Imposts, p. 17. pl. 14.
Intaglia's, carved ornaments of the frize and architrave.
Intavolato, or Cima, or Gola reversa, p. 22.
Intercolumniation, the space between columns.

L

Listello, fillet.
Loggia, or Vestibulo, p. 27. and p. 42. pl. 18.

M

Metopa, p. 18. pl. 15.
Mezato, a half story, p. 40. pl. 8.
Modeno, p. 70. pl. 8.
Modiglion, p. 20. pl. 20.
Module, p. 13.
Mutule, p. 29.

O

Oeci, small halls, p. 43, 44.
Orlo, Zocco, or Plinth, p. 14. pl. 10.
Ovolo, p. 14. pl. 10.

P

Palestra, p. 77. pl. 21.
Pedestal, p. 14. pl. 10.
Peridromis, p. 21.
Peripteros, winged round with columns, p. 83.
Peristilio, p. 44. pl. 23.
Picnostilos, thick of columns, p. 83.
Piano, p. 32. pl. 30.
Plinth, Orlo, or Zocco, p. 17. pl. 14.
Poggio, or Pedestal, p. 42.
Portico, p. 42. pl. 18.
Profile, side view.
Prostilos, fronted with columns, p. 21.
Pseudodipteros, false-winged round with columns, p. 83.

R

Regolo, or Orlo, p. 31.
Remenati, p. 84.

b   Reticula,

EXPLANATORY INDEX.

++++++++++++:+++

ERRATA.

Beſides a few literal Miſtakes, the Reader will be pleaſed to take notice of the following :

Page 14. line 14. read *beſides the being.* P. 15. l. 11. r. *Gocciolatoio.* P. 19. l. 10. r. *Euſtilos.* Ibid. l. 17. r. *fourth and an eigth.* P. 21. l. 6. r. *nine modules and an half.* Ibid. l. 21. r. *Siſtilos.* P. 24. l. 10. r. *Picnoſtilos.* P. 25. l. 45. r. *thinner at the top.* P. 32. l. 10. r. *two parts in three.* P. 52. l. ult. r. *delight.* Every where read *mezato* and *mezati.* P. 55. l. 21. r. *as there are.* P. 85. l. 30. r. *Aereoſtilos.* P. 96. l. 44. r. *Fuſarolo.* P. 97. l. 19. r. *elegance.* P. 97. l. 42. r. *Martiris.*

Plate 10. firſt Book, for 8 *minutes* in Cavetto of impoſt, read 5 *minutes.*

ADVERTISEMENT.

THE works of the famous ANDREA PALLADIO, publifhed by himfelf at *Venice* in the year 1570. have been univerfally efteemed the beft ftandard of architecture hitherto extant. The original work written in Italian being very fcarce, feveral have attempted to tranflate the fame into Englifh, and to copy his excellent and moft accurate wooden prints on copper plates.

IN particular, two perfons have publifhed what they honour with the title of PALLADIO's works: The firft, and in all refpects the beft of the two, was done in the year 1721. by Mr. LEONI; who has thought fit not only to vary from the fcale of the originals, but alfo in many places to alter even the graceful proportions prefcribed by this great mafter, by diminifhing fome of his meafures, enlarging others, and putting in fanciful decorations of his own : and indeed his drawings are likewife very incorrect; which makes this performance, according to his own account in the preface, feem rather to be itfelf an original, than an improvement on PALLADIO.

THE other work (publifhed in the year 1735.) is done with fo little underftanding, and fo much negligence, that it cannot but give great offence to the judicious, and be of very bad confequence in mifleading the unfkilful, into whofe hands it may happen to fall.

To do juftice therefore to PALLADIO, and to perpetuate his moft value-able remains amongft us, are the principal inducements to my undertaking fo great and laborious a work ; in executing of which, I have ftrictly kept to his proportions and meafures, by exactly tracing all the plates from his originals, and engraved them with my own hands : So that the reader may depend upon having an exact copy of what our author publifhed, without diminution or increafe ; nor have I taken upon me to alter, much lefs to correct, any thing that came from the hands of that excellent artift.

FROM the fame motive I have chofen to give a ftrict and literal tranflation, that the fenfe of our author might be delivered from his own words.

Scotland-Yard,
June, 1737.

THE AUTHOR'S
PREFACE
TO THE READER.

GUIDED *by a natural inclination, I gave myself up in my most early years to the study of architecture: and as it was always my opinion, that the antient* Romans, *as in many other things, so in building well, vastly excelled all those who have been since their time,* I proposed to myself VITRUVIUS *for my master and guide, who is the only antient writer of this art, and set myself to search into the reliques of all the antient edifices, that, in spight of time and the cruelty of the Barbarians, yet remain; and finding them much more worthy of observation, than at first I had imagined, I began very minutely with the utmost diligence to measure every one of their parts; of which I grew at last so sollicitous an examiner, (not finding any thing which was not done with reason and beautiful proportion) that I have very frequently not only travelled in different parts of* Italy, *but also out of it, that I might intirely, from them, comprehend what the whole had been, and reduce it into design.*

Whereupon perceiving how much this common use of building was different from the observations I had made upon the said edifices, and from what I had read in VITRVIUS, LEON BATTISTA ALBERTI, *and in other excellent writers who have been since* VITRUVIUS, *and from those also which by me have lately been practised with the utmost satisfaction and applause of those who have made use of my works; it seemed to me a thing worthy of a man, who ought not to be born for himself only, but also for the utility of others, to publish the designs of those edifices, (in collecting which, I have employed so much time, and exposed myself to so many dangers) and concisely to set down whatever in them appeared to me more worthy of consideration; and moreover, those rules which I have observed, and now observe, in building; that they who shall read these my books, may be able to make use of whatever will be good therein, and supply those things in which (as many perhaps there may be) I shall have failed; that one may learn, by little and little, to lay aside the strange abuses, the barbarous inventions, the superfluous expence, and (what is of greater consequence) avoid the various and continual ruins that have been seen in many fabricks.*

I applied myself the more willingly to this undertaking, as I see great numbers of persons at this time applying themselves to the study of this profession, many of which are worthily and honourably mentioned in the books of Messer GIORGIO VASARI ARETINO, *a painter and rare architect.*

I therefore hope, that the manner of building may with universal utility be reduced, and soon brought to that pitch of perfection, which in all the arts is greatly desired, and to which it seems that this part of Italy *is very nearly arrived; since that not only in* Venice, *where all the good arts flourish, and*

which

PREFACE.

which only remains as an example of the grandeur and magnificence of the Romans, one begins to see fabricks that have something good in them, since Meſſer GIACOMO SANSOVINO, a celebrated ſculptor and architect, firſt began to make known the beautiful manner, as is ſeen (not to mention many other beautiful works of his) in the new Procuratia, which is the richeſt and moſt adorned edifice, that perhaps has been made ſince the antients; but alſo in many other places of leſs fame, particularly in Vicenza, a city of no very large circumference, but full of moſt noble intellects, and abounding ſufficiently with riches; and where I had firſt an opportunity to practiſe what I now publiſh for common utility, where a great number of very beautiful fabricks are to be ſeen, and where there have been many gentlemen very ſtudious in this art, who, for their nobility and excellent learning, are not unworthy to be numbered among the moſt illuſtrious; as Signor GIOVAN GIORGIO TRISSINO, the ſplendor of our times; the Counts MARC' ANTONIO and ADRIANO DE THIENI, brothers; Signor ANTENORE PAGELLO, Knight; and beſides theſe, who are paſſed to a better life, having eternized their memory in their beautiful and moſt adorned fabricks, there is now Signor FABIO MONZA, intelligent in a great many things; Signor ELIO DE BELLI, ſon of Signor VALERIO, famous for the artifice of camei's and engraving in cryſtal; Signor ANTONIO FRANCESCO OLIVIERA, who, beſides the knowledge of many ſciences, is an architect, and an excellent poet, as he has ſhewn in his Alemana, a poem in heroick verſe, and in a fabrick of his at Boſchi di Nanto, a place in the Vicentine; and laſtly, (to omit many more, who might very deſervedly be placed in the ſame rank) Signor VALERIO BARBARANO, a moſt diligent obſerver of all that belongs to this profeſſion.

But to return to our ſubject : As I am to publiſh thoſe labours that I have from my youth hitherto undergone, in ſearching and meaſuring (with the greateſt care and diligence I could) all thoſe antient edifices that came to my knowledge; and upon this occaſion, in a few words, to treat of architecture, as orderly and diſtinctly as was poſſible for me; I thought it would be very convenient to begin with private houſes, becauſe one ought to believe, that thoſe firſt gave riſe to publick edifices; it being very probable, that man formerly lived by himſelf; but afterwards, ſeeing he required the aſſiſtance of other men, to obtain thoſe things that might make him happy, (if any happineſs is to be found here below) naturally ſought and loved the company of other men: whereupon of ſeveral houſes, villages were formed, and then of many villages, cities, and in theſe publick places and edifices were made.

And alſo becauſe of all the parts of architecture there is none ſo neceſſary to mankind, nor that is oftener uſed than this, I ſhall therefore firſt treat of private houſes, and afterwards of publick edifices; and ſhall briefly treat of ſtreets, bridges, piazze, priſons, baſiliche (which are places of juſtice) xiſti, paleſtre (which are places where men exerciſed themſelves) of temples, theatres, amphitheatres, arches, baths, aqueducts; and laſtly, of the manner of fortifying cities and ſea-ports.

And in all theſe books I ſhall avoid the ſuperfluity of words, and ſimply give thoſe directions that ſeem to me moſt neceſſary, and ſhall make uſe of thoſe terms which at this time are moſt commonly in uſe among artificers.

And

PREFACE.

And because I cannot promise any more myself, (save the long fatigue, great diligence, and the love that I have bestowed to understand and practise what I now offer,) if it pleases GOD that I may not have laboured in vain, I shall heartily thank his goodness; acknowledging withal, myself obliged to those, that from their beautiful inventions, and from the experience they had, have left the precepts of such an art, because they have opened a more easy and expeditious way to the discovery of new things, and that by their means we have attained to the knowledge of many things, which perhaps had otherwise been hid.

The first part shall be divided into two books; in the first shall be treated of the preparation of the materials, and when prepared, how, and in what manner, they ought to be put to use, from the foundation up to the roof: where those precepts shall be, that are universal, and ought to be observed in all edifices, as well private as publick.

In the second I shall treat of the quality of the fabricks that are suitable to the different ranks of men: first of those of a city; and then of the most convenient situation for villa's, and in what manner they are to be disposed.

And as we have but very few examples from the antients, of which we can make use, I shall insert the plans and elevations of many fabricks I have erected, for different gentlemen, and the designs of the antients houses, and of those parts which are most remarkable in them, in the manner that VITRUVIUS *shews us they were made.*

ERRATA.

PAGE 5. line 24. read *Giovanni*. l. 29. r. *Damiano*. l. 30. r. *St. Agnes*, now called *Santa Agnesa*. l. 31. r. *Numentana*. p. 6. l. ult. r. *Tofo*. p. 10. l. 18. r. modiglions. p. 22. l. 6. r. *dentelli* only. p. 25. l. 5. *dele* may. p. 27. l. 38. r. *Paduan*. p. 31. l. 44. r. *regolo*. p. 32. l. 1. r. triangle.

THE

THE FIRST BOOK

OF

Andrea Palladio's

ARCHITECTURE.

CHAPTER I.

Of the several particulars that ought to be consider'd and prepar'd before we begin to build.

GREAT care ought to be taken, before a building is begun, of the several parts of the plan and elevation of the whole edifice intended to be raised: For three things, according to VITRUVIUS, ought to be confidered in every fabrick, without which no edifice will deferve to be commended; and thefe are utility or convenience, duration and beauty. That work therefore cannot be called perfect, which fhould be ufeful and not durable, or durable and not ufeful, or having both thefe fhould be without beauty.

AN edifice may be efteemed commodious, when every part or member ftands in its due place and fit fituation, neither above or below its dignity and ufe; or when the *loggia's*, halls, chambers, cellars and granaries are conveniently difpofed, and in their proper places.

THE ftrength, or duration, depends upon the walls being carried directly upright, thicker below than above, and their foundations ftrong and folid: obferving to place the upper columns directly perpendicular over thofe that are underneath, and the openings of the doors and windows exactly over one another; fo that the folid be upon the folid, and the void over the void.

BEAUTY will refult from the form and correfpondence of the whole, with refpect to the feveral parts, of the parts with regard to each other, and of thefe again to the whole; that the ftructure may appear an entire and compleat body, wherein each member agrees with the other, and all neceffary to compofe what you intend to form.

WHEN thofe feveral particulars have been duly examined upon the model or draught, then an exact calculation ought to be made of the whole expence, and a timely provifion made of the money, and of thofe materials that fhall feem moft neceffary, to the end that nothing may be wanting, or prevent the compleating of the work. In fo doing, the builder will not only be commended; but it will alfo be of the utmoft advantage to the whole ftructure, if the walls are equally and expeditioufly carried up: for being thus difpatch'd, they will fettle proportionably, every where alike, and not be fubject to thofe clefts fo commonly found in buildings that have been finifh'd at divers times.

THEREFORE, having made choice of the moft fkilful artifts that can be had, by whofe advice the work may the more judicioufly be carried on, you muft then provide a fufficient quantity of timber, ftone, fand, lime and metals; concerning which provifion I intend to lay down fome very ufeful directions. There muft alfo be a fufficient number of joyfts, to frame the floors of the halls and chambers; which ought to be difpofed and placed in fuch a manner, that the diftance betwixt each joyft may be the width of one joyft and an half when they are framed together.

YOU

Y o u muſt likewiſe obſerve, that when the jambs of doors and windows are to be made, not to chuſe ſtones bigger than a fifth, or leſs than a ſixth part of the void or opening. And if you intend to adorn the building with columns or pilaſters, make the baſes, capitals, and architraves of ſtone, and the other parts of brick.

W i t h reſpect to the walls, care muſt be taken, as they are raiſed, that they may proportionably be diminiſhed in the thickneſs. Which obſervation, if rightly applied, may be of ſingular ſervice, and enable you to make a truer eſtimate of the charge, and avoid great part of the expence.

B u t as I ſhall treat more diſtinctly of theſe ſeveral particulars under their reſpective heads, this general hint may ſuffice at preſent, and may ſerve as a ſketch of the whole fabrick.

T h e ſame regard is likewiſe to be had to the quality and goodneſs of thoſe materials, that the beſt may be choſen. The experience gained from the buildings of others, will very much help to determine what is fit and expedient to be done.

A n d although V i t r u v i u s, L e o n B a p t i s t a A l b e r t i, and other excellent writers, have laid down very uſeful rules with reſpect to the choice of the materials, I ſhall nevertheleſs take notice of ſuch as are moſt eſſential, that nothing may appear to be wanting in this treatiſe.

C H A P. II.

O f T i m b e r.

V I T R U V I U S tells us, in the ninth chapter of his ſecond book, that timber ought to be felled in autumn, or during the winter ſeaſon, in the wane of the moon; for then the trees recover the vigour and ſolidity that in ſpring and ſummer was diſperſed among their leaves and fruit. It will, moreover, be free from a certain moiſture, very apt to engender worms, and rot it, which at that time will be conſumed and dried up. It ought likewiſe to be cut but to the middle of the pith, and ſo left until it is thoroughly dry, that the moiſture, the cauſe of putrefaction, may gradually diſtil and drop away.

W h e n fell'd, it muſt be laid in a proper place, where it may be ſhelter'd from the ſouth ſun, high winds, and rain. That of a ſpontaneous growth eſpecially ought to be fully dried, and daubed over with cow-dung, to prevent its ſplitting. It ſhould not be drawn through the dew, but removed rather in the afternoon; nor wrought when wet and damp, or very dry: the one being apt to cauſe rottenneſs, and the other to make clumſy work. Neither will it in leſs than three years be dry enough to be made uſe of in planks for the floors, windows, and doors.

T h o s e therefore who are about to build, ought to be inform'd from men thoroughly acquainted with the nature of timber, that they may know which is fit for ſuch and ſuch uſes, and which not.

I n the above-mention'd chapter V i t r u v i u s gives many other uſeful directions, beſides what other learned men have written upon that ſubject.

C H A P. III.

O f S t o n e s.

S T O N E S are either natural, or artificially made by the induſtry of men. The former are taken out of quarries, and ſerve to make lime (of which more hereafter) and alſo to raiſe walls. Thoſe of which walls are commonly made, are marble and hard ſtone, alſo called live ſtone; or ſoft, and tender.

M a r b l e and live ſtone ought to be wrought as ſoon as they are taken out of the quarry, which then may be done with much more eaſe than after they have continued ſome time expofed to the air. But the fofter kind muft be dug in fummer, and placed under a proper fhelter for the fpace of two years before they are ufed, that they may more gradually harden, being thus defended from high winds, rain, and frofts (efpecially when the nature of the ftone is not well known, or if it be dug out of a place that never was open'd before) by which means they will be made much fitter to refift the inclemencies of the weather.

THE reafon for keeping them fo long is, that being forted, thofe which have receiv'd damage, may be placed in the foundations; and the others, which have not been injured, fhould be ufed above ground: and thus they will laft a long time.

THE ftones artificially made are commonly called *quadrelli*, or bricks, from their fhape. Thefe ought to be made of a chalky, whitifh, and foft earth, dug up in autumn, and temper'd in winter, that, in the fpring following, it may the more conveniently be work'd up into bricks; always avoiding that earth that is over fat or fandy. But if neceffity obliges to make them in the winter or fummer time, they muft carefully be cover'd during the former feafon with dry fand, and in the latter with ftraw. When made, they require a long time to dry; for which reafon a good fhelter is the moft proper place, to caufe the outfide and infide to dry or harden equally, which can't be accomplifhed in lefs than two years.

AND as bricks are made either larger or fmaller, according to the quality of the building, and their intended ufe; fo the antients made them larger for publick and great buildings than for fmall and private ones; and therefore holes ought to be made here and there through the larger, that they may dry and burn the better.

CHAP. IV.

OF SAND.

THERE are three forts of fand commonly found; pit, river, and fea fand. The beft of all is pit fand, and is either black, white, red, or afh-colour'd; which laft is a kind of earth calcined by fubterraneous fires pent up in the mountains, and taken out of pits in *Tufcany*.

THEY alfo dig out of the earth in *Terra di Lavoro*, in the territories of *Baia* and *Cuma*, a fort of fand, called *Pozzolana* by VITRUVIUS, which immediately cements in the water, and makes buildings very ftrong. But long experience has fhewn, that of all the feveral kinds of pit fand, the white is the worft. The beft river fand is that which is found in rapid ftreams, and under water-falls, becaufe it is moft purged. Sea fand, although the worft, ought to be of a blackifh colour, and fhine like glafs: that which is large grained, and neareft to the fhore, is beft. Pit fand, being fatteft, makes, for that reafon, the moft tenacious cement, and is therefore employ'd in walls and long vaults; but it is apt to crack.

RIVER fand is very fit for covering and rough-cafting of walls. Sea fand foon wets and foon dries, and waftes by reafon of its falt, which makes it very unfit to fuftain any confiderable weight.

EVERY kind of fand will be good that feels crifp when handled, and, if laid upon white clothes, will neither ftain or leave earth behind it. But that fand is bad, which, being mix'd with water, makes it turbid and dirty: As alfo fuch as has remain'd a long while expofed to the weather; for then it will contain fo much earth and corrupt moifture, that it will be apt to produce fhrubs and wild fig-trees, which are very prejudicial to buildings.

CHAP. V.

Of LIME, *and of the method of working it into mortar.*

THE ftones of which lime is made, are either dug out of hills, or taken out of rivers. All thofe taken out of hills are good where dry, brittle, free from moifture, or the mixture of any fubftance, which being confumed by the fire, diminifhes the ftone. That lime will
therefore

therefore be beſt which is made of the moſt hard, ſolid, white ſtone, and which, being burnt, is left a third part lighter than the ſtone of which it was made.

THERE is alſo a ſpungy ſort of ſtone, the lime of which is very good for covering and rough-caſting of walls; likewiſe a ſcaly rugged ſtone, taken out of the hills of *Padua*, that makes an excellent lime for ſuch buildings as are moſt expoſed to the weather, or ſtand under water, becauſe it immediately ſets, grows hard, and is very laſting.

ALL ſtones taken out of the earth are much better to make lime of, than thoſe which are collected; and rather taken from a ſhady moiſt pit, than from a dry one. The white are better than the brown, as being the moſt eaſily work'd. The pebbles found in rivers and rapid ſtreams, are excellent for lime, and make very white neat work; therefore it is chiefly uſed in the rough-caſting of walls. All ſtones, either dug out of the hills or rivers, burn quicker or ſlower, in proportion to the fire given them, but are generally calcined in ſixty hours. When calcined, they muſt be wetted, in order to ſlack them; obſerving not to pour on the water all at once, but at ſeveral times, to prevent its burning before it be well-tempered, and afterwards muſt be laid in a moiſt ſhady place, only covering it lightly with ſand, taking care not to mix any thing with it; and when uſed, the more it is work'd up with the ſand, the better it will cement; except that made of a ſcaly ſtone, like that from *Padua*, becauſe that muſt be uſed as ſoon as it is ſlacked, to prevent its burning and conſuming away; it will otherwiſe be uſeleſs.

To make mortar, lime ſhould be mix'd with ſand in this proportion; three parts of pit ſand to one of lime, and but two of ſea or river ſand to one of lime.

C H A P. VI.

OF METALS.

THE metals commonly employ'd in buildings, are iron, lead, and copper. Iron ſerves to make nails, hinges, bars, gates, bolts for faſtenings, and ſuch like works.

THERE is no iron any where found pure; nor any, when taken out of the earth, but muſt firſt be melted, and then purged of its droſs by the fire, to make it fit for uſe. For then it will eaſily be made red-hot, will be ſoft enough to be wrought, and ſpread under the hammer; but cannot ſo eaſily be melted again, except it is put into a furnace made for that purpoſe: And if not well hammer'd when red-hot, it will burn and waſte away.

IT is a ſign the iron is good, if, when reduced into bars, you ſee the veins run ſtreight and uninterrupted, and that the ends of the bars be clean and without droſs: For theſe veins will ſhew that the iron is free from lumps and flaws; by the ends we may know the goodneſs of the middle; and, when wrought into ſquare plates, or any other ſhape, if its ſides are ſtreight and even, we may conclude it is equally good in all its parts, as it has equally in every part endured the hammer.

MAGNIFICENT palaces, churches, towers, and other publick edifices, are generally covered with lead. The pipes and gutters to convey the water, are alſo made of the ſame. It likewiſe ſerves to faſten the hinges and iron-work in the jambs of doors and windows. The three ſorts of lead uſually found, are the white, black, and that of a colour between both, by ſome called aſh-colour'd. The black is ſo called, not becauſe it is really ſuch, but becauſe it is intermix'd with ſome blackneſs; therefore the antients, to diſtinguiſh it from the white, gave it very properly that name. The white is much more perfect, and of greater value than the black. And the aſh-colour'd holds the middle rank betwixt both.

LEAD is either taken out of the earth in a great maſs, without any mixture, or in ſmall, ſhining, blackiſh lumps; and is ſometimes found ſticking in ſmall flakes to the rocks, to marble, and to ſtones. All the different ſorts melt very eaſily, becauſe the heat of the fire liquifies it before it can be made red-hot; and if thrown into an extreme hot furnace, it will not preſerve its ſubſtance, but be converted into litharge and droſs. Of the three ſorts the black is the ſofteſt and moſt weighty, and therefore will eaſily ſpread under the hammer. The white is harder and lighter. The aſh-colour'd is much harder than the white, and is of a middle weight between both.

PUBLICK buildings are sometimes cover'd with copper; and the antients also made nails and cramps thereof, which were fix'd in the stone below, and to that above, to unite and tie them together, and prevent them from being pushed out of their place. And by means of these nails and cramps, a building, which can't possibly be made without a great number of pieces of stone, is so join'd and fix'd together, that it appears to be one entire piece, and for the same reason is much stronger and more durable.

THESE nails and cramps were likewise made of iron; but the antients most commonly made them of copper, because it is less subject to rust, and consequently will last much longer. The Letters for inscriptions, that were placed in the frizes of buildings without, were made of copper; and history informs us, that the hundred famous gates of *Babylon*, and HERCULES' two pillars, eight cubits high, in the island of *Gades*, were also made of that metal.

THE best and most excellent copper is that which is extracted and purged from the ore by fire. If it is of a red colour, inclining to yellow, well-grained, and full of pores, we may then be pretty certain it is freed from dross.

COPPER will heat red-hot in the fire, like iron, and so liquify that it may be cast. If thrown into an extreme hot furnace, it will not endure the flames, but totally consume and waste away. Although it be hard, it will nevertheless bear the hammer, and may be wrought into very thin plates. The best method to preserve it is to dip it into tar; for tho' it does not rust like iron, yet it has a peculiar rust, called verdigreafe, especially if it be touched with any sharp liquor.

THIS metal mix'd with tin, lead and brass (which last is only copper coloured with *lapis calaminaris*) makes *bronze*, or bell-metal, which is often used by architects in making bases, columns, capitals, statues, and such-like ornaments. There are to be seen in the church of *St. Giovani Laterano* in *Rome* four brass columns (one of which only has its capital) made by the order of AUGUSTUS of the metal that was found in the prows of those ships he had taken in *Egypt* from MARK ANTHONY.

THERE also remains in *Rome* to this day four antient gates; *viz.* the *Rotunda*, formerly the *Pantheon*; that of *St. Adriano*, formerly the temple of SATURN; that of *St. Cosmo* and *St. Domiano*, formerly the temple of CASTOR and POLLUX, or rather of ROMULUS and REMUS; and that of *St. Agnas*, now called *St. Agnese*, without the gate *Viminalis su la via Numenta.*

THE most beautiful of these is that of *Santa Maria Rotunda*; wherein the antients endeavoured to imitate by art that sort of *Corinthian* metal in which the natural colour of gold did mostly predominate: For we read, that when *Corinth*, now called *Coranto*, was burnt and destroy'd, the gold, silver, and copper were melted and united into one mass, which was so temper'd and mix'd together, that it composed the three sorts of brass afterwards called *Corinthian*. In the first, silver prevailed, of which it retained the whiteness and lustre; the second, as it partook more of the gold, retained mostly its yellow colour; the third was that in which all the three metals were pretty equally mix'd. All these have afterwards been imitated by various workmen.

HAVING sufficiently explained the several particulars and materials most necessary to be consider'd and prepared before we begin to build; it is proper, in the next place, to say something of the foundations, since it is from them the whole work must be raised.

CHAP. VII.

Of the qualities of the ground where foundations ought to be laid.

THE foundations are properly called the basis of the fabrick, *viz.* that part of it under ground which sustains the whole edifice above; and therefore of all the errors that can be committed in building, those made in the foundation are most pernicious, because they at once occasion the ruin of the whole fabrick, nor can they be rectified without the utmost

C
difficulty.

difficulty. For which reason the architect should apply his utmost diligence in this point; in-asmuch as in some places there are natural foundations, and in other places art is required.

WE have natural foundations when we build on a chalky soil, which in some degree re-sembles stone *; for these, without digging or any other assistance from art, are of themselves very strong and sufficient foundations, and capable to sustain any great edifice, either on land or in water.

BUT when nature does not furnish foundations, then art must be made use of; because the places to build on are sometimes either solid ground, gravel, sand, or a moist and marshy soil. Where it is solid, the foundation need be no deeper than what the quality of the building, and the solidity of the ground shall require (according as the judicious architect shall think proper) and must not exceed the sixth part of the height of the whole edifice, if there are no cellars or subterraneous offices wanted.

OBSERVATIONS made in digging of wells, cisterns, and such like, are of great use, and very much help us to know the solidity of the ground; as do also the herbs that spontaneously grow thereon, especially if they are such as spring up only in a hard and firm soil. The so-lidity may likewise be known by throwing a great weight upon the earth, provided it neither shakes or resounds (which may easily be observed by the help of a drum set upon the ground, if the percussion only gently moves it, without making it sound, or without moving the water in a vessel set near it:) It may also be judged of by the adjacent places.

BUT when the place is either sandy or gravelly, regard must be had whether it be on land or in the water. If it be on land, that only is to be observed which has before been said con-cerning dry ground. But if buildings are to be in rivers, the sand and gravel will be alto-gether useless; because the water, by its continual current and flood, is always shifting their bed : We must therefore dig until a firm and solid bottom be found. If that cannot easily be done, let some of the sand and gravel be taken out, and then piles, made of oak, must be driven in, until their ends reach the solid ground, upon which one may build.

BUT if a building is to be raised upon a boggy soil, then it must be dug out, until firm ground be come at, and so deep therein as is in proportion to the thickness of the walls, and the largeness of the fabrick.

SOUND and firm soils, fit to sustain buildings, are of various kinds : For, as ALBERTI well observes, in some places the soil is so hard, that iron can scarce cut its way into it, and sometimes still harder; in others blackish or whitish, which is esteem'd the weakest; some are like chalk, or otherwise soft : But the best is that which is cut with the most labour, and when wet does not dissolve into mud.

NO buildings should be erected on ruins before their depth is first known, and whether they are sufficient to sustain the edifice.

WHEN the ground is soft, and sinks very much, as it commonly does in bogs, then piles are to be used, whose length ought to be the eighth part of the height of the walls, and their thickness the twelfth part of their length. The piles are to be driven so close to one another, as not to leave space for others to come in between. Care must also be taken to drive them rather with blows frequently repeated, than such as are violent; that so the earth may bind the better to fasten them.

THE pilings are to be not only under the outside walls, which are placed upon the canals; but also under those which are placed on the earth, and divide the fabrick: For if the foun-dations of the middle walls are made different from those on the outside, it will often happen, that when the beams are placed by each other in length, and the others over them crossways, the inside walls will sink, and the outside ones, by being piled, will remain unmov'd; which, besides its being very disagreeable to the sight, will occasion all the walls to open, and ruin the whole edifice. This danger therefore is to be avoided by a trifling expence in piling; for according to the proportion of the walls, the piles in the middle will be smaller than those for the outside.

* There are strictly no proper words in *English* for *Tofo* or *Scaranto*.

CHAP.

CHAP. VIII.

Of foundations.

FOUNDATIONS ought to be twice as thick as the wall to be built on them ; and regard in this should be had to the quality of the ground, and the largeness of the edifice ; making them greater in soft soils, and very solid where they are to sustain a considerable weight.

THE bottom of the trench must be level, that the weight may press equally, and not sink more on one side than on the other, by which the walls would open. It was for this reason the antients paved the said bottom with *Tivertino*, and we usually put beams or planks, and build on them.

THE foundations must be made sloping, that is, diminished in proportion as they rise ; but in such a manner, that there may be just as much set off on one side as on the other, that the middle of the wall above may fall plumb upon the middle of that below : Which also must be observed in the setting off of the wall above ground ; because the building is by this method made much stronger than if the diminutions were done any other way.

SOMETIMES (especially in fenny places, and where columns intervene) to lessen the expence, the foundations are not made continued, but with arches, over which the building is to be.

IT is very commendable in great fabricks, to make some cavities in the thickness of the wall from the foundation to the roof, because they give vent to the winds and vapours, and cause them to do less damage to the building. They save expence, and are of no little use if there are to be circular stairs from the foundation to the top of the edifice.

CHAP. IX.

Of the several sorts of walls.

THE foundations being laid, we are next to treat of the upright wall above ground.

THE antients had six sorts of walls : The first called *reticulata* ; the second of baked earth, or square bricks ; the third of rough stones, either from mountains or rivers ; the fourth of irregular stones ; the fifth of squared stones ; the sixth called *riempiuta*.

THE first, called *reticulata*, is not in use in our time ; but because VITRUVIUS mentions its being commonly used in his, I have given a draught of it.

THEY made the corners or angles of the building of bricks ; and between every two foot and a half, three courses of square bricks were laid, which bound the thickness of the wall together.

Plate I

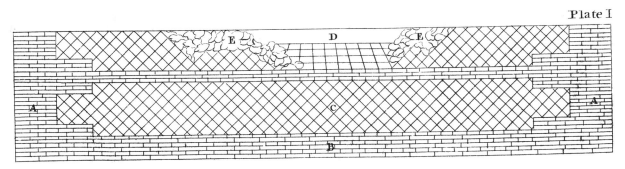

A, *the angles made of brick.*
B, *courses of bricks that bind the whole wall.*
C, *the net-work.*
D, *courses of bricks through the thickness of the wall.*
E, *the inner part of the wall, made of cement.*

THE

THE brick walls of a city, or any other great building, fhould be made with fquare bricks on both fides, and the middle filled up with cement and pounded bricks. To every three foot in height there muft be three courfes of larger bricks than the others, which take the whole thicknefs of the wall. The firft courfe muft be with headers, that is, the fmalleft end of the brick outwards; the fecond longway, or ftretchers; and the third headers again. After this manner are the walls of the *Rotunda*, the baths of D I O C L E S I A N, and all the antient buildings that are at *Rome*.

II

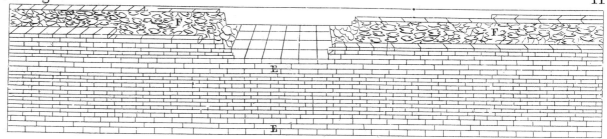

E, *the courfes of bricks that bind the whole wall.*
F, *the middle part of the wall, made of cement, between the feveral courfes and the outward bricks.*

THE walls built of cement muft be fo made, that to every two foot, at leaft, there may be three courfes of bricks, placed according to the method above-mentioned. Thus in *Piedmont* are the walls of *Turin*, which are built with large river-pebbles, fplit in the middle, and placed in the wall with the fplit-fide outwards, making the work very upright and even.

THE walls of the *arena*, or amphitheatre, in *Verona*, are alfo of cement, and at every three feet diftance are three courfes of bricks. In like manner are other antient fabricks made, as may be feen in my *Books of Antiquity*.

III

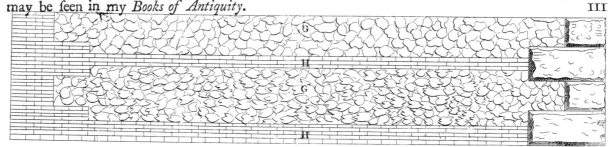

G, *cement, or river-pebbles.*
H, *courfes of bricks, that bind the whole wall.*

THOSE walls were faid to be uncertain, which were made of ftones of unequal angles and fides. To make thofe walls they ufed a fquaring rule of lead, which being bent where the ftone was to be placed, ferved them in fquaring it. This they did that the ftones fhould join well together, and that they might not be obliged to make frequent tryals whether the ftone was rightly placed. There are feen at *Præneſte* walls after this manner; and the antient roads and ftreets were thus paved.

IIII

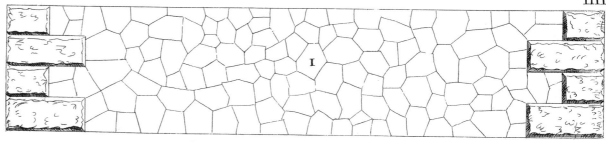

I, *irregular or rough ftones.*

WALLS may be seen, built with squared stones, at *Rome*, where stood the piazza and the temple of AUGUSTUS, in which the lesser stones are key'd in with some courses of the larger.

V

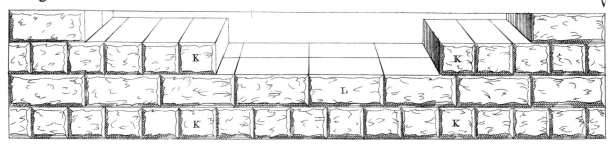

K, *courses of the lesser stones.*
L, *courses of the larger stones.*

THE method the antients made use of to build the walls called *riempiuta*, or coffer-work, was by placing two rows of planks edgeways, distant the one from the other according to the thickness they intended to give the walls, and then filled the void with cement, mix'd with all kinds of stones, and continued it in this manner from course to course. Walls of this kind may be seen at *Sirmion*, upon the lake of *Garda*.

VI

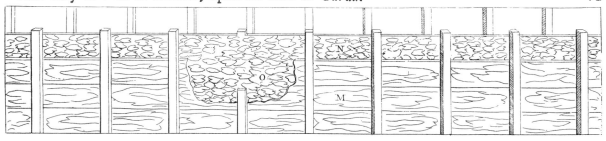

M, *planks laid edgeway.*
N, *inward part of the wall.*
O, *face of the wall, the planks being taken away.*

THE walls of *Naples*, that is, the antient ones, may be said to be after this manner; which have two walls of squared stones, four foot thick, and six foot distant the one from the other, bound together with others that run cross them. The coffers that remain between the traverse and out-walls are six foot square, which are filled up with stones and earth.

VII

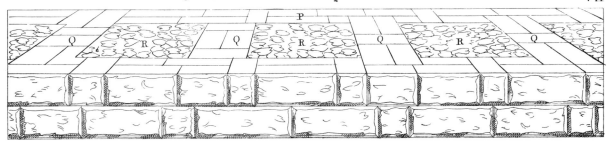

P, *the outward stone walls.*
Q, *the traverse stone walls to bind them together.*
R, *the coffers, filled with stones and earth.*

THESE, in fine, are the different sorts of walls the antients made use of, footsteps of which still remain: From which we may conclude, that all walls, let them be of what kind soever, ought to have some cross courses, as so many ligaments to bind all the other parts together. This must particularly be observed in brick walls, that, should the middle of the walls, through length of time, sink or decay, the rest may not be subject to ruin; as we see happens in many walls, particularly on the side facing the north.

CHAP.

C H A P. X.

Of the method obferved by the antients in erecting ftone edifices.

AS it fometimes happens that an edifice is either to be in part or entirely built with marble or with large pieces of other ftone, it feems reafonable that I fhould in this place mention what method the antients obferved on fuch occafions; becaufe it appears in their works, fuch exact care was taken in the joining of their ftones, that the junctures in many places are fcarce to be difcerned, to which every one ought to be very attentive, who, befides beauty, defires the folidity and duration of the fabrick.

B u t as far as I could ever comprehend, they firft wrought and fquared thofe fides of the ftones that were to be laid upon one another, leaving the other fides rough, and thus employ'd them in the building: For as the edges were then thicker and ftronger, they could the more conveniently manage and move them backwards and forwards, until they were placed and well united together, with lefs danger of breaking them than if all the fides had been fquared and polifhed, which would have made them too thin, and confequently more apt to be fpoiled.

A n d in this manner they built rough or ruftick edifices; and when thus finifhed, they then polifhed all thofe fides of the ftones that were expofed to view. As the rofes between the modilions, and the other ornaments carved in the cornice, could not however be fo conveniently made after the ftones were fix'd, thefe were work'd whilft they lay upon the ground. This is manifeft by the many ftones found unwrought and unpolifhed in a great many antient buildings.

T h e arch near the old caftle in *Verona*, and all the other arches and antient edifices in that place, are made after the fame manner; which is very perceptible to any one that will take notice of the marks the tools have made upon the ftones, which plainly fhew how they were wrought. The *Trajan* column in *Rome* and the *Antonine* were made in this manner; it would have been otherwife impoffible to fix the ftones fo exactly as to make the joints meet fo clofe together athwart the heads and other parts of the figures. The fame may alfo be faid of the other arches that are feen there.

W h e n the antients had any very large fabrick to build, fuch as the *Arena* in *Verona*, the amphitheatre of *Pola*, or any other of that kind, to fave time and expence, they only wrought the impofts of the arches, the capitals and cornices, leaving all the reft ruftick, having a regard only to the beautiful form of the whole edifice.

B u t in temples, and other ftructures that require more delicacy, they were not fparing of their labour in working of them; but fmoothed and polifhed, even to the very flutes of the columns, with the utmoft care and accuracy.

B u t it is my opinion, that brick walls ought never to be made ruftick; nor the mantles of chimneys, which require to be wrought very neat: For, befides being there mifapplied, it would follow, that a work, which naturally ought to be one entire piece, would appear to be divided into feveral parts. But, according to the largenefs and quality of the building, it may either be made ruftick or very neat; for what the antients judicioufly practifed (being thereto compelled by the largenefs of their ftructures) muft not be imitated by us in buildings in which neatnefs is particularly required.

C H A P.

CHAP. XI.

Of the diminution of walls, and of their several parts.

IT ought to be obſerved, that walls ſhould diminiſh in proportion as they riſe; therefore thoſe which appear above ground muſt be but half as thick as the walls in the foundations; thoſe of the ſecond ſtory half a brick thinner than the walls of the firſt; and in this manner to the top of the building; but with diſcretion, that the upper part be not too thin.

THE middle of the upper walls ought to fall directly upon the middle of the lower, which will give the whole wall a pyramidal form. But when you are willing to make the ſuperficies or face of the upper walls to fall directly upon the lower, it muſt be done towards the inſide of the building; becauſe that the floors, beams or rafters, vaults, and other ſupports of the fabrick, will keep them from falling or giving way.

THE diſcharged part, or ſet-off, which is on the outſide, may be covered with a faſcia and a cornice; which, ſurrounding all the building, will be both an ornament, and a kind of bond to the whole. And becauſe the angles partake of the two ſides, in order to keep them upright, and united together, they ought to be made very ſtrong and ſolid with long hard ſtones, holding them as it were with arms.

THE windows, and other openings, ought be as far diſtant from the angles as poſſible; or at leaſt ſo much ſpace muſt be left between the aperture and the angles as the width of the opening or void.

HAVING thus treated of plain walls, we ſhall next conſider their ornaments; among which none are more conſiderable than columns, when they are properly placed, and in a juſt proportion to the whole edifice.

CHAP. XII.

Of the five orders made uſe of by the antients.

THE Tuſcan, Dorick, Ionick, Corinthian, and Compoſite, are the five orders made uſe of by the antients. Theſe ought to be ſo diſpoſed in a building, that the moſt ſolid may be placed undermoſt, as being the moſt proper to ſuſtain the weight, and to give the whole edifice a more firm foundation : Therefore the Dorick muſt always be placed under the Ionick; the Ionick under the Corinthian; and the Corinthian under the Compoſite.

THE Tuſcan being a plain rude order, is therefore very ſeldom uſed above ground, except in villas, where one order only is employ'd. In very large buildings, as amphitheatres, and ſuch like, where many orders are required, this, inſtead of the Dorick, may be placed under the Ionick.

BUT if you are deſirous to leave out any of theſe orders, as, for inſtance, to place the Corinthian immediately over the Dorick, you may, provided you always obſerve to place the moſt ſtrong and ſolid undermoſt, for the reaſons above-mention'd.

THE meaſures and proportions of each of theſe orders I ſhall ſeparately ſet down; not ſo much according to VITRUVIUS, as to the obſervations I have made on ſeveral antient edifices. But I ſhall firſt mention ſuch particulars as relate to all of them in general.

CHAP.

CHAP. XIII.

Of the swelling and diminution of columns, and of the intercolumniations and pilasters.

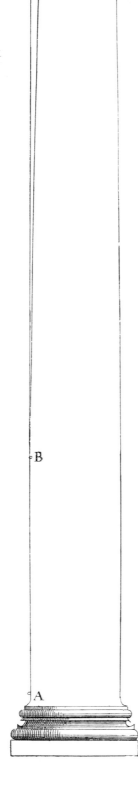

THE columns in each order ought to be form'd in such a manner, that the diameter of the upper part of the column may be smaller than at the bottom, with a kind of a swelling in the middle.

IT is to be obferved in the diminutions, that the higher the columns are, the lefs they muft diminifh; becaufe the height, by reafon of the diftance, has that effect.

THEREFORE, if the column be fifteen foot high, the thicknefs at the bottom muft be divided into fix parts and a half, five and a half of which will be the thicknefs for the top. If from fifteen to twenty foot high, divide the diameter at the bottom into feven parts, and fix and a half will be the diameter above. The fame muft alfo be obferved in thofe from twenty to thirty foot high; the lower diameter of which muft be divided into eight parts, and feven given to the upper. And fo in proportion, columns of a greater altitude ought in the fame manner to be diminifhed, as VITRUVIUS tells us in the fecond chapter of his third book.

As to the manner of making the fwelling in the middle, we have no more to fhew from VITRUVIUS but his bare promife; which is the reafon that moft writers differ from one another upon that fubject.

THE method I ufe in making the profile of the fwellings is this; I divide the fuft of the column into three equal parts, and leave the lower part perpendicular; to the fide of the extremity of which I apply the edge of a thin rule, of the fame length, or a little longer than the column, and bend that part which reaches from the third part upwards, until the end touches the point of the diminution of the upper part of the column under the *collarino*. I then mark as that curve directs, which gives the column a kind of fwelling in the middle, and makes it project very gracefully.

AND although I never could imagine a more expeditious and fuccefsful method than this, I am neverthelefs confirmed in my opinion, fince Signor PIETRO CATANEO was fo well pleafed when I told him of it, that he gave it a place in his Treatife of Architecture, with which he has not a little illuftrated this profeffion.

A B, *the third part of the column, which is left directly perpendicular.*
B C, *the two thirds that are diminifhed.*
C, *the point of diminution under the* collarino.

THE intercolumniations, or the fpaces between the columns, may be of one diameter and a half of the column (the diameter being taken at the loweft part of the column.) They alfo may be of two, two and a quarter, three, or more diameters; but the antients never allow'd more to thefe fpaces than three times the diameter of the column, except in the Tufcan order, where the architrave was made of timber, the intercolumniations were then very large. Neither did they ever allow lefs than one diameter and a half, which was the diftance they ufually obferv'd, efpecially when the columns were very high.

BUT, above all other, they approved of thofe intercolumniations that were of two diameters and a quarter; and they reckon'd this a

beautiful

beautiful and elegant manner of intercolumniation. And it ought to be obferved, that there fhould be a proportion and correfpondence between the intercolumniations or fpaces, and the columns; becaufe if fmall columns are placed in the larger fpaces, the greateft part of their beauty will be taken away, by the quantity of air, or the vacuity between the fpaces, which will diminifh much of their thicknefs. On the contrary, if large columns are placed in fmall intercolumniations, the ftraitnefs or narrownefs of the fpaces will make them appear clumfy, and without grace. Therefore if the fpaces exceed three diameters, the thicknefs of the columns ought to be a feventh part of their height; as I have obferved in the following Tufcan order.

But if the fpaces are three diameters, the columns ought to be feven and a half or eight diameters high; as in the Dorick order: If two and a quarter, the height of the columns muft be nine diameters; as in the Ionick: If but two, the height of the columns fhould be nine diameters and a half; as in the Corinthian: And, laftly, if of one diameter and a half, the height of the columns muft be ten; as in the Compofite. In which orders I have taken this care, that they may ferve as an example for the different intercolumniations mention'd by Vitruvius in the aforefaid chapter.

An even number of columns ought always to be placed in the fronts of edifices, that an intercolumniation may be made in the middle fomewhat larger than the others, that the doors and entries, ufually placed in the middle, may be the better feen. And this is fufficient as to fimple colonades.

But if loggia's are made with pilafters, they ought to be fo difpofed, that the thicknefs of the pilafters be not lefs than one third of the void or fpace between pilafter and pilafter; and the thicknefs of thofe placed in the corners to be two thirds of the faid fpace, that fo the angles of the fabrick may be both ftrong and folid.

And when they are to fuftain an exceeding great weight, as in very large buildings, they ought then to be made as thick as half the void, like thofe of the theatre of *Vicenza*, and the amphitheatre at *Capua*; otherwife their thicknefs may be two thirds of the faid fpace, as thofe of the theatre of *Marcellus* at *Rome*, and that of *Ogubio*, now in poffeffion of Signor Ludovico de Gabrielli, a gentleman of that city.

The antients fometimes made them as thick as the whole void, as thofe are in that part of the theatre of *Verona* which is not upon the Mountain. But in private buildings they muft not be lefs in thicknefs than the third part of the void, nor more than the two thirds, and ought to be fquare. But to leffen the expence, and to make the place to walk in larger, they may be made lefs thick in the flank than front, to adorn which, half columns and pilafters may be placed in the middle, to fupport the cornice over the arches of the loggia's, whofe thicknefs muft be proportionable to their height, according to each order; as may be feen in the following chapters and defigns.

For the better underftanding of which, and to avoid my repeating the fame thing often, it is to be obferved, that in the dividing and meafuring the faid orders, I would not make ufe of any certain and determinate meafure peculiar to any city, as a cubit, foot, or palm, knowing that thefe feveral meafures differ as much as the cities and countries; but imitating Vitruvius, who divides the Dorick order with a meafure taken from the thicknefs or diameter of the columns, common to all, and by him called a module, I fhall therefore make ufe of the fame meafure in all the orders.

The module fhall be the diameter of the column at bottom, divided into fixty minutes; except in the Dorick Order, where the module is but half the diameter of the column, divided into thirty minutes, becaufe it is thus more commodious in the divifions of the faid order.

From whence every one may, by either making the module greater or lefs, according to the quality of the building, make ufe of the proportions and profiles belonging to each order.

E   CHAP.

CHAP. XIV.

Of the TUSCAN ORDER.

THE Tuscan order, according to VITRUVIUS, and as in effect it appears, is the most simple and plain of all the orders in architecture; because it retains something of the former antiquity, and is deprived of those ornaments that make the others so sightly and beautiful.

IT was first invented in *Tuscany*, a most noble part of *Italy*, from whence its name is derived.

THE columns, with their base and capital, ought to be seven modules in height, and to be diminished at top a fourth part of their thickness.

IF simple colonades are made of this order, the spaces or intercolumniations may be very wide, because the architraves are made of wood, which will therefore be very commodious for villa's, because it admits of passage for carts, and other country implements, besides being of little expence.

BUT if gates or loggia's with arches are to be made, then the measures marked in the design are to be used in which the stones are bonded, as I think they ought to be. I have also been mindful of this in the designs of the other four orders. And this way of disposing and bonding the stones I have taken from many antient arches; as will be seen in my *Book of arches*; and in this I have used great diligence.

> A, *the architrave of wood.*
> B, *the joysts which form the corona or drip.*

THE pedestals placed under the columns of this order are to be made plain, and one module in height. The height of the base is half the diameter of the column; and this height is to be divided into two equal parts, one to be given to the plinth, which is made with the compass, and the other divided into four parts, one to be given to the fillet, also called the *cimbia*, which may sometimes be made less, and in this order only is part of the base, which in all the other is part of the column; the other three parts are for the *torus* or bastone. The projection of this base is the sixth part of the diameter of the column.

THE height of the capital is half the diameter of the lower part of the column, and is divided into three equal parts; one is given to the *abaco*, (which from its form is usually called the *dado*) the other to the *ovolo*, and the third is divided into seven parts; of one the fillet under the ovolo is made, and the remaining six are for the *collarino*. The height of the astragal is double that of the listello or fillet under the *listello*, and its center is made upon the line that falls perpendicularly upon the said listello, upon which also falls the projection of the cimbia, which is as thick as the listello.

THE projection of this capital answers to the shaft of the column below; the architrave is made of wood, equal in height as in width, and not to exceed in width the shaft of the column at top. The projecture of the joysts that form the *gronda* or drip, is a fourth part of the length of the column.

THESE are the measures of the Tuscan order, according to VITRUVIUS.

A, *Abaco.*	F, *the shaft of the column below.*
B, *Ovolo.*	G, *Cimbia or Cincture.*
C, *Collarino.*	H, *Toro or Bastone.*
D, *Astragal.*	I, *Orlo.*
E, *the shaft of the column at top.*	K, *Pedestal.*

THE profiles placed near the plan of the base and capital are the imposts of the arches.

BUT

BUT when the architraves are to be made of ftone, then what has been faid before, with refpect to the intercolumniations, muft be obferved.

THERE are antient buildings ftill to be feen, which, as they partly retain the fame mea-fures, may be faid to have been formed of this order, like the arena of *Verona*, the arena and theatre of *Pola*, and many others; from which I have taken the profiles of the bafe, capital, architrave, frize, and cornices, placed upon the laft plate of this chapter, as alfo thofe of the impofts of arches, and fhall infert the defigns of all thefe feveral edifices in my *books of antiquity*.

A, *Gola diritta.*
B, *Corona.*
C, *Gocciolatrio e Gola diritta.*
D, *Cavetto.*
E, *Fregio, or frize.*
F, *Architrave.*
G, *Cimacio*
H, *Abaco*
I, *Gola diritta*   } *of the capital.*
K, *Collarino.*

L, *Aftragal.*
M, *Shaft of the column under the capital.*
N, *Shaft of the column at bottom.*
O, *Cimbia of the column.*
P, *Baftone and Gola,*
    or Torus   } *of the bafe.*
Q, *Orlo*

DIRECTLY oppofite to the architrave marked F, there is the profile of an architrave formed with more delicacy.

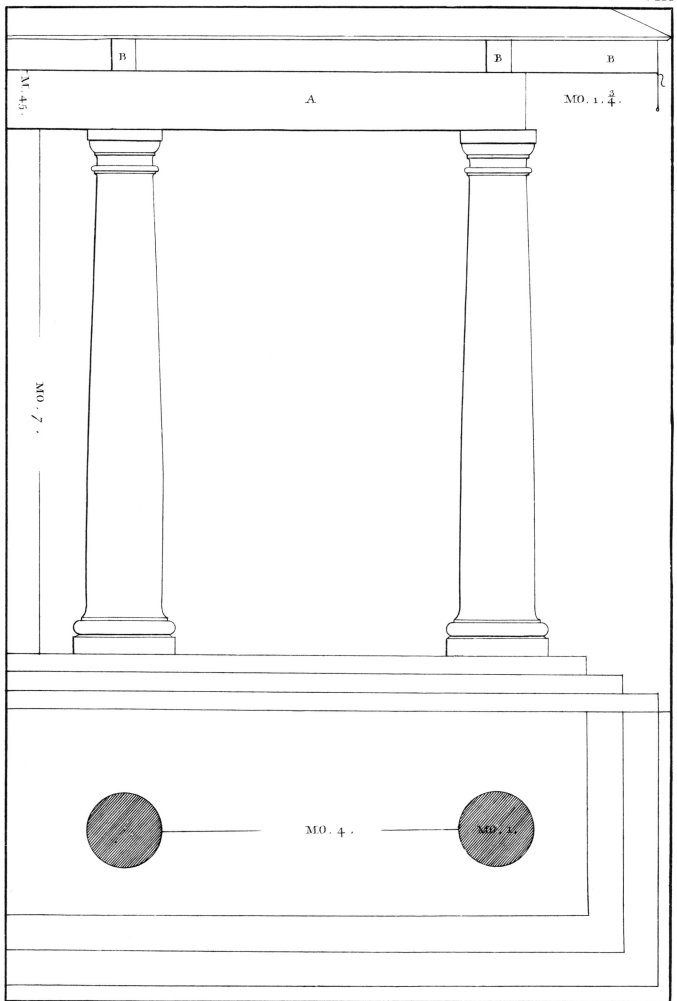

B

B

B

M. 45.

A

MO. 1. $\frac{3}{4}$.

MO. 7.

MO. 4.

MO. 1.

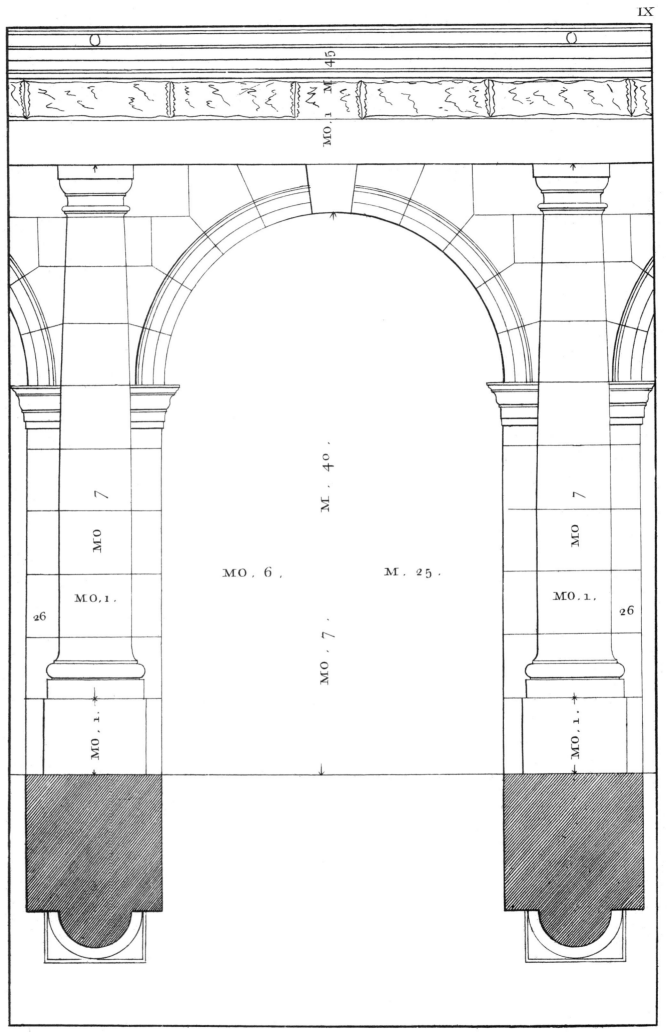

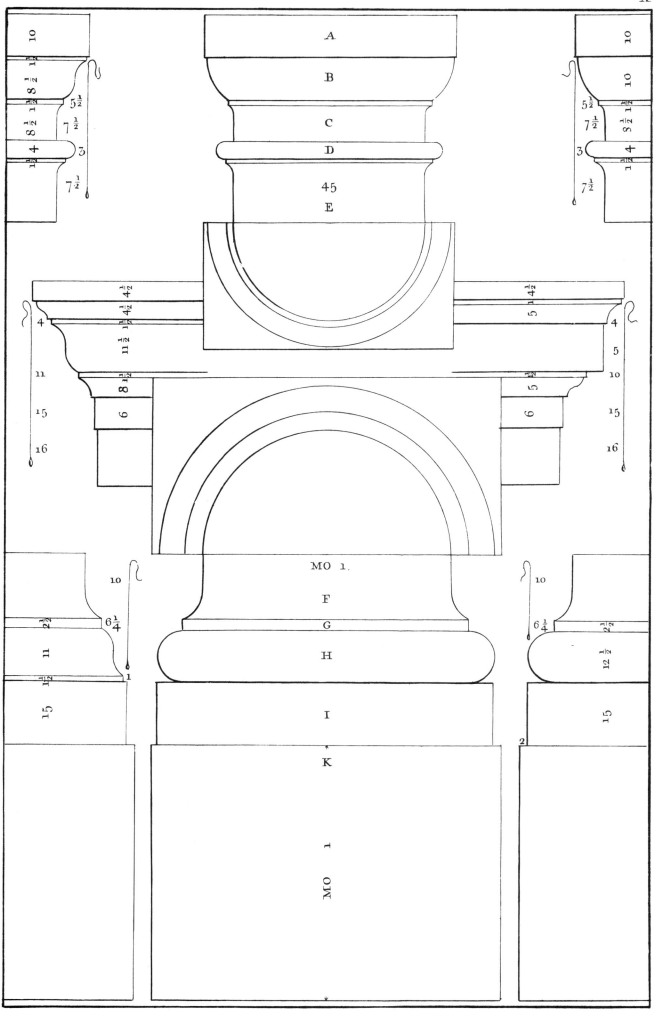

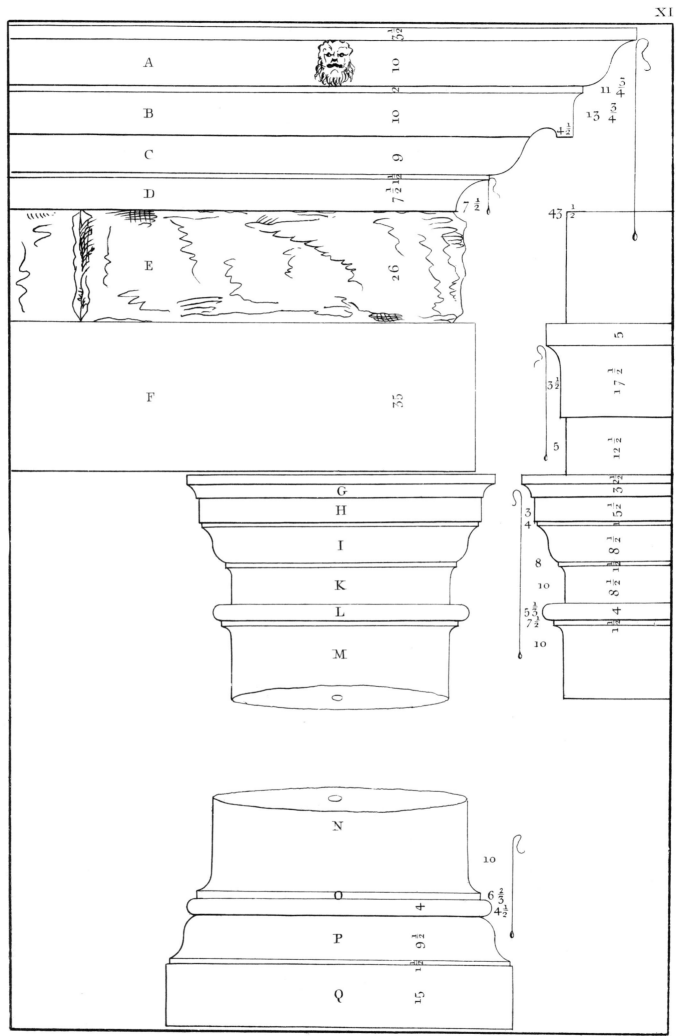

CHAP. XV.

Of the DORICK ORDER.

THE Dorick order had both its name and origin from the *Dorians*, a *Greek* nation in *Asia*. If the columns of this order are made alone, and without pilasters, they ought to be seven diameters and a half or eight in height : the intercolumniations are something less than three diameters of the column ; which manner of placing columns, to form colonades, is called by VITRUVIUS diastilo's.

BUT when they are supported with pilasters, their height ought to be seventeen modules and one third, including the base and capital. And it is to be observed, as I have said before in *chap.* xiii. that the module in this order, only, is but half the diameter of the column divided into thirty minutes, and in all the other orders it is the whole diameter divided into sixty minutes.

NO pedestal is to be seen in antient buildings to this order, although there are in the modern ; therefore when a pedestal is required, the dado ought to be made square, from which the measures of all its ornaments must be taken, because it is to be divided into four equal parts ; two of them shall be for the base with its *zocco* or plinth, and one for the cimacia, to which the orlo of the base must be joined. Some pedestals of this kind are still to be seen in the Corinthian order, at *Verona*, in the arch called *de Leoni*.

I HAVE inserted different profiles, that may be adapted to the pedestals of this order ; all of them beautiful, and taken from the antients, and measured with the utmost diligence.

THIS order has no base peculiar to it, which is the reason that in a great many edifices the columns are to be seen without bases : As at *Rome*, in the theatre of *Marcellus* ; in the temple *de la Pieta*, near the said theatre ; in the theatre of *Vicenza* ; and in divers other places.

BUT the Attick base is sometimes joined to it, which adds very much to its beauty ; and the measures are thus. The height must be half the diameter of the column, which is to be divided into three equal parts ; one goes to the plinth or zocco, the other two are divided into four parts, one of which is for the upper bastone ; the remaining three are again divided into two equal parts, one of which is for the lower torus, the other to the cavetto with its listello's, therefore must be divided into six parts, the first for the upper listello, the second for the lower, and four remain for the cavetto.

THE projecture is the sixth part of the diameter of the column. The cimbia is half the upper torus. If it is divided from the base, its projecture is one third part of the whole projecture of the base ; but if the base and part of the column make one entire piece, the cimbia must be made thin : As may be seen in the third design of this order, where there are also two different sorts of imposts of arches.

A, *Shaft of the column.*	F, *Plinth or Zocco.*
B, *Cimbia or fillet.*	G, *Cimacia* ⎫
C, *Upper Torus.*	H, *Dado* ⎬ *of the pedestals.*
D, *Cavetto with its Listello's.*	I, *Base* ⎭
E, *Lower Torus.*	K, *Imposts of arches.*

THE capital ought to be in height half the diameter of the column, and is to be divided into three parts. The upper part is given to the abaco and cimacio. The cimacio is two of the five parts thereof, which must be divided into three parts ; with the one the listello is made, and with the other two the gola. The second principal part is divided into three equal parts ; one to be given to the annelli or annulets, or gradetti, which three are equal ; the other two remain for the ovolo, which projects two thirds of its height. The third part is for the collarino.

THE whole projecture is the fifth part of the diameter of the column. The astragal or tondino is as high as all the three annelli, and projects equal to the lower part of the shaft of the column. The cimbia is half the height of the astragal or tondino, and its projecture is directly plumb with the centre of the said astragal.

F THE

T H E architrave is placed upon the capital, the height of which muſt be half the diameter of the column, that is, a module. It is divided into ſeven parts. With one the *tenia* or *henda* is made, whoſe projecture muſt be equal to its height; then the whole is again divided into ſix parts, one is given to the *goccie*, which ought to be ſix, and to the liſtello under the tenia, which is a third part of the ſaid goccie.

F R O M the tenia downwards the remainder is again divided into ſeven parts; three are to be given to the firſt faſcia, and four to the ſecond. The frize is a module and a half in height. The breadth of the triglyph is one module, and its capital the ſixth part of a module. The triglyph is to be divided into ſix parts; two of which are for the two channels in the middle, one for the two half channels at the ends, and the other three for the ſpaces between the ſaid channels.

T H E *metopa*, or ſpace between triglyph and triglyph, ought to be as broad as it is high. The cornice muſt be a module and one ſixth in height, and divided into five parts and a half, two of which are given to the cavetto and ovolo. The cavetto is leſs than the ovolo by the width of its liſtello. The remaining three parts and a half are to be given to the corona or cornice, which is vulgarly called *gocciolatoio*, and to the gola or cima recta and reverſa.

T H E corona ought to project four parts in ſix of the module, and have on its ſoffit, that looks downwards, and projects forward, ſix drops, or *guttæ*, in length, and three in breadth, with their liſtelli over the triglyphs, and ſome roſes over the metopæ. The guttæ are round, ſhaped like bells, and anſwer to thoſe under the tenia.

T H E gola muſt be an eighth part thicker than the corona, and divided into eight parts; two are to be given to the orlo, and ſix remain for the gola, whoſe projecture is ſeven parts and a half.

T H E R E F O R E the height of the architrave, frize and cornice is a fourth part of the altitude of the column.

T H E S E are the dimenſions of the cornice, according to V I T R U V I U S ; from which I have deviated in altering ſome of the members, and making them ſomewhat larger.

A, *Gola recta.*
B, *Gola reverſa.*
C, *Gocciolatoio or Corona.*
D, *Ovolo.*
E, *Cavetto.*
F, *Capital of the Triglyph.*
G, *Triglyph.*

H, *Metopa.*
I, *Tenia.*
K, *Goccie.*
L, *Firſt Faſcia.*
M, *Second Faſcia.*
Y, *Soffit of the Gocciolatoio.*

Parts of the capital.

N, *Cimacio.*
O, *Abaco.*
P, *Ovolo.*
Q, *Gradetti or Annulets.*
R, *Collarino.*

S, *Aſtragal.*
T, *Cimbia.*
V, *Shaft of the column.*
X, *Plan of the capital, and the module divided into thirty minutes.*

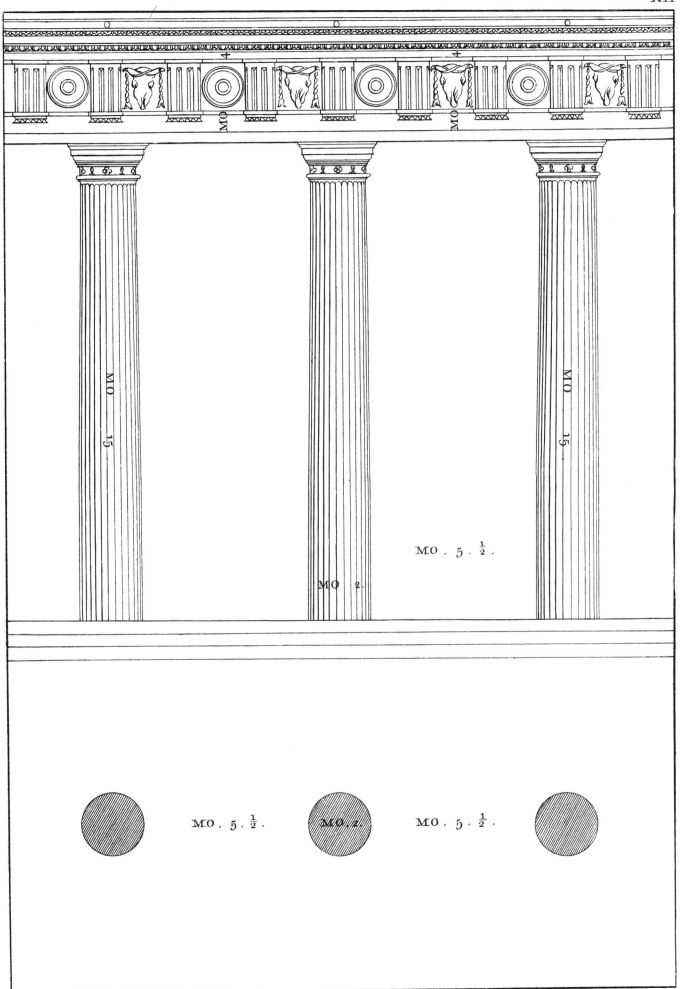

MO . 5 . ½ .

MO 2 .

MO . 5 . ½ .   MO . 2 .   MO . 5 . ½ .

4

MO

Hight of the Arch is 20 Mod. $\frac{1}{2}$

17 $\frac{1}{3}$

17 $\frac{1}{3}$

26   MO   26

26   MO   26

From middle of one column to middle of the other is 15 Mod.

MO. 4 $\frac{2}{3}$

MO 4 $\frac{2}{3}$

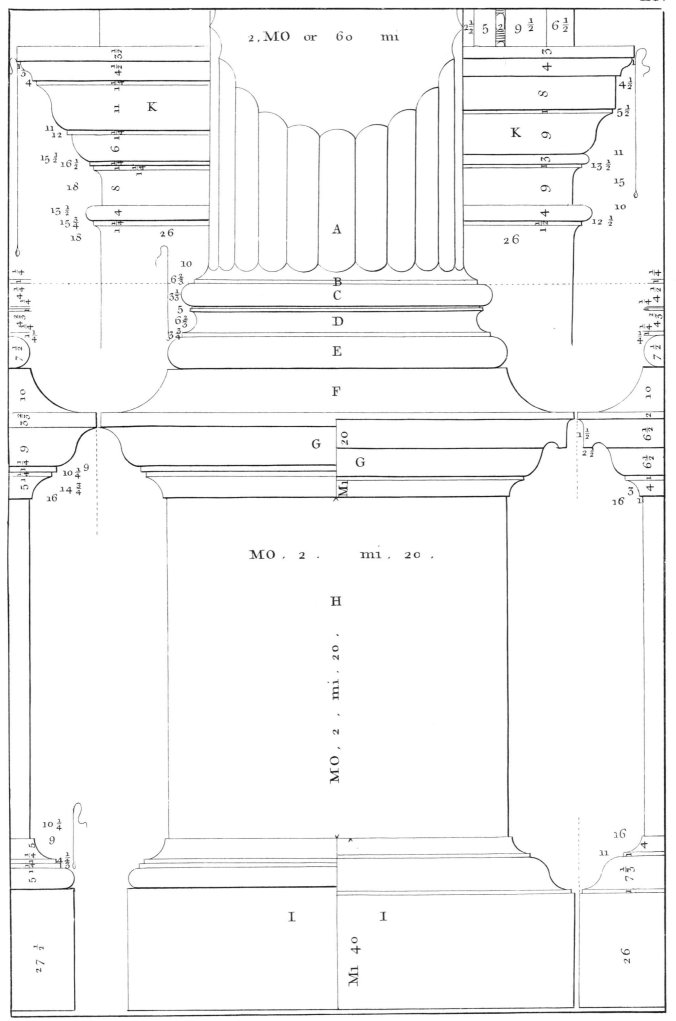

2, MO or 60 mi

2½ 5 9½ 6½

K

K

A

B
C
D
E
F

G

G

MO, 2. mi, 20,

H

MO, 2, mi, 20,

I I

Mi 40

27½

26

A

B

C

D

E

F

G

H

I

K

L

M

N

O

P

Q

R

S

T

V

X

Y

CHAP. XVI.

Of the IONICK ORDER.

THE Ionick order had its origin from *Ionia*, a province in *Afia*, of which it is faid that the temple of DIANA at *Ephefus* was built. The columns, with the capital and bafe, are nine modules high. By a module is underftood the lower diameter of the column.

THE architrave, frize, and cornice are a fifth part of the altitude of the column. In the defigns of fimple colonades, the intercolumniations are of two diameters and a quarter, which is the moft beautiful and commodious manner of intercolumniations, and by VITRUVIUS called *Euftilo's*. In the defign of arches the pilafters are a third part of the void, and the arches are two fquares high.

IF a pedeftal is to be put to Ionic columns, as in the defign of arches, it muft be made as high as half the width of the arch, and divided into feven parts and a half; two of which are for the bafe, one for the cimacia, and the remaining four and a half for the dado, that is, the middle plain.

THE bafe of the Ionick order muft be half a module in thicknefs, and divided into three parts; one to be given to the plinth, whofe projecture is the fourth and eighth part of the module; the other two are divided into feven parts, three of which are for the baftone or torus; the other four are again divided into two, of one is made the upper cavetto, and with the other the lower, which muft project more than the other.

THE aftragal muft be the eighth part of the cavetto. The cimbia of the column is the third part of the baftone or torus of the bafe. But if the bafe is joined with part of the column, then the cimbia muft be made thinner, as I have faid in the Dorick order. Thefe are the dimenfions of the Ionick bafe, according to VITRUVIUS.

BUT as in many antient buildings Attick bafes are feen placed under the columns of this order, and they pleafe me better fo, I have drawn the faid bafe upon the pedeftal, with a little torus under the cimbia; but at the fame time I have not omitted the defign of that order'd by VITRUVIUS.

THE defigns marked L are two different profiles, to make the impofts of arches, the dimenfions of each of which are marked in numbers, fhewing the minutes of the module, as it has been obferved in all the other defigns. Thefe impofts are half as high again as the pilafter is thick, which fupports the arch.

A, *Shaft of the column.*
B, *Tondino or Aftragal, with the Cimbia, and are members of the column.*
C, *upper Baftone or Torus.*
D, *Cavetto.*
E, *lower Baftone or Torus.*

F, *Orlo joined to the Cimacia of the pedeftal.*
G, *the Cimacia in two different forms* ⎫
H, *Dado* ⎬ *of the pedeftal.*
I, *Bafe in two different forms* ⎭
K, *Orlo or Plinth of the Bafe.*
L, *Impofts of the arches.*

TO form the capital, the foot of the column muft be divided into eighteen parts, and nineteen of thefe parts is the height and width of the abaco, half thereof is the height of the capital with the volute, which is therefore nine parts and a half high; one part and half muft be given to the abaco with its cimacio, the other eight remain for the volutæ, which is thus made.

ONE of the nineteen parts is to be allowed from the extremity to the infide of the cimacio, and from that place where the point was made, a line muft fall perpendicular, which divides the voluta in the middle, called *catheto*. And where the point is upon the line which feparates the fuperior four parts and a half from the inferior three and a half, the centre of the eye of the voluta muft be made, whofe diameter is one of the eight parts. And from the faid point a line muft be drawn, which interfecting with the catheto at rectangles, divides the voluta into four parts.

THEN

THEN a fquare ought to be formed in the eye of the voluta, half the diameter of the faid eye in bignefs, and diagonal lines drawn. Upon which lines the points are marked whereon the fixed foot of the compaffes muft be placed in forming the voluta. Thefe are thirteen in number, including the centre of the eye of the faid voluta. The order that ought to be obferved in them will plainly appear by the numbers placed in the defign.

THE aftragal of the column is in a direct line with the eye of the voluta. The thicknefs of the voluta in the middle muft be equal to the projecture of the ovolo, which projects beyond the abaco juft as much as the eye of the voluta is. The channel of the voluta is even with the fhaft of the column.

THE aftragal of the column goes quite round under the voluta, and is always feen, as appears by the plan: For it is natural, that a thing fo tender as the voluta is fuppofed to be, fhould give way to a hard one, fuch as the aftragal, from which it muft always be equally diftant.

CAPITALS are generally made in the angles of colonades and portico's of this order, with volutæ not only in front, but alfo in that part which, if the capital was made as ufual, would be the flank; by which means they have the fronts on two fides, and are called angular capitals. I fhall fhew how thefe are made in my *book of temples*.

A, *Abaco.*
B, *Channel or hollow of the Voluta.*
C, *Ovolo.*
D, *Tondino or Aftragal under the Ovolo.*
E, *Cimbia.*
F, *Shaft of the column.*
G, *The line called Catheto.*

IN the plan of the capital the faid members are countermarked with the fame letters.

S, *The eye of the Voluta in a larger form.*

MEMBERS of the bafe, according to VITRUVIUS.

K, *Shaft of the column.*
L, *Cimbia.*
M, *Baftone or Torus.*
N, *Firft Cavetto.*
O, *Tondini or Aftragals.*
P, *Second Cavetto.*
Q, *Orlo or Plinth.*
R, *Projecture of the bafe.*

THE architrave, frize and cornice are, as I have faid, a fifth part of the height of the column, the whole to be divided into twelve parts, of which the architrave is four parts, the frize three, and the cornice five.

THE architrave is to be divided into five parts; of one its cimacio is made, and the remaining four divided into twelve parts, three of which are given to the firft fafcia and its aftragal; four to the fecond and its aftragal, and five to the third.

THE cornice is to be divided into feven parts and three fourths; two muft be given to the cavetto and ovolo, two to the modiglion, and three and three fourths to the corona and gola or cima. Its projecture is equal to its height. I have defigned the front, flank, and plan of the capital; as alfo the architrave, frize, and cornice, with their proper ornaments.

A, *Gola or Cima recta.*
B, *Gola, or Cima reverfa.*
C, *Gocciolatoio or Corona.*
D, *Cimacio of the Modiglions.*
E, *Modiglions.*
F, *Ovolo.*
G, *Cavetto.*
H, *Fregio or frize.*
I, *Cimacio of the architrave.*
K, *Firft Fafcia.*
L, *Second Fafcia.*
M, *Third Fafcia.*

MEMBERS of the capital.

N, *Abaco.*
O, *Hollow of the Voluta.*
P, *Ovolo.*
Q, *Tondino of the column or Aftragal.*
R, *Shaft of the column.*

THE foffit of the cornice is where the rofes are between one modiglion and the other.

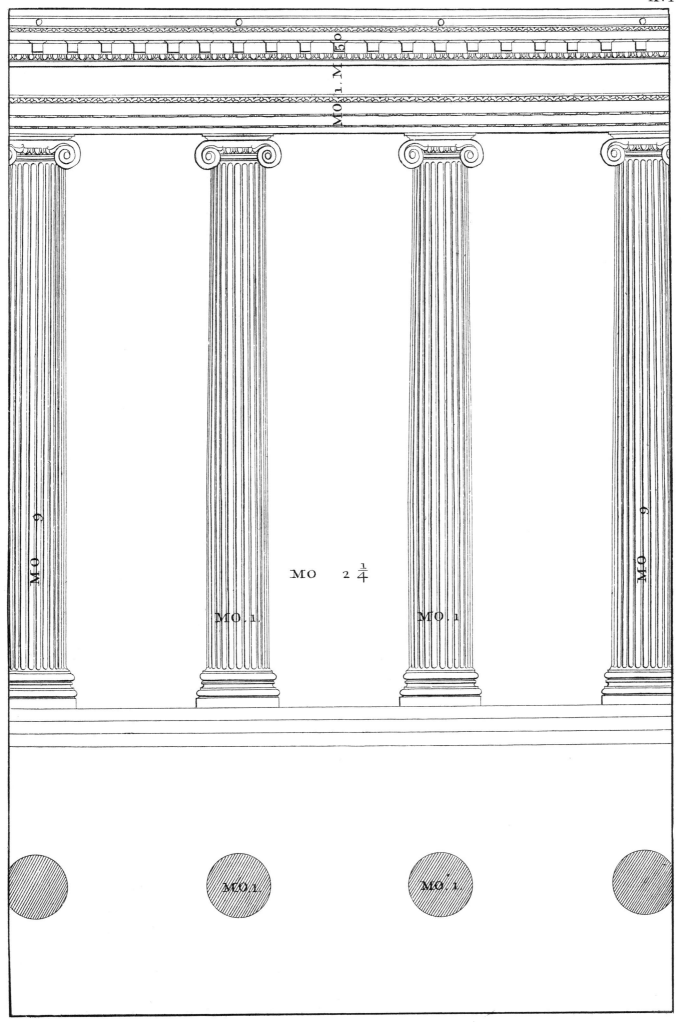

MO. 1. M. 5.°

MO. 9

MO 2 ¼

MO. 9

MO. 1

MO. 1

MO. 1

MO. 1

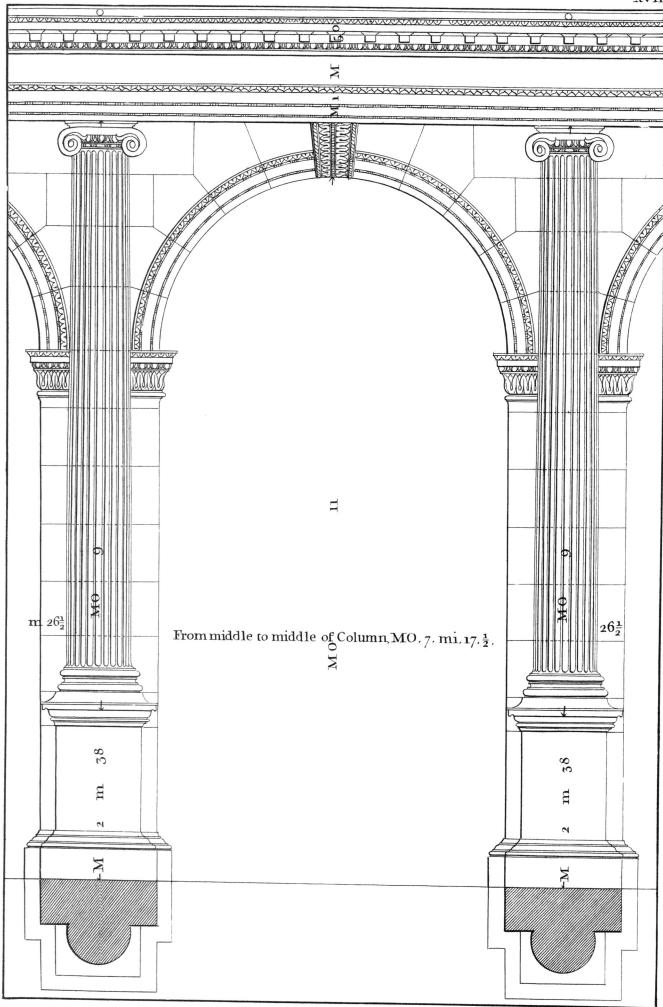

From middle to middle of Column, MO, 7, mi, 17, ½.

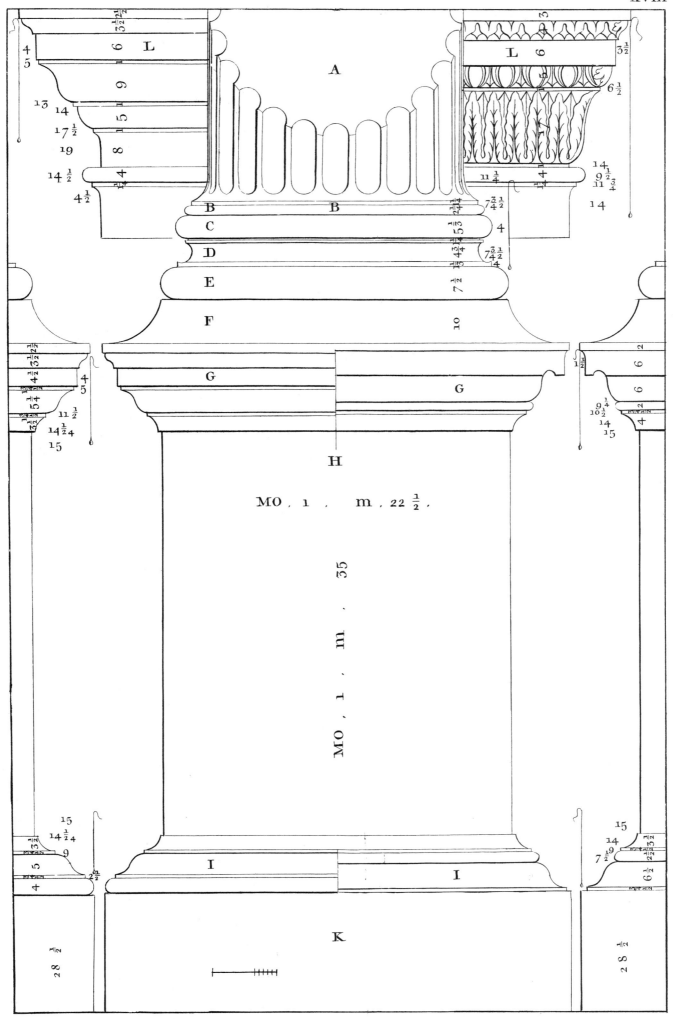

A

L

6

3½ 2½

4

5

13 14

17½

19

14½

4½

6

9

5

8

4

4

B   B

C

D

E

F

L

6

3½

5

6½

14½
9½
11

14

11¼   4 4

7¾ 4½

2¼
2¼

4
1¼
5 3

4¾
¾
3

7¾ 4½
4

7½

10

G

G

H

MO . 1 .   m . 22 ½ .

35

MO . 1 . m . 22 ½

1½
4½ 3½ 2½

4
5

5¼
5 4

3½
14½ 4

15

4 5

11½

2

6

6

9¼
10½

4 2

14

15

15
14½ 4

9

4 5

3¾

2½

I

I

15

14

7½

9

3½ 3½

2¼ 2½

6½

K

28 ½

28 ½

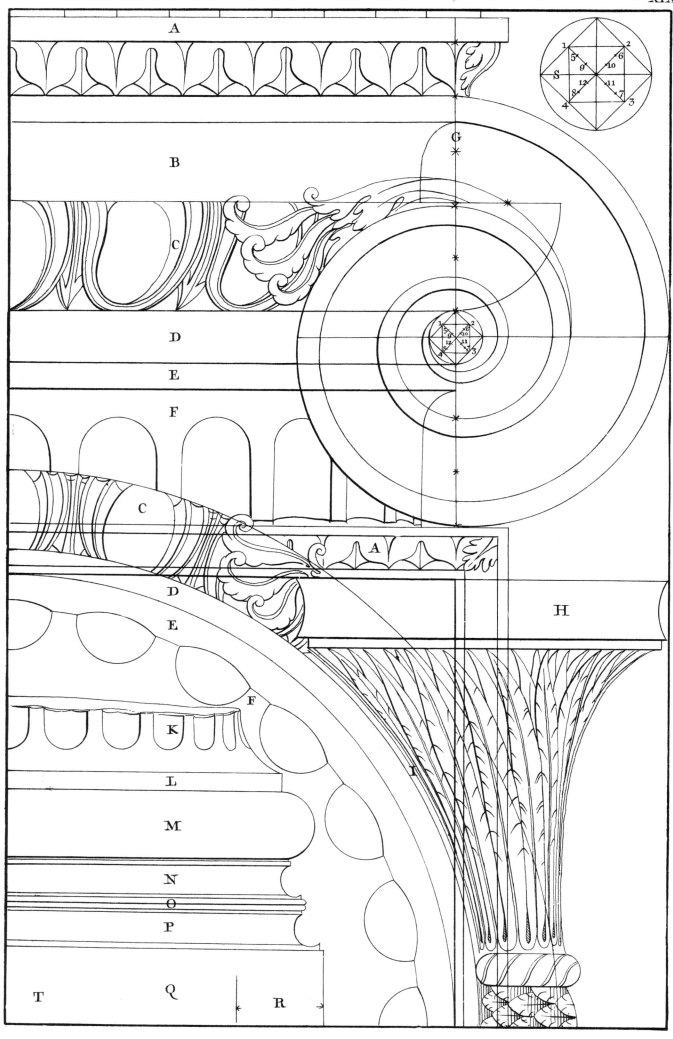

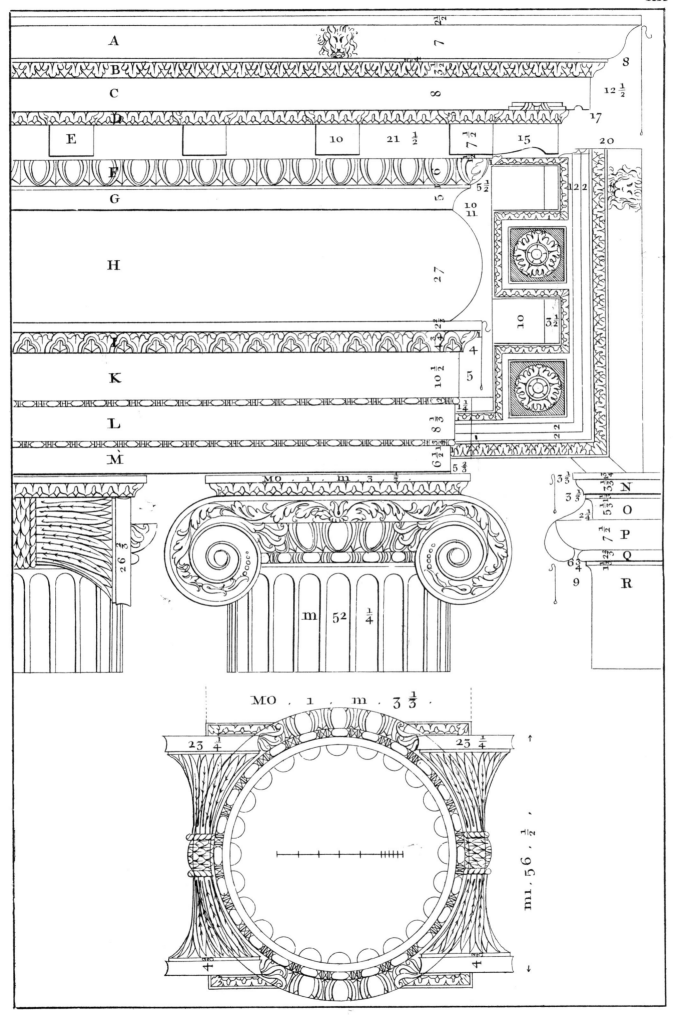

A

B

C

D

E 10 21 ½ 7 ½ 15 20

F 6 5 ½

G 5

H 27

I 4

K 5

L

M 5 ⅔

2 ½ 7

8

12 ½

17

12 2

10 3 ½

2 2

10 ½

8 ⅓

6 ½

MO . 1 . m . 3 ¼

26 ⅔

m 52 ¼

3 ⅓ N
3 ½ O
2 ¼ P 7 ½
Q 6 ¾
R 9

MO . 1 . m . 3 ⅓ .

23 ¼   23 ¼

4   4

m1 . 56 . ½ .

CHAP. XVII.

Of the CORINTHIAN ORDER.

THE Corinthian order, which is more beautiful and elegant than any of the foregoing orders, was firſt invented in *Corinth*, a moſt noble city in *Peloponeſus*.

THE columns are like thoſe of the Ionic order, being five modules and a half in height, including their baſe and capital. When they are to be fluted, they ought to have twenty four channels or flutes, whoſe depth muſt be half of their width. The ſpaces between two flutes muſt be one third of the width of the ſaid flutes.

THE architrave, frize and cornice are a fifth part of the height of the whole column. In the deſign of a ſimple colonade the intercolumniations are of two diameters, as they are in the portico of *St. Maria la Rotunda* at *Rome*; which manner of placing columns is by VITRUVIUS called *Siſtilo's*. In that of arches the pilaſters are two fifths of the void, which void is two ſquares and a half, including the thickneſs of the arch.

THE pedeſtals to be placed under Corinthian columns ought to be one fourth of the height of the columns, and divided into eight parts; one to be given to the cimacia, two to its baſe, and the remaining five for the dado. The baſe muſt be divided into three parts; two to be given to the zocco or plinth, and one to the cornice or molding.

THE Attick is the baſe to theſe columns, but differs from that which is placed under the Dorick order, its projecture being but one fifth part of the diameter of the column. It may alſo vary in ſome other parts; as is ſeen in the deſign, where the impoſts of the arches are alſo profiled, whoſe height is half as much again as the thickneſs of the members or pilaſters that ſupport the arch.

A, *the ſhaft of the column.*	F, *Orlo of the baſe joined to the Cimacia of the pedeſtal.*
B, *the Cimbia or Cincture, and Tondino or Aſtragal of the column.*	G, *Cimacia*
C, *the upper Baſtone or Torus.*	H, *Dado* ⎫ *of the pedeſtal.*
D, *Cavetto with its Aſtragal.*	I, *Cornice of the baſe* ⎬
E, *lower Baſtone or Torus.*	K, *Orlo of the baſe.*

The impoſts of the arches is by the ſide of the column.

THE height of the Corinthian capital ought to be the diameter of the column below, and a ſixth part more, which is allowed to the abaco. The remainder is divided into three equal parts; the firſt is given to the firſt leaf, the ſecond to the ſecond, and the third is again divided into two parts. In that part neareſt to the abaco muſt be made the *caulicoli* or ſtems, with their leaves, that ſeem to be ſupported by them, and from which they ariſe; therefore the ſhaft or ſtem from whence they ſpring ſhould be thick, and diminiſh gradually in their foldings, imitating thereby the plants, which are thicker in the part from whence they ſprout, than at the extremities of their branches.

THE *campana*, which is the body of the capital under the leaves, ought to fall directly perpendicular with the bottom of the flutes of the columns. To form the abaco, and to give it a ſuitable projecture, a ſquare is to be made, every ſide whereof muſt be a module and a half, within which let diagonal lines be drawn, and in the middle or centre where they interſect, the fix'd point of the compaſſes ought to be placed, and towards every angle of the ſquare a module is to be marked; then, where the points are, lines that interſect the ſaid diagonals at rectangles muſt be drawn, ſo as to touch the ſides of the ſquare, and theſe will be the bounds of the projecture, the length of which will alſo give the width of the horns of the abaco.

THE curvature, or diminution, is made by drawing a thread from one horn to the other, and taking the point where the triangle is formed whoſe baſe is the diminution, then a line is to be drawn from the extremities of the ſaid horn to the extremity of the aſtragal or tondino of the column, which line the tip of the leaves is to touch, or they may come out a little more, and this is their projecture. The width of the rofe ought to be a fourth part of the lower diameter of the column.

T H E architrave, frize, and cornice, as I have faid, are one fifth of the height of the column, and the whole to be divided into twelve parts, as in the Ionick ; but with this difference, that in this the cornice is to be divided into eight parts and a half, one of which is given to the *intavolato* or cima reverfa, another to the *dentello* or dentels, the third to the ovolo, the fourth and fifth to the modiglion, and the remaining three and a half to the corona and gola.

T H E projecture of the cornice is equal to its height.

T H E pannels for the rofes placed between the modiglions muft be fquare, and the modiglions half as broad as the plane of the faid rofes.

T H E members of this order are not marked with letters, as the foregoing ; becaufe by them thefe may eafily be known.

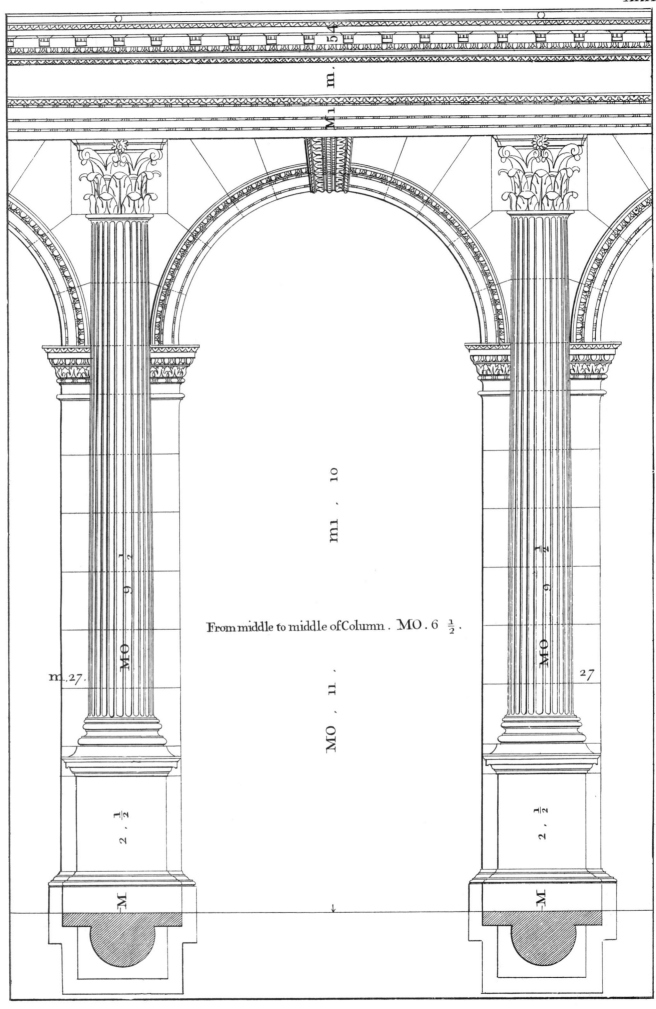

From middle to middle of Column . MO . 6 ½ .

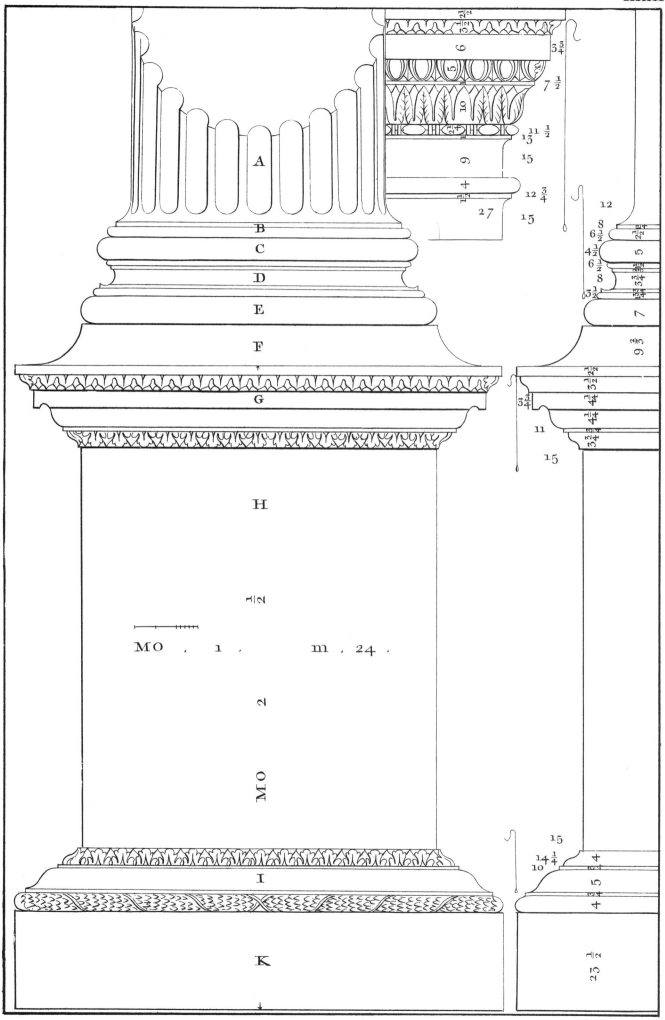

CHAP. XVIII.

Of the COMPOSITE ORDER.

THE Compofite order, which is alfo called *Latin* from its having been the antient *Romans* invention, and alfo becaufe it partakes of two of the foregoing orders. The moft regular and beautiful is that which is compofed of the Ionic and Corinthian.

IT is made more flender than the Corinthian, and may be formed like that in all its parts, except the capital. The columns ought to be ten modules high.

IN the defigns of fimple colonades the intercolumniations are of one diameter and a half, which is called by VITRUVIUS *Picnoftilo's*. In that of arches the pilafters are half the void of the arch, and the arches are two fquares and a half high under the vault.

AND becaufe this order, as I have faid, ought to be formed more flender than the Corinthian, its pedeftal is a third part of the height of the column divided into eight parts and a half; of one the cimacia of that bafe is made, and five and a half remain for the dado. The bafe of the pedeftals is divided into three parts; two are given to the zocco or plinth, and one to its baftone and gola.

THE Attick may ferve for the bafe of this column, as in the Corinthian; and alfo may be form'd compofed of the Attick and Ionick, as appears by the defign.

THE profile of the impoft of the arches is on one fide of the dado of the pedeftal, the height of which is equal to the thicknefs of the *membretto*.

THE dimenfions of the Compofite capital are the fame as thofe of the Corinthian, but differs from it in the voluta, ovolo, and *fufarolo*, which members are attributed to the Ionick. The method of forming which is thus: From the abaco downwards the capital is to be divided into three parts, as in the Corinthian; the firft to be given to the firft leaf, the fecond to the fecond, and the third to the voluta, which is formed in the fame manner, and with the fame points with which it was faid the Ionick was made, and takes up fo much of the abaco that it feems to grow out of the ovolo near the flower, which is placed in the middle of the curvature of the faid abaco, and is as thick in front as the blunt part that is made over the horns thereof, or a little more.

THE thicknefs of the ovolo is three parts in five of the abaco. Its lower part begins parallel with the lower part of the eye of the voluta, and projects three parts of four of its height, and is with its projecture perpendicular to the curvature of the abaco, or a little more.

THE fufarolo is one third part of the height of the ovolo, and its projecture a little more than half its thicknefs, and goes round the capital under the voluta always in fight.

THE *gradetto*, which is placed under the fufarolo that forms the orlo of the campana of the capital is half the fufarolo. The body of the campana anfwers directly to the bottom of the flutes of the columns.

I HAVE feen one of this kind at *Rome*, from which I have taken the faid dimenfions, becaufe I thought it extremely beautiful, and exceedingly well contrived.

THERE are alfo capitals to be feen formed in another manner, that may be called Compofite, of which mention fhall be made and the defigns placed in my *books of antiquity*.

THE architrave, frize and cornice are a fifth part of the height of the column. Their proportions and divifions may eafily be known by what has been laid in the other orders, and by the numbers placed in the defigns.

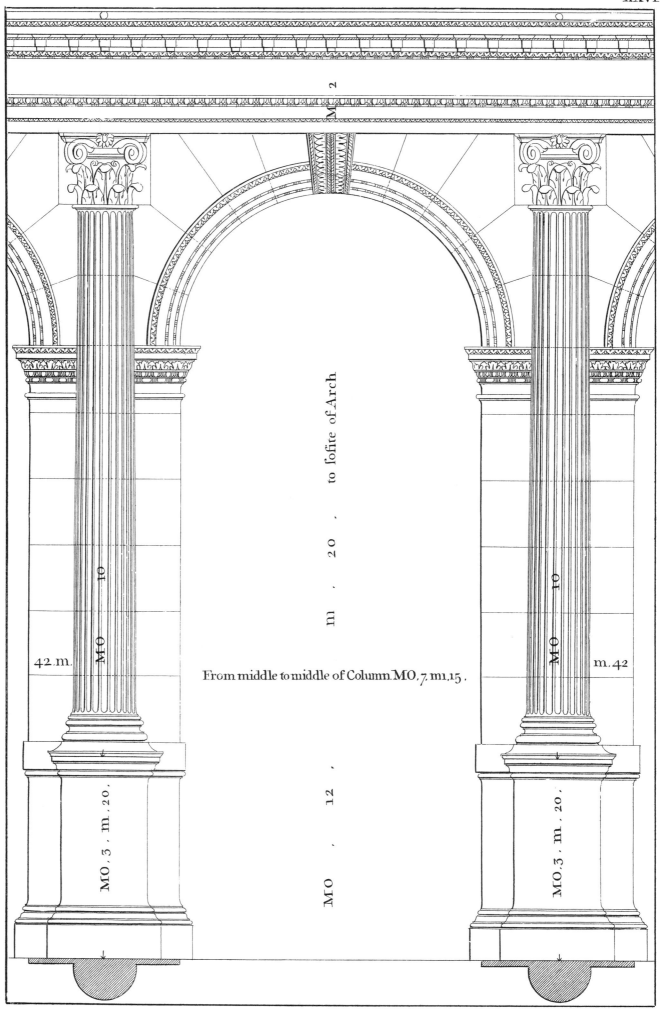

From middle to middle of Column MO, 7, m1, 15.

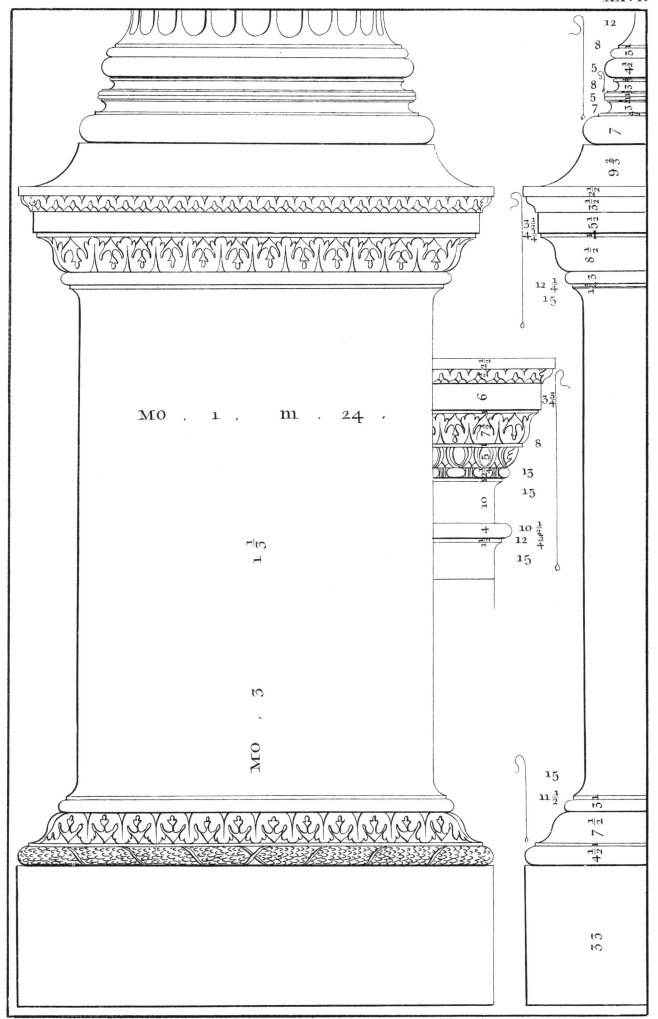

MO . 1 . m . 24 .

$1\frac{1}{3}$

MO . 3

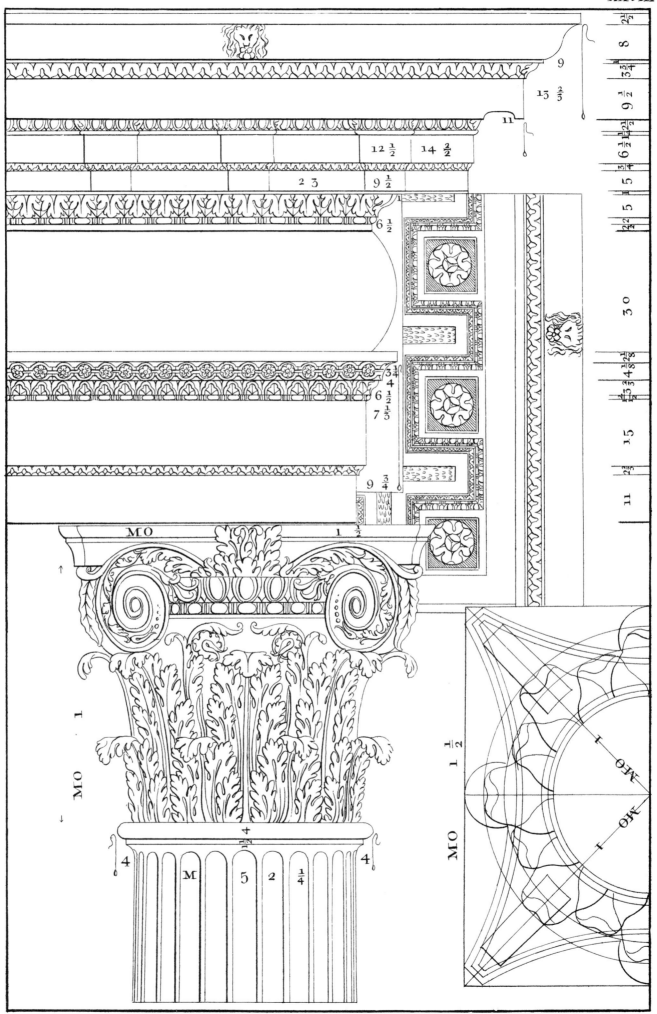

CHAP. XIX.

Of PEDESTALS.

I HAVE hitherto faid as much as I thought neceffary with refpect to plain walls, and their ornaments; and have particularly touched upon the feveral pedeftals that may be applied to each order.

BUT tho' the antients may feem to have had no regard to form a pedeftal larger for one order than another; yet this member is a very great addition both in point of ornament and beauty when it is made with judgment, and in due proportion to the other parts.

IN order that the architect may have a perfect knowledge of pedeftals, and be able to ufe them upon all occafions; it is to be obferved, that the antients made them fometimes fquare, equal in height and width, as in the arch of *Leoni* at *Verona*. Thefe I have given to the Dorick order, becaufe it requires folidity.

THEY fometimes made them by taking the meafure from the opening, as in the arch of *Titus* at *Santa Maria Nova* in *Rome*, and that of *Trajan* over the port of *Ancona*, where the height of the pedeftal is half the void of the arch. Which kind of pedeftal I have placed in the Ionick order.

THEY fometimes took the dimenfion from the height of the column, as may be feen in an arch that was erected in honour of AUGUSTUS CÆSAR, at *Sufa*, a city fituated at the foot of the mountains that part *France* and *Italy*; in the arch of *Pola*, a city in *Dalmatia*; and in the amphitheatre at *Rome*, in the Ionick and Corinthian orders; in which edifices the pedeftal is one fourth of the height of the columns, as I have obferved in the Corinthian order. In the arch of *Caftel Vecchio* at *Verona*, which is exceeding beautiful, the pedeftal is a third part of the height of the column, as I have placed it in the Compofite order. Thefe are the moft beautiful forms of pedeftals, and fuch as have a fine proportion to the other parts.

WHEN VITRUVIUS, in his fixth book, fpeaking of theatres, makes mention of the *poggio*, it is to be obferved, that the poggio is the fame as the pedeftal, which is a third of the length of the column, placed as an ornament to the fcene.

BUT pedeftals that exceed a third part of the columns may be feen in the arch of *Conftantine* at *Rome*, where the pedeftals are two fifths of the height of the columns. And it was obferv'd in almoft all the antient pedeftals to form the bafe twice as thick as the cimacia; as fhall be feen in my *book of arches*.

CHAP. XX.

Of ABUSES.

HAVING laid down the ornaments of architecture, that is, the five orders, and fhewn how they ought to be made; and having placed the profiles of every one of their parts as I found the antients did obferve them; it feems to me not improper to inform the reader in this place of many abufes introduc'd by the Barbarians, which are ftill followed, that the ftudious in this art may avoid them in their own works, and be able to know them in thofe of others.

I SAY therefore, that architecture, as well as all other arts, being an imitatrix of nature, can fuffer nothing that either alienates or deviates from that which is agreeable to nature; from whence we fee, that the antient architects, who made their edifices of wood, when they began to make them of ftone, inftituted that the columns fhould be left thicker at the top than at the bottom, taking example from the trees, all which are thinner at the top than in the trunk, or near the root.

A N D because it is very probable, that thofe things are depreffed upon which fome great weight is put, bafes were placed under the columns, which, with their baftoni and cavetti, feem to be crufhed with the burden laid upon them.

S o likewife in the cornice they introduced the triglyphs, modiglions and dentels, which reprefent the ends of thofe beams that are put for a fupport to the floors and roofs.

T H E fame alfo may be obferved in all the other parts, if they are confider'd. Being thus, that manner of building cannot but be blamed, which departs from that which the nature of things teacheth, and from that fimplicity which appears in the things produced by her; framing as it were another nature, and deviating from the true, good and beautiful method of building.

F O R which reafon one ought not, inftead of columns or pilafters, that are to fuftain fome great weight, to place *cartelli*, alfo called *cartocci*, being a kind of a fcroll, which to the intelligent appear very fhocking, and to thofe that are not fo it gives rather a confufion than a pleafure; nor have they any other effect befides encreafing the builder's expence.

F O R the fame reafon none of thefe cartocci ought to project from the cornices; for it is requifite that all the parts of the cornices fhould be made for fome purpofe and fhew, like what they would feem to be if the whole work was of wood.

B E S I D E S, it is neceffary that a great weight fhould be fuftained by fomething folid and ftrong enough to fupport it: now it is certain that thofe cartocci would be altogether fuperfluous, becaufe it is impoffible that any beams or timber fhould produce the effect reprefented; and fince they are fuppofed to be foft and tender, I cannot conceive with what reafon they can be placed under a thing both hard and heavy.

B U T, in my opinion, the moft important error is that of making the frontifpieces of doors, windows, and loggia's broken in the middle, fince thefe were made to keep the rain from the fabricks, and which the antient builders, inftructed by neceffity itfelf, made to clofe and fwell in the middle.

I K N O W therefore nothing that can be done more contrary to natural reafon, than to divide that part which is fuppofed to fhelter the inhabitants and thofe that go into the houfe from rain, fnow, and hail.

A N D altho' variety and things new may pleafe every one, yet they ought not to be done contrary to the precepts of art, and contrary to that which reafon dictates; whence one fees, that altho' the antients did vary, yet they never departed from the univerfal and neceffary rules of art, as fhall be feen in my *books of antiquities*.

A L S O as to the projection of the cornices, and the other ornaments, the making them come out too much is no fmall abufe; becaufe when they exceed that which is reafonably proper for them, efpecially if they are in a clofe place, they will make it narrow and difagreeable, and frighten thofe that ftand under them, as they always threaten to fall.

N O R ought the making cornices which are not in proportion to the columns lefs to be avoided; becaufe if upon little columns great cornices are placed, or little cornices upon great columns, who doubts but that fuch a building muft have a very unpleafing afpect?

B E S I D E S which, the fuppofing of the columns to be divided, making certain annulets and garlands round them, that may feem to hold them firmly united together, ought as much as poffible to be avoided; becaufe the more folid and ftrong the columns appear, the better they feem to execute the purpofe for which they were erected, which is to make the work thereon both ftrong and fecure.

I C O U L D mention many other fuch abufes, as fome members in the cornices that are made without any proportion to the others, which, by what I have fhewn above, and by that which has been already faid, may very eafily be known.

I T remains now, to come to the difpofition of the particular and principal places of the fabricks.

C H A P.

CHAP. XXI.

Of the loggia's, entries, halls, rooms, and of their form.

THE loggia's, for the moſt part, are made in the fore and back front of the houſe, and are placed in the middle, when only one is made, and on each ſide when there are two.

THESE loggia's ſerve for many uſes, as to walk, eat in, and other recreations; and are either made larger or ſmaller, according as the bigneſs and conveniency of the fabrick requires; but, for the moſt part, they are not to be made leſs than ten foot wide, nor more than twenty.

BESIDES, all the well-contrived houſes have in the middle, and in their more beautiful part, ſome places, by which all the others have a communication: theſe in the under part are called entries, and in the upper halls. Theſe places are publick.

THE entries are the firſt parts, except the loggia's, which offer to thoſe that enter the houſe, and are the moſt convenient for thoſe to ſtay in who wait the maſter's coming out, to ſalute or do buſineſs with him.

THE halls ſerve for feaſts, entertainments and decorations, for comedies, weddings, and ſuch like recreations; and therefore theſe places ought to be much larger than the others, and to have the moſt capacious form, to the end that many perſons may be therein commodiouſly placed, and ſee whatever is done there.

IN the length of halls I uſe not to exceed two ſquares, made from the breadth; but the nearer they come to a ſquare, the more convenient and commendable they will be.

THE rooms ought to be diſtributed on each ſide of the entry and hall; and it is to be obſerved, that thoſe on the right correſpond with thoſe on the left, that ſo the fabrick may be the ſame in one place as in the other, and that the walls may equally bear the burden of the roof; becauſe if the rooms are made large in one part, and ſmall in the other, the latter will be more fit to reſiſt the weight, by reaſon of the nearneſs of the walls, and the former more weak, which will produce in time very great inconveniences, and ruin the whole work.

THE moſt beautiful and proportionable manners of rooms, and which ſucceed beſt, are ſeven, becauſe they are either made round (tho' but ſeldom) or ſquare, or their length will be the diagonal line of the ſquare, or of a ſquare and a third, or of one ſquare and a half, or of one ſquare and two thirds, or of two ſquares.

CHAP. XXII.

Of pavements and cielings.

HAVING ſeen the forms of the loggia's, halls, and rooms, it is proper to ſpeak of their pavements and cielings.

THE pavements are uſually made either of *terrazzo*, as is uſed in *Venice*, bricks or live ſtones. Thoſe terrazzi are excellent which are made of pounded bricks, and ſmall gravel, and lime of river pebbles, or the *paduan*, well pounded; and ought to be made in ſpring or in ſummer, that they may be well dry'd.

THE brick floors, becauſe the bricks may be made of divers forms and of divers colours by reaſon of the diverſity of the chalks, will be very agreeable and beautiful to the eye.

THOSE of live ſtones are very ſeldom made in chambers, becauſe they are exceeding cold in winter; but they do very well in the loggia's and publick places.

IT is to be obſerved, that the chambers which are one behind the other muſt have their

floors

floors even, and in fuch a manner that the threfholds of the doors be not higher than the remaining part of the chamber-floor; and if any little room or clofet fhould not join with its height to that mark, a *mezato* or falfe floor ought to be made upon it.

T H E cielings are alfo diverfly made, becaufe many take delight to have them of beautiful and well-wrought beams. Where it is neceffary to obferve, that thefe beams ought to be di-ftant one from another one thicknefs and a half of the beam, becaufe the cielings appear thus very beautiful to the eye, and there remains fo much of the wall between the ends of the beams, that it is more able to fuftain what is over it. But if they are made more di-ftant, they'll not be an agreeable fight; and if they are made lefs, it will be in a manner di-viding the wall above from that below, whereupon, the beams being rotted or burnt, the upper wall muft be ruined.

O T H E R S are for having compartments of *ftucco*, or of wood, in which pictures are placed; and thus being adorn'd according to different inventions, therefore in this no certain and determinate rule can be given.

C H A P. XXIII.

Of the height of the rooms.

T H E rooms are either made with a vaulted or flat cieling. If with a flat cieling, the height from the floor to the cieling muft be equal to their breadth; and the rooms above muft be a fixth part lefs in height than thofe below. If vaulted (as thofe of the firft order are ufually made, becaufe they thus appear more beautiful, and are lefs expofed to fires) the height of the vaults in rooms that are fquare is a third part more than the breadth of the room.

B u T in thofe which are longer than they are broad, it will be neceffary from the length and breadth to feek for the height, that they may bear a proportion to each other. This height will be found in adding the breadth to the length,

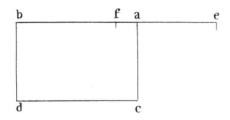

and dividing the whole into two equal parts, becaufe one of thofe halves will be the height of the vault. As for example, let *b c* be the place to be arched; add the breadth, *a c*, to *a b*, the length, and let the line *e b* be made, which is to be divided into two equal parts, in the point *f,* we'll fay *f b* is the height we feek. Otherwife, let the room to be vaulted be twelve foot long and fix broad, add fix to twelve, and it will make eighteen, the half of which is nine, the vault ought therefore to be nine foot high.

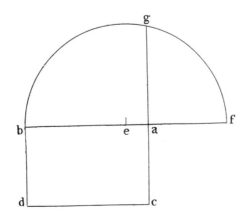

A N O T H E R height, that will be proportionable both to the length and breadth of the room, will alfo in this manner be found. *c b*, the place to be vaulted, being fet down, we'll add the breadth to the length, and make the line *b f*; we'll afterwards divide it into two equal parts in the point *e*, which being made the centre, we'll make the half circle *b g f*, and lengthen *a c* until it touches the circumference in the point *g*, and *a g* will give the height of the vault of *c b*.

B Y numbers it will thus be found: The length and breadth of the room in feet being known, we'll find a number that has the fame proportion to the breadth as the length has to the number fought. This we find by multiplying the leffer extreme with the greater; becaufe the fquare root of the number which will proceed from the faid multiplication, will be the height we feek. As for example, if the place that we intend to vault be nine foot long, and four wide, the height of the vault will be fix foot; and the fame proportion that nine has to fix, fix alfo has to four, that is the fefquialteral.

B u T

BUT it is to be obferved, that it will not be poffible always to find this height in whole numbers.

ANOTHER height may be found that will fall fhort of this, but neverthelefs will be proportionable to the room. Draw the lines *a b*, *a c*, *c d*, and *b d*, that defcribe the breadth and length of the room, and the height will be found as in the firft method, which is *c e*, this join to *a c*, then draw the line *e d f*, and lengthen *a b* until it touches *e d f* in the point *f*, and *b f* will be the height of the vault.

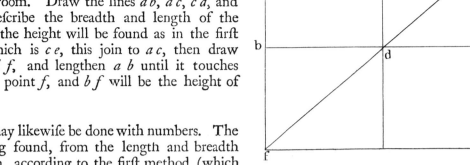

THIS may likewife be done with numbers. The height being found, from the length and breadth of the room, according to the firft method (which in a foregoing example was nine) the length, breadth and height muft be placed as they are in the figure; then nine is to be multiplied with twelve and with fix, and that which will proceed from twelve is to be placed under the twelve, and the product of fix under the fix; afterwards the fix is to be multiplied with twelve, and the product, which is feventy two, placed under the nine; then a number being found which multiplied by nine amounts to feventy two, which in our cafe would be eight, we'll fay eight foot to be the height of the vault.

$$12 - 9 - 6$$
$$108 - 72 - 54$$
$$8$$

THESE heights run in this manner between themfelves, *viz.* the firft is greater than the fecond, and the fecond is greater than the third; we'll however make ufe of each of thefe heights, according as they may fuit with convenience, that feveral rooms of different dimenfions may be fo made as to have all their vaults of an equal height, and the faid vaults to be neverthelefs proportionable to them; from which will refult both beauty to the eye, and convenience for the floors that are placed thereon, fince they'll all be level.

THERE are alfo other heights for vaults, which do not come under any rule, and are therefore left for the architect to make ufe of as neceffity requires, and according to his own judgment.

CHAP. XXIV.

Of the feveral manners of vaults.

THERE are fix manners of vaults, *viz.* crofs'd, fafciated, flat (fo they call vaults which are a portion of a circle, and do not arrive to a femicircle) circular, groined, and fhelllike; all which are a third part of the breadth of the room in height.

THE two laft manners have been invented by the moderns, but the four firft were ufed by the antients.

THE circular vaults are made in fquare rooms, and the manner of making them is thus: In the angles of the room are left fome mutules that fupport the femicircle of the vault, which in the middle is flat, but more circular the nearer it comes to the angles.

THERE is one of this kind in the baths of *Titus* at *Rome*, which was partly ruin'd when I faw it.

I   I HAVE

I Have here put under the forms of all thefe different manners, applied to the different fhapes of the rooms.

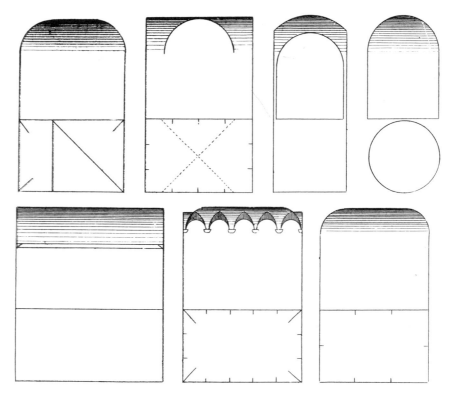

C H A P.   XXV.

Of the dimenfions of the doors and windows.

NO certain and determinate rule can be given for the height and breadth of the principal doors of fabricks, or concerning the doors and windows of rooms; becaufe, in making the principal doors, the architect ought to accommodate them to the bignefs of the fabrick, to the quality of the mafter, and to thofe things that are to be carried in and out of the fame.

THE beft way, in my opinion, is to divide the fpace from the floor to the fuperficies of the joyfts, into three parts and a half, (as Vitruvius teacheth in the fixth chapter of his fourth book) and allow two to the height, and one to the breadth of the opening, wanting the twelfth part of the height.

THE antients ufed to make their doors narrower at top than at bottom, as is feen in a temple at *Tivoli*, and which Vitruvius alfo teacheth, perhaps for greater ftrength.

THE place to be chofen for principal doors, is where a free accefs may be had to it from all parts of the houfe.

THE doors of rooms are not to be made wider than three foot, and fix and a half high; nor lefs than two foot in breadth, and five in height.

IT is to be obferved in making the windows, that they fhould not take in more or lefs light, or be fewer or more in number, than what neceffity requires: therefore great regard ought to be had to the largenefs of the rooms which are to receive the light from them; becaufe it is manifeft, that a great room requires much more light to make it lucid and clear, than a fmall one: and if the windows are made either lefs or fewer than that which is convenient, they will make the places obfcure, and if too large, they will fcarce be habitable, becaufe they will let in fo much hot and cold air, that the places, according to the feafon of the year, will either be exceeding hot or very cold, in cafe the part of the heavens which they face, does not in fome manner prevent it.

There-

THEREFORE the windows ought not to be wider than the fourth part of the breadth of the rooms, or narrower than the fifth, and are to be made two fquares and a fixth part of their breadth more in height. And altho' the rooms in a houfe are made large, middling, and fmall, the windows, neverthelefs, ought to be all equal in the fame order or ftory.

To take the dimenfions of the faid windows, I like thofe rooms very much whofe length is two thirds more than the breadth, that is, if the breadth be eighteen foot, the length fhould be thirty, and I divide the breadth into four parts and a half, one I give to the breadth of the void of the window, and two to the height, adding one fixth part of the breadth more; and according to the largenefs of thefe I make thofe of the other rooms.

THE windows above thefe, that is, in the fecond ftory, ought to be a fixth part lefs in the height of the void, than thofe underneath; and in the fame manner, if other windows are placed higher, they ought to diminifh ftill a fixth part.

THE windows on the right hand ought to correfpond to thofe on the left, and thofe above directly over them that are below; and the doors likewife ought to be directly over one another, that the void may be over the void, and the folid upon the folid, and all face one another, fo that ftanding at one end of the houfe one may fee to the other, which affords both beauty and cool air in fummer, befides other conveniencies.

FOR greater ftrength, it is ufual that the lintels or architraves of the doors and windows may not be overcharged with the weight, to make certain arches which are vulgarly called fegments, which contribute very much to the duration of the fabrick.

THE windows ought to be diftant from the angles or corners of the building, as has been faid before, becaufe that part ought not to be opened and weakened, which is to keep the whole edifice upright and together.

THE pilafters or jambs of the doors and windows muft not be lefs in thicknefs than the fixth part of the breadth of the void, nor more than the fifth.

IT remains now that we look into their ornaments.

CHAP. XXVI.

Of the ornaments of doors and windows.

HOW the ornaments of the principal doors of a building ought to be made, may eafily be known by what VITRUVIUS teacheth in the fixth chapter of the fourth book, (adding withal what the moft reverend BARBARO fays and fhews in his defign upon that fubject) and by what I have hitherto faid and defigned in all the five orders.

BUT fetting thefe afide, I fhall only give fome profiles of the ornaments of the doors and windows of rooms according as they may be differently made, and fhew how to mark each member in particular, that it may be graceful and have a due projection.

THE ornaments given to doors and windows, are the architrave, frize, and cornice: the architrave goes round the door, and muft be as thick as the jambs or pilafters, (which I have faid ought not to be lefs thick than the fixth part of the breadth of the void, nor thicker than the fifth) from which alfo the frize and cornice take their thicknefs.

THE firft or uppermoft of the two defigns which follow, has thefe meafures: the architrave is divided into four parts, three of which are for the height of the frize, and five for that of the cornice. The architrave is again divided into ten parts, three of which go to the firft fafcia, four to the fecond, and the remaining three parts are fubdivided into five, two are given to the *regolo* or orlo, and the remaining three to the gola reverfa, which is otherwife called intavolato. Its projection is equal to its height. The orlo projects lefs than half its thicknefs.

THE intavolato is in this manner marked; a ftrait line muft be drawn that ends at the extremities of that under the orlo, and upon the fecond fafcia, and to be divided in the middle,

dle, making each of the halves the bafe of a triangle of two equal fides; then placing the fixed foot of the compaffes in the angle oppofite to the bafe, draw the curve lines which form the faid intavolato.

T H E frize is three parts of the four of the architrave, and is to be marked with a fegment of a circle lefs than half a circle, and with its fwelling comes directly to the cimacio of the architrave.

T H E five parts which are given to the cornice, are in this manner diftributed to its members; one is given to the cavetto with its liftello, which is a fifth part of the cavetto: the cavetto projects three parts in two of its height. To mark it a triangle muft be formed of two equal fides, and the angle C made the center, fo that the cavetto will be the bafe of the triangle: another of the faid five parts is given to the ovolo, whofe projection is two parts in three of its height; to mark it a triangle muft be formed of two equal fides, and the point H made the center: the other three are divided into feventeen parts, eight are given to the corona or gocciolatoio, with its liftelli, of which that above is one of the faid eight parts, and that below which makes the hollow of the gocciolatoio, is one of the fix parts of the ovolo: the other nine are given to the gola dlritta, and to its orlo, which is one part of the three of the faid gola. To form it well, and make it graceful, the ftraight line A B muft be drawn, and divided into two equal parts, in the point C; one of thefe muft be divided into feven parts, fix of which muft be taken in the point D, to form the two triangles A E C, and C B F, and in the points E and F the fixed foot of the compaffes muft be placed to defcribe the fegments of a circle A C and C B, which form the gola.

T H E architrave likewife, in the fecond invention, is to be divided into four parts, three of which make the height of the frize, and five that of the cornice.

T H E architrave muft be divided into three parts, two of which muft be fubdivided into feven, and three given to the firft fafcia, and four to the fecond; the third part muft be divided into nine; with two the tondino is made, and the other feven are to be fubdivided into five, three of which form the intavolato, and two the ovolo.

T H E height of the cornice is divided into five parts and three quarters, one of thefe muft be divided into fix, and five given to the intavolato over the frize, and one to the liftello; the projection of the intavolato is equal to its height, as alfo of the liftello. Another is given to the ovolo, whofe projection is three parts of four of its height: the gradetto over the ovolo is a fixth part of the ovolo, and its projection the fame: the other three are divided into feventeen, eight of which are given to the gocciolatoio, whofe projection is four parts of three of its height; the other nine are divided into four, three of which are given to the gola, and one to the orlo: the three quarters that remain muft be divided into five parts and a half; with one is made the gradetto, and with the other four and a half its intavolato over the gocciolatoio. The projection of this cornice is equal to its thicknefs.

The members of the cornice of the firft invention.

I, *Cavetto.*   N, *Gola.*
K, *Ovolo.*   O, *Orlo.*
L, *Gocciolatoio.*

Members of the architrave.

P, *Intavolato or Gola reverfa.*   R, *Orlo.*
Q, *firft Fafcia.*   S, *fwelling of the Frize.*
V, *fecond Fafcia.*   T, *part of the Frize that goes into the wall.*

B Y means of thefe the members of the fecond invention may alfo be known.

O F thefe two other inventions, the architrave of the firft, marked with F, muft likewife be divided into four parts; three and a quarter are given to the height of the frize, and five to the height of the cornice. The architrave muft be divided into eight parts, five go to the *piano*, and three to the cimacio; which is alfo divided into eight parts, three of which are given to the intavolato, three to the cavetto, and two to the orlo. The height of the cornice muft be divided into fix parts; two are given to the gola diritta with its orlo, and one to the intavolato; then the faid gola muft be divided into nine parts, with eight of which is made

the

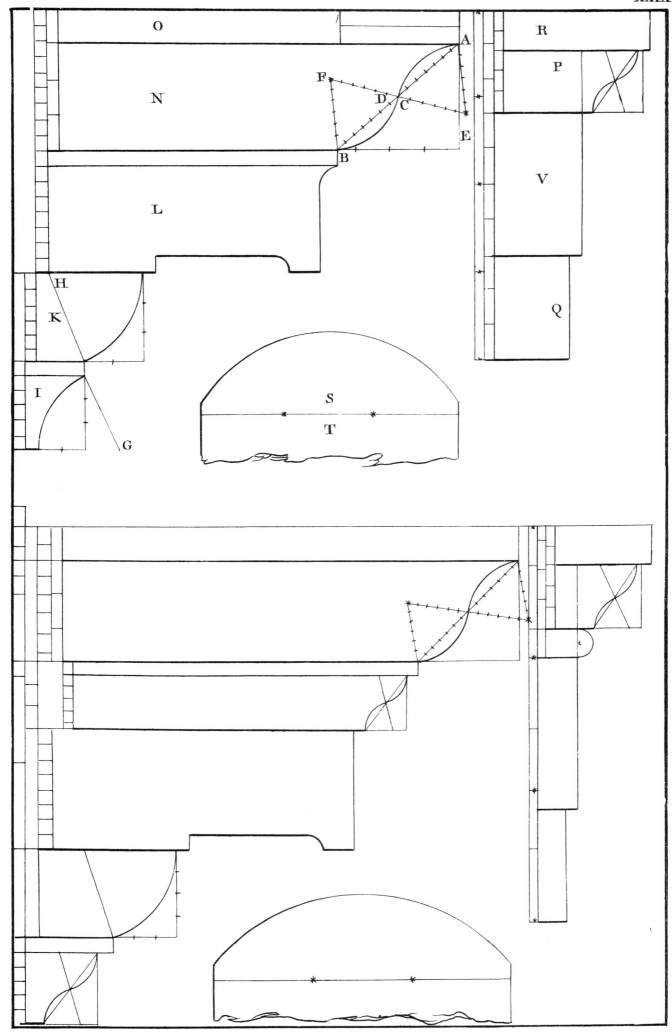

E

F

G

H

the gocciolatoio and gradetto : the aftragal or tondino over the frize, is a third of one of the faid fix parts, and that which remains between the gocciolatoio and tondino is left to the cavetto.

In the other invention the architrave marked with H, is divided into four parts ; three and a half are given to the height of the frize, and five to the height of the cornice : the architrave is divided into eight parts ; five go to the piano, and three to the cimacio : the cimacio is divided into feven parts ; with one is made the aftragallo, and what remains is divided again into eight parts, three are given to the gola reverfa, three to the cavetto, and two to the orlo : the height of the cornice muft be divided into fix parts and three quarters ; with three parts are made the intavolato, the dentello and ovolo. The projection of the intavolato is equal to its thicknefs ; of the dentello two parts of three of its height, and of the ovolo three parts of four : with the three quarters the intavolato between the gola and gocciolatoio is made ; and the other three parts are to be divided into feventeen, nine of which make the gola and orlo, and eight the gocciolatoio.

The projection of this cornice is equal to its height, as alfo the abovefaid cornices.

CHAP. XXVII.

Of Chimneys.

THE antients ufed to warm their rooms in this manner. They made their chimneys in the middle, with columns or modiglions that fupported the architraves, upon which was the pyramid of the chimney, from whence the fmoke iffued. There was one of thefe to be feen at *Baie* near Nero's pifcina, and another not far from *Civita Vecchia*.

And when they were not willing to have chimneys, they then made in the thicknefs of the walls fome tubes or pipes, through which they conveyed the heat of the fire that was under thofe rooms, and which came out of certain vents or holes that were made at the top of thofe pipes.

Almost in the fame manner the Trenti, *Vicentine* gentlemen at *Coftoza*, their villa cooled the rooms in the fummer, becaufe there are in the mountains of the faid villa fome very large caves, which the inhabitants of thofe places call *Couali*, that formerly were quarries, (which I believe Vitruvius means, when in the fecond book, wherein he treats of ftones, he fays, that in the *Marca Trivigiana* a fort of ftone was dug up, which was cut with a faw like wood) in which fome very cool winds were generated, and which thofe gentlemen conveyed to their houfes through certain fubterraneous vaults, by them called ventiducts, and with pipes like the abovefaid, they convey that cool wind through all the rooms, by ftopping and unftopping them at pleafure, to receive more or lefs of that cool air according to the feafons.

And altho' this very great convenience makes this place wonderful, what makes it ftill more worthy our admiration, is the prifon of the winds, which is a fubterraneous room built by the moft excellent Signor Francesco Trento, and by him called Eolia, where a great number of thofe ventiducts difcharge themfelves ; to beautify which, and make it worthy of the name, he has neither fpared coft or care.

But to return to the chimneys ; we make them in the thicknefs of the walls, and raife their funnels above the roofs, that they may carry the fmoke into the air : obferving not to make their funnels too wide, nor too narrow ; becaufe if they are made wide, the air wandering through them, will drive the fmoke down, and hinder its afcending and going out freely ; when too narrow, the fmoke not having a free paffage, will choak it up, and return.

Therefore in the chimneys of rooms the funnels are not to be made lefs wide than half a foot, nor wider than nine inches, and two foot and a half long ; and the mouth of the pyramid, where it joins to the funnel, muft be made a little narrower, that the fmoke returning down, may meet with that impediment to hinder its coming into the room.

Some make the funnel crooked, in order that by this crookednefs, and the force of the fire, which drives the fmoke up, they may prevent the fmoke from returning back.

THE top of the chimneys, or the holes thro' which the fmoke is to go out, ought to be wide, and far from any combuftible matter. The mantle-trees upon which the pyramid of the chimneys are made, ought to be very neatly wrought, and in every thing far from being ruftick ; becaufe ruftick work is not proper, unlefs it be in very great edifices, for the reafons already mentioned.

C H A P.   XXVIII.

Of ftairs, and the various kinds of them; and of the number and fize of the fteps.

GREAT care ought to be taken in the placing of ftair-cafes, becaufe it is no fmall diffi- culty to find a fituation fit for them, and that doth not impede the remaining part of the fabrick: A proper place muft therefore be principally given them, that they may not obftruct other places, nor be obftructed by them.

THREE openings are required in ftair-cafes; the firft is the door thro' which one goes up to the ftair-cafe, which the lefs it is hid to them that enter into the houfe, fo much the more it is to be commended. And it would pleafe me much, if it was in a place, where before that one comes to it, the moft beautiful part of the houfe was feen; becaufe it makes the houfe (altho' it fhould be little) feem very large; but however, let it be manifeft, and eafily found. The fecond opening is the windows that are neceffary to give light to the fteps; they ought to be in the middle, and high, that the light may be fpread equally every where alike. The third is the opening thro' which one enters into the floor above; this ought to lead us into ample, beautiful, and adorned places.

THE ftair-cafes will be commendable if they are clear, ample, and commodious to afcend, inviting, as it were, people to go up: They will be clear, if they have a bright light, and if (as I have faid) the light be diffufed equally every where alike: They will be fufficiently ample, if they do not feem fcanty and narrow to the largenefs and quality of the fabrick; but they are never to be made lefs wide than four foot, that if two perfons meet, they may conveniently give one another room: They will be convenient with refpect to the whole building, if the arches under them can ferve to lodge fome neceffaries; and with refpect to men, if their afcent is not too fteep and difficult: therefore their length muft be twice their height.

THE fteps ought not to be made higher than fix inches of a foot; and if they are made lower, particularly in long and continued ftairs, it will make them the more eafy, becaufe in rifing one's felf the foot will be lefs tired; but they muft never be made lower than four inches: the breadth of the fteps ought not to be made lefs than one foot, nor more than one and a half.

THE antients obferved to make the fteps uneven in number, that beginning to go up with the right foot, one might end with the fame; which they look'd upon as a good omen, and of greater devotion when they entered the temple: The number of fteps is not to exceed eleven, or thirteen at moft, before you make a floor or refting-place, that the weak and weary may find where to reft themfelves, if obliged to go up higher, and be able more eafily to ftop any thing that fhould happen to fall from above.

STAIR-CASES are either made ftraight or winding; the ftraight are either made to fpread into two branches, or fquare, which turn into four branches: To make thefe, the whole place is to be divided into four parts, two are given to the fteps, and two to the void in the middle, from which thefe ftairs would have light, if it was left uncovered: They may be made with the wall within, and then in the two parts which are given to the fteps, this wall is alfo included; and they may alfo be made without.

THESE two forts of ftair-cafes were invented by the magnificent Signor LUIGI COR- NARO, a gentleman of an excellent judgment, as may be known by the moft beautiful log- gia, and the moft elegantly adorned rooms which he built for his habitation at *Padua*.

THE winding ftair-cafes (that are alfo called *a chiocciola*) are in fome places made round, in others oval, fometimes with a column in the middle, and fometimes void, in narrow places

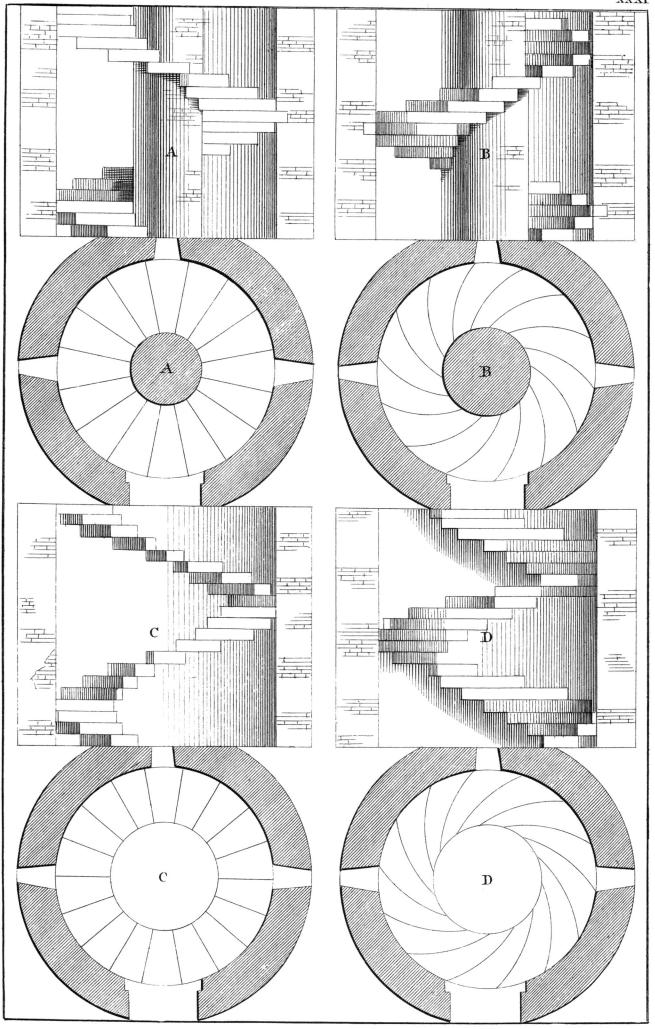

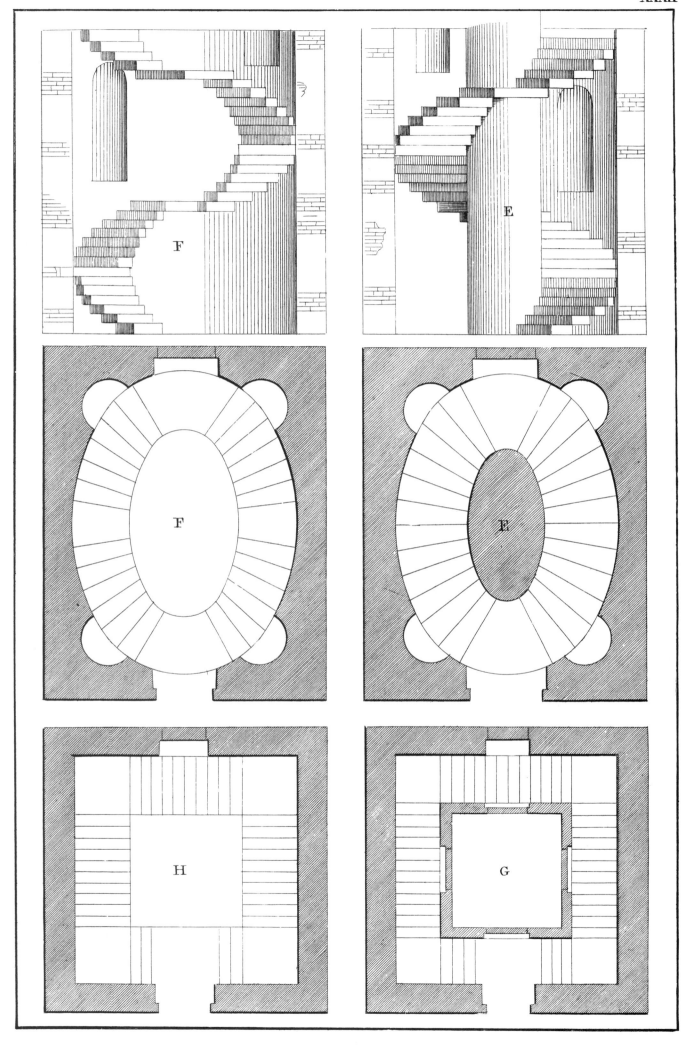

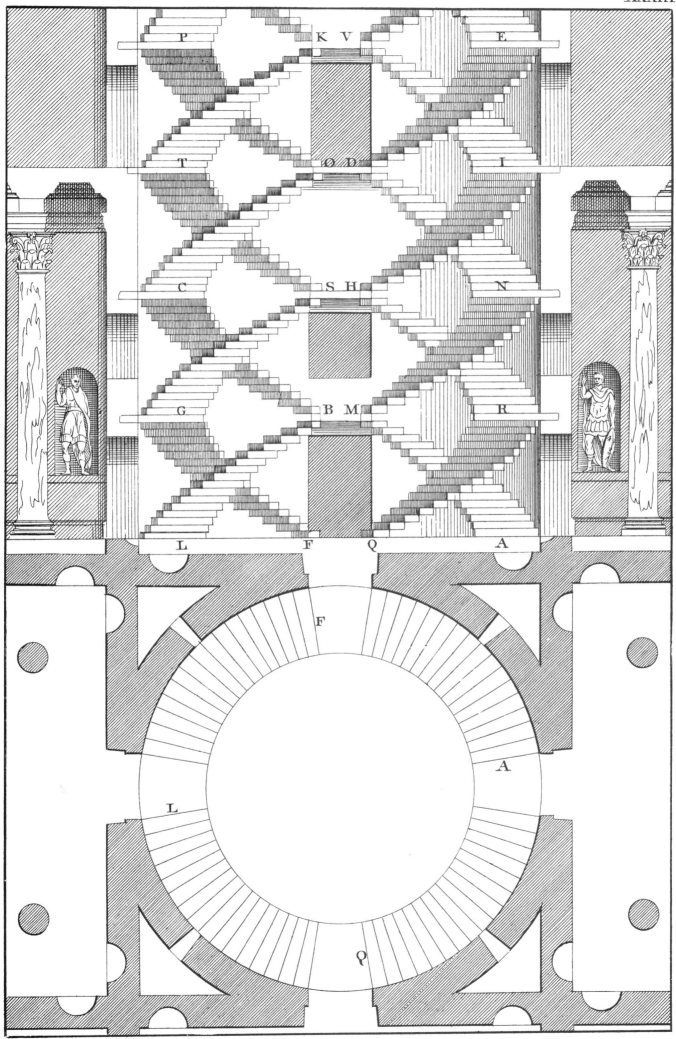

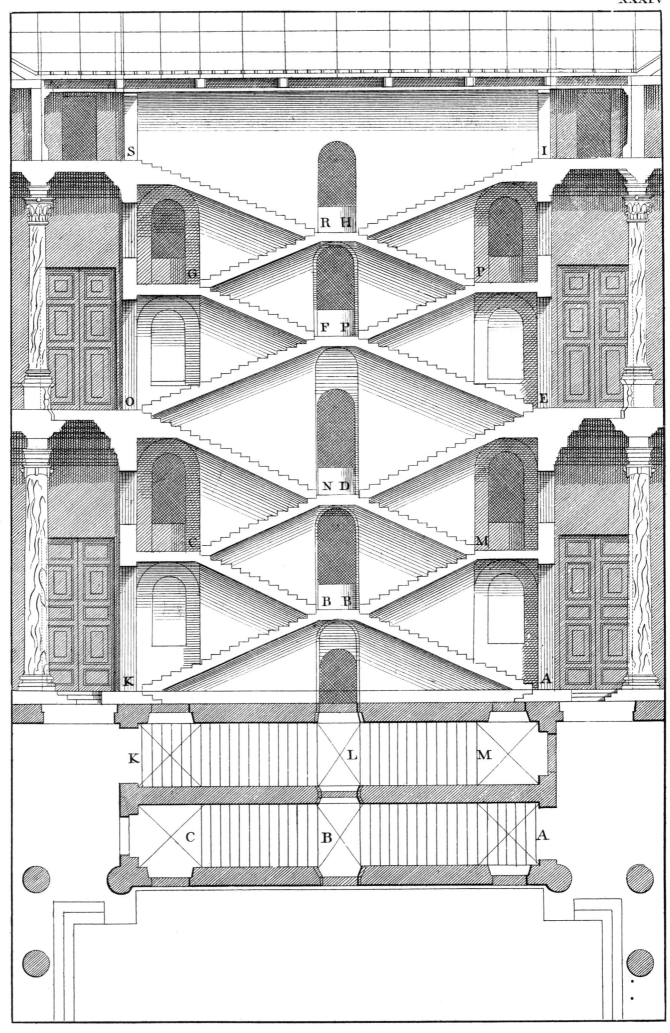

particularly, becaufe they occupy lefs room than the ftraight, but are fomewhat more difficult to afcend. They fucceed very well that are void in the middle, becaufe they can have the light from above, and thofe that are at the top of the ftairs, fee all thofe that come up, or begin to afcend, and are likewife feen by them: Thofe that have a column in the middle, are made in this manner; the diameter being divided into three parts, let two be left to the fteps, and one given to the column, as in the defign A, or let the diameter be divided into feven parts, and three given to the column in the middle, and four to the fteps; and in this manner exactly is made the ftair-cafe of the column of TRAJAN. And if the fteps are made crooked, as in the defign B, they will be very beautiful to look at, and longer than if they are made ftraight: but in thofe that are void, the diameter muft be divided into four parts; two are given to the fteps, and two remain for the place in the middle.

BESIDES the ufual manners of ftairs, there was another fort of winding ftair-cafe invented by the Clariffimo Signor MARC' ANTONIO BARBARO, a *Venetian* gentleman of a fine genius, which in very narrow places ferves very well: it has no column in the middle; and becaufe the fteps are crooked, they are very long, and muft be divided as the abovefaid.

THE oval ftair-cafes are alfo divided in the very fame manner as the round; they are very beautiful and agreeable to fee, becaufe all the windows and doors come to the head of the oval, and in the middle, and are fufficiently commodious.

I HAVE made a ftair-cafe void in the middle, in the monaftery *de la Carita* in *Venice*, which fucceeds admirably.

A, *The winding ftair-cafe with a column in the middle.*
B, *The winding ftair-cafe with a column, and with crooked fteps.*
C, *The winding ftair-cafe void in the middle.*
D, *The winding ftair-cafe void in the middle, and with crooked fteps.*
E, *The oval ftair-cafe with the column in the middle.*
F, *The oval ftair-cafe without a column.*
G, *The ftraight ftair-cafe with the wall within.*
H, *The ftrait ftair-cafe without the wall.*

ANOTHER beautiful fort of winding ftairs was made at *Chambor*, (a place in *France*) by order of the magnanimous King FRANCIS, in a palace by him erected in a wood, and is in this manner: there are four ftair-cafes, which have four entrances, that is, one each, and afcend the one over the other in fuch a manner, that being made in the middle of the fabrick, they can ferve to four apartments, without that the inhabitants of the one go down the ftair-cafe of the other, and being open in the middle, all fee one another going up and down, without giving one another the leaft inconvenience: and becaufe it is a new and a beautiful invention, I have inferted it, and marked the ftair-cafes with letters in the plan and elevation, that one may fee where they begin, and how they go up.

THERE were alfo in the portico's of POMPEY in *Rome*, going into the piazza *Giudea*, three winding ftair-cafes of a very laudible invention, becaufe being placed in the middle, where they could receive no light but from above, they were made upon columns, that the light might fpread equally every where.

IN imitation of thefe, BRAMANTE, a moft excellent architect in his time, made one in *Belvedere* without fteps, and with the four orders in architecture, that is, the Dorick, Ionick, Corinthian and Compofite. To make fuch ftair-cafes, the whole fpace is to be divided into four parts; two are given to the void in the middle, and one of a fide to the fteps and columns.

MANY other forts of ftair-cafes are to be feen in antient edifices, fuch as triangular; of this kind are the ftairs that lead to the cupulo of *Santa Maria Rotonda*, and are void in the middle, and receive the light from above. Thofe were alfo very magnificent that are at *Santo Apoftolo* in the faid city, and go up to *Monte Cavallo*: thofe ftair-cafes were double, from which many have fince taken example, and did lead to a temple placed on the top of the mountain, as I fhall fhew in my *book of temples*; and the laft defign is of this fort.

CHAP.

C H A P. XXIX.

Of R O O F S.

THE walls being raiſed up to their ſummit, the vaults made, the joyſts of the floors laid, the ſtair-caſes, and all thoſe things accommodated of which mention has been made before, it is neceſſary to make the roof; which embracing every part of the fabrick, and with its weight preſſing equally upon the walls, is a kind of a ligament to the whole work, and beſides defending the inhabitants from rain, ſnow, the ſcorching ſun, and moiſture of the night, it is no ſmall aſſiſtance to the fabrick, in caſting off the water from the walls when it rains, which altho' they may ſeem to be but of little prejudice, are, nevertheleſs, in time the cauſe of great damages.

OUR forefathers (as may be read in VITRUVIUS) uſed to make the roofs of their habitations flat; but perceiving that they were not ſheltered from rain, compelled by neceſſity, began to make them ridged, or raiſed in the middle.

THESE ridges ought to be made higher or lower, according to the regions where one builds; therefore in *Germany*, by reaſon of the great quantity of ſnow that falls there, the roofs are made very acute, and covered with ſhingles, which are ſmall pieces of boards, or with very thin tiles; which roofs, if they were otherwiſe made, would be deſtroyed by the weight of the ſnow: But we that live in temperate regions, ought to chuſe that height which makes a roof appear agreeable and with a beautiful form, and that eaſily carries off the rain.

THEREFORE the breadth of the place to be roofed, muſt be divided into nine parts, and two given to the height of the ridge; for if it is made with a fourth of the breadth, the roof will be too ſteep, whereby the tiles will be faſtened with great difficulty; and if a fifth is given, it will be too flat, and therefore the tiles and ſhingles would be very much charged when the ſnows fall.

GUTTERS are uſually made round the houſes, into which the water falling from the tiles, is by ſpouts thrown away a great diſtance from the walls: theſe ought to have a foot and a half of wall over them, which, beſides holding them firm, will defend the timber of the roof from receiving damage in any part from the water.

THERE are various manners of diſpoſing the timber of the roofs; but when the middle walls ſupport the beams, they are very eaſily accommodated; which method pleaſeth me very much, becauſe the out-walls do not bear ſo much weight, and altho' the head of ſome beam ſhould rot, the roof is notwithſtanding in no danger.

The E N D *of the* F I R S T   B O O K.

REGINA VIRTUS

THE SECOND BOOK OF
ARCHITECTURE
by
ANDREA PALLADIO
wherein the Designs of Several Houses
Ordered by him both within and out of
the City are contained,
And the Designs of the Antient Houses
of the GREEKS and LATINS.

LONDON,
Published by
ISAAC WARE,
Anno MDCCXXXVIII.

THE SECOND BOOK

O F

Andrea Palladio's

ARCHITECTURE.

CHAPTER I.

Of the decorum or conveniency that ought to be obferved in private fabrics.

I HAVE explained in the foregoing book all thofe things, that to me feemed moft worthy of confideration for the building of public edifices, and private houfes, that the work might be beautiful, graceful and durable: I have there alfo mentioned fome things belonging to the conveniency of private houfes, to which this other book fhall chiefly be applied: for that houfe only ought to be called convenient, which is fuitable to the quality of him that is to dwell in it, and whofe parts correfpond to the whole and to each other.

BUT the architect ought above all to obferve, that (as VITRUVIUS fays in the firft and fixth book) for great men, and particularly thofe in a republic, the houfes are required with loggia's and fpacious halls adorned, that in fuch places thofe may be amufed with pleafure, who fhall wait for the mafter to falute, or afk him fome favour: and for gentlemen of a meaner ftation, the fabrics ought alfo to be lefs, of lefs expence, and have fewer ornaments. For judges and advocates, they ought likewife to be fo built, that in their houfes there may be handfome and well adorned places to walk in, that their clients may remain there without inconvenience.

MERCHANTS houfes ought to have places facing the north, where their merchandizes may be lodged; and to be fo difpofed, that the mafter may not be in fear of thieves.

DECORUM is alfo to be obferved in regard to the work, if the parts fo anfwer to the whole, as that in great edifices there may be great members, in the little, fmall, and middling in the middle-fized: for what a difagreeable and unfeemly thing wou'd it be, if in a very large fabric there fhould be fmall halls and rooms; and, on the contrary, in a little one, there fhould be two or three rooms that took up the whole.

As much as poffible, one ought therefore, as has been faid, to have a regard to thofe who are inclined to build; and not fo much to mind what they can afford to lay out as the quality of the building that is proper for them: when that is fettled, the parts are to be fo difpofed, that they may be fuitable to the whole, and to each other, and fuch ornaments are to be applied as fhall feem moft proper. But an architect is very often obliged, to conform more to the will of thofe who are at the expence, than to that which ought to be obferved.

CHAP. II.

Of the compartment or difpofition of rooms, and of other places.

THAT the houfes may be commodious for the ufe of the family, without which they wou'd be greatly blame-worthy, far from being commendable, great care ought to be taken, not only in the principal parts, as the loggia, halls, courts, magnificent rooms, and ample ftairs, light and eafy of afcent; but alfo, that the moft minute and leaft beautiful parts be accommodated to the fervice of the greateft and more worthy: for as in the human body there are fome noble and beautiful parts, and fome rather ignoble and difagreeable, and yet we fee that thofe ftand in very great need of thefe, and without them they cou'd not fubfift; fo in fabricks, there ought to be fome parts confiderable and honoured, and fome lefs elegant; without which the other cou'd not remain free, and fo confequently wou'd lofe part of their dignity and beauty. But as our Bleffed Creator has ordered thefe our members in fuch a manner, that the moft beautiful are in places moft expofed to view, and the lefs comely more hidden; fo in building alfo, we ought to put the principal and confiderable parts, in places the moft feen, and the lefs beautiful, in places as much hidden from the eye as poffible; that in them may be lodged all the foulnefs of the houfe, and all thofe things that may give any obftruction, and in any meafure render the more beautiful parts difagreeable. I approve therefore that in the loweft part of the fabric, which I make fomewhat under-ground, may be difpofed the cellars, the magazines for wood, pantries, kitchens, fervants-halls, wafh-houfes, ovens, and fuch like things neceffary for daily ufe. From which difpofi-tion follow two conveniencies, the one, that the upper part remains all free; and the other and no lefs important, is, that the faid upper apartments are wholefomer to live in, the floor being at a diftance from the damps of the ground; befides as it rifes, it is more agreeable to be looked at, and to look out of. It is alfo to be obferved, that in the remaining part of the fabric there may be great, middle-fized, and fmall rooms, and all near one another, that they may reciprocally be made ufe of.

THE fmall rooms may be divided off, to make clofets where ftudies or libraries may be placed, riding accoutrements and other lumber, which may be every day wanted, and which wou'd not be fo proper to be in rooms, where one either fleeps, eats, or where ftrangers are received.

WHAT contributes alfo to conveniency is, that the rooms for fummer be ample, fpacious and turned to the north; and thofe for the winter to the fouth and weft, and rather fmall than otherwife: becaufe we feek the fhades and winds in fummer, and in winter the fun; befides fmall rooms are much more eafily warmed than large.

BUT thofe which we wou'd make ufe of in fpring and autumn, muft be turned to the eaft, and ought to look over greens and gardens. In this particular part, ftudies and libra-ries ought alfo to be; becaufe the morning is the moft proper time of all other to make ufe of them.

BUT the large rooms with the middling, and thofe with the fmall, ought to be fo diftri-buted, that, as I have elfewhere faid, one part of the fabric may correfpond with the other; and that fo the body of the edifice, may have in itfelf a certain convenience in its mem-bers, that may render the whole beautiful and graceful.

BUT as moft commonly in cities, either the neighbours walls, the ftreets, or publick places, prefcribe certain limits, which the architect cannot furpafs, it is proper he fhou'd con-form himfelf to the circumftances of the fituation; to which, if I miftake not, the following plans and elevations will give a great infight, and which may alfo ferve as an example of what has been faid in the foregoing book.

CHAP.

CHAP. III.

Of the defigns of town-houfes.

I AM convinced, that in the opinion of thofe, who fhall fee the following fabrics, and know how difficult it is to introduce a new cuftom, efpecially in building, of which profeffion every one is perfuaded that he knows his part, I fhall be efteemed very fortunate, to have found gentlemen of fo noble and generous a difpofition, and of fuch excellent judgment, as to have hearkened to my reafons, and departed from that antiquated cuftom of building without grace or any beauty at all; and, indeed, I cannot but very heartily thank God, as we ought in all our actions to do, for granting me fuch a fhare of his favour, as to have been able to put in practice many of thofe things, which I have learnt from my very great fatigues and voyages, and by my great ftudy.

AND altho' fome of the defigned fabrics are not entirely finifhed, yet may one by what is done comprehend what the whole will be when finifhed. I have prefixed to each the name of the builder, and the place where they are, that every one may, if he pleafes, really fee how they fucceed.

AND here the reader may take notice, that in placing the faid defigns, I have had refpect neither to the rank or dignity of the gentlemen to be mentioned; but I have inferted them where I thought moft convenient: not but they are all very honourable.

LET us now come to the fabrics, of which the following is in *Udene* the metropolis Plate 1. of *Friuli*, and was raifed from the foundation by Signor FLORIANO ANTONINI, a gentleman of that city. The firft order of the front is of ruftic work, the columns of the front, of the entrance, and of the loggia backwards are of the Ionick order. The firft rooms are vaulted; the greater have the height of the vaults according to the firft method beforementioned, for the height of vaults in places that are longer than they are broad. The rooms above have flat ceilings, and fo much wider than thofe below, as the contraction or diminution of the walls, and the height of the ceilings, equal to their breadth. Over thefe are other rooms which may ferve for granaries. The height of the hall reaches to the roof. The kitchen is out of the houfe, but very commodious neverthelefs. The neceffary places are on the fides of the ftairs, and although they are in the body of the fabric, they do not give any offenfive fmell; becaufe they are placed in a part remote from the fun, and have vents from the bottom of the pit all through the thicknefs of the wall, to the very fummit of the houfe.

THIS line is half the *Vicentine* foot, with which the following fabrics have been meafured.

THE whole foot is divided into twelve inches, and each inch into four minutes.

IN *Vicenza* upon the *Piazza*, which is vulgarly called the *Ifola*, the Count VALERIO CHIERICATO, an honourable gentleman of that city, has built according to the following Plate 2. invention.

THIS fabric has in the part below a loggia forwards, that takes in the whole front: the pavement of the firft order rifes above ground five foot; which has been done not only to put the cellars and other places underneath, that belong to the conveniency of the houfe, which wou'd not have fucceeded if they had been made intirely under ground, becaufe the river is not far from it; but alfo that the order above might the better enjoy the beautiful fituation forwards. The larger have rooms the height of their vaults, according to the firft method for the height of vaults: the middle-fized are with groined vaults, and their vaults as high as thofe of the larger. The fmall rooms are alfo vaulted, and are divided off. All thefe

vaults

vaults are adorned with moſt excellent compartments of ſtucco, by Meſſer BARTOLOMEO RI-
DOLFI, a *Veroneſe* ſculptor; and paintings by Meſſer DOMENICO RIZZO, and Meſſer BAT-
TISTA VENETIANO, men ſingular in this profeſſion. The hall is above in the middle of
the front, and takes up the middle part of the loggia below. Its height is up to the roof; and
becauſe it projects forward a little, it has under the angles double columns. From one part
to the other of this hall, there are two loggia's, that is, on each ſide one; which have their
ſoffites or ceilings adorned with very beautiful pictures, and afford a moſt agreeable ſight. The
firſt order of the front is Dorick, and the ſecond Ionick.

Plate 3.   HERE follows the deſign of part of the front in a large form.

Plate 4.   THE following deſigns are of the houſe of the Count ISEPPO DE PORTI, a very noble
family of the ſaid city. This houſe fronts two publick ſtreets, and therefore has two entrances, which have four columns each, that ſupport the vault, and render the place above it
ſecure. The firſt rooms are vaulted. The height of thoſe, that are on each ſide the ſaid entrances, is according to the laſt method for the height of vaults. The ſecond rooms, that is, of
the ſecond order, are with flat cielings: and thus the firſt, as well as the ſecond of that part
of the fabrick, which has been done, are adorned with paintings, and moſt beautiful ſtucco's,
by the hands of the aforeſaid excellent artiſts, and of Meſſer PAOLO VERONESE, a moſt excellent painter. The court encompaſſed with portico's, to which one goes from the ſaid entrances by a paſſage, is to have columns ſix and thirty foot and an half high, that is, as high
as the firſt and ſecond order. Behind theſe columns there are pilaſters one foot and three
quarters broad, and one foot and two inches thick, which ſupport the pavement of the loggia above. This court divides the whole houſe into two parts: that forwards is for the uſe
of the maſter, and the women belonging to him; and that backward to lodge ſtrangers in;
whereby thoſe of the houſe, and the ſtrangers will remain free in every reſpect: to which the
ancients, and eſpecially the *Greeks*, had a very great regard.

BESIDES which, this partition will alſo ſerve in caſe the deſcendants of the ſaid gentleman,
ſhou'd chuſe to have their apartments ſeparate.

I HAVE placed the principal ſtairs under the portico, that they may anſwer to the middle of
the court; that thoſe who have a mind to go up, may as it were be compelled to ſee the
moſt beautiful part of the fabrick; and alſo, that being in the middle, they may ſerve one
part as well as the other. The cellars and ſuch-like places are under ground. The ſtables are
out of the ſquare of the houſe, and have their entrance under the ſtairs. Of the deſigns in
Plate 5,6. a large form, the firſt is of part of the front, and the ſecond of the part towards the court.

Plate 7.   THE following fabrick is in *Verona*, and was begun by the Count GIOVIANNI BATTIS-
TA DELLA TORRE, a gentleman of that city, who being overtaken by death, could not
finiſh it; but there is a great part of it done. One goes into this houſe by the flanks, where
the paſſages are ten feet wide; from which one comes into the courts, each fifty feet long;
and from theſe into an open hall, which has four columns for the greater ſecurity of the
vault above. From this hall one goes to the ſtairs, which are oval, and open in the middle. The ſaid courts have corridors or balconies round them, level with the floor of the
ſecond rooms. The other ſtairs ſerve for the greater conveniency of the whole houſe. This
compartment ſucceeds extremely well in this ſituation; which is long and narrow, and has
the principal ſtreet towards one of the leſſer fronts.

Plate 8.   THE following deſigns are of a fabrick in *Vicenza*, of the Count OTTAVIO DE THIENI:
It belonged to Count MARC' ANTONIO, who began it. This houſe is ſituated in the middle
of the city, near the piazza, and therefore I have thought proper to diſpoſe of that part towards the piazza into ſhops: becauſe the architect is alſo to conſider the advantage of
the builder, when it can be done conveniently, and where the ſituation is ſufficiently large.
Every ſhop has over it a mezato for the uſe of the ſhop-keeper; and over them are the rooms
for the maſter.

THIS houſe is inſular, that is, encompaſſed by four ſtreets. The principal entrance, or as one
may ſay, the maſter-gate, has a loggia forwards, and fronts the moſt frequented ſtreet of the
city. The great hall is to be above; which will project even with the loggia. There are
two

Plate I.

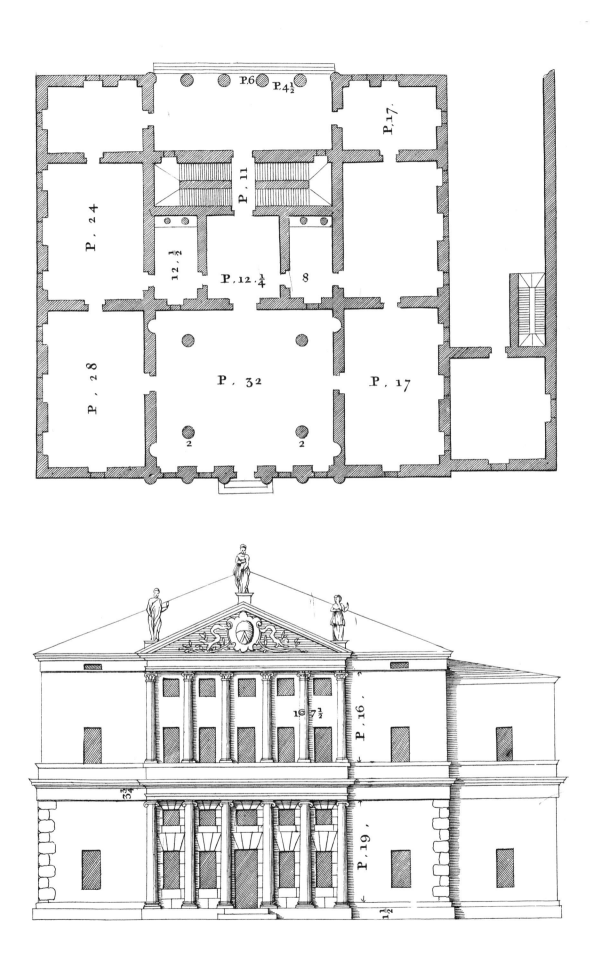

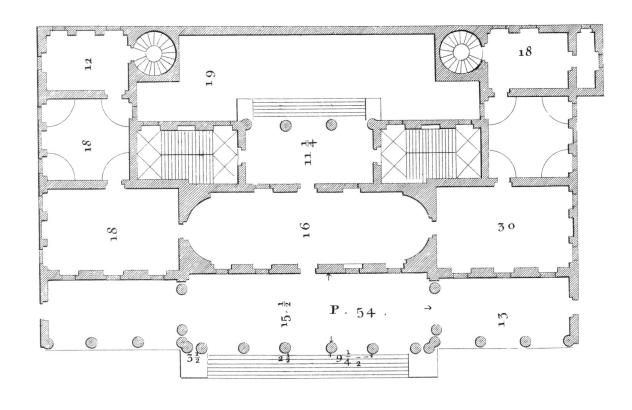

P . 54 .

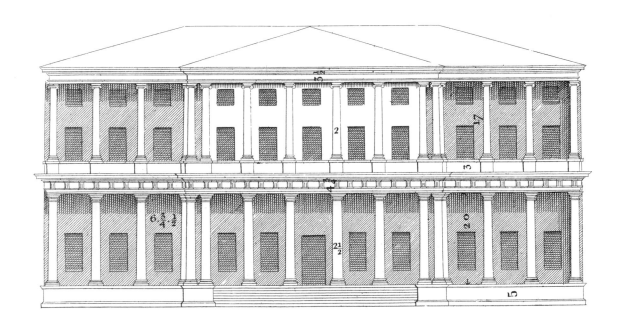

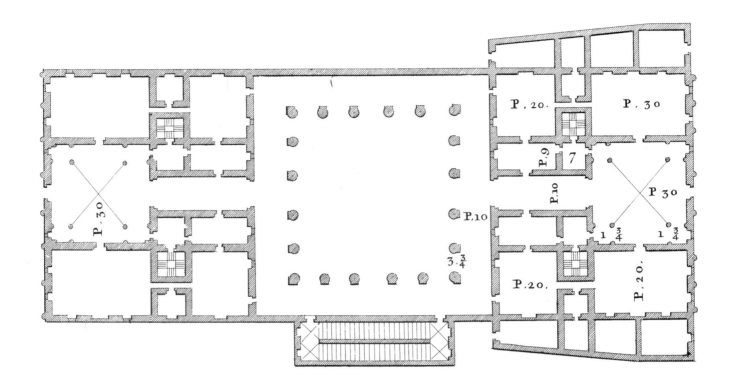

P. 20.
P. 30
P. 9
7
P. 10
P. 30
P. 10
3. 3/4
1 3/4   1 3/4
P. 30
P. 20.
P. 20.

P. 30.
P. 20
P. 40
P. 24
P. 24
P. 15
P. 20
P. 30
P. 3/4

V.

P 3¾

P 4

P 7½

P 4½

P 2

P 8

P 4

P 18

P 19¼

P

P I¼

P I¼

P 8¼

P 4

P 18¾

P — 23½

P 5

P 19¼

P 10 9

P. 35

P. 3. ½

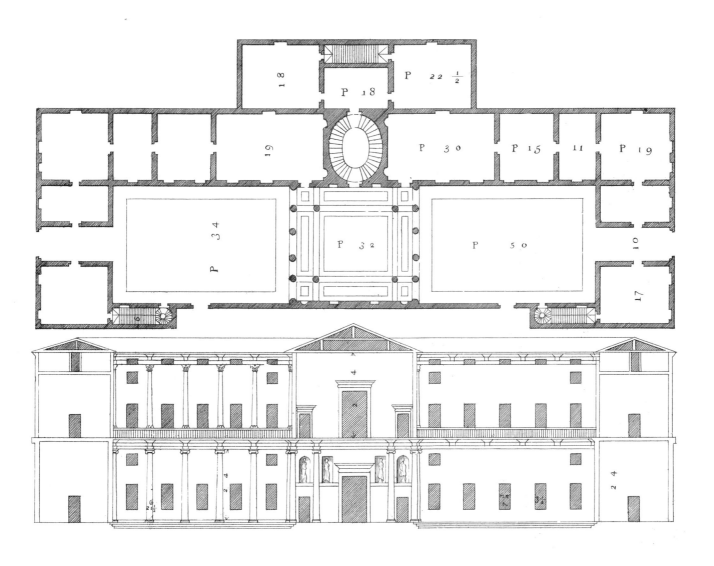

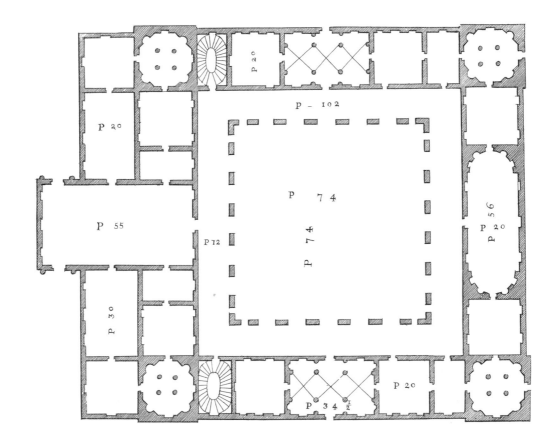

P _ 102

P 20

P 74

P 20

P 55

P 74

P 12

P 56

P 74

P 20

P 30

P 20

P 34

P 20

P 12

P 20

P 20

two entrances in the wings, which have columns in the middle, placed there not fo much for ornament, as they are to render the part above it fecure, and to make the height proportionable to the breadth. From thefe entrances one goes into the court encompaffed all round with loggia's of pilafters. In the firft order they are Ruftick, and in the fecond of the Compofite order. In the angles, there are octangular rooms, that fucceed well, as well with refpect to their form, as for diverfe ufes to which they may be accommodated. The rooms of this fabrick that are now finifhed, have been adorned with the moft beautiful ftucco's, by Meffer ALESSANDRO VITTORIA, and Meffer BARTOLOMEO RIDOLFI; and with paintings, by Meffer ANSELMO CANERA, and Meffer BERNARDINO INDIA of *Verona*, not inferior to any of the prefent age. The cellars, and fuch like places, are under ground; becaufe this fabrick is in the higheft part of the city, where there is no danger that water fhould prove any inconvenience.

OF the following defigns, in a larger form of the above inferted fabrick; the firft is part of the front; the fecond is of the part towards the court. Plate 9. Plate 10.

THE Counts VALMARANA, very honourable gentlemen, for their own honour and conveniency, and the ornament of their native country, have built in the faid city, according to the following defigns: in which fabrick there is no want of any ornaments that can be thought of; as ftucco's and paintings. This houfe is divided into two parts by the middle court; about which there is a corridor, or balcony, which leads from the fore-part to that which is backwards. The firft rooms are vaulted; the fecond with flat cielings, and they are as high as they are broad. The garden, which is before one comes to the ftables, is much larger than it is marked; but it has been made fo fmall becaufe the leaf wou'd not have contained the ftables and all the other parts. Thus much as to this fabrick, having in this, as well as in all the others, inferted the meafure of each part. Plate 11.

THE following defign is of half the front. Plate 12.

AMONGST many honourable *Vicentine* gentlemen, there is Monfignor PAOLO ALMERICO, an ecclefiaftick, and who was referendary to two fupreme Popes, PIO the fourth and fifth, and who for his merit, deferved to be made a *Roman* citizen with all his family. This gentleman after having travelled many years out of a defire of honour, all his relations being dead, came to his native country, and for his recreation retired to one of his country-houfes upon a hill, lefs than a quarter of a mile diftant from the city, where he has built according to the following invention: which I have not thought proper to place amongft the fabricks of villa's, becaufe of the proximity it has with the city, whence it may be faid to be in the very city. The fite is as pleafant and as delightful as can be found; becaufe it is upon a fmall hill, of very eafy accefs, and is watered on one fide by the *Bacchiglione*, a navigable river; and on the other it is encompaffed with moft pleafant rifings, which look like a very great theatre, and are all cultivated, and abound with moft excellent fruits, and moft exquifite vines: and therefore, as it enjoys from every part moft beautiful views, fome of which are limited, fome more extended, and others that terminate with the horizon; there are loggia's made in all the four fronts; under the floor of which, and of the hall, are the rooms for the conveniency and ufe of the family. The hall is in the middle, is round, and receives its light from above. The fmall rooms are divided off. Over the great rooms (the vaults of which are according to the firft method) there is a place to walk round the hall, fifteen foot and a half wide. In the extremity of the pedeftals, that form a fupport to the ftairs of the loggia's, there are ftatues made by the hands of Meffer LORENZO VICENTINO, a very excellent fculptor. Plate 13.

Signor GIULIO CAPRA, likewife a moft noble cavalier, and a *Vicentine* gentleman, for an ornament to his native country, rather than from any neceffity he was under of fo doing, has prepared the materials to build, and has begun according to the following defigns, in a moft beautiful fite, in the principal ftreet of the city. This houfe will have courts, loggia's, halls and rooms; fome of which will be great, fome middling, and others fmall. The form will be beautiful, and diverfified; and certainly that gentleman will have a very ftately and magnificent houfe, fuitable to his noble mind. Plate 14.

C, *an open court.*
D, *a court likewife uncovered.*
L, *the court.*
S, *the hall which in the lower part has columns, and free above, that is, without columns.*

I MADE the prefent invention for a fite, belonging to the Count MONTANO BARBARANO at *Vicenza*; in which, by reafon of the fituation, I did not obferve the fame order on one part, as Plate 15.

M I did

I did on the other. Now this gentleman has bought the neighbouring piece of ground, and therefore the fame order is obferved in both parts; and as in one part the ftables are placed, and the lodgings for fervants (as may be feen in the defign) fo in the other there are rooms that will ferve for a kitchen, and places for women, and for other conveniencies. They have already be-
Plate 16. gun to build, and have raifed the front according to the following defign, in a large form. I have not yet inferted the defign of the plan, according as it was finally concluded on, and according as the foundations are already laid, fince I could not get it graved time enough to have it printed. The entrance of this invention has fome columns which fupport the vault, for the reafons already mentioned. On the right and left there are two rooms one fquare and a half long; and after thefe, two fquare ones; and befides thefe, two clofets. Oppofite to the entrance there is a paffage, from which one comes into a loggia over the court. This paffage has a clofet on each fide, and over them mezati's, to which the principal ftairs of the houfe ferve. All the vaults of thefe places are one and twenty foot and a half high. The hall above, and all the other rooms, are with flat cielings; the fmall rooms only have their vaults as high as the cielings of the rooms. The columns of the front have pedeftals under them, and fupport the balcony; into which one enters by the fofita. The front is not to be made in this manner (as
Plate 16. was faid) but according to the following defign, in a large form.

C H A P. IV.

Of the TUSCAN ATRIO, *or porch.*

AFTER having fet down fome of thofe fabricks I have directed in cities, it is very proper that, to keep my promife, I fhould infert the defigns of fome of the principal parts of the houfes of the antients. And becaufe the Atrio was a very remarkable part of them, I fhall firft make mention of the Atrio's, or porches, and then of the places adjoined to them, and fo proceed to the halls.

VITRUVIUS fays, in his fixth book, that there were five kinds of Atrio's among the Antients, that is, the Tufcan, of four columns; the Corinthian, Teftuginato, and Uncover'd,
Plate 17. of which I do not intend to fpeak. The following defigns are of the Tufcan Atrio. The breadth of this Atrio is two thirds of the length. The breadth of the Tablino is two fifths of that of the Atrio, and of the fame length. From this one paffes into the Periftilio, that is, into the court with portico's round it; which is one third longer than it is broad. The portico's are as wide as the columns are long. On the fides of the Atrio fmall halls might be made, that would look over the gardens; and if they were made as one fees in the defign, their columns would be of the Ionick order, twenty foot long, and the portico would be as wide as the intercolumniation. Above them there would be other columns, of the Corinthian order, one fourth part lefs than thofe below; between which there would be windows to receive light. Over the Anditi there fhould be no covering, but they fhould have baluftrades round them; and according to the fituation, they might be made either longer or fhorter than what I have defigned, according as it fhould be neceffary for the ufe and conveniency of thofe who were to dwell there.

Plate 18.   HERE follows the defign of this Atrio in a larger form.

B, *Atrio.*	I, *Portico of the Periftillio.*
D, *Frize, or beam of limitation.*	K, *Loggia before the Atrio, which we may call*
G, *the door of the Tablino.*	*Veftibulo.*
F, *Tablino.*	

C H A P. V.

Of the ATRIO *with four columns.*

Plate 19.   THE following defign is of the Atrio with four columns; which is in breadth three parts of five of its length. The wings are the fourth part of the length. The columns are Corinthian; their diameter is half the breadth of the wings. The uncover'd part is a third part of the breadth of the Atrio, and as long. From the Atrio through the Tablino one paffes into the Periftilio; which is in length one fquare and a half. The columns of the firft order are Dorick, and the portico's are as broad as the faid columns are long. Thofe above, that is, of the fecond order, are Ionick, one fourth part lefs than thofe of the firft, under which there is a Poggio, or pedeftal, two foot and three quarters high.

A, *Atrio.*

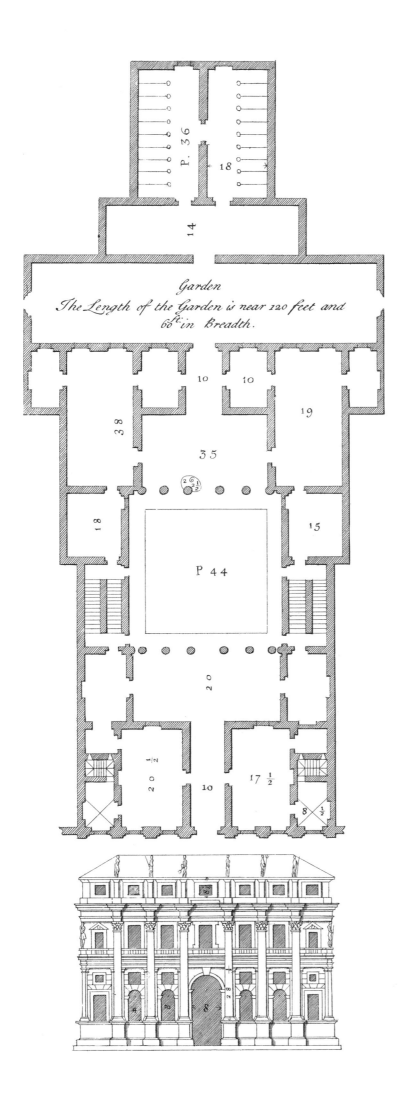

P. 36

18

14

Garden
The Length of the Garden is near 120 feet and
66^{ft} in Breadth.

10   10

38   19

35

2 6 1
2 2

18   15

P 44

20

20 ½   17 ½

10   8 ½

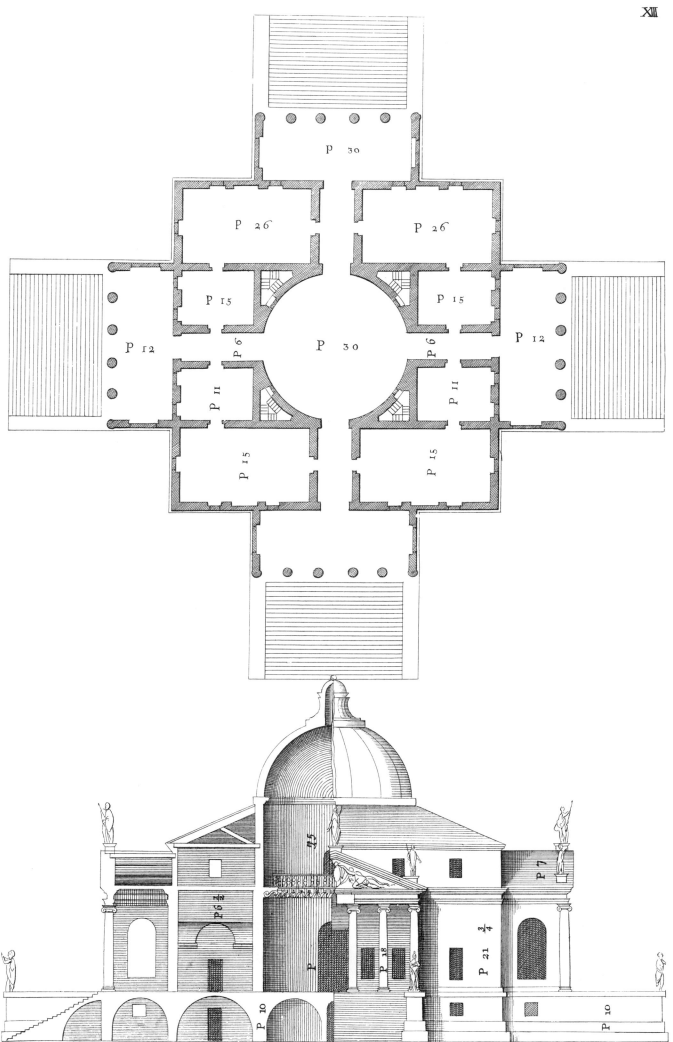

P 30

P 26   P 26

P 15   P 15

P 12   P 6   P 30   P 6   P 12

P 11   P 11

P 15   P 15

P 7

P 6½   P 21 ¾   P 18   P 10

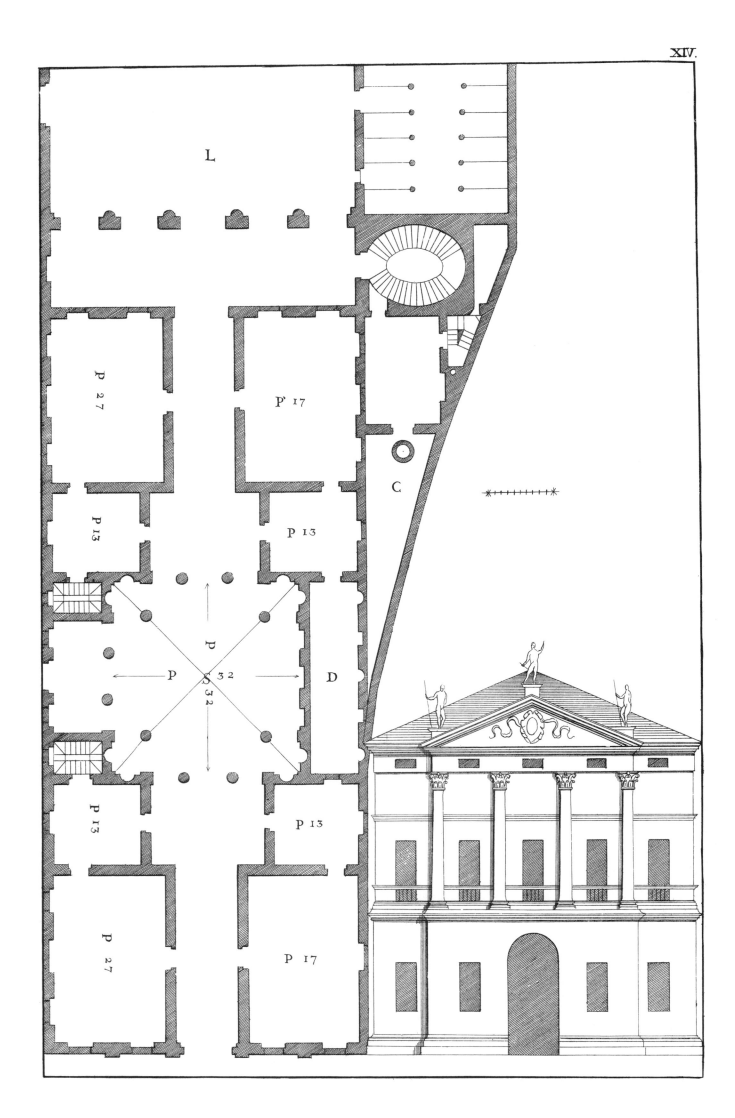

L

P 27

P' 17

P 13

P 13

C

P

P S 32

P S 32

D

P 13

P 13

P 27

P 17

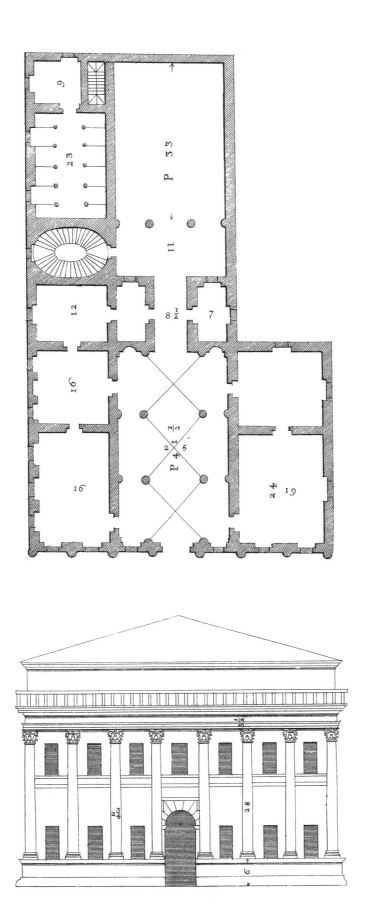

P 6 $\frac{3}{4}$

P 3 6 5

P 16 $\frac{1}{2}$

P 3 $\frac{3}{4}$

P 4

P 16 8 $\frac{1}{2}$

P 3 6 10 $\frac{1}{2}$

P 19

P 4 $\frac{1}{8}$

P 2 6 1 $\frac{1}{2}$

P 2 6 1 $\frac{1}{2}$

P — 8

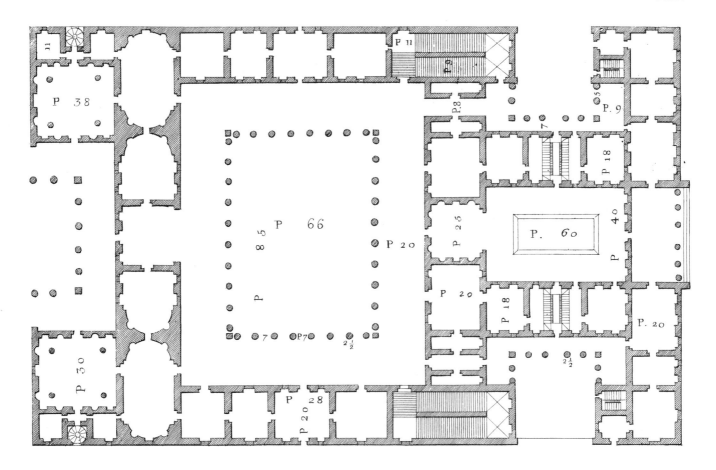

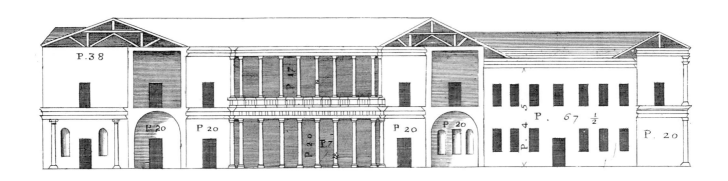

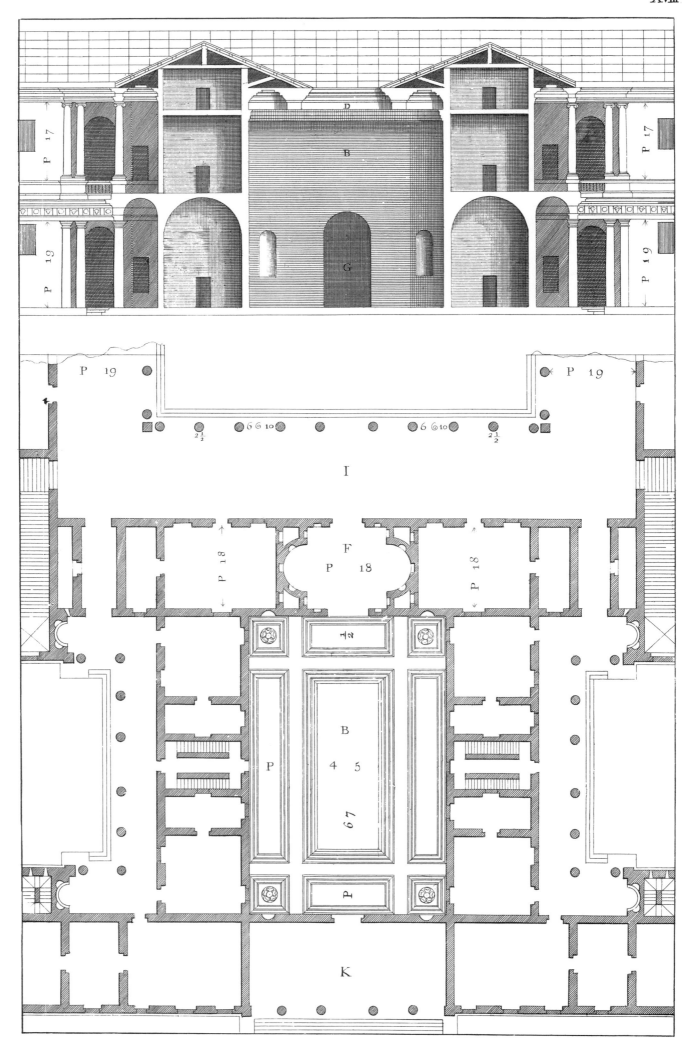

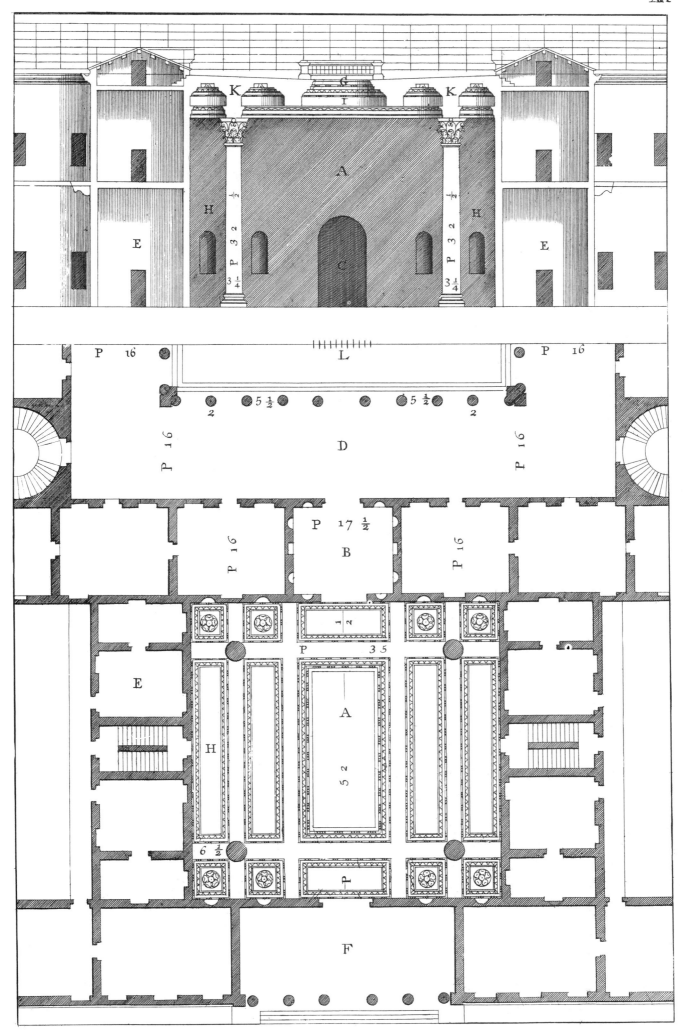

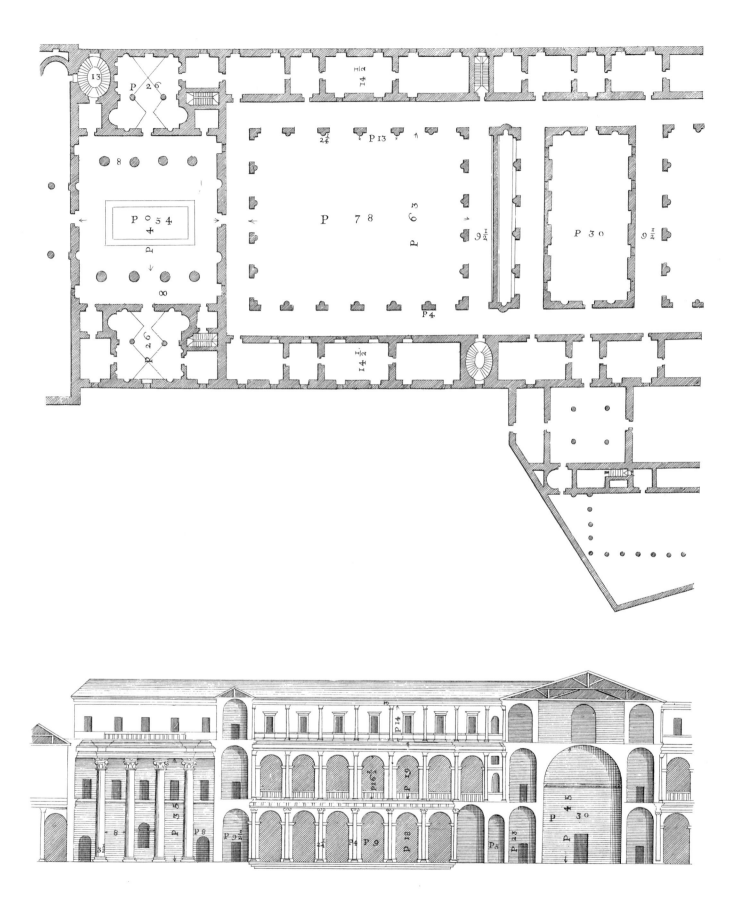

A, *Atrio.*
B, *Tablino.*
C, *door of the Tablino.*
D, *portico of the Periftilio.*
E, *rooms near the Atrio.*
F, *Loggia thro' which one enters the Atrio.*

G, *the uncover'd part of the Atrio, with baluftrades round it.*
H, *the wings of the Atrio.*
I, *frize of the cornice of the Atrio.*
K, *folid part over the columns.*
L, *meafure of ten feet.*

CHAP. VI.

Of the CORINTHIAN ATRIO.

THE following fabrick is of the convent *de la Carita* where are regular canons at *Venice*. Plate 20. I have endeavoured to make this houfe like thofe of the antients; and therefore I have made a Corinthian Atrio to it, whofe length is the diagonal line of the fquare of its breadth. The wings arc one part of three and a half, or two fevenths of its length. The columns are of the Compofite order, three foot and a half thick, and five and thirty foot long. The uncovered part in the middle is the third part of the breadth of the Atrio. Over the columus there is an uncovered terrace level with the floors of the third order of the cloifter where the Friar's cells are. The facrifty is on one fide near the Atrio, incompaffed with a Dorick cornice, which fupports the vaults. The columns there feen, fupport that part of the wall in the cloifter, which in the part above, divides the chambers or cells from the loggia's. This facrifty ferves for a tablino (fo they called the place where they lodged the images of their anceftors) tho' for conveniency, I have placed it on one fide of the Atrio. On the other fide is the place for the chapter, which anfwers to the facrifty. In the part near the church there is an oval ftair-cafe, void in the middle, which is very convenient and pleafant. From the Atrio one enters into the cloifter, which has three orders of columns, one over the other. The firft is Dorick, and the columns project from the pilafters more than one half. The fecond is Ionick; the columns are one fifth part lefs than thofe of the firft. The third is Corinthian, and the columns are a fifth part lefs than thofe of the fecond. In this order, inftead of pilafters, there is the continued wall; and directly over the arches of the inferior orders, there are windows which give light to the entrance into the cells, the vaults of which are made with reeds, that they may not overcharge the walls. Oppofite to the Atrio and cloifter, beyond the ftairs, one finds the refectory, which is two fquares long, and as high as the floor of the third order of the cloifter: It has a loggia on each fide, and underneath a cellar made in the fame manner as cifterns are, that the water may not get in. At one end it has the kitchen, ovens, a yard for poultry, a place for wood, a place to wafh clothes in, and a very agreeable garden; and at the other end, other kind of places.

THERE are in this fabrick, befides places for ftrangers, and others that ferve for different purpofes, forty four rooms, and forty fix cells.

OF the defigns that follow, the firft is of part of this Atrio in a larger form, and the fecond Plate 21, of part of the cloifter. and 22.

CHAP. VII.

Of the ATRIO TESTUGGINATO, *and of the private houfes of the antient* Romans.

BESIDES the abovefaid different manners of Atrio's, there was another very much in ufe among the antients, by them called Teftugginato: and becaufe this part is very difficult, from the obfcurity of VITRUVIUS, and worthy of a particular regard, I fhall mention what I think of it, adjoining thereto the difpofition of the Oeci, or fmall halls, Cancellarie, Tinelli, baths, and other places; fo that in the following defign there will be all the parts of Plate 23. the private houfe fet in their proper places according to VITRUVIUS. The Atrio is as long as the diagonal of the fquare of the breadth, and as high as it is broad, up to the limitary beam. The rooms on the fide thereof, are fix foot lefs in height; and upon the walls, which divide them from the Atrio, there are fome pilafters that fupport the Teftudine, or covering of the Atrio; and through the diftances between them it receives light; and the rooms have an open terrace over them. Oppofite to the entrance is the Tablino, which is one part of two and a half, or two fifths of the breadth of the Atrio; and thofe places

ferved,

ferved, as I before faid, to place the images and ftatues of their anceftors in. Farther on, is the Periftilio, which has portico's round it, as broad as the columns are long. The rooms are of the fame breadth, and are as high to the impoft of the vaults as they are broad, and the vaults are in height a third part of the breadth.

SEVERAL forts of Oeci are defcribed by VITRUVIUS (it was thefe halls, or Salotte, in which they made their feftivals and entertainments, and where the women worked) that is, Tetraftili; fo called, becaufe there were four columns; the Corinthian, which had femi-columns round them; the Egyptian, which over the firft columns were inclofed with a wall with femi-columns directly over the firft, and one fourth part lefs. In the inter-columnia-tions there were windows, from which the part in the middle received light. The height of the loggia's that were round them, did not pafs the firft columns, and over that it was uncovered, and encompafs'd with a corridor or balcony. The defigns of each of thefe fhall be feparately fet down. The fquare Oeci were places to be in the cool in the fummer: and looked upon gardens and other green places. There were alfo other Oeci made, which they called Ciziceni, which alfo proved for the conveniencies abovefaid. The Cancellarie, and libraries were in proper places towards the eaft; and alfo the Ticlini, which were places where they did eat. There were alfo baths for the men and women, which I have defigned in the fartheft part of the houfe.

A, *Atrio.*
B, *Tablino.*
C, *Periftilio.*
D, *Corinthian Salotti.*
E, *Salotti with four columns.*

F, *Bafilica.*
G, *places for fummer.*
H, *rooms.*
K, *library.*

Plate 24.   THE following defign is of this fame Atrio in a larger form.

D, *Atrio.*
E, *windows which give light to the Atrio.*
F, *door of the Tablino.*
G, *Tablino.*
H, *portico of the Cortile.*
I, *Loggia before the Atrio.*
K, *Cortile.*

L, *rooms round the Atrio.*
M, *Loggia.*
N, *beam of limitation, or frize of the Atrio.*
O, *part of the Corinthian hall.*
P, *uncovered place, over which the light comes into the Atrio.*

CHAP. VIII.

Of the HALLS *with four columns.*

Plate 25.   THE following defign is of the halls, which were called Tetraftili, becaufe they had four columns. Thefe were made fquare; and the columns were put to make the breadth proportionable to the height, and to make the place above fecure; which I have done my felf in many fabricks, as has been feen in the foregoing defigns, and will be in thofe that follow.

CHAP. IX.

Of CORINTHIAN HALLS.

Plate 26.
Plate 27.   THE Corinthian halls were made in two manners, that is, either with columns which rofe from the ground, as may be feen in the firft defign; or with columns upon pedeftals, as they are in the fecond: But in the one as well as the other, the columns were made clofe to the wall; and the architraves, frizes and cornices were wrought with ftucco, or made of wood, and there was but one order of columns. The vault was made either of a femi-circle, or a Schiffo, that is, it had as much in height, as was the third part of the breadth of the hall, and ought to be adorned with compartments of ftucco and paintings. The length of thefe halls would be very beautiful of one fquare and two thirds of the breadth.

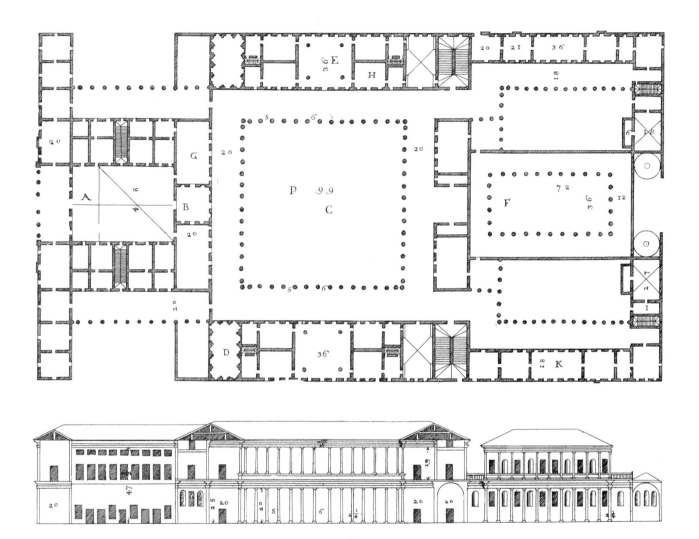

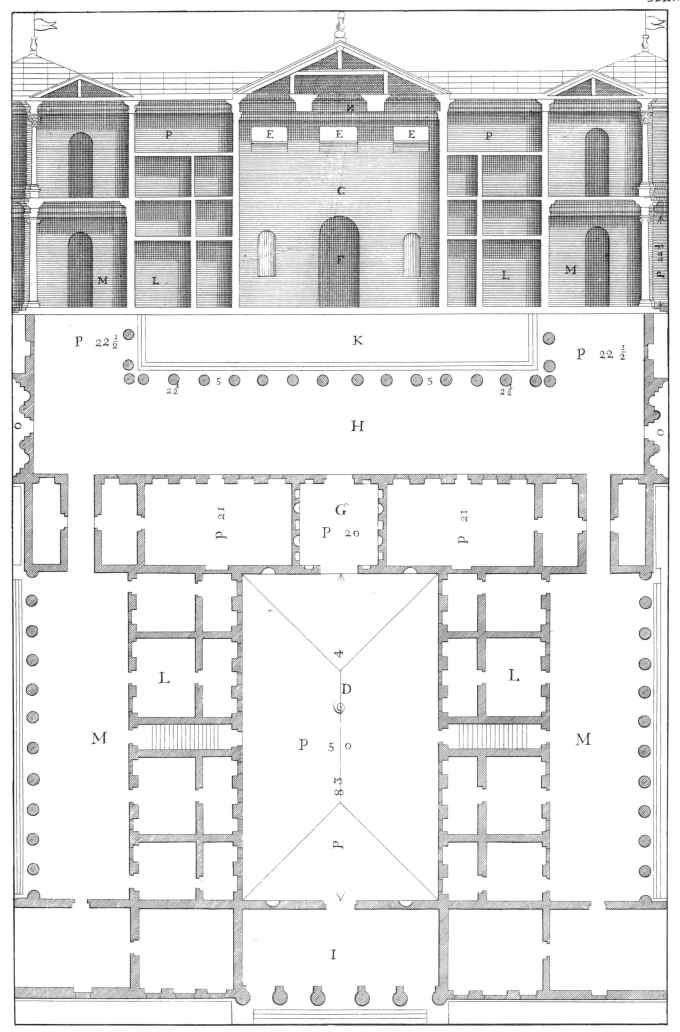

CHAP. X.

Of EGYPTIAN HALLS.

THE following defign is of the Egyptian halls, which refembled Bafilica's very much, Plate 28. (that is, places where juftice was adminifter'd) of which mention fhall be made when we treat of the piazza's: becaufe in thefe halls there was a portico commonly made with the columns at a diftance from the wall, as they are in the Bafilica's; and over the columns there were the architraves, the frizes, and the cornices. The fpace between the columns and the wall was covered with a pavement. This pavement was uncovered, and formed a Corridor, or balcony, round. Above the faid columns there was a continued wall, with femi-columns on the infide, one fourth part lefs than the abovefaid; and between the inter-columniations there were windows, which gave light to the hall, and through which, from the faid uncover'd pavement, one might fee into it. Thefe halls muft needs have been of an admirable magnificence, as well by reafon of the ornament of the columns, as alfo for its height; becaufe the foffit lay over the cornice of the fecond order, and muft have been very commodious when feftivals and entertainments were made there.

CHAP. XI.

Of the PRIVATE HOUSES of the Greeks.

THE Greeks held a different manner of building from the Latins; becaufe, as VITRUVIUS fays, omitting the loggia's and atrio's, they made the entrance of the houfe little and narrow; and on one part placed the ftables for horfes, and on the other the porter's rooms. From this firft paffage one enter'd the court; which had on three fides portico's, and on the part fronting the fouth they made two Anti, i. e. pilafters, which fupported the beams of the more inward cielings; becaufe fome fpace being left on the one fide, and the other, there were very large places appointed for the mothers of families, wherein they dwell with their men and women fervants. And even with the faid Anti were fome rooms, which we may call antichamber, chamber, and back room, as they are one behind the other. Round the portico's were places for eating, fleeping, and for other like neceffary things to the family. To this edifice they annexed another, of much greater fize, and ornament, with more ample courts; in which they either made four portico's of an equal height, or one that was greater, viz. that which fronted the fouth, and the court which had this higher portico was called Rhodiaco; perhaps becaufe the invention came from the Rhodians. Thefe courts had magnificent loggia's forwards, with particular gates of their own, wherein the men only dwelt. Near this fabrick, on the right and left, they made other houfes, which had particular gates of their own, and all the conveniences neceffary to make them habitable; and in thefe ftrangers were lodged: for it was the cuftom among thefe people, when a ftranger came, to conduct him the firft day to eat with them, and then to affign him a lodging in the faid houfes, and fend him thither all the neceffaries of life; whereby the ftrangers were in every refpect as free, as if they had been in their own houfe.

LET it fuffice to have faid thus much concerning the houfes of the Greeks, and of city houfes.

Of the parts of the houfes of the Greeks.

A, paffage.
B, ftables.
C, places for the porters.
D, firft court.
E, entrance to the rooms.
F, places where the women did their work.
G, firft great room, which we fhall call the antichamber.
H, middling chamber.
I, fmall room.
K, fmall halls to eat in.
L, the rooms.
M, fecond court, larger than the firft.
N, portico greater than the three others, from which the court is called Rhodiaco.

O, place leading from the leffer into the Plate 29. greater court.
P, the three portico's, having fmall co-lumns
Q, Triclini, Ciziceni, and Cancelarie, or the places to be painted.
R, hall.
S, library.
T, fquare halls, where they ufed to eat.
V, the houfes for the ftrangers.
X, little alleys, which parted the faid houfes from thofe of the mafter.
Y, fmall uncovered courts.
Z, principal ftreet.

CHAP.

CHAP. XII.

Of the SITE *to be chofen for the fabricks of* VILLA'S.

THE city houfes are certainly of great fplendour and conveniency to a gentleman who is to refide in them all the time he fhall require for the adminiftration of the republick, or for directing his own affairs. But perhaps he will not reap much lefs utility and confolation from the country houfe; where the remaining part of the time will be paffed in feeing and adorning his own poffeffions, and by induftry, and the art of agriculture, improving his eftate; where alfo by the exercife which in a villa is commonly taken, on foot and on horfe-back, the body will the more eafily preferve its ftrength and health; and, finally, where the mind, fatigued by the agitations of the city, will be greatly reftor'd and comforted, and be able quietly to attend the ftudies of letters, and contemplation.

HENCE it was the antient fages commonly ufed to retire to fuch like places; where being oftentimes vifited by their virtuous friends and relations, having houfes, gardens, fountains, and fuch like pleafant places, and above all, their virtue, they could eafily attain to as much happinefs as can be attained here below.

HAVING now, by the help of God, gone through what I had to fay concerning city houfes; it is juft that we proceed to thofe of the country, in which private and family affairs are chiefly tranfacted.

BUT before we come to the defigns of thefe, it feems not improper to fay fomething concerning the fituation or place to be chofen for thofe fabricks, and of their difpofition; becaufe, as we are not confined (as commonly happens in cities) by publick walls, or thofe of our neighbours, to certain and determinate bounds, it is the bufinefs of a wife architect, with the utmoft care and diligence, to feek and find out a convenient and healthy place: fince we are, for the moft part, in the country during the fummer feafon; at which time, even in the moft healthy places, our bodies become weak and fickly, by reafon of the heat.

IN the firft place therefore, let a place be chofen as convenient as poffible, and in the middle of the eftate, that the owner, without much trouble, may view and improve it on every fide, and that the fruits thereof may be the more conveniently carried by the labourers to his houfe.

IF one may build upon a river, it will be both convenient and beautiful; becaufe at all times, and with little expence, the products may be convey'd to the city in boats, and will ferve for the ufes of the houfe and cattle. Befides the cooling the air in fummer very much, it will afford a beautiful profpect, with which the eftates, pleafure and kitchen gardens may with great utility and ornament be water'd, which are the fole and chief recreation of a villa.

BUT if navigable rivers cannot be had, one muft endeavour to build near fome other running water; and above all to get at a diftance from ftanding waters, becaufe they generate a very bad air: which we may very eafily avoid, if we build upon elevated and chearful places, where the air is, by the continual blowing of the winds, moved; and the earth, by its declivity, purged of all ill vapours and moifture: and where the inhabitants are healthy and chearful, and preferve a good colour, and are not molefted by gnats and other fmall animals, which are generated by the putrefaction of ftill fenny waters.

AND becaufe the waters are very neceffary to human life, and according to their various qualities they produce in us different effects; fome generating the fpleen, others glandulous fwellings in the neck, others the ftone, and many other difeafes:

GREAT care ought therefore to be taken, not to build near thofe waters which have any odd tafte, or which partake of any colour; but be clear, limpid, and fubtile, and which, being fprinkled upon a white cloth, do not ftain it: becaufe thefe will be certain figns of their goodnefs.

THERE are many methods to find whether the waters are good, taught us by VITRUVIUS: but that water is deemed perfect which makes good bread, and in which greens are quickly boiled; and which, being boiled, does not leave any fur or fediment at bottom of the veffel.

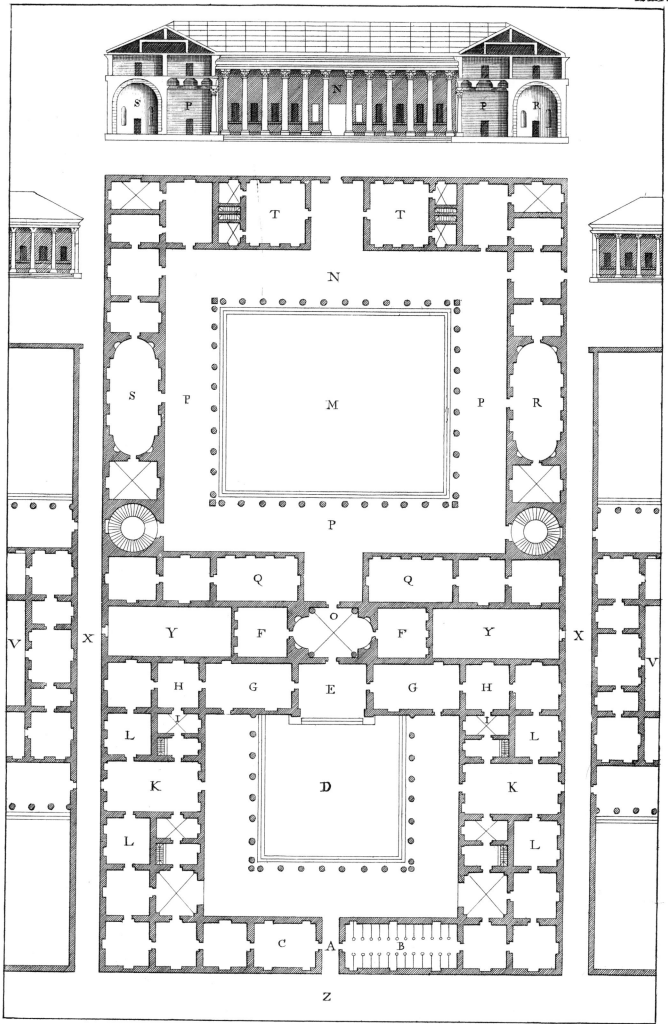

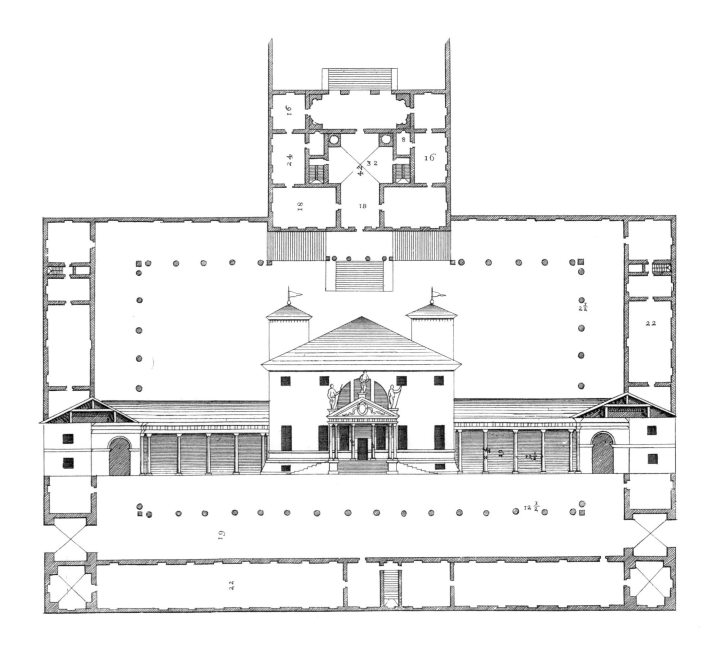

IT will be an excellent fign of the goodnefs of the water, if, where it paffes, one does not fee mofs or rufhes grow; but the place is clean, beautiful, and has fand or gravel at the bottom, and is not foul and muddy.

THE animals which are accuftomed to drink of them, will alfo be an indication of the goodnefs and falubrity of the waters, if they are lively, robuft, and fat, and not weak and lean.

BUT with regard to the wholefomnefs of the air, befides the aforefaid particulars, the antient edifices will give an indication thereof, if they are not corroded and fpoiled: if the trees are well nourifhed and beautiful, and not bent in any part by the winds, and if they are not fuch as grow in fenny places.

AND if the ftones produced in thofe places do not appear on the furface to be putrified; and alfo if the colour of the inhabitants be natural, and fhews a good temperature.

ONE ought not to build in valleys enclofed between mountains; becaufe edifices in valleys are there hid, and are deprived of feeing at a diftance, and of being feen. Thefe are without dignity and grandure, and alfo entirely contrary to health; becaufe the earth being impregnated by the rains that fettle there, fends forth peftiferous vapours, infecting both the body and mind; the fpirits being by them weaken'd, the joints and nerves emafculated: and what is lodged in the granaries will corrupt through the too great moifture.

BESIDES which, if the fun happens to fhine, the reflection of its rays will caufe exceffive heats; and if it doth not, the continual fhade will render the people in a manner ftupid and difcoloured.

AND when the winds enter into the faid valleys, it will be with too much fury, as if it were through narrow channels; and when they do not blow, the collected air will grow grofs and unhealthy.

WHEN there is a neceffity of building upon a mountain, let a fituation be chofen facing a temperate part of the heaven, and which is not by higher mountains continually fhaded, nor fcorched (as it were by two funs) by the fun's reverberation from fome neighbouring rock, for in either of thefe cafes it will be exceeding bad to dwell in.

AND, finally, in the choice of the fituation for the building a villa, all thofe confiderations ought to be had, which are neceffary in a city houfe; fince the city is as it were but a great houfe, and, on the contrary, a country houfe is a little city.

CHAP. XIII.

Of the compartment or difpofition of the VILLA's.

THE agreeable, pleafant, commodious, and healthy fituation being found, attention is to be given to its elegant and convenient difpofition. There are two forts of fabricks required in a villa: one for the habitation of the mafter, and of his family; and the other to manage and take care of the produce and animals of the villa. Therefore the compartment of the fite ought to be in fuch a manner, that the one may not be any impediment to the other.

THE habitation for the mafter ought to be made with a juft regard to his family and condition, and as has been obferved in cities, of which mention has been made.

THE covertures for the things belonging to a villa, muft be made fuitable to the eftate and number of animals; and in fuch manner joined to the mafter's habitation, that he may be able to go to every place under cover, that neither the rains, nor the fcorching fun of the fummer, may be a nuifance to him, when he goes to look after his affairs; which will alfo be of great ufe to lay wood in under cover, and an infinite number of things belonging to a villa, that would otherwife be fpoiled by the rains and the fun: befides which thefe portico's will be a great ornament.

REGARD muft be had in lodging the men employ'd for the ufe of the villa, the animals, the products, and the inftruments, conveniently, and without any conftraint. The rooms for the steward, for the bailiff or farmer, and for the labourers, ought to be in a convenient place near to the gates, for the safeguard of all the other parts.

THE stables for the working animals, such as oxen and horses, must be at a distance from the master's habitations, that the dunghills may be at a distance from it, and be placed in very light and warm places.

THE places for breeding animals, as hogs, sheep, pidgeons, fowls, and such like, are to be disposed according to their quality and nature: and in this the custom of different countries ought to be observed.

THE cellars ought to be under ground, inclosed, and far from any noise, moisture, or ill smell, and ought to receive their light from the east, or from the north; because that having it from any other part, where the sun might heat them, the wines being thereby warmed would grow weak, and be spoiled. They must be made somewhat sloping in the middle, and have their floors of terazzo, or paved in such a manner, that should the wine happen to run out, it may be taken up again. The tubs in which the wine is fermented must be placed under the covertures that are made near the said cellars, and so raised, that their out-lets may be something higher than the bung-holes of the barrels, that the wine may be the more easily convey'd, either through leather pipes or wooden channels, from the said tubs into the barrels.

THE granaries ought to have their light towards the north, because the corn cannot so easily be heated, but rather cooled by the winds; and thereby it will be a long time preserv'd, and none of those little animals will breed there, which damage it very much. Their floor, or pavement, ought to be of terrazzato, if it can be had, or at least of boards; because the corn will be spoiled by touching of lime.

THE other store-rooms ought also, for the said reasons, to look towards the same part of the heaven.

HAY-LOFTS ought to face the south or west; because the hay being dried by the heat of the sun, it will not be in danger of corrupting and taking fire. The instruments necessary to the husband-men, must be in convenient places under cover towards the south. The grange, where the corn is threshed, ought to be exposed to the sun, ample, spacious, paved, and a little raised in the middle, with portico's round it, or at least on one side; that in case of sudden rains, the corn may be immediately conveyed under cover; and must not be too near the master's house, by reason of the dust, nor so far off as to be out of sight.

THIS in general will suffice concerning the election of sites, and their compartments. It remains (as I have promised) that I insert the designs of some of the fabricks which I have directed in the country, according to several inventions.

C H A P. XIV.

Of the DESIGNS of the country-houses belonging to some noble Venetians.

Plate 30. THE following fabrick is at *Bagnolo*, a place two miles distant from *Lonigo*, a castle in the *Vicentine*, and belongs to the magnificent Counts VITTORE, MARCO, and DANIELE DE PISANI, brothers. The stables, the cellars, the granaries, and such like other places, for the use of the villa, are on each side of the court. The columns of the portico's are of the Dorick order. The middle part of this fabrick is for the master's habitation. The pavement of the first rooms, are seven foot high from the ground; under which are the kitchen and such like places for the family. The hall is vaulted, in height once and half its breadth. To this height also joins the vault of the loggia's. The rooms are with flat cielings, and their height equal to their breadth: the length of the greater is one square and two thirds, and of the others one square and an half. And it is to be observed, that great attention has not been given, in putting the lesser stairs in a place where they might have a strong light, (as we have recommended in the first book) because they being to serve to places below, and to those above, which are for granaries and mezzati; wherefore, regard has been chiefly had to accommodate well the middle order, which is for the master's habitation, and for strangers. The stairs that lead to this order, are put in a very proper place, as may be seen by the designs.

THIS

THIS is said also for an hint to the prudent reader, with respect to all the other fabricks of one order only; because, in those which have two, beautiful and well adorned, I have taken care that the stairs should be light, and put in commodious places: I say two, because that which goes under-ground for the cellars, and such like uses, and that which goes to the part above, and serves for granaries and mezzati, I do not call a principal order, as it does not lead to the habitation of the gentlemen.

THE following fabrick belongs to the magnificent Signor FRANCESCO BADOERO, in the Plate 31. *Polesine*, at a place called *La Frata*, on a site somewhat elevated, and washed by a branch of the *Adige*, where formerly stood a castle, belonging to SALINGUERRA DE ESTE, brother-in-law to EZZELINO DA ROMANO.

THE base to the whole edifice is a pedestal, five feet high; the pavement of the rooms is level with this height, which are all with flat cielings, and have been adorned with grotesque work of a beautiful invention, by GIALLO FIORENTINO. The granaries are above, and the kitchen, cellars, and other places belonging to its convenience, are below. The columns of the loggia's of the master's house, are of the Ionick order. The cornice, like a crown, encompasses the whole house. The frontispiece, over the loggia's, forms a beautiful sight, because it makes the middle part higher than the sides. Lower on the plane are found the places for the steward, bailiff or farmer, stables, and other suitables for a villa.

THE magnificent Signor MARCO ZENO has built according to the following invention Plate 32. at *Cesalto*, a place near to the *Motta*, a castle in the *Trevigiano*. The pavement of the rooms, all which are vaulted, is level with a basement which encompasses the whole fabrick. The height of the vaults of the greater, is according to the second manner for the height of vaults. Those that are square, have lunetti in the angles over the windows. The little rooms next the loggia, are cov'd *à fascia*, as also the hall. The vault of the loggia is as high as that of the hall, and both exceed the height of the rooms. This fabrick has gardens, a court, a dove-house, and all that is necessary for a villa.

NOT very far from the *Gambarare*, on the *Brenta*, is the following fabrick, belonging Plate 33. to the magnificent Signors NICOLO' and LUIGI DE FOSCARI. This fabrick is raised eleven foot from the ground; and underneath are the kitchens, servants halls, and such like places, and vaulted above as well as below. The height of the vaults of the greater rooms, is according to the first manner for the height of vaults. The square rooms have their vaults *à cupola*. Over the small rooms, there are mezzati. The vaults of the hall is crossed semicircularly: the height of its impost, is as high as the hall is broad; which has been adorned with most excellent paintings, by Messer BATTISTA VENETIANO. Messer BATTISTA FRANCO, a very great designer of our times, had begun to paint one of the great rooms; but being overtaken by death, has left the work imperfect. The loggia is of the Ionick order. The cornice goes round the house, and forms a frontispiece over the loggia; and on the opposite part below the main roof, there is another cornice, which passes over the frontispiece. The rooms above are like mezzati, by reason of their lowness; because they are but eight foot high.

THE following fabrick is at *Masera*, a village near *Asolo*, a castle in the *Trevigiano*; Plate 34. belonging to Monsignor Reverendissimo ELETTO DE AQUILEIA, and to the magnificent Signor MARC' ANTONIO DE BARBARI, brothers. That part of the fabrick which advances a little forward, has two orders of rooms. The floor of those above is even with the level of the court backwards, where there is a fountain cut into the mountain opposite to the house, with infinite ornaments of stucco and paintings. This fountain forms a small lake, which serves for a fish-pond. From this place the water runs into the kitchen; and after having watered the gardens that are on the right and left of the road, which leads gradually to the fabrick, it forms two fish-ponds, with their watering places upon the high-road; from whence it waters the kitchen garden, which is very large, and full of the most excellent fruits, and of different kinds of pulse. The front of the master's house has four columns, of the Ionick order. The capitols of those in the angles face both ways. The method of making which capitols, I shall set down in the book of temples. On the one, and on the other part, there are loggia's, which, in their extremities, have two dove-houses; and under them there are places to make wines, the stables, and other places for the use of the villa.

THE following fabrick is near the gate of *Montagnana*, a castle in the *Padoano*; Plate 35. and was built by the magnificent Signor FRANCESCO PISANI; who being gone to a better life, could not finish it. The large rooms are one square and three quarters in length; the vaults are *à schiffo*, and in height according to the second manner for the height of

O   vaults.

vaults. The middle fized are fquare, and vaulted *à cadino*. The fmall rooms, and the paffage, are of an equal breadth : their vaults are two fquares in height ; the entrance has four columns, one fifth lefs than thofe without, which fupport the pavement of the hall, and make the height of the vaults beautiful, and fecure. In the four niches that are feen there, have been carved the four feafons of the year, by Meffer ALESSANDRO VITTORIA, an excellent fculptor. The firft order of the columns is Dorick, the fecond Ionick. The rooms above, are with flat cielings. The height of the hall reaches up to the roof.

THIS fabrick has two ftreets on the wings, where there are two doors ; over which there are paffages that lead to the kitchen, and places for fervants.

Plate 36.   THE following fabrick belongs to the magnificent Signor GIORGIO CORNARA, at *Piombino*, a place in *Caftelfranco*. The firft order of the loggia's is Ionick. The hall is placed in the moft inward part of the houfe, that it may be far from the heat and cold. The wings where the niches are feen, are in breadth the third part of its length. The columns anfwer directly to the laft, but one, of the loggia's, and are as far diftant from one another, as they are high. The large rooms are one fquare and three quarters long. The height of the vaults is according to the firft method for the height of vaults. The middle fized are fquare, one third higher than they are broad : their vaults are *à lunetti*. Over the fmall rooms there are mezzati. The loggia's above are of the Corinthian order. The columns are one fifth lefs than thofe underneath. The rooms are with flat cielings, and have fome mezzati over them. On one part is the kitchen, and places for houfewifery ; and on the other, places for fervants.

Plate 37.   THE fabrick beneath belongs to the Clariffimo Cavalier il Signor LEONARDO MOCENICO, at a village called *Marocco*, on the road from *Venice* to *Trevigi*. The cellars are above-ground, and over them, in one part, are the granaries, and on the other, conveniencies for the family ; and over thefe places, are the mafter's rooms, divided into four appartments. The vaults of the larger, are one and twenty foot high, and made of cane, that they may be light. The vaults of the middle-fized are as high as thofe of the greater. The vaults of the fmaller rooms, or clofets, are *à crociera*, and feventeen foot high. The loggia below is of the Ionick order. There are four columns in the ground hall, that the height may be proportionable to the breadth. The loggia above is of the Corinthian order, and has a poggio two foot and three quarters high.

THE ftairs are placed in the middle, and divide the hall from the loggia, and go up, one contrary to the other, whereby one may go up and down on the right and left ; and are both very convenient and beautiful, and fufficiently light.

THIS fabrick has on the wings, the places to make wine, the ftables, portico's, and other conveniencies, proper for the ufe of a villa.

Plate 38.   THE under fabrick is at *Fanzolo*, a village in the *Trevigiano*, three miles diftant from *Caftelfranco*, belonging to the Magnificent Signor LEONARDO ERNO. The cellars, the granaries, the ftables, and the other places belonging to a villa, are on each fide of the mafter's houfe ; and at the extremity of each of them, is a dove-houfe, which affords both profit to the mafter, and an ornament to the place ; and to all which, one may go under cover : which is one of the principal things required in a villa, as has been before obferved.

BEHIND this fabrick there is a fquare garden of eighty *campi trevigiani* ; in the middle of which runs a little river, which makes the fituation very delightful and beautiful.

IT has been adorned with paintings by Meffer BATTISTA VENETIANO.

CHAP. XV.

Of the DESIGNS of the VILLA's *belonging to fome gentlemen of the* TERRA FIRMA.

Plate 39.   AT a place in the *Vicentine*, called *Finale*, is the following building belonging to Signor BIAGIO SARRACENO. The floor of the rooms is raifed five foot above the ground ; the larger rooms are one fquare and five eighths in length, and in height equal to their breadth, and with flat cielings. This height alfo continues to the hall. The fmall rooms, near the loggia, are vaulted ; the height of the vaults is equal to that of the rooms.

The

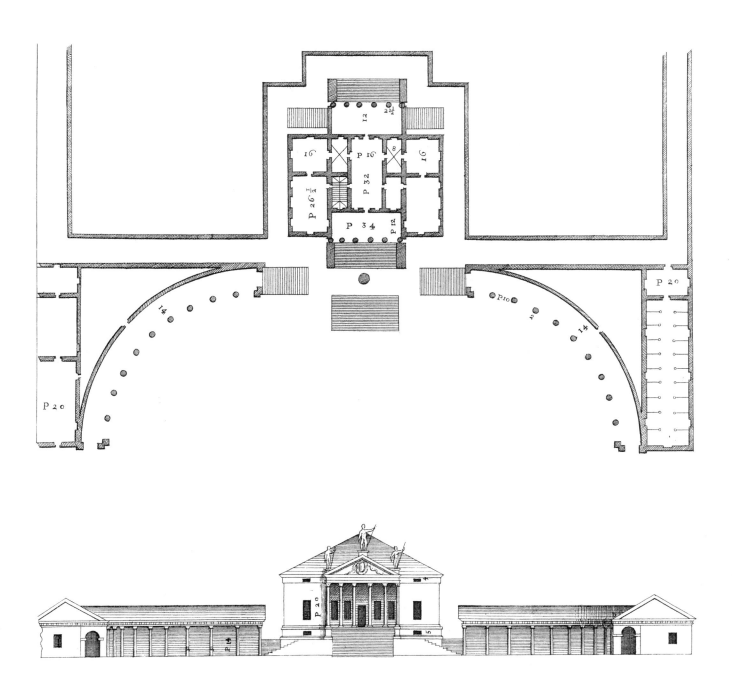

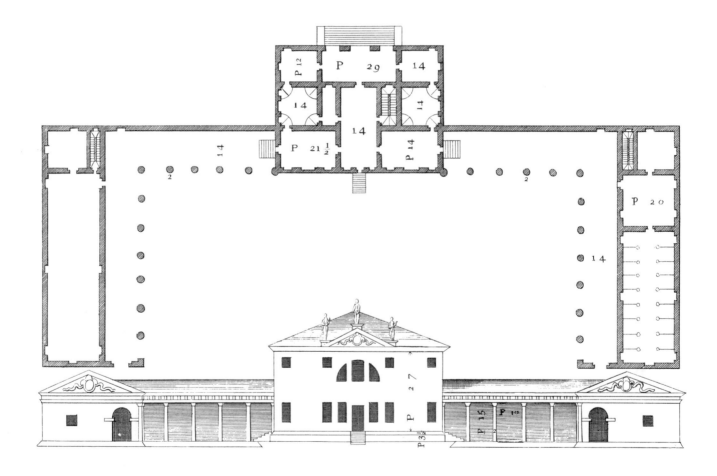

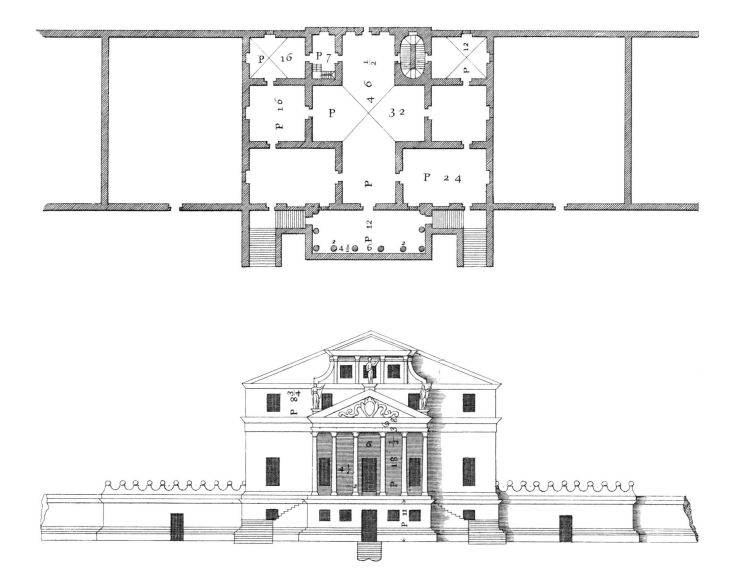

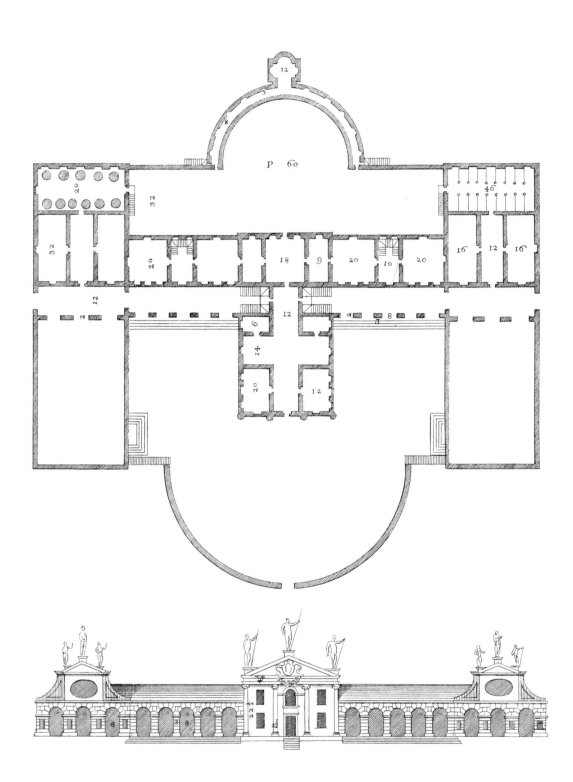

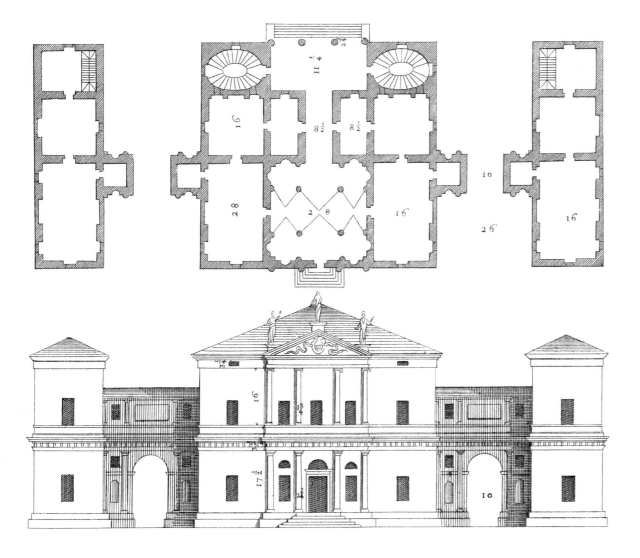

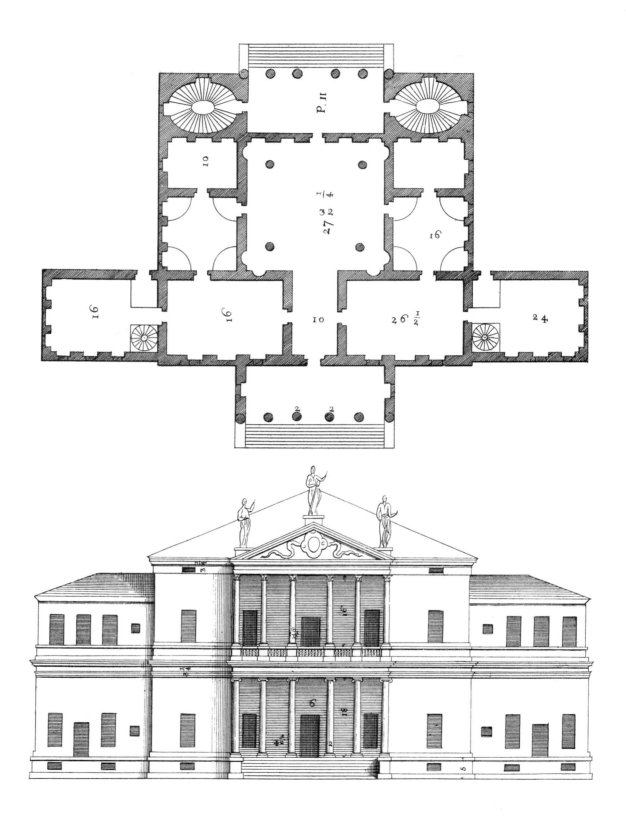

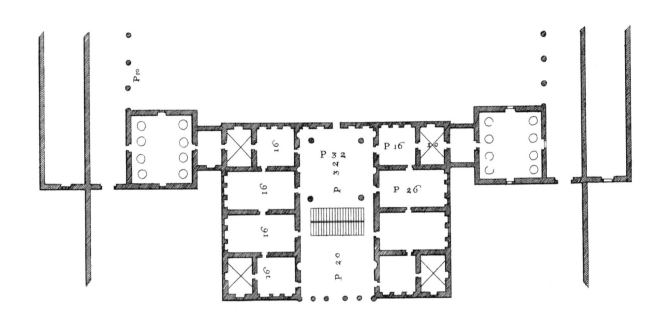

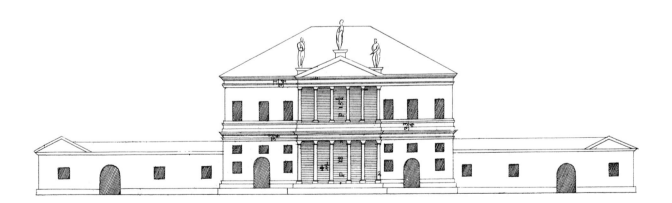

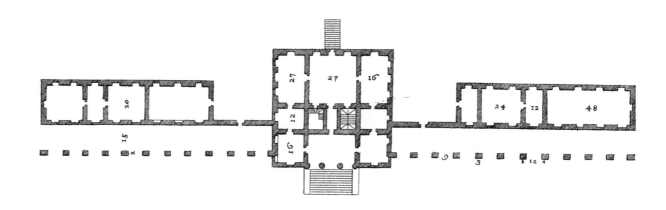

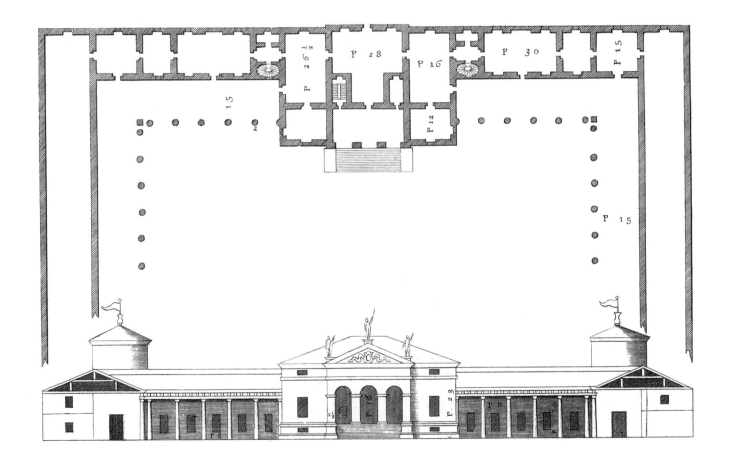

P 26½ P 28 P 16 P 30 P 15

15

2

P 12

P 15

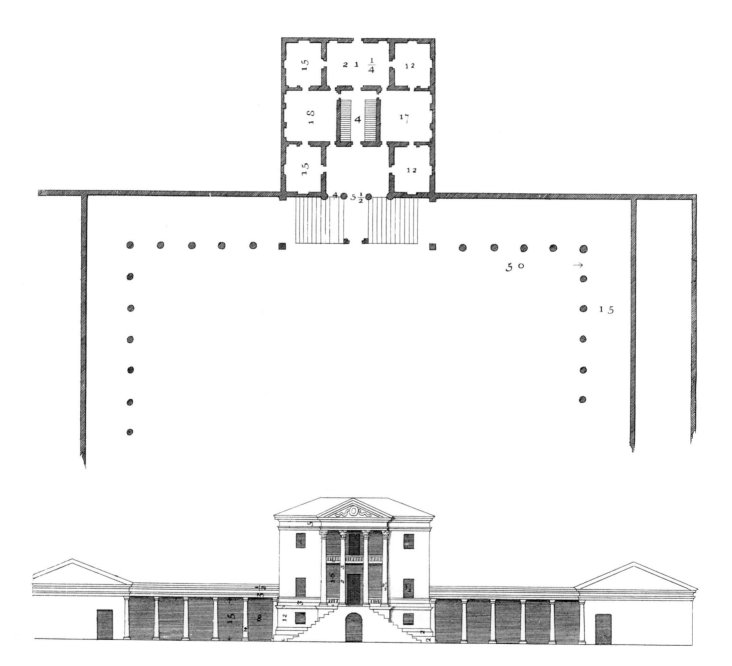

The cellars are underneath, and the granaries above, which take up the whole body of the houfe. The kitchens are without the houfe, but fo joined, that they are convenient. On each fide there are all the neceffary places for the ufe of a villa.

THE following defigns are of the fabrick of Signor GIORALAMO RAGONA, a *Vicen-* Plate 40. *tine* gentleman, built by him at *Le Ghizzole,* his villa. This fabrick has the conveniencies before mention'd, that is, one may go every where under cover. The pavement of the rooms for the mafter's ufe, is twelve foot above the ground : under thefe rooms, are the conveniencies for the family ; and above them, other rooms which may ferve for granaries, and alfo for places to lodge in on occafion. The principal ftairs are in the fore front of the houfe, and anfwer under the portico's of the court.

IN *Pogliana,* a village, is the following fabrick of the Cavalier POGLIANA. Its rooms Plate 41. have been adorned with paintings and moft beautiful ftucco's, by Meffer BERNARDINO INDIA, and Meffer ANSELMO CANERA, *Veronefe* painters, and by Meffer BARTO- LOMEO RIDOLFI, a *Veronefe* fculptor. The large rooms are one fquare, and two thirds long, and are vaulted. The fquare ones have the lunetti in their angles. Over the fmall rooms there are mezzati. The heigth of the hall, is one half more than it is broad ; and even with the height of the loggia the hall is vaulted *à fafcia,* and the loggia *à crociera.* Over all thefe places are the granaries, and underneath them the cellars and the kitchen, becaufe the floor is raifed five foot above ground. On one fide it has the court, and other places for the neceffaries of a villa ; on the other there is a garden, which anfwers to the faid court ; and backwards a kitchen-garden, and a fifh-pond : fo that this gentleman, as he is magnificent, and of a moft noble mind, has not fpared any of thofe ornaments, or any of the conveniencies poffible, that might render this place of his, beautiful, delightful, and commodious.

AT *Lifiera,* a place near *Vicenza,* is the following fabrick, built by Signor FRANCESCO Plate 42. VALMARANA, of happy memory. The loggia's are of the Ionick order : the columns have a fquare bafe under them, which goes round the houfe. Level with this height is the floor of the loggia's, and of the rooms, which are all with flat cielings. In the angles of the houfe there are four towers, which are vaulted. The hall is vaulted *à fafcia*

THIS fabrick has two courts ; one forward, for the ufe of the mafter, and the other backward, where the corn is threfhed : and has covertures, in which are accommodated all the places belonging to the ufe of a villa.

THE following fabrick was begun by Count FRANCESCO, and Count LODOVICO DE Plate 43. TRISSINI, brothers, at *Meledo,* a village in the *Vicentine.* The fituation is very beautiful, becaufe it is upon a hill, which is wafhed by an agreeable little river, in the middle of a very fpacious plain, and near to a well frequented road. Upon the fummit of the hill, there is to be a round hall, encompaffed with the rooms, but fo high, that it may receive its light from above them. There are fome half columns in the hall, that fupport a gallery, into which one goes from the rooms above ; which by reafon they are but feven feet high, ferve for mezzati. Under the floor of the firft rooms, there are the kitchens, fervant's halls, and other places. And becaufe every front has a very beautiful profpect, there are four loggia's, of the Corinthian order ; above the frontifpieces of which the cupola of the hall rifes. The loggia's that tend to the circumference, form an agreeable profpect. Nearer to the plain, are the hay-lofts, the cellars, the ftables, the granaries, the places for the farmer, and other rooms for the ufe of the villa. The columns of thefe portico's are of the Tufcan order. Over the river, in the angles of the court, are two dove-houfes.

THE under-placed fabrick is at *Campiglia,* a place in the *Vicentine,* and belongs to Sig- Plate 44. nor MARIO REPETA, who has executed, in this fabrick, the will of his father, Signor FRANCESCO, of happy memory. The columns of the portico's are of the Dorick order : the intercolumniations are four diameters of a column. In the extream angles of the roof, where the loggia's, are feen without the whole body of the houfe, there are two dove-houfes, and the loggia. On the flank, oppofite to the ftables, there are rooms, of which, fome are ftill dedicated to continency, others to juftice, and others to other virtues, with elogiums and paintings adapted to the fubject ; part of which is the work of Meffer BATTISTA MA- GANZA, a *Vicentine* painter, and an excellent poet. This was done, that this gentleman, who very courtioufly receives all thofe who go and fee him, may lodge his vifitors and friends in the rooms infcribed to that virtue to which he thinks them moftly inclined. This fa- brick has this conveniency, that one can go every where under cover. And becaufe the part for the mafter's dwelling, and that for the ufe of the villa, are of the fame order ;

as much at that lofes in grandeur, for not being more eminent than this, fo much this of the villa increafes in its proper ornament and dignity, by being made equal to that of the mafter, which adds beauty to the whole work.

Plate 45.   THE following fabrick belongs to the Count OLEARDO and Count THEODORO DE THIENI, brothers, and is at *Cigogna*, his villa; which fabrick was begun by Count FRANCESO their father. The hall is in the middle of the houfe, and has round it fome Ionick columns, over which there is a gallery, level with the floor of the rooms above. The vault of this hall reaches up to the roof. The large rooms are vaulted *à fchiffo* and the fquare ones *à mezzo cadina* and rife in fuch a manner, that they form four little towers in the angles of the fabrick. The fmall rooms have their mezzati over them, the doors of which anfwer to the middle of the ftairs. The ftairs are without a wall in the middle; and becaufe the hall by receiving the light from above, is very clear, thefe alfo have light enough: as they are void in the middle befides, they alfo receive light from above. In one of the covertures, on the fides of the court, there are the cellars, and the granaries; on the other, the ftables, and the places for a villa. Thofe two loggia's, which like arms come out of the fabrick, are made to join the mafter's houfe with that of the villa. Near this fabrick, there are two courts of old building, with portico's; the one to threfh the corn in, and the other for the under part of the family.

Plate 46.   THE following fabrick belongs to the Count GIACOMO ANGARANO, and was built by him at his villa at *Angarano* in the *Vicentine*. On the fides of the court there are the cellars, granaries, places to make wines, places for the farmer, ftables, dove-houfe; and farther, in one part of the court, places for the neceffaries of a villa; and on the other a garden. The mafter's houfe, which is placed in the middle, is vaulted in the lower part, and in that above cieled. The fmall rooms above, as well as thofe below, have mezzati. Near to this fabrick the *Brenta* runs, a river abounding with excellent fifh. This place is celebrated for the good wines that are made there, and the fruits that grow there, but much more for the courtefy of the mafter.

Plate 47.   THE defigns that follow, are of the fabrick belonging to Count OTTAVIE THIENE, at *Quinto*, his villa. It was begun by the Count MARC' ANTONIO, his father, of happy memory, and by Count ADRIANO, his uncle. The fituation is very beautiful, having on one part the *Tefina*, and on the other a branch of the faid river, which is pretty large. This palace has a loggia before the gate, of the Dorick order: through this one paffes into another loggia, and from that into a court, which has on the fides two loggia's; on the one, and on the other end of thefe loggia's, are the apartments or rooms, fome of which have been adorned with paintings by Meffer GIOVANI INDEMIO VINCENTINO, a man of a very fine genius. Oppofite to the entrance one finds a loggia, like that at the entrance; from which one enters into an atrio of four columns; and from that into the court, which has portico's of the Dorick order, and ferves for the ufe of the villa. There are no principal ftairs that correfpond with the whole fabrick, becaufe the part above is intended only for ftores, and places for fervants.

Plate 48.   AT *Lonedo*, a place in the *Vicentine*, is the following fabrick, belonging to Signor GIROLAMO DE GODI. It is placed upon a hill that has a beautiful profpect, and near a river that ferves for a fifh-pond. To make this place commodious for the ufe of a villa, courts have been made, and roads upon vaults, at no fmall expence. The fabrick in the middle, is for the habitation of the mafter, and of the family. The mafter's rooms have their floor thirteen feet high from the ground, and are with cielings; over thefe are the granaries, and the part underneath, that is, in the height of the thirteen foot, are difpofed the cellars, the places to make wines, the kitchens, and fuch like other places. The hall reaches, in height, up to the roof, and has two rows of windows. On either fide of this body of the fabrick, there are courts, and the covered places for the neceffaries of a villa. This fabrick has been adorned with paintings of a beautiful invention by Meffer GUALTIERA PADOVANO, by Meffer BATTISTA DEL MORO VERONESE, and by Meffer BATTISTA VENETIANO. Becaufe this gentleman, who is a very judicious man, in order to bring it to all the excellency and perfection poffible, has not fpared any coft, and has pitched on the moft fingular and excellent painters of our time.

Plate 49.   AT *Santa Sofia*, a place five miles from *Verona*, is the following fabrick belonging to Signor Conte MARC' ANTONIO SAREGO. It is placed in a very beautiful fituation, that is, upon a hill of a moft eafy afcent, which difcovers a part of the city, and between two fmall vales. All the hills about it are very agreeable, and abound with moft excellent water, therefore this fabrick is adorned with gardens and marvellous fountains. This place, for its agreeablenefs, was the delights of the Seinora DALLA SCALLA; and by fome veftigia, that

are

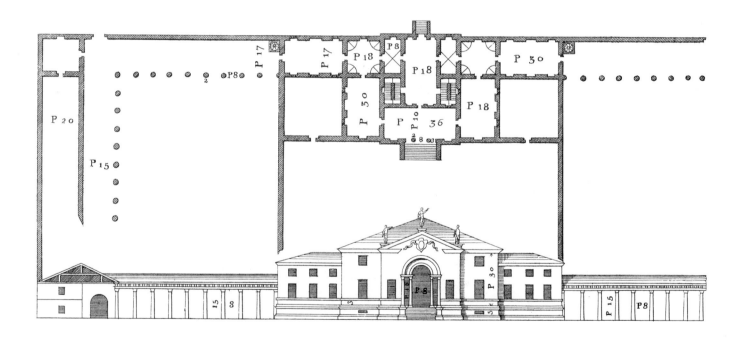

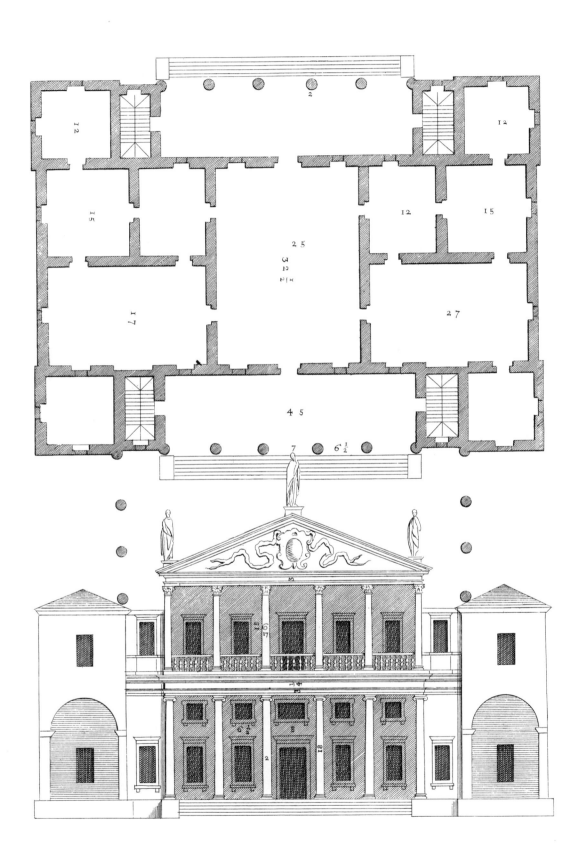

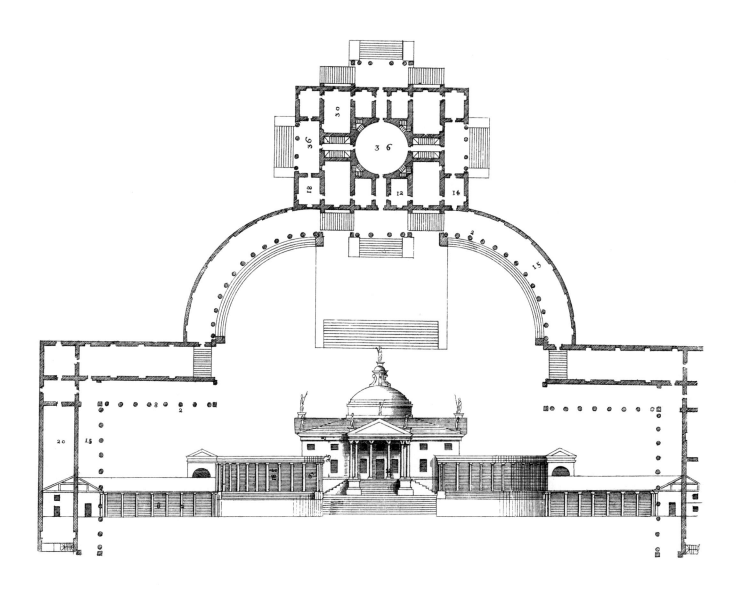

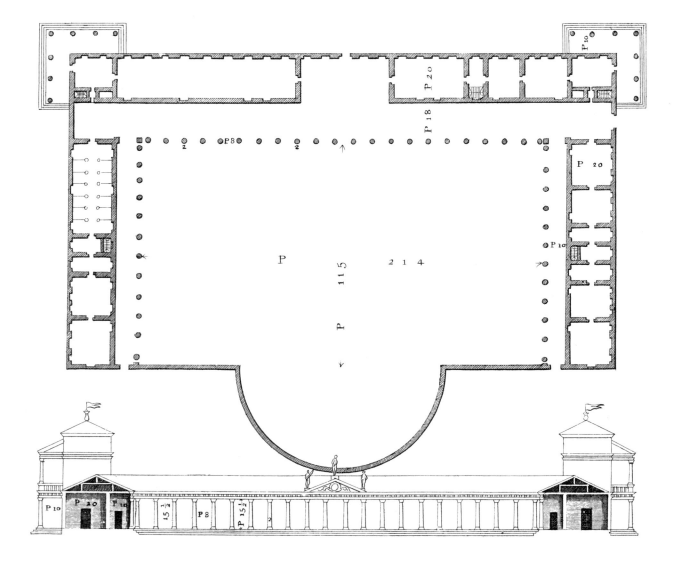

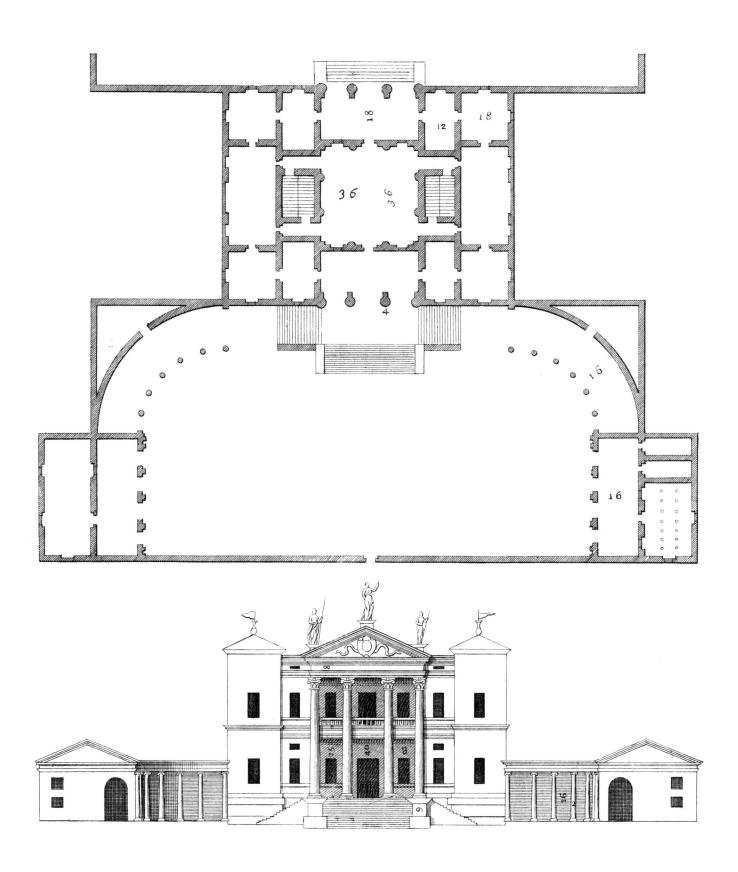

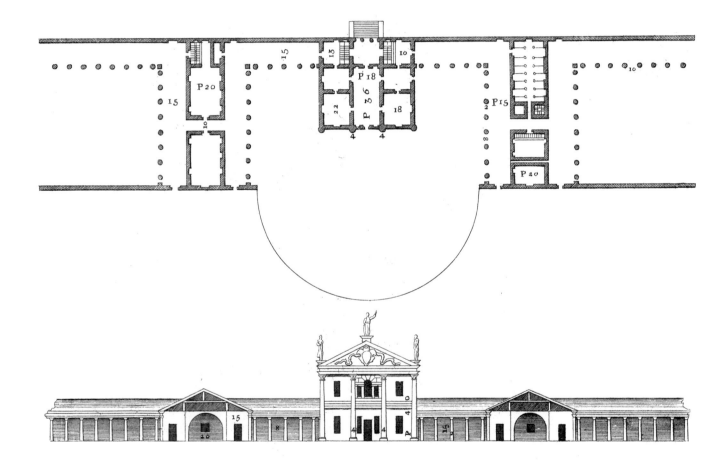

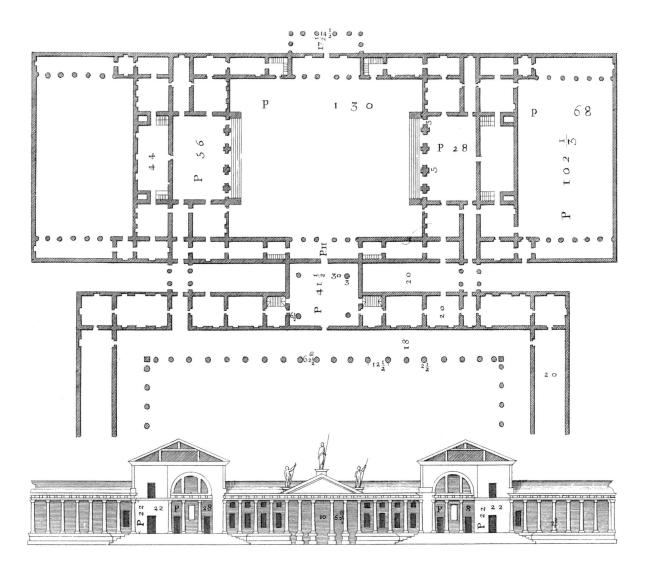

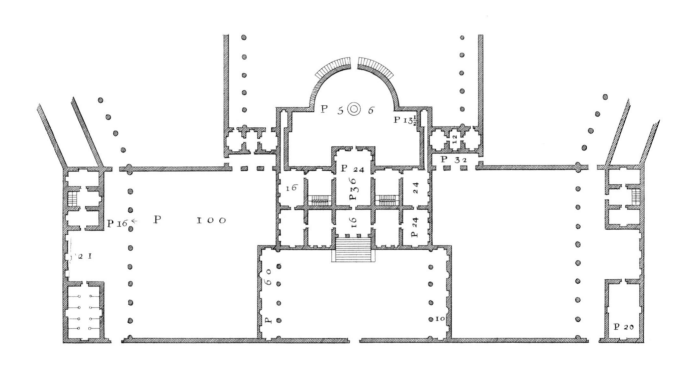

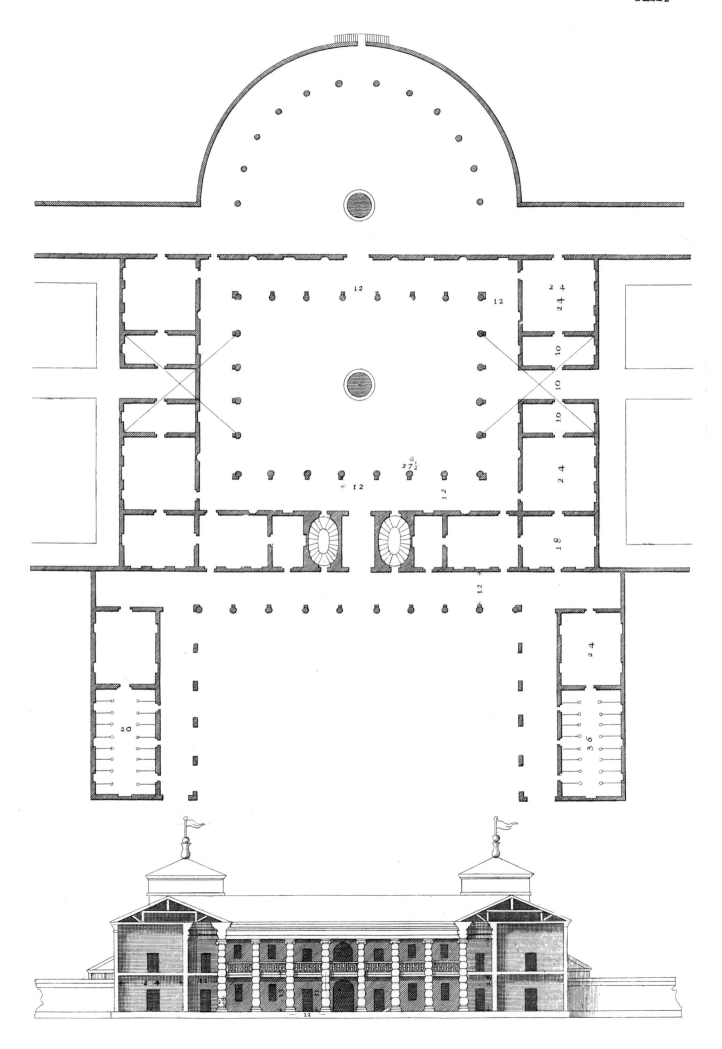

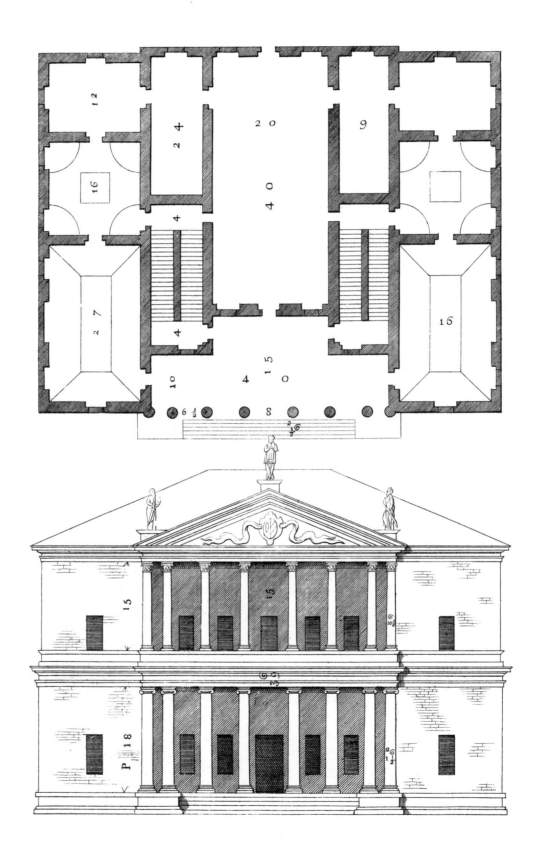

are there to be feen, one may comprehend, that in the time of the *Romans,* it was alfo held by the antients in no fmall efteem.

THE part of this houfe which ferves for the ufe of the mafter, and of the family, has a court, round which are portico's. The columns are of the Ionick order, made of unpolifhed ftones; as it fhould feem a villa requires, to which plain and fimple things are more fuitable than thofe that are delicate. Thefe columns fupport the outward cornice, that forms a gutter; into which the water falls from the roof. Behind thefe columns, that is, under the portico's, there are pilafters which fupport the pavement of the loggia above, that is, of the fecond floor. In this fecond floor there are two halls, the one oppofite to the other; the largenefs of which is expreffed in the defign of the plan, with lines that interfect one another, and are drawn from the outward walls of the fabrick to the columns. On the fide of this court is that for the ufe of the villa; on the one and on the other part of which, there are covertures for thofe conveniencies that are required in villa's.

THE following fabrick belongs to Signor Conte ANIBALE SAREGO, at a place in the Plate 50, *Colognefe,* called *la Miga.* A pedeftal, four foot and a half high, forms a bafement to the whole fabrick; and at this height is the pavement of the firft rooms; under which there are the cellars, the kitchens, and other rooms for the ufe of the family. The faid firft rooms are vaulted, and the fecond cieled. Near this fabrick there is the court for the neceffaries of a villa, with all thofe places that are fuitable to fuch a ufe.

CHAP. XVI.

Of the VILLA's *of the antients.*

I HAVE hitherto put the defigns of many fabricks, for villa's done by my direction. It remains that I fhou'd alfo put the defign of a houfe for a villa, which, as VITRUVIUS fays, the antients ufed to make; becaufe all the places belonging to the habitation, and to the ufes of the villa, may be feen in it expofed to that region of the heaven which is fuitable for them. Nor fhall I expatiate in referring to what PLINY fays upon this fubject; becaufe my chief intent at this time, is only to fhew how VITRUVIUS ought to be underftood in this place. The principal front is turned to the fouth, and has a loggia, from which one goes into the Plate 51. kitchen through a paffage, which receives its light from above the places adjacent, and has the chimney in the middle. On the left hand there are the ftables for oxen, whofe mangers are turned to the fire, and to the eaft. The baths are alfo on the fame part, which, for the rooms that thefe require, are at a diftance from the kitchen, even with the loggia. On the right hand is the prefs, and other places for the oil, anfwerable to the places for the baths, and front the eaft, fouth, and weft. Backwards there are the cellars, which receive their light from the north, and are far from noife, and from the heat of the fun. Over the cellars are the granaries, which receive their light from the fame part of the heaven. On the right and left part of the court, there are the ftables for horfes, fheep, and other animals; the hay-lofts, the places for ftraw, and the bake-houfes; all which ought to be far from the fire. Backwards one fees the mafter's habitation, the principal front of which is oppofite to the front of the houfe for the ufes of the villa: fo that in thefe houfes, built out of the city, the atrio's were in the back part. In this are obferved all thofe confiderations of which mention has been made before, when the defign of the antient private houfe was given; and therefore we have now only confidered what regards the villa.

I HAVE made the frontifpiece in the fore-front in all the fabricks for villa's, and alfo in fome for the city, in which are the principal gates; becaufe fuch frontifpieces fhew the entrance of the houfe, and add very much to the grandeur and magnificence of the work. Befides, the fore-part being thus made more eminent than the reft, is very commodious for placing the enfigns or arms of the owners, which are commonly put in the middle of the front. The antients alfo made ufe of them in their fabricks, as is feen in the remains of the temples, and other publick edifices; from which, as I have faid in the preface to the firft book, it is very likely that they took the invention, and the reafons for private edifices or houfes. VITRUVIUS, in the laft chapter of his third book, teaches how they are to be made.

CHAP. XVII.

Of some INVENTIONS, *according to divers situations.*

MY intention was to speak only of those fabricks which were either compleated, or begun, and carried on so far that one might soon expect them to be finished : but knowing that it is very often necessary to conform one's self to the situation, as one does not always build in open places, I was afterwards persuaded that the annexing to the afore-going designs some few inventions, made by me at the request of divers gentlemen, would not be deviating from our purpose; and which they have not executed, for those reasons which ordinarily happen; because of their difficult situations, and the method I have observed in accommodating in them the rooms, and the other places, that they might have a correspondence and proportion the one to the other, may (as I imagine) be of no small utility.

Plate 52.   THE situation of the first invention is pyramidal. The base of the pyramid comes to the principal front of the house, which has three orders of columns, that is, the Dorick, the Ionick, and the Corinthian. The entrance is square, and has four columns, which support the vault, and make the height proportionable to the breadth. On the one, and on the other part, there are two rooms, one square and two thirds long, and in height according to the first method for the heights of vaults. Near each there is a small room, and stairs to go up to the mezzati. At the head of the entrance I intended to make two rooms, one square and an half long, and then two small rooms in the same proportion with the stairs that should lead to the mezzati; and, a little farther, the hall, one square and two thirds long, with columns equal to those of the entrance. There would have been a loggia, in the flanks of which should have been the stairs in an oval form; and a little farther the court, on the side of which wou'd have been the kitchens. The second rooms, that is, those of the second order, wou'd have had twenty feet in height, and those of the third eighteen; but the height of each hall wou'd have been up to the roof. And these halls wou'd have had, even with the floor of the upper rooms, some corridors, which wou'd have served to place persons of respect in, at the time of festivals, banquetings, and such like diversions.

Plate 53.   I MADE the following invention for a situation at *Venice*. The principal front has three orders of columns; the first is Ionick, the second Corinthian, and the third Composite. The entrance advances a little outwards, and has four columns equal to, and like those in the front. The rooms that are on the flanks have the height of their vaults according to the first method for the height of vaults. Besides these there are small rooms, closets, and the stairs that serve to the mezzati. Opposite to the entrance, there is a passage, through which one goes into another smaller hall, which on one side has a small court, from whence it receives light, and on the other, the principal and larger stairs, of an oval form, void in the middle, and with columns round them, that support the steps. Farther, one enters into a loggia, through a passage, the columns of which are of the Ionick order, equal to those of the entrance. This loggia has an apartment on each side, like those of the entrance; but that which is on the left lessens a little by reason of the situation. Near this there is a court, with columns round it, that form a corridor, which serve the rooms backwards, where the women were to have been; and there the kitchen should have stood. The part above is like that below, except the hall over the entrance, which has no columns, and joins in height up to the roof, and has a corridor, or balcony, even with the third rooms, that wou'd also have served to the windows above, because there wou'd have been two orders of them in this hall. The smaller hall wou'd have had the beams even with the vaults of the second rooms; and these vaults wou'd have been three and twenty feet high. The rooms of the third order wou'd have been cieled, and eighteen feet high. All the doors and windows wou'd have faced, and have been over one another; and all the walls wou'd have had their share of the weight. The cellars, the places to wash clothes in, and the other magazines, wou'd have been accommodated under ground.

Plate 54.   I MADE the following invention at the request of the Count FRANCESCO, and Count LODOVICO DE TRISSINI, brothers, for a situation belonging to them at *Vicenza*; according to which, the house wou'd have had a square entrance, divided into three spaces by columns of the Corinthian order, that its vault might have had strength and proportion. On the flanks there wou'd have been two apartments, with seven rooms in each, including three mezzati, to which the stairs wou'd have served that were on one side of the small rooms. The height of the greater rooms wou'd have been seven and twenty feet, and of the middling and smaller eighteen. Farther in wou'd the court have been found, encompassed with

loggia's

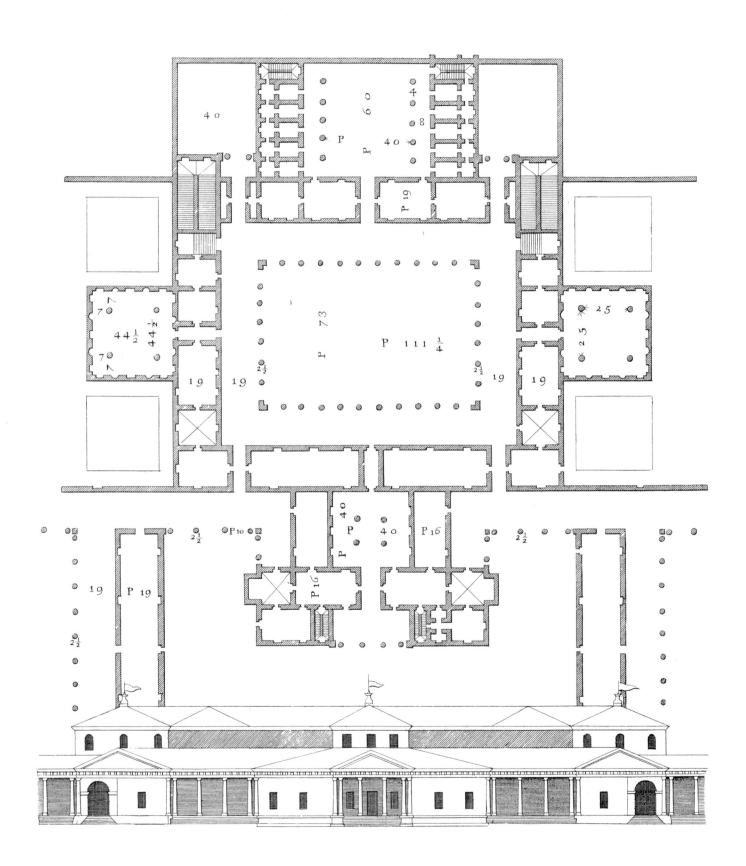

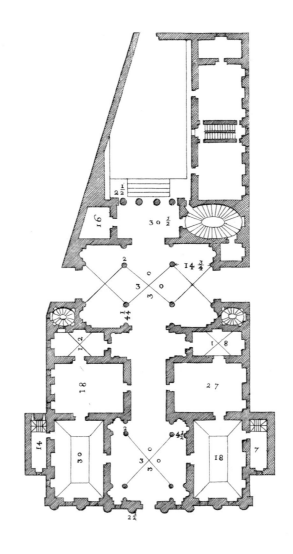

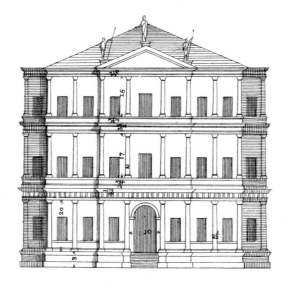

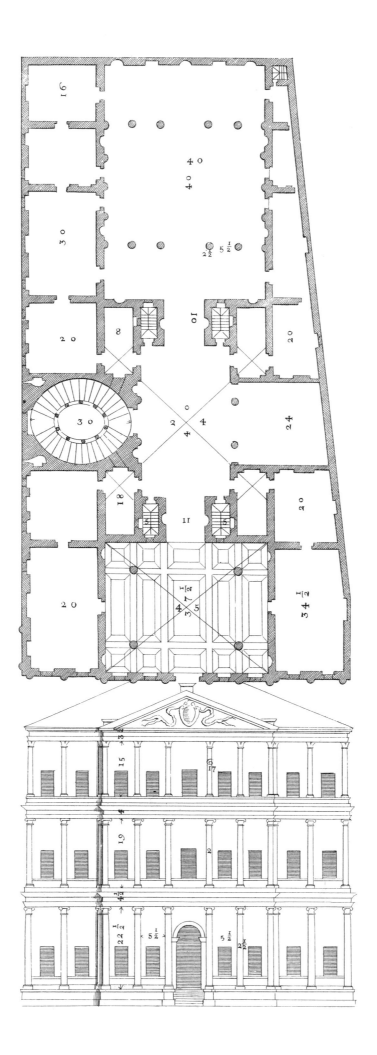

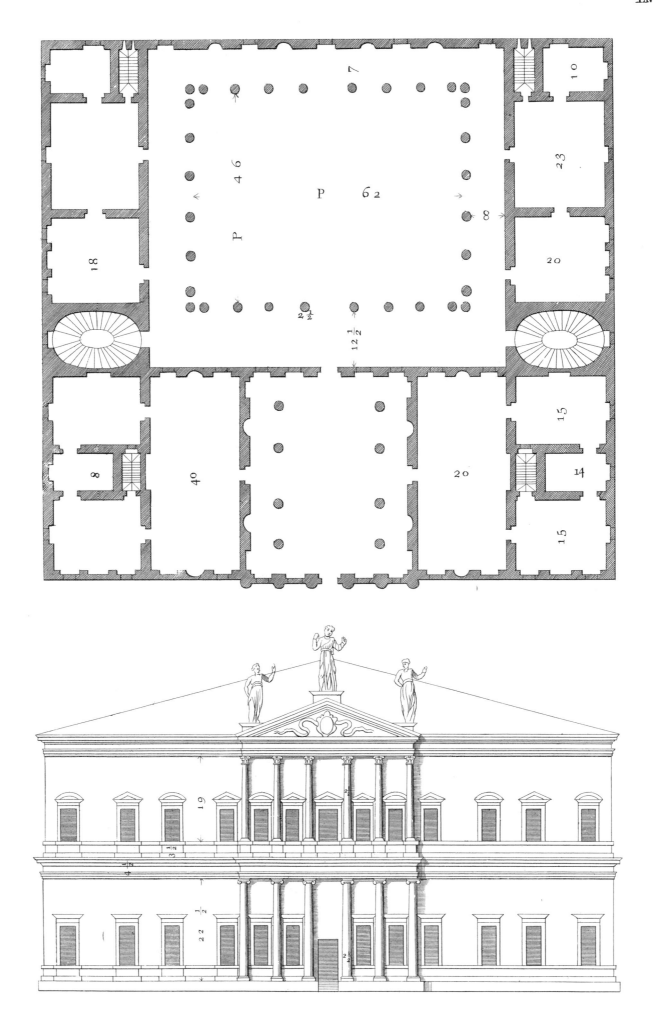

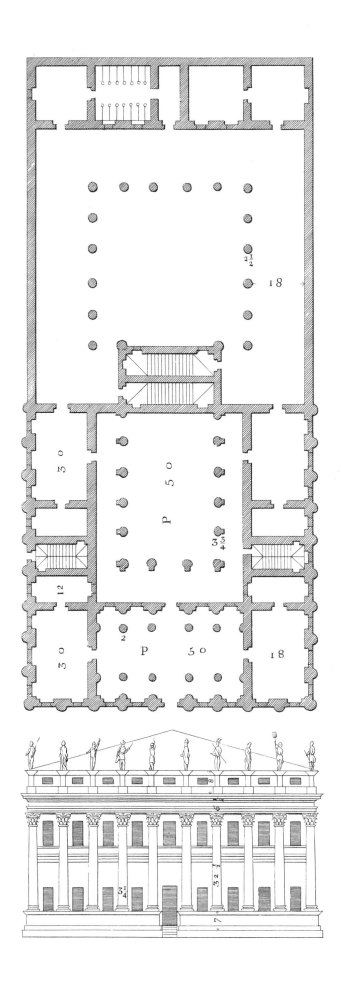

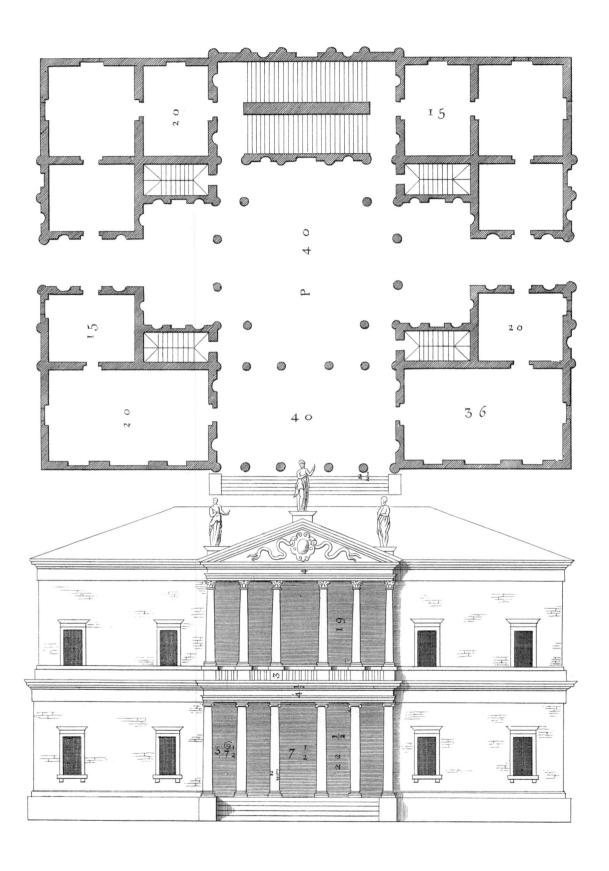

20

15

15

20

P 40

20

36

40

2½

19

4

3

4½

37½

7½

2½

2¾

2¼

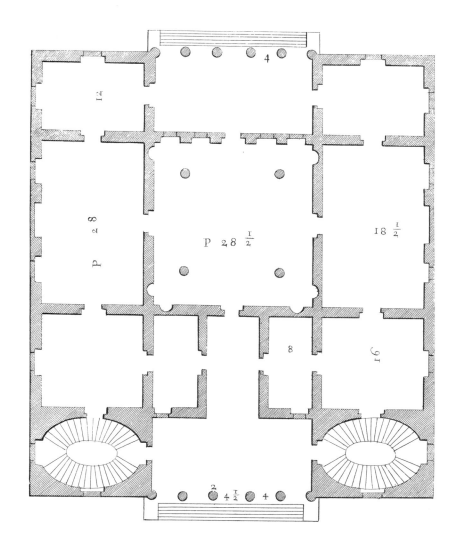

P 28

P 28 $\frac{1}{2}$

18 $\frac{1}{2}$

4

12

8

19

2 4 $\frac{1}{2}$ 4

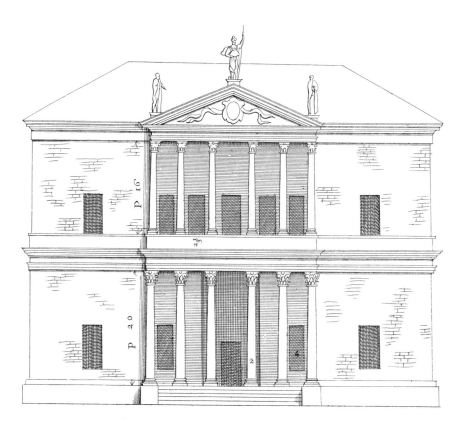

P 16

P 20

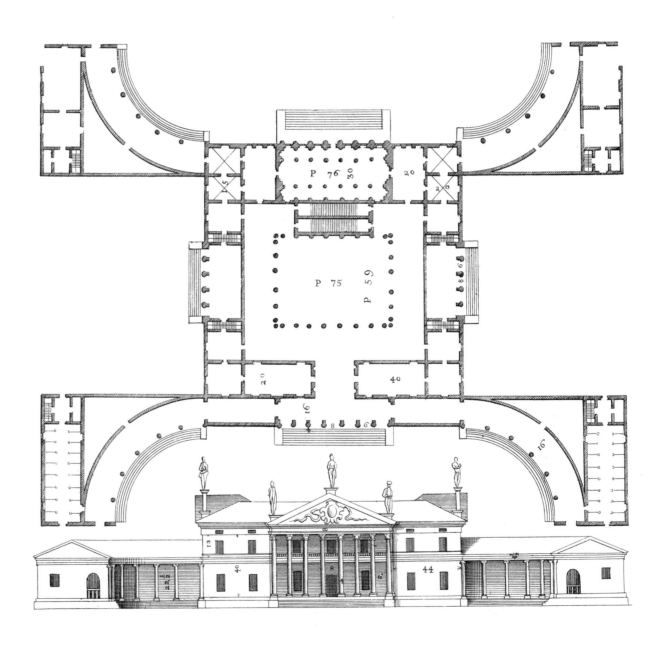

loggia's of the Ionick order. The columns of the firft order of the front wou'd have been Ionick, and equal to thofe of the court; and thofe of the fecond, Corinthian. The hall wou'd have been quite free, of the fize of the entrance, and raifed up to the roof. Even with the floor of its foffita, it wou'd have had a corridor. The greater rooms wou'd have been ceiled, and the middling and fmaller vaulted. On one fide of this court wou'd have been rooms for the women, kitchen, and other places; and under ground, the cellars, the places for wood, and other conveniencies.

THE invention here placed, was made for the Count GIACOMO ANGARANO, for a fite Plate 55. of his in the fame city. The columns of the front are of the Compofite order. The rooms near the entrance are one fquare and two thirds long. Next to them is a clofet, and over that a mezzato. One then paffes into a court incompaffed with portico's. The columns are fix and thirty feet long, and have behind them fome pilafters, by VITRUVIUS called Parafta-tice, that fupport the pavement of the fecond loggia; over which there is another uncover'd, even with the floor of the laft cieling of the houfe, and has corridors round it. Farther one finds another court, encompaffed likewife with portico's. The firft order of the columns is Dorick, the fecond Ionick, and in this the ftairs are placed. In the oppofite part to the ftairs, there are the ftables, and the kitchens might be made there, and the places for fer-vants. As to the part above, the hall wou'd have been without columns, and its cieling wou'd have reached up to the roof. The rooms wou'd have been as high as they are broad; and there wou'd have been clofets and mezzati, as they are in the lower part. Over the columns in the front a corridor might have been made, which on feveral occafions would have been very commodious.

IN *Verona*, at the *Portoni*, vulgarly called *Della Brà*, a moft notable fituation, the Count Plate 56. GIO. BATTISTA DELLA TORRE, fometime fince intended to make the under placed fa-brick, which wou'd have had gardens, and all thofe parts required in a commodious and delightful place. The firft rooms wou'd have been vaulted, and over all the fmall ones there wou'd have been mezzati; to which the fmall ftairs wou'd have ferved. The fecond rooms, that is, thofe above, wou'd have been cieled. The height of the hall wou'd have reached up to the roof; and even with the plane of the foffita, there wou'd have been a corridor or balcony; and from the loggia, and the windows placed in the flanks, it wou'd have received light.

I MADE alfo the following invention for the Cavalier GIO. BATTISTA GARZADORE, a *Vi*- Plate 57. *centine* gentleman, in which are two loggia's, one forwards, and the other backwards, of the Co-rinthian order. Thefe loggia's have foffites, as alfo the ground hall; which is in the inmoft part of the houfe, that it may be cool in the fummer, and has two orders of windows. The four columns that appear, fupport the foffita, and make the pavement of the hall above ftrong and fecure; which is fquare, and without columns, and as high as it is broad, and as much as the thicknefs of the cornice more. The height of the vaults of the greater rooms is according to the third manner for the height of vaults. The vaults of the clofets are fixteen foot high. The rooms above are cieled. The columns of the fecond loggia's are of the Compofite order, the fifth part lefs than thofe underneath. The loggia's have fron-tifpieces, which (as I have faid,) give no fmall grandeur to the fabrick; making it more elevated in the middle, than it is in the flanks, and ferve to place the enfigns.

I MADE the following invention at the requeft of the Clariffimo Cavalier il Sig. LEO- Plate 58. NARDO MOCENICO, for a fite of his upon the *Brenta*. Four loggia's, which like arms tend to the circumference, feem to receive thofe that come near the houfe. Near thefe loggia's are the ftables, in the part forwards that looks over the river; and on the part backwards, the kitchens, and the places for the fteward, and the farmer. The loggia in the middle of the front is thick of columns, which, becaufe they are forty foot high, have behind them fome pilafters two feet wide, and one foot and a quarter thick, that fupport the floor of the fecond loggia. And farther in, one finds the court encompaffed with loggia's of the Ionick order. The portico's are as wide as the columns are long; one diameter of the column excepted. The loggia's and the rooms that look over the gardens, are alfo of the fame breadth, that the wall which divides one member from the other, may be placed in the middle to fuftain the weight of the roof. The firft rooms wou'd have been very convenient to eat in, when a great number of perfons fhould happen to have been there, and are in a double proportion. Thofe of the angles are fquare, and have their vaults *à fchiffo*, as high up to the impoft as the room is broad, and are cover'd one third of the breadth. The hall is two fquares and an half long. The columns are put there to proportion the length and breadth to the height; and thofe columns wou'd have been in the ground hall only, that the hall above might have been quite free. The columns of the upper loggia's over the court are one fifth lefs than thofe underneath them, and are of the Corinthian order. The rooms

above

above are as high as they are broad. The ftairs are at the end of the court, and afcend one oppofite to the other.

AND with this invention, praife be to God, I have put an end to thefe two books; in which, with as much brevity as poffible, I have endeavoured to put together, and teach eafily, with words and figures, all thefe things that feemed to me moft neceffary, and moft important for building well; and particularly for building private houfes, that they may in themfelves contain beauty, and be of credit and conveniency to the owners.

The END of the SECOND BOOK.

THE

REGINA   VIRTUS

THE THIRD BOOK OF
ARCHITECTURE
by
ANDREA PALLADIO
WHEREIN
the WAYS, BRIDGES, PIAZZAS, BASILICAS,
and XISTI are treated of.

LONDON,
Published by
ISAAC WARE,
Anno MDCCXXXVIII.

THE THIRD BOOK

OF

Andrea Palladio's

ARCHITECTURE.

The PREFACE *to the* READER.

HAVING fully treated of private edifices, and taken notice of all the moſt neceſſary advertencies that ought in them to be had; and having, beſides this, put the
deſigns of many of thoſe houſes, that have been by me directed, both within and
without cities, and of thoſe which (according to VITRUVIUS) were made by the antients;
it is very proper, that, in directing my diſcourſe to more excellent, and to more magnificent fabricks, I ſhould now paſs on to the publick edifices: in which, as they are made
more ſtately, and with more exquiſite ornaments than the private, and ſerve for the uſe
and conveniency of every body, princes have therein a very ample opportunity to make the world
acquainted with the greatneſs of their ſouls, and architects a very fine one to ſhew their
capacity in beautiful and wonderful inventions.

I DESIRE therefore in this book, in which my antiquities begin, and in the others,
which, God willing, ſhall follow, that ſo much the more attention may be applied, in
conſidering the little that ſhall be ſaid, and the deſigns that ſhall be given, as I have, with
far greater fatigue, and much longer vigilancy, reduced thoſe fragments that remained of
the antient edifices, to ſuch a form, that the obſervers of antiquity may (I hope) take
delight therein, and the lovers of architecture may thence receive very great utility; there
being much more to be learnt from good examples in a little time, by meaſuring and
ſeeing the entire edifices, with all their parts, upon a ſmall leaf, than in a long time from
words, by which, with the imagination only, and ſtill ſome difficulty, the reader is able to
attain to a firm and certain knowledge of what he reads, and with much more difficulty will
he put it in practiſe.

AND to every one, that is not altogether void of judgment, it may be very manifeſt,
how good the method was, which the antients obſerved in building; ſince after ſo much
time, and after ſo many ruins and mutations of empires, there ſtill remain both in
Italy and out of it, the veſtigies of ſo many of their ſumptuous edifices, by which we are
able to get at a certain knowledge of the *Roman* virtue and grandeur, which perhaps had not
otherwiſe been believed. I therefore, in this third book, (in placing the deſigns of the
edifices contained in it) ſhall obſerve this order.

IN the firſt place, I ſhall put thoſe of the ſtreets, and of the bridges, as belonging to
that part of architecture which regards the ornaments of cities and of provinces, and which
ſerves for the univerſal conveniency of mankind. For, as in the other fabricks which
the antients made, one may eaſily apprehend that they had no regard either to expence,
or to any labour to bring them to that pitch of excellency, which has been granted
them from our imperfection; ſo, in directing the roads, they took very great care,
that they ſhould be made in ſuch a manner, that alſo in them might be known the
grandeur and the magnificence of their minds. Wherefore, to make them both commo-

dious

dious and ſhort, they cut through mountains, dried up fens, and joined with bridges, and ſo made eaſy and plain, thoſe places, that had been ſunk, either by vales or torrents.

I SHALL, afterwards, treat of piazza's in the manner that VITRUVIUS ſhews us the *Greeks* and *Latins* made them, and of thoſe places that ought to be diſtributed round the piazza's. And becauſe, among theſe, that place is worthy of great conſideration, where the judges adminiſter juſtice, called by the antients *Baſilica*, the deſigns of it ſhall be particularly ſet down. But becauſe it is not ſufficient, that the regions and the cities be well diſpoſed and governed by moſt ſacred laws, and have magiſtrates, who, as executors of the laws, keep the citizens in awe; if men are not alſo made prudent by learning, and ſtrong and hearty by bodily exerciſe, that they may be able to govern both themſelves and others, and to defend themſelves from thoſe who wou'd oppreſs them; which is one principal reaſon why the inhabitants of ſome countries, when diſperſed in many ſmall places, unite themſelves, and form cities: wherefore the antient *Greeks* made in their cities (as VITRUVIUS relates) ſome edifices, which they called *Paleſtrae* and *Xiſti*, in which the philoſophers aſſembled to diſpute concerning the ſciences, and the younger men were every day exerciſed; and at certain appointed times the people aſſembled there to ſee the wreſtlers contend.

THE deſigns of thoſe edifices ſhall alſo be inſerted, and an end ſo put to this third **book.** After which, ſhall follow that of the temples belonging to religion, without which it wou'd be impoſſible that civil ſociety cou'd be maintained.

THIS line is half of the *Vicentine* foot, with which the following edifices have been meaſured.

THE whole foot is divided into twelve inches, and each inch into four minutes.

CHAPTER I.

Of ROADS.

THE roads ought to be ſhort, commodious, ſafe, delightful and beautiful; they will be ſhort and commodious if made in a ſtrait line, and if they be made ample, that ſo the carts and the cattle meeting, do not impede one another. And therefore it was an eſtabliſh'd law among the antients, that the roads ſhould not be narrower than eight foot, where they were ſtrait; nor leſs than ſixteen wide where they were crooked and winding. They will, beſides this, be commodious if they are made even, that is, that there may not be any places, in which one cannot eaſily march with armies, and if they are not obſtructed by water or rivers. We therefore read that the Emperor TRAJAN, regarding theſe two qualities, neceſſarily required in roads, when he repaired the moſt celebrated *Appian* way, which in many places was damaged by length of time, dried up fenny places, levelled mountains, filled up valleys, and erecting bridges where neceſſary, made travelling thereon very expeditious and eaſy.

ROADS will be ſafe if made on hills, or if, when made through fields, according to antient cuſtom, they have a cauſeway to travel on, and if they have no places near them in which robbers and enemies can conveniently hide themſelves; that ſo the travellers and the armies may be able to look about them, and eaſily diſcover if there ſhould be any ambuſcade laid for them. Thoſe roads that have the three aboveſaid qualities, are alſo neceſſarily beautiful and delightful to travellers, becauſe of their ſtrait direction from the city. The conveniency they afford, and beſides being in them able to ſee at a great diſtance, and beſides to diſcover a good deal of the country, whereby great part of the fatigue is alleviated, and our minds (having always a new proſpect before our eyes) find great ſatisfaction and delight. A ſtrait ſtreet in a city affords a moſt agreeable view, when it is ample and clean; on each ſide of which there are magnificent fabricks, made with thoſe ornaments, which have been mentioned in the forgoing books.

As in cities beauty is added to the ftreets by fine fabricks: fo without, they are adorn'd with trees; which being planted on each fide of them, by their verdure enliven our minds, and by their fhade afford very great conveniency. Of thefe kinds of roads there are many in the *Vicentine*; and among the reft, thofe that are at *Cigogna*, a villa belonging to the Signor Conte ODOARDO THIENI, are celebrated; and at *Quinto*, a villa belonging to the Signor Conte OTTAVIO, of the fame family: which being defigned by me, have been fince adorned, by the diligence and induftry of the faid gentlemen. The roads that are thus made, afford very great conveniencies, becaufe that by their ftrait direction, and by being fomewhat raifed above the remaining part of the fields, fpeaking of thofe which are without the city, in time of war, as I have faid, the enemies may be difcovered from a great diftance, and fo that refolution, which fhall feem moft convenient to the commander, may be taken; befides all which, at other times, with regard to the affairs that commonly happen among men, their brevity and conveniency will afford infinite advantages.

BUT becaufe the ftreets are either within or without a city, I fhall, in the firft place, make particular mention of the qualities which thofe of a city ought to have; and then how thofe without are to be made. And fince there are fome that are called military, which pafs through the middle of the city, and lead from one city to another, and ferve for the univerfal conveniency of travellers, and are thofe through which armies march, and carriages are conveyed; and others not military, which departing from the military, either lead to another military way, or are made for the ufe and particular conveniency of fome villa: I fhall, in the following chapters, only treat of the military ones, omitting the non-military, becaufe thefe ought to be regulated by them; and the more they fhall be like them, the more they'll be commended.

CHAP. II.

Of the COMPARTMENT *of ways within the cities.*

IN the compartment or difpofition of the ways within a city, regard ought to be had to the temperature of the air, and to the region of the heaven, under which the city is fituated. For in thofe of a temperate and cool air, the ftreets ought to be made ample and broad; confidering, that by their breadth the city will be much wholefomer, more commodious, and more beautiful; feeing that the lefs fubtile, and the more freely the air comes, fo much the lefs it will offend the head. The more the city, therefore, is in a cold place, and hath a fubtile air, and where the edifices are made very high, fo much the wider the ftreets ought to be made, that they may, in each of their parts, be vifited by the fun. And as to conveniency, there is no doubt, that, as much better room may be allowed to men, to cattle, and to carriages in broad than in the narrow ftreets, broad ones are much more convenient than the narrow; it being manifeft, that as there is much more light in the broad ones, and alfo that as one fide is not fo much obftructed by the other, its oppofite, one is able, in the large ones, much better to confider the beauty of the temples, and of the palaces, whereby the eye receives greater contentment; it adds befides a greater ornament to the city.

BUT the city being in a hot country, its ftreets ought to be made narrow, and the houfes high, that by their fhade, and by the narrownefs of the ftreets, the heat of the fite may be tempered; by which means it will be more healthy. This is known by the example of *Rome*, which, according to CORNELIUS TACITUS, grew hotter, and lefs healthy, after NERO, to make it beautiful, had widened its ftreets. In fuch cafe, however, for the greater ornament and conveniency of the city, the ftreets moft frequented by the principal arts, and by paffengers, ought to be made fpacious, and adorned with magnificent and fumptuous fabricks, that foreigners who pafs through it, may eafily incline to believe, that to the beauty and largenefs of this, the other ftreets of the city may alfo correfpond.

THE principal ftreets, which we have called military, in the cities ought to be fo comparted, that they may be ftreight, and lead from the gates of the city in a direct line to the greateft and principal piazza; and fometimes alfo, the fite permitting it, lead in the fame manner directly to the oppofite gate; and according to the greatnefs of the city, by the fame line. Of fuch ftreets, between the faid principal piazza, and any of the gates you pleafe, there ought to be one or more piazza's, made fomewhat lefs than the before-faid principal piazza.

THE other ftreets, efpecially the more noble of them, ought alfo to be made, not only to lead to the principal piazza, but alfo to the moft remarkable temples, palaces, portico's, and other publick fabricks.

BUT in this compartment of the ftreets, it ought to be obferved, with the utmoft diligence (as VITRUVIUS teaches us in the fixth chapter of his firft book) that they fhould not in a direct line face fome winds; that through them furious and violent winds may not be felt; but that they may, with more falubrity to the inhabitants, come broken, gentle, purified and fpent, left the fame inconveniency fhould be incurred which happened to thofe who in the ifland of *Lesbos* laid out the ftreets of *Mitylene*, from which city the whole ifland has now taken the name.

THE ftreets in a city ought to be paved; and we read, that under the confulfhip of M. ÆMILIUS, the cenfors began to pave in *Rome*, where fome are ftill to be feen, which are all even, and are paved with irregular ftones; which manner of paving, how it was done, fhall be mentioned hereafter. But if one is willing to divide the place where men are to walk, from that which ferves for the ufe of carts and of cattle, I fhould like that the ftreets were divided, that on the one and on the other part there were portico's made, through which the citizens might, under cover, go and do their bufinefs, without being molefted by the fun, by the rains and fnow: in which manner are almoft all the ftreets of *Padua* difpofed, a very antient city, and celebrated for learning. Or if no portico's be made, (in which cafe the ftreets will be more ample and pleafant) fome margins are to be made on each fide, paved with mattoni, which are baked ftones, thicker and narrower than bricks, becaufe they do not at all offend the feet in walking; and the middle part is to be left for the carts and cattle, and to be paved with flints, or any other hard ftones.

THE ftreets ought to be fomewhat concave in the middle, and flanting, that the water which falls from the houfes may all run to one place, and have a freer courfe, whereby the ftreets are left clean, and are not the caufe of bad air; as is the cafe when it ftops in any place, and there putrifies.

C H A P. III.

Of the W A Y S *without the city.*

THE ways without the city ought to be made ample, commodious, having trees on either fide, by which travellers may be defended from the fcorching heats of the fun, and their eyes receive fome recreation from the verdure. The antients took great care of thefe ways: that they might therefore always be in good repair, they eftablifhed proveditors and curators of them; by whom many of them were made, of which there ftill remains fome memory of their beauty and conveniency, although they have been impaired by time. But the *Flaminian* and the *Appian* are the moft famous of them all; the firft was made by FLAMINIUS, while he was conful, after the victory he had over the *Genoefe*. This way began from the gate *Flumentana*, now called *del Popolo*, and paffing through *Tufcany*, and through *Umbria*, led to *Rimini*; from which city it was afterwards continued to *Bologna* by M. LEPIDUS, his colleague; and near the foot of the *Alps*, by windings, to avoid the fens, he carried it to *Aquileia*. The *Appian* took its name from APPIUS CLAUDIUS, by whom it was made with much fkill and at great expence: thence, for its magnificence and wonderful artifice, it was by the poets called the *Queen of ways*. This ftreet began from the *Colifeo*, and through the gate *Capena* reached to *Brindifi*. It was continued only to *Capua* by APPIUS; from thence forwards, there is no certainty who made it; and it is the opinion of fome, that it was CÆSAR: becaufe we read in PLUTARCH, that the care of this way being given to CÆSAR, he fpent thereon a great deal of money. It was laftly repaired by the Emperor TRAJAN, who (as I have faid before) by drying up fenny places, levelling mountains, filling up valleys, and by making bridges where it was neceffary, made the travelling thereon both expeditious and agreeable. The *Via Aurelia* is alfo very much celebrated. It was fo called from AURELIUS, a Roman citizen, who made it. It began from the gate *Aurelia*, now called *San. Pacratio*, and extending itfelf through all the maritime places of *Tufcany*, led to *Pifa*.

THE *Via Numentana*, the *Praeneftina*, and the *Libicana*, were of no lefs renown. The firft began from the gate *Viminalis*, now called *S. Agnefa*, and reached to the city of *No-*
mentum;

mentum; the fecond began from the gate *Efquilina*, which is now called *S. Lorenzo*; and the third from the gate *Nevia*, that is, from the *Porta Maggiore*; and thefe ways led to the city of *Prænefte*, now called *Peleftrino*, and to the famous city of *Labicana*.

THERE were alfo many other ways mentioned and celebrated by writers, that is, the *Salara*, the *Collatina*, the *Latina*, and others; all which took their names either from thofe who ordered them, or from the gates where they began, or from the places whither they led. But among them all, the *Via Portuenfe* muft have been of the utmoft beauty and conveniency, which led from *Rome* to *Oftia*; becaufe (as ALBERTI faith he has obferved) it was divided into two ftreets; between the one and the other of which there was a courfe of ftones a foot higher than the remaining part of the way, and which ferved for a divifion: by one of thefe ways people went, and by the other they returned, avoiding thereby the inconvenience of meeting; an invention very commodious for the very great concourfe of people that, from all parts of the world, was at *Rome* in thofe times.

THE antients made thefe their military ways in two manners; that is, either paving them with ftones, or by covering them all over with fand and gravel. The ways after the firft manner, (from what one has been able to conjecture by fome *veftigia*) were divided into three fpaces. Upon that in the middle, which was higher than the other two, and which was fomewhat raifed toward the middle, that the water might run off and not fettle there, thofe who were on foot travelled. This was paved with irregular ftones, that is, of unequal fides and angles; in which manner of paving (as it has been elfewhere faid) they made ufe of a leaden rule, which they opened and fhut according to the fides and angles of the ftones: they therefore joined them exceeding well together, and that with great expedition. The other two fpaces that were on each fide, were made fomewhat lower, and were covered with fand and fmall gravel, and on thefe went the horfes.

EACH of thefe margins were as wide as half the breadth of the fpace in the middle, from which they were divided by rows of ftones placed edge-ways, and there was at every fuch diftance fome ftones placed end-ways, a foot higher than the remaining part of the ftreet. Upon thefe the antients ftepped when they were willing to mount on horfe-back, as they did not make ufe of ftirrups.

BESIDES thefe ftones placed for the faid ufe, there were other ftones much higher, upon which, from place to place, were marked the miles of the whole journey; and thefe ways were meafured, and the faid ftones fixed by CNEUS GRACCHUS.

THE military ways after the fecond manner, that is, made of fand and gravel, were made by the antients fomewhat raifed in the middle, by means of which the water could not lodge there; and being of a fubftance apt to dry quickly, and of itfelf, they were always clean, that is, without dirt or duft. Of this fort there is one to be feen in *Friuli*, which is called by the inhabitants of thofe places *la Pofthuma*, and leads into *Hungary*. There is another alfo in the *Padouan*, which beginning from the faid city, in the place named *l'Argere*, paffes through the middle of *Gigogna*, a villa belonging to Count ODOARDO, and to Count THEODORE DE THIENI, brothers, and leads to the *Alps*, which divide *Italy* from *Germany*.

Plate I.

THE following defign is of the ways according to the firft manner, from which one may know how the *Via Hoftienfis* muft have been made. It did not appear to me neceffary to give a defign of the fecond manner, becaufe it is a very eafy thing, as there is no need of any induftry, provided they are but made rifing in the middle, that the water may poffibly not ftand there.

A, *is the fpace in the middle, on which the people on foot travelled.*
B, *are the ftones that ferved to mount on horfe-back.*
C, *are the margins covered with fand and gravel, on which the horfes went.*

R CHAP.

C H A P. IV.

Of what ought to be observed in the building of BRIDGES, *and of the site that ought to be chosen.*

FORASMUCH as many rivers, by reason of their breadth, height, and rapidity, cannot be forded, the conveniency of bridges was first thought on. It may therefore be said, that they are a principal part of the way, and that they are but a street above water. They ought to have the same qualities that we have said were required in all other fabricks, that is, to be commodious, beautiful, and for a long time durable. They will be commodious when they are not raised above the rest of the way, and if they be raised, to have their ascent easy; and such place is to be chosen to build them in, as ought to be most convenient to the whole province, or to the whole city, according as they are to be built, either within or without the walls.

CHOICE ought therefore to be made of that place to which one may go from all parts easily, that is, in the middle of the province, or in the middle of the city, as NITOCRE Queen of *Babylon* did in the bridge she built over the *Euphrates*; and not in an angle, where it can be of use only to a few. They'll be beautiful and durable for a long time, if they are made after the manner, and with those measures that shall particularly be mentioned hereafter.

BUT in pitching on the site for building them, one ought to observe to chuse it so as may give hopes that the bridge there built will be perpetual, and where it may be made with as little expence as possible. That place therefore is to be chosen, in which the river shall be less deep, and shall have its bed or bottom even and durable, that is, of rock or stone, because (as has been said in the first book, when I spoke of the places to lay foundations on) stone and rock make very good foundations in waters : besides which, gulphs and whirlpools ought to be avoided, as also that part of the bottom, or bed of the river, which shall be gravelly or sandy; for sand and gravel being continually moved by the floods, this changes the bed of the river, and the foundations being thereby undermined, wou'd of necessity occasion the ruin of the work. But when the whole bed of the river is gravel and sand, the foundations ought to be made as shall be directed hereafter, when I come to treat of stone bridges.

REGARD also is to be had, to chuse that site in which the river's course is direct; since the windings and crooked parts of the banks are subject to be carried away by the water; in such a case therefore the bridge wou'd remain like an island, disunited from the banks : and also, because during the floods, the waters carry into the said windings, all the matter they wash from the banks and fields, which not being able to go directly down, stops other things, and clogging the pilasters, fills up the opening of the arches; whereby the work suffers in such a manner, that by the weight of the water only, it falls in time to ruin.

THE place therefore to be chosen for building bridges, ought to be in the middle of the country or of the city, and as convenient to all the inhabitants as possible, and where the river has a direct course, and its bed equal, perpetual, and shallow. But as bridges are either made of wood or of stone, I shall particularly mention the manner of both the one and the other, and shall give some designs of them, both antient and modern.

C H A P. V.

Of WOODEN BRIDGES, *and of the advertencies which ought to be had in the building of them.*

BRIDGES are made of wood, either upon one occasion only, like those which are made for all those accidents that usually happen in war; of which sort that is the most celebrated which JULIUS CÆSAR directed over the *Rhine*; or secondly, that they may perpetually serve for the conveniency of every body. After this manner we read that HERCULES built the first bridge that ever was made, over the *Tiber*, in the place where *Rome* was

afterwards

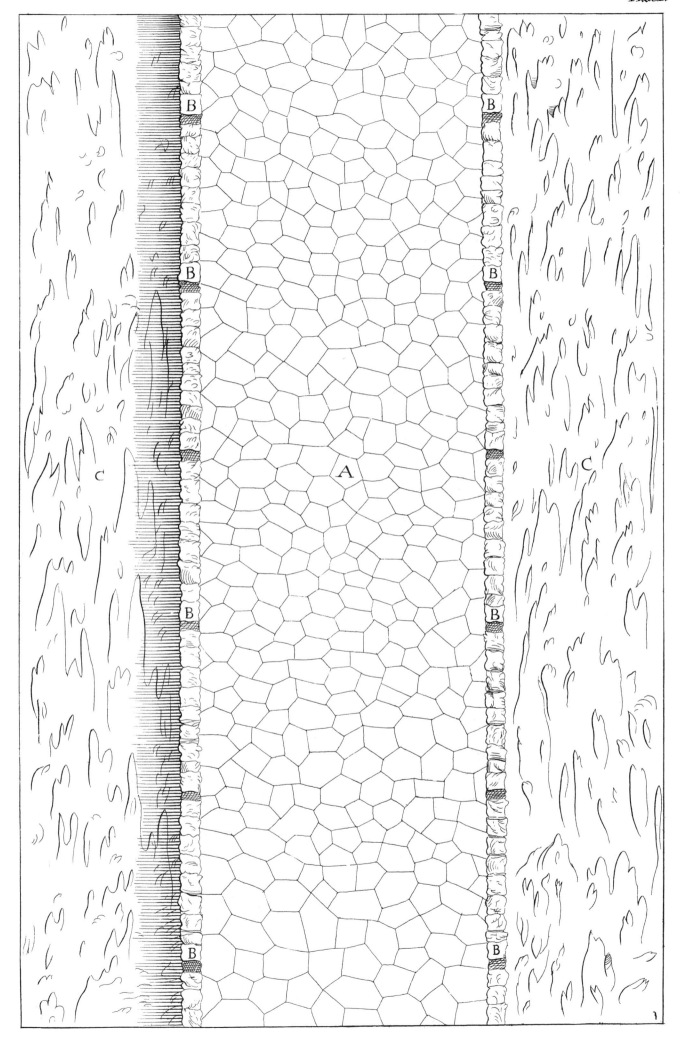

Plate I.

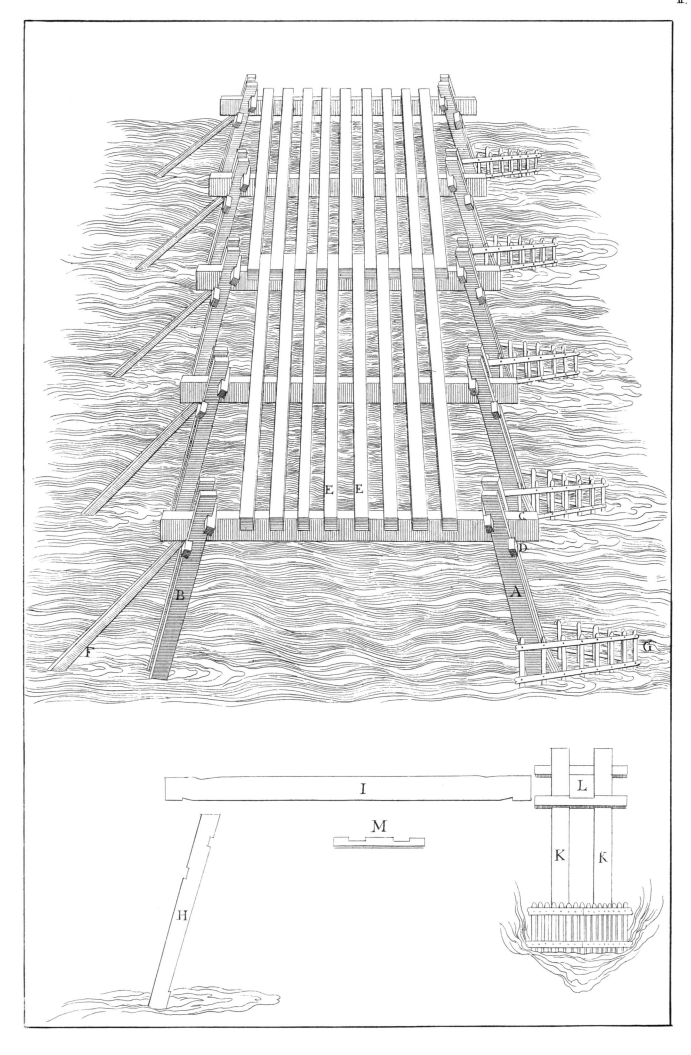

afterwards built; when, after having killed GERYON, he victoriously led his herd through *Italy*. It was called the holy bridge, and was situated in that part of the *Tiber*, where afterwards the *Pons Sublicius* was built by ANCUS MARTIUS the King, which was likewise all of timber, and its beams were joined together with so much art, that one could take them away, and replace them according as necessity should require, there being neither nails nor any iron whatsoever in it. How it was constructed is not known; but by what writers say of it, that it was made upon great pieces of timber, which supported others, from which it took the name of *Sublicius*; because such timbers in the *Volscian* tongue were called *Sublices*.

THIS was the bridge that was defended by HORATIUS COCLES, with so much advantage to his native country, and glory to himself. This bridge was near *Ripa*, where there are still *vestigia* to be seen in the middle of the river, because it was afterwards made of stone by ÆMILIUS LEPIDUS the prætor, and restored by the Emperor TIBERIUS, and by ANTONINUS PIUS.

WOODEN bridges of this kind ought to be made in such a manner, that they may be very strong, and so tied together by large strong timbers, that there may not be any danger of their breaking, either thro' the great multitude of people, and of animals, or by the weight of the carriages and of the artillery that shall pass over them, nor liable to be ruined by the inundations and the floods in rivers. Those that are made at the gates of the cities, however, which we call draw-bridges, because they may be raised and let fall according to the will of those within, are usually paved, or covered with bars or plates of iron, that they may not be spoiled or broken by the wheels of carriages, and by the feet of cattle.

THE timbers, as well those which are fixed in the water, as those that form the length and breadth of the bridge, ought to be long and thick, according as the depth, the breadth, and the velocity of the river shall require.

BUT because the particulars are infinite, one cannot give a certain and determinate rule for them. Wherefore I shall give some designs, and shall mention their measures, from which every one may easily be able, according as occasion shall offer, of exercising the acuteness of his understanding, to take his measures and form a work that is worthy of praise.

CHAP. VI.

Of the BRIDGE *directed by* JULIUS CÆSAR *over the* Rhine.

JULIUS CÆSAR having (as he says in the fourth book of his Commentaries) resolved to pass the *Rhine*, that the Roman power might also be felt in *Germany*, and judging that it was not a very safe thing, nor worthy either of him, or of the Romans, to pass it in barks, ordered a bridge, an admirable work, and most difficult by reason of the breadth, height, and rapidity of the river. But how this bridge was built, (although he describes it) is, nevertheless, not known, as the force of some of the words by him used in the description of it, is not understood; so has it been variously set down in designs, according to diverse inventions. As I have also thought a little upon it, I would therefore not omit this opportunity of setting down the manner of it, which I imagined in my youth, when first I read the said Commentaries, because it agrees pretty much (in my opinion) with CÆSAR's words, and because it succeeds admirably well, as the effect has been seen in a bridge I have directed just without *Vicenza*, over the *Bachiglione*.

IT is not my intention to confute the opinions of others, as they are all very learned men, and worthy of the utmost praise. For having left it in their writings as they understood it, and by means of their industry and fatigue, they have greatly facilitated the understanding of it to us. But before we come to the designs, I shall give the words of CÆSAR, which are these:

RATIONEM *igitur pontis hanc instituit. Tigna bina sesquipedalia, paululum ab imo præacuta, dimensa ad altitudinem fluminis, intervallo pedum duorum inter se jungebat. Hæc cum machinationibus demissa in flumen defixerat, fistucisque adegerat, non sublicæ modo directa ad perpendiculum, sed prona, ac fastigiata, ut secundum naturam fluminis procumberent : his item contraria duo ad eundem modum juncta intervallo pedum quadragenum ab inferiore parte contra* vim

*vim atque impetum fluminis converfa ftatuebat. Hæc utraque infuper bipedalibus trabibus im-
miffis, quantum eorum tignorum junctura diftabat, binis utrinque fibulis ab extrema parte dif-
tinebantur. Quibus difclufis, atque in contrariam partem revinctis, tanta erat operis firmitudo,
atque ea rerum natura, ut quo major vis aquæ fe incitaviffet, hac arctius illigata tenerentur.
Hæc directa injecta materia contexebantur, ac longuriis, oratibufque confternebantur. Ac nihilo
fecius fublicæ ad inferiorem partem fluminis oblique adigebantur, quæ pro pariete fubjectæ,
& cum omni opere conjunctæ, vim fluminis exciperent. Et aliæ, item fupra pontem mediocri
fpatio, ut fi arborum trunci, five naves dejiciendi operis caufa effent à Barbaris miffæ, his defen-
foribus, earum rerum vis minuerentur, neu ponti nocerent.*

THE fenfe of which words is, that he ordered a bridge in this manner. He joined two
beams, each a foot and an half thick, two foot diftant from each other, fomething fharp
in the part below, and as long as the height of the river required; and having with ma-
chines fixed thefe beams in the bottom of the river, he drove them into it with a rammer,
not directly plumb, but leaning in fuch a manner, as to be flanting according to the current of the water. Oppofite to thefe, in the inferior part of the river, and at the diftance
of forty foot, he fixed two others, joined together in the fame manner, flanting thefe againft
the ftrength and impetuofity of the river. Between thefe two beams he faftened other
beams two foot thick, that is, equal to their diftance from each other. They were held at
each end by two braces, which being open, and bound contrary to each other, fo great
was the ftrength of the work, and fuch was the nature of the things, that by how much
greater the ftrength of the water was, fo much the firmer the whole kept braced together.
Thefe timbers were intermixed with other timbers, and covered with poles and hurdles.
Befides which, in the lower part of the river, there were pofts joined flanting, which were
placed underneath inftead of buttreffes, and being united to the whole work, ferved to
refift the ftrength of the river. There were others alfo joined in the part above the
bridge, at a moderate fpace, that in cafe trunks of trees, or fhips, fhou'd be fent down
the river by the Barbarians to ruin the work, it might by thefe ramparts avoid their violence, and prevent them from hurting the bridge.

THUS CÆSAR defcribes the bridge by him ordered over the *Rhine*; to which defcrip-
tion the following invention feems to me very conformable, all the parts of which are
marked with letters.

Plate 2.

A, *Are the two beams joined together one foot and an half thick, fomething fharp
in the lower part, fixed in the bottom of the river, not upright, but leaning
with the current, and two foot diftant from each other.*

B, *Are two other beams placed in the lower part of the river oppofite to the above-
mentioned, and diftant from them the fpace of forty foot, and flanting againft
the current of the river.*

H, *Is the form of one of the beams by itfelf.*

C, *Are the beams two foot thick every way, that formed the breadth of the bridge,
which was forty foot.*

I, *Is one of the faid beams.*

D, *Are the beams, which being open, that is, divided one from the other, and bound
contrary to each other, that is, one in the part within, and the other in the
part without; the one above, and the other below the beams, two foot thick,
that formed the breadth of the bridge, and give fo great a firmnefs to the
work, that the greater the violence of the water, and the more the bridge was
laden, fo much the more it united, and the firmer it was.*

M, *Is one of the beams.*

E, *Are the beams that were put length-ways on the bridge, and were covered with
plates and hurdles.*

F, *Are the pofts placed in the lower part of the river, which being flanting, and
joined with the whole work, refifted the violence of the ftream.*

G, *Are the pofts placed in the part above the bridge to defend it in cafe the enemy
fhould fend trees or fhips down the river to ruin it.*

K, *Are two of thofe beams that were joined together, and not driven in the river
directly plumb, but flanting.*

L, *Is the head of the beams that formed the breadth of the bridge.*

C H A P. VII.

Of the BRIDGE *of* CISMONE.

THE *Cifmone* is a river, which falling from the mountains that divide *Italy* from *Germany*, runs into the *Brenta*, a little above *Baſſano*. And becauſe it is very rapid, and that by it the mountaineers ſend great quantities of timber down, a reſolution was taken to make a bridge there, without fixing any poſts in the water, as the beams that were fixed there were ſhaken and carried away by the violence of the current, and by the ſhock of the ſtones and trees that by it are continually carried down : wherefore Count GIACOMO ANGARANO, who owns the bridge, was under the neceſſity of renewing it every year.

THE invention of this bridge is, in my opinion, very worthy of attention, as it may Plate 3. ſerve upon all occaſions, in which the ſaid difficulties ſhall occur ; and becauſe that bridges thus made, are ſtrong, beautiful, and commodious: ſtrong, becauſe all their parts mutually ſupport each other ; beautiful, becauſe the texture of the timbers is very agreeable and commodious, being even and in the ſame line with the remaining part of the ſtreet. The river where this bridge was ordered, is one hundred foot wide ; the breadth is divided into ſix equal parts ; and at the end of each part (excepting at the banks, which are ſtrengthned with pilaſters of ſtone) the beams are placed, that form the bed, and breadth of the bridge ; upon which, a little ſpace being left at their ends, were placed other beams lengthways, which form the ſides. Over theſe, directly upon the firſt, the *colonelli* on each ſide were diſpoſed (ſo we call thoſe beams vulgarly, that in ſuch works are placed directly upright.) Theſe colonelli are bound with the beams (which, as was ſaid, formed the breadth of the bridge) with irons which we call cramps, paſſing through a hole, made for that purpoſe in the heads of the ſaid beams, in that part which advances beyond the beams that form the ſides.

THESE cramps, becauſe they are in the upper part along the ſaid upright and plain colonelli, are preforated in ſeveral places. And in the under part, near the ſaid thick beams, by one hole only, ſufficiently large, they were driven into the colonello, and faſtened afterwards underneath with iron bolts, made for that purpoſe ; they therefore made the whole work to be in a manner united. The beams that form the breadth, and thoſe of the ſides being as it were, of one piece with the colonelli, ſupport the beams that form the breadth of the bridge ; and thoſe are alſo ſupported by the arms that go from one colonello to the others, whereby all the parts are ſupported the one by the other ; and their nature is ſuch, that the greater the weight upon the bridge, ſo much the more they bind together, and increaſe the ſtrength of the work. All the ſaid arms, and the other beams that form the texture of the bridge, are but one foot broad, and but three quarters thick. But thoſe beams that form the bed of the bridge, that is, thoſe that are laid long ways, are a great deal ſmaller.

A, *The flank of the bridge.*
B, *The pilaſters that are on the banks.*
C, *The heads of the beams that form the breadth.*
D, *The beams that form the ſides.*
E, *The colonelli.*
F, *The heads of the cramps, with the iron bolts.*
G, *Are the arms, which bearing contrary to each other, ſupport the whole work.*
H, *Is the plan of the bridge.*
I, *Are the beams that form the breadth, and advance beyond the ſides, near which the holes are made for the cramps.*
K, *Are ſmall beams that form the bed of the bridge.*

CHAP. VIII.

Of three other INVENTIONS, *according to which wooden bridges may be made, without fixing any posts in the water.*

WOODEN bridges may be made, without posts in the water, like the bridge on the *Cismone*, after three other manners; of which I would not omit giving the designs, because they are of a most beautiful contrivance, and may be more easily understood by every one who shall have made himself master of the terms made use of in the said bridge on the *Cismone*; because these also consist of beams placed crofs ways, of colonelli, of cramps, and of beams placed long ways, that form the sides.

THE bridges, therefore, after the first invention, are to be made after this manner: the banks being first fortified with pilasters, as necessity shall require, one of the beams that forms the breadth of the bridge is to be placed at some distance from them, and then the beams that form the sides, are to be disposed upon it, which with one of their heads are to lie upon the bank, and be fastened to it; after which, upon these, directly plumb with the beams placed for the breadth, the colonelli are to be fixed, which are to be fastened to the said beams with cramps of iron, and supported by the braces well fastened to the heads of the bridge; that is, in the beams that form the sides upon the bank: then leaving as much space as has been left from the said beam for the breadth to the bank, the other beam for the breadth is to be placed, and fastened in the same manner with the beams that shall be placed upon them lengthways of the bridge, and with the colonelli, and the colonelli to be supported by their braces, and thus continue from one order to another, as far as shall be requisite. Observing always in such bridges as these, that in the middle of the breadth of the river, there may be a colonello, in which the braces in the middle meet, and that other beams be fixed in the upper part of the colonelli, which joining from one colonello to the other will keep them united, and will form, with the braces in the head of the bridge, the portion of a circle, less than a semicircle. And in this manner, making every brace support its colonello, and every colonello support the beam for the breadth, and those that make the sides, whereby every part bears its own weight.

BRIDGES made after this manner, are wide at the heads, and grow narrow towards the middle of their length. There are none in *Italy* made after this manner; but conversing with Messer ALESSANDRO PICHERONI, a *Mirandolese*, he told me he had seen one in *Germany*.

Plate 4.
A, *Is the elevation of the flank of the bridge.*
B, *Are the heads of the beams that form the breadth.*
C, *Are the beams placed for the length.*
D, *Are the colonelli.*
E, *Are the braces, which being fixed in the beams for the length, support the colonelli.*
F, *Are the beams that bind one colonello with the other, and form a portion of a circle.*
G, *Is the bottom of the river.*
H, *Is the plan of the said bridge.*
I, *Are the first beams, which at one end are supported by the bank, and at the other by the first beams for the breadth.*
K, *Are the second beams, which are supported by the first and by the second beam for the breadth.*
L, *Are the third beams, which are supported by the second and by the third beam for the breadth.*
And then there are those beams that form the breadth (as I have said) supported by the colonelli, to which they are fastened, and the colonelli by the braces.

Plate 4.
THE invention of the following bridge has the upper part, which is what supports all the weight, made of a portion of a circle less than a semicircle, and has the braces, that go from one colonello to another, so disposed, that in the middle of the spaces which are between the colonelli, they crofs each other.

THE beams that form the floor of the bridge, are bound to the colonelli with cramps, as they are in the above mentioned invention. And for a greater strength, one might add

two

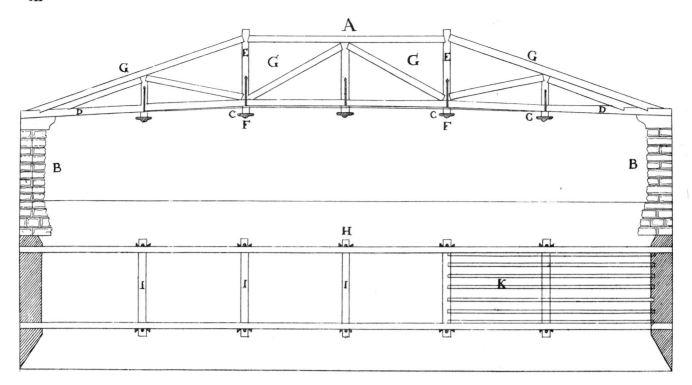

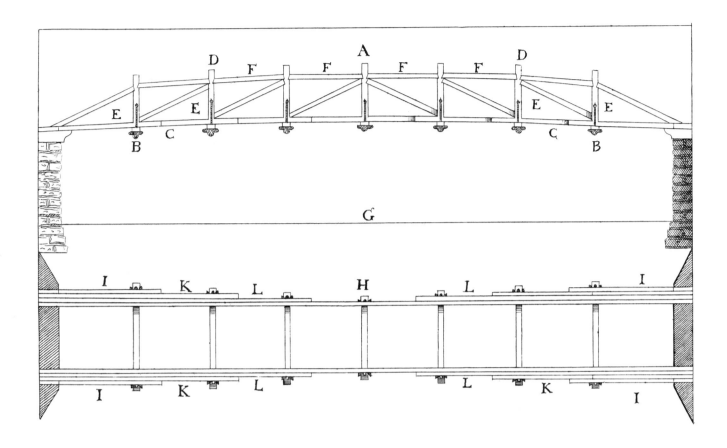

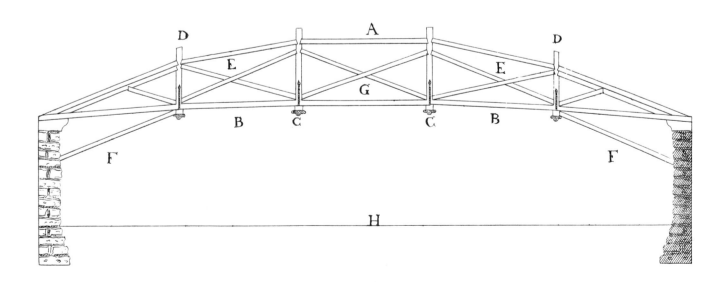

two beams at each end of the bridge, which being faftened with one end in the pilafters, and the other reaching under the firft colonelli, they would help very much to fupport the weight of the bridge.

A, Is the upright of the bridge in flank.
B, Are the beams that form the fides of the bridge.
C, Are the heads of the beams that form the breadth.
D, Are the colonelli.
E, Are the braces, that is, the fence of the bridge.
F, Are the beams placed under the bridge, at each end, that help to fupport the weight.
G, Is the floor of the bridge.
H, The bottom of the river.

THIS laft invention may be made with a greater or a fmaller arch than it is here defigned, Plate 5, according to the quality of the fite, and as the greatnefs of the river fhall require. The height of the bridge, in which are the fences, or the braces that go from one colonello to another, muft be an eleventh part of the breadth of the river. All the mortices that are made, ought, from the colonelli, to anfwer exactly to the centre, which will make the work very ftrong; and the colonelli will fupport the beams for the breadth, and for the length of the bridge, as in the abovefaid. The bridges, after thefe four manners, may be inlarged as neceffity fhall require, making all their parts ftronger in proportion.

A, Is the upright of the bridge in flank.
B, Is the floor of the bridge.
C, Are the colonelli.
D, Are the braces that fence and fupport the colonelli.
E, Are the heads of the beams that form the breadth of the bridge.
F, Is the bottom of the river.

C H A P. IX.

Of the bridge of BASSANO.

NEAR Baffano, a country fituated at the foot of the Alps which feparates Italy from Plate 6. Germany, I have directed the following wooden bridge over the Brenta, a moft rapid river, that difcharges itfelf into the fea near Venice, and was by the antients called Medoacus, to which, (as LIVY relates in his firft Decad) CLEONIMUS the Spartan came with a naval army before the Trojan war. The river, in the place where the bridge was made, is one hundred and eighty foot wide. This breadth is divided into five equal parts, becaufe the two banks being very well fortified, that is, the heads of the bridge, with beams of oak and of larix, four orders of piles were made in the river, thirty four foot and an half diftant the one from the other. Each of thefe orders confifts of eight beams thirty foot long, and a foot and an half thick every way, and diftant two foot one from the other: hence the whole length of the bridge comes to be divided into five fpaces, and its breadth is twenty fix foot. Upon the faid orders were placed fome crofs beams, according to the faid breadth (this fort of beams fo placed, are vulgarly called correnti) which being nailed to the beams driven in the river, hold them all together, joined and united. Upon thefe correnti, plumb on the faid beams, were placed eight other beams, which make the length of the bridge, and reach from one order to the other. And becaufe the diftance between the faid orders is very great, hence with difficulty the beams placed length ways, could have been able to fupport the weight that might have been put upon them, when it fhould have been great, fome beams were placed between thefe and the correnti, that ferve for modiglions, and fupport part of the weight: befides which, other beams were placed, which being faftened in thofe that were driven into the river, and leaning the one towards the other, were united with another beam placed in the middle of the faid diftance under each beam for the length. Thefe beams fo placed, reprefent an arch, having the fourth part of its diameter in height; and fo the work becomes beautiful in its form; and ftrong, becaufe the beams that form the length of the bridge, are thereby doubled in the middle.

UPON thefe are put other beams crofs ways, which make the plan or floor of the bridge, and project fomething more than the remaining part of the work, and appear like the
modiglions

modiglions of a cornice. On each fide of the bridge are placed the columns that fupport the roof, and ferve as a loggia, and make the whole work very commodious and beautiful.

+ *Is the line of the furface of the water.*

A, *Is the upright of the flank of the bridge.*

B, *Are the orders of piles driven into the river.*

C, *Are the heads of the correnti.*

D, *Are the beams that make the length of the bridge, upon which are feen the heads of thofe that form the floor.*

E, *Are the beams, which leaning one towards the other, are united with other beams placed in the middle of the diftance, that is, between the orders of piles; hence in the faid place the beams come to be double.*

F, *Are the columns that fupport the roof.*

G, *Is the upright of one of the heads of the bridge.*

H, *Is the plan of the orders of piles with the buttreffes which hinder the faid piles being fhaken by the timber that comes down the river.*

I, *Is the fcale of ten feet, with which the whole work is meafured.*

CHAP. X.

Of STONE BRIDGES, *and what ought to be obferved in the building of them.*

MEN at firft made bridges of wood, as being attentive to their prefent neceffity only; but fince they have begun to have a regard for the immortality of their name, and when riches gave them fpirit, and conveniency to do greater things, they began to build with ftone, which is more durable, of greater expence, and of more glory to the builders. In thefe, four things ought to be confidered; that is, the heads, made in the banks; the pilafters, that are funk into the rivers; the arches, that are fupported by the pilafters; and the pavement, which is made upon the arches. The heads of bridges ought to be made very firm and folid, fince they not only ferve to fupport the weight of the arches as the other pilafters do, but they keep the whole bridge united befides, and prevent the arches from opening; and therefore they muft be made where the banks are of ftone, or at leaft of a folid foil. And if banks thus made very firm by nature cannot be had, they muft be made firm and ftrong by art; making there other pilafters and other arches, fo that if the banks fhould be ruined by the water, the way to the bridge may not be interrupted.

THE pilafters that are made for the breadth of the river, ought to be in number even; as well becaufe we fee that nature has produced all thofe things of this number, which being more than one, are to fupport any weight, as the legs of men, and all the other animals can juftify: as alfo becaufe this fame compartment is more agreeable to be looked at, and renders the work more firm; becaufe the courfe of the river in the middle, (in which place it is naturally more rapid, as being farther from the banks) is free, and doth not damage the pilafters by continually fhaking them. The pilafters ought to be fo comparted, as to fall in that part of the river where the ftream is lefs rapid.

THE greateft current of the waters, is where thofe things gather together that fwim upon it, which may eafily be known at the increafe of the river. Their foundations muft be made in that time of the year when the waters are loweft, that is, in autumn: and if the bottom of the river be of ftone, or of tofo, or of fcaranto, which as I have faid (in the firft book) is a fort of earth, that is partly ftone, the foundations will be had without the fatigue of digging; becaufe thefe forts of bottoms are an excellent foundation of themfelves. But if the bottom of the river be of gravel or fand, one muft dig until the folid ground is found; and if that be difficult, fome of the gravel or fand muft be dug out, and then piles, made of oak, muft be driven there, which, with the iron points that are made to them, muft reach the folid and firm bottom.

To lay the foundations of the pilafters, one ought to inclofe but one part of the river only, and build in that, that the water may have its courfe by the other part left open; and thus proceed from one part to another. The pilafters ought not to be thinner than the fixth part of the breadth of the arch; nor ordinarily thicker than the fourth. They muft be made with large ftones, which are to be joined together with cramps, and with iron or

metal

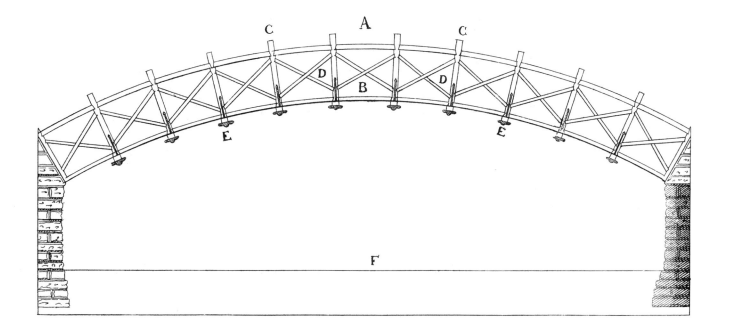

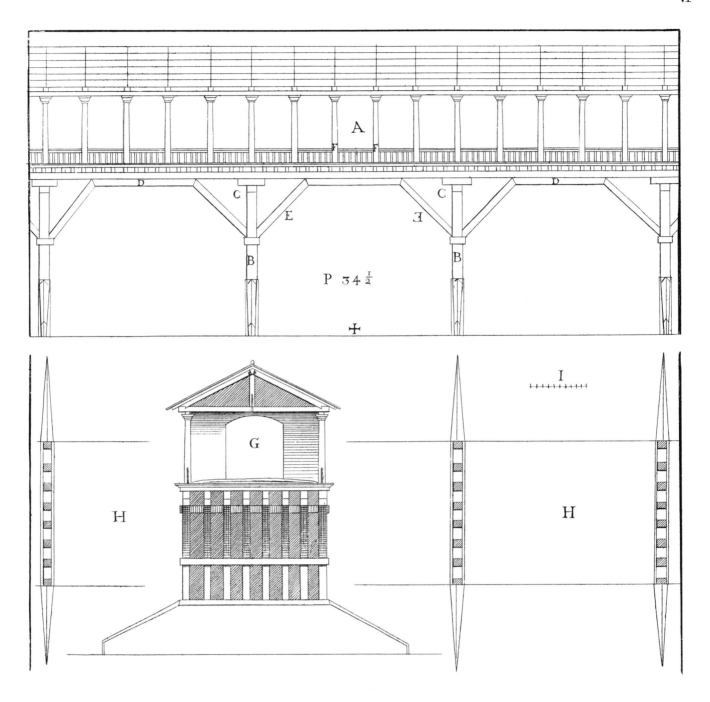

A

F F

D C C D

E E

B B

P 34 ½

✝

G

I

H H

metal nails, that by such concatenations they may come to be all as of one piece. The fronts of the pilasters are commonly made angular, that is, that they have in their extremity a rectangle; and some are also made sometimes semicircular, that they may cut the water, and that those things which are carried down by the impetuosity of the river, may, by striking against them, be thrown off from the pilasters, and pass through the middle of the arch.

THE arches ought to be made firm and strong, and with large stones, which must be well joined together, that they may be able to resist the continual passing of carts, and support the weight, that occasionally may be conveyed over them. Those arches are very firm that are made semi-circular, because they bear upon the pilasters, and do not shock one another. But if by reason of the quality of the site, and the disposition of the pilasters, the semicircle should offend by reason of the too great height, making the ascent of the bridge difficult, the diminished must be made use of, by making arches, that have but the third part of their diameter in height ; and, in such case, the foundations in the banks must be made very strong. The pavement of bridges must be made after the same manner, as the ways are paved, of which mention has been made before. Hence, as all that is to be observed in the building of stone bridges has been seen, it is time that we pass on to the designs.

CHAP. XI.

Of some celebrated BRIDGES *built by the antients, and of the designs of the bridge of* RIMINO.

MANY bridges were built by the antients in divers places. But in *Italy*, especially over the *Tyber*, they built a great many, of which some are still to be seen intire; and of some others there are the antient vestigia only remaining. Those that are still to be seen intire, over the *Tyber*, are that of the castle *Santo Angelo*, formerly called *Ælius*, from the name of the Emperor ÆLIUS ADRIANUS, who built thereon his own sepulchre. The *Fabricius*, built by FABRICIUS, now called *Ponte Quatro Capi*, from the four heads of JANUS, or of TERMINUS, which are placed on the left hand going upon this bridge. By means of this bridge, the island of the *Tyber* is joined to the city. The *Cestius*, now called of *San. Bartolomeo*, which from the other side of the island passes to *Transtevere*. The bridge called *Senatorius* from the senators, and *Palatinus* from the mountain that is near it, made of rustick work, which at present is called of *Santa Maria*. But those bridges of which the antient vestigia are only seen in the *Tyber*, are, the *Sublicius*, called also *Lepidus*, from ÆMELIUS LEPIDUS, which being first of wood, he made it of stone, and it was near *Ripa*. The *Triumphal*, the pilasters of which are to be seen opposite to the church of *Santo Spirito*. The *Janiculensis*, so called for being near mount *Janiculus*, which as it was rebuilt by Pope SIXTUS IV. now is called *Ponte Sisto*. And the *Milvius*, now called *Ponte Molle*, placed in the *Via Flaminia*, somewhat less than two miles distant from *Rome*; which does not retain any thing antient besides the foundations; and they say, that it was built in the time of SILLA, by M. SCAURUS the censor. There are also the ruins of a bridge built by AUGUSTUS CÆSAR, to be seen of rustick work, over the *Nera*, a very rapid river near *Narni*. And over the *Metauro* in *Umbria* at *Galgi*, another is to be seen of rustick work likewise, with some spurs in the banks, that support the street, and make it very strong.

BUT among all the celebrated bridges, that is recorded as a marvellous thing which CALIGULA made from *Pozzuolo* to *Baie*, in the middle of the sea, in length somewhat less than three miles; in which, they say, that he spent all the money of the empire. Exceeding great, and worthy of admiration, was that which TRAJAN built, to subdue the Barbarians over the *Danube*, opposite to *Transilvania*, on which were read these words:

PROVIDENTIA AUGUSTI VERE PONTIFICIS VIRTUS ROMANA QUID NON DOMET ?

SUBJUGO ECCE RAPIDUS ET DANUBIUS.

THIS bridge was afterwards ruined by ADRIAN, that the Barbarians might not be able to pass it, to the damage of the Roman provinces; and its pilasters are still to be seen in the

T

middle

middle of the river. But confidering, that of all the bridges I have feen, that at *Rimino*, a city in *Flaminia*, feems to me to be the moft beautiful, and the moft worthy of confideration, as well for its ftrength, as for its compartment and difpofition. It was built, I Plate 7. judge, by AUGUSTUS CÆSAR. I have given the defigns of it, which are thofe that follow. It is divided into five arches, the three middle ones are equal, and five and twenty foot in breadth, and the two next the banks are lefs, that is, only twenty foot broad. All thofe arches are femicircular, and their modeno is the tenth part of the void of the greater, and the eighth part of the void of the lefser. The pilafters are in thicknefs, a little lefs than half the void of the greater arches. The angle of the fpurs, that cut the water, is a right one, which I have obferved that the antients made in all their bridges; becaufe it is ftronger than the acute one, and therefore lefs expofed to be ruined by the trees, or by other matters that fhould be carried down by the river. Directly over the pilafters, in the fides of the bridge, are fome tabernacles, in which formerly there muft have been ftatues. Over thefe tabernacles, according to the length of the bridge, there is a cornice, which although it is plain, affords a beautiful ornament to the whole work.

A, *Is the faid cornice over the tabernacles of the bridge.*
B, *Is the furface of the water.*
C, *Is the bottom of the river.*
D, *A fcale of ten foot, with which this bridge is meafured.*

C H A P. XII.

Of the BRIDGE *of* Vicenza, *that is over the* Bacchiglione.

THERE run through *Vicenza* two rivers, one of which is called the *Bacchiglione*, and the other the *Rerone*. The *Rerone*, as it goes out of the city, enters into the *Bacchiglione*, and immediately lofes its name. Over thefe rivers are two antient bridges; of that over the *Bacchiglione*, the pilafters and one arch, ftill intire, are to be feen near the church of *S. Maria de gli Angioli*. The remaining part is all modern work. This bridge Plate 8. is divided into three arches; that in the middle is thirty foot wide, the other two are but two and twenty foot and an half in breadth; which was done that the river might have in the middle a freer courfe. The pilafters are in thicknefs the fifth part of the void of the lefser arches, and the fixth of the greater. The arches have in height the third part of their diameter. Their modeno is in thicknefs the ninth part of the lefser arches, and the twelfth of that in the middle, and are wrought in the manner of an architrave. In the extream parts of the length of the pilafters, under the impofts of the arches, fome ftones project forward, which in building of the bridge, ferved to fupport the beams, upon which were made the centerings of the arches. And, in this manner, the danger of the floods carrying away the beams, to the ruin of the work, was avoided; which had it been done otherwife, it would have been neceffary to drive them into the river, to make the faid centerings.

A, *Is the breaftwork of the bridge.*
C, *Is the modeno of the arches.*
D, *Are the ftones that project from the remaining part of the pilafters, and ferve for the centring of the arches.*
E, *Are the heads of the bridge.*

C H A P. XIII.

Of a STONE BRIDGE *of my invention.*

Plate 9, and 10. THE invention of the following bridge, is, in my opinion, very beautiful, and well adapted to the place where it was to have been built; which was in the middle of a city, that is one of the greateft, and of the moft noble in *Italy*, and is the metropolis of many other cities, and where there is a very great traffick carried on, almoft from every part of the world. The river is very broad, and the bridge would have been in the very fpot
                                                                                                           where

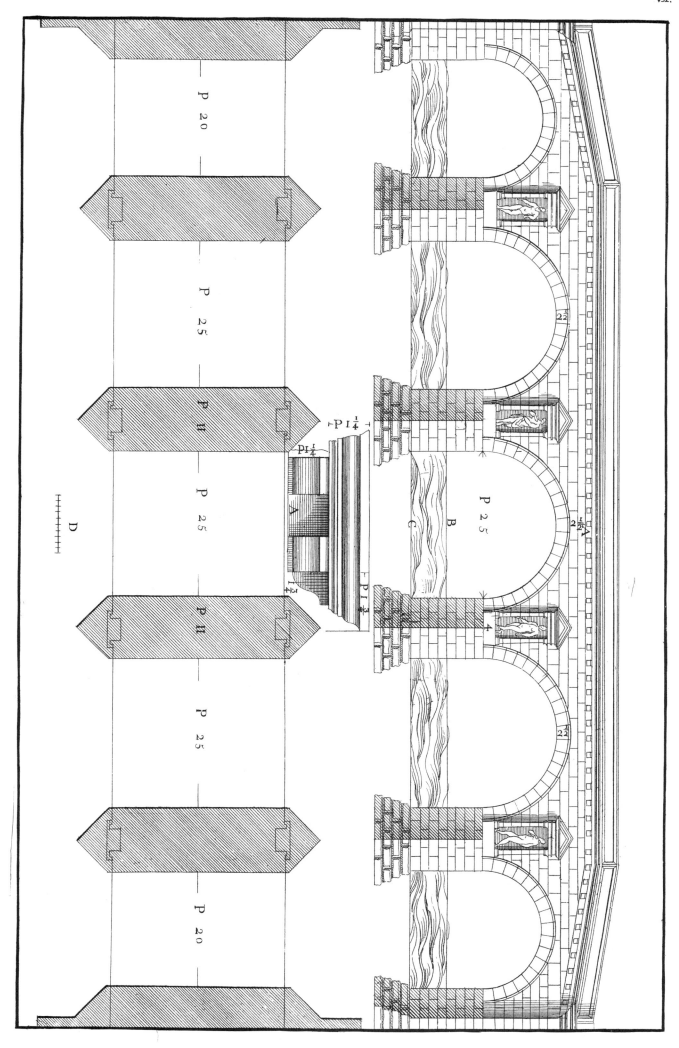

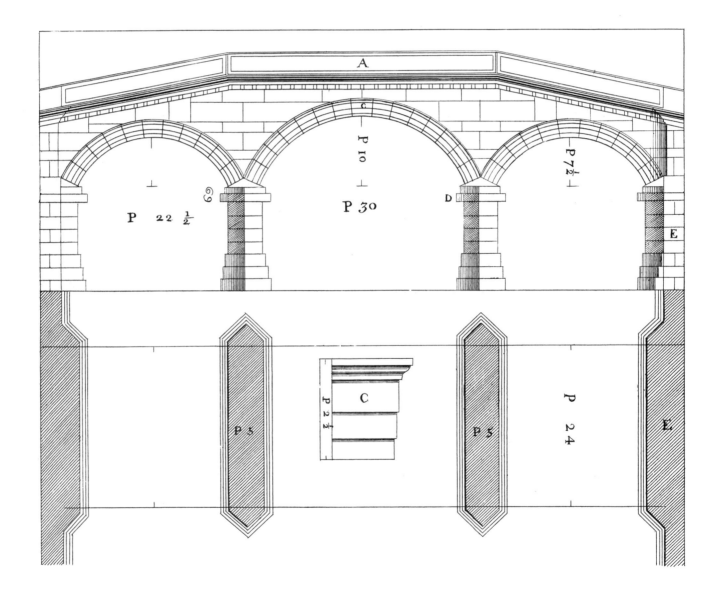

A

P 10

P 7½

P 22 ½

69

P 30

D

E

P 5

C

P 2½

P 5

P 24

E

IX.

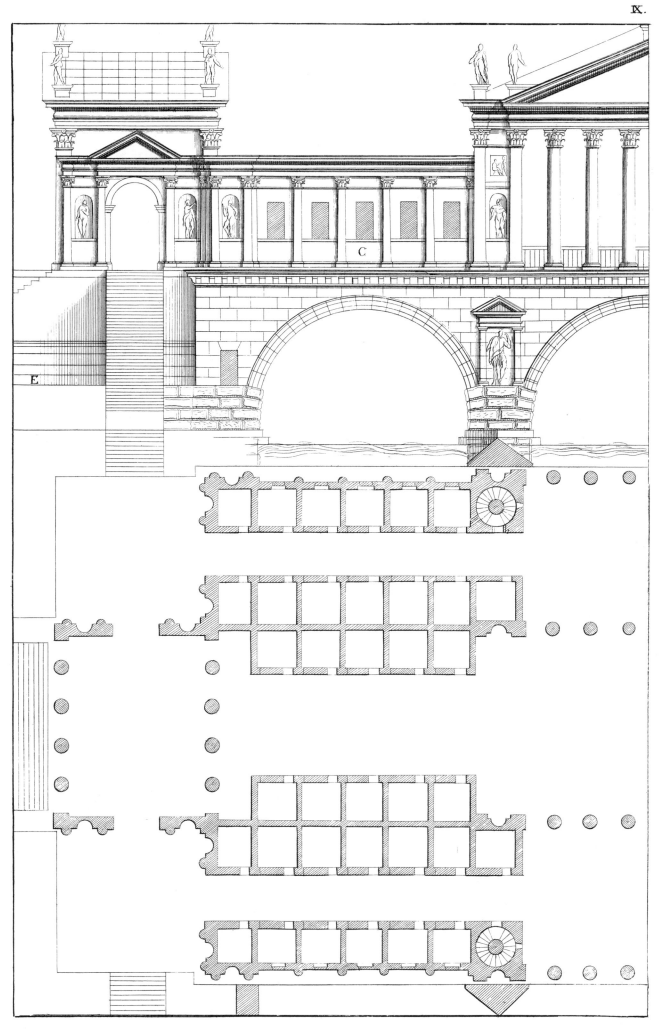

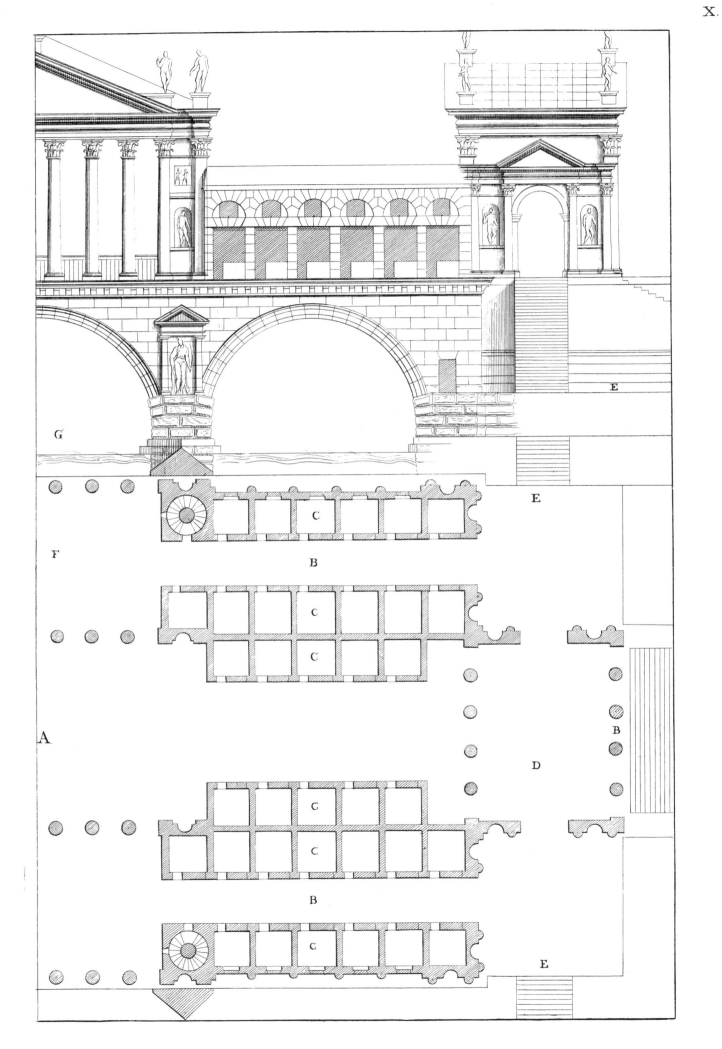

G

F

A

B

C

C

C

C

C

C

E

E

E

E

B

B

D

where the merchants affemble to treat of their affairs. Therefore, to keep up to the grandeur and dignity of the faid city, and alfo to add a very great income to it, I made upon the bridge, in its full breadth, three ftreets; that in the middle, ample and beautiful, and the other two, one on each fide, fomewhat lefs. On each fide of thefe ftreets I ordered fhops, fo that there would have been fix rows of them. Befides this, in the heads of the bridge, and in the middle, that is, upon the greateft arch, I made loggia's, in which the merchants might have affembled to negotiate together; and it would have afforded conveniency, and very great beauty. One might have gone up to the loggia's, in the heads, by a few fteps; and level with them would have been the floor of all the remaining part of the bridge. It ought not to feem a novelty that loggia's are made upon bridges, becaufe the bridge *Ælius* in *Rome*, of which mention has been made in its place, was covered over with loggia's, with columns of bronzo, with ftatues, and with other curious ornaments. Befides which, on this occafion, for the above-mentioned reafons, it was almoft neceffary to make them. In the proportions of the pilafters, and of the arches, the fame order has been obferved, and the fame rules that have been laid down in the above-mentioned bridges, which every one may eafily find out of himfelf.

Parts of the plan.

A, *Is the beautiful and ample ftreet made in the middle of the breadth of the bridge.*
B, *Are the leffer ftreets.*
C, *Are the fhops.*
D, *Are the loggia's in the heads of the bridge.*
E, *Are the fteps that go up to the faid loggia's.*
F, *The loggia's in the middle upon the greateft arch of the bridge.*

THE parts of the upright correfpond to thofe of the plan, and therefore may eafily be underftood, without any farther explication.

C, *The upright of the fhops, in the part without, that is over the river; and in the plate appears the upright of the fame fhops towards the ftreet.*
G, *Is the line of the furface of the water.*

C H A P. XIV.

Of another BRIDGE *of my invention.*

MY opinion being afked by fome gentlemen concerning a bridge they defigned to Plate 11. build of ftone, I made them the following invention. The river where the bridge was intended, is one hundred and eighty foot wide. I divided this whole breadth into three voids, making that in the middle fixty foot wide, and the other two forty eight foot apiece.

THE pilafters that fupport the arches were twelve foot thick, and fo were in thicknefs the fifth part of the void of that in the middle, and the fourth of the fmaller voids. I fomewhat altered, in thefe, the ordinary meafures, making them very thick, that they might project out from the body of the breadth of the bridge; and that they might the better refift the impetuofity of the river, which is very rapid, and the ftones and timber that might be carried down by it. The arches would have been a fegment of a circle lefs than a femicircle, that the afcent of the bridge might have been eafy and plain. I made the modeno of the arches the feventeenth part of the void of the arch in the middle, and the fourteenth of the void of the other two.

THIS bridge might have been adorned with niches directly over the pilafters and with ftatues; and a cornice along its fides would have had a good effect: which was alfo fometimes done by the antients, as one may fee in the bridge of *Rimino*, ordered by AUGUSTUS CÆSAR, the defigns of which have been given before.

A, *The furface of the water.*
B, *The bottom of the river.*
C, *The ftones that project, for the ufe abovefaid.*
D, *The fcale of ten foot, by which the whole work is meafured.*

C H A P.

C H A P. XV.

Of the Bridge *of* Vicenza, *that is upon the* Rerone.

Plate 12.   THE other antient bridge, that (as I have faid) is in *Vicenza*, over the *Rerone*, is vulgarly called *Il ponte dalle Beccarie*, becaufe it is near the greateft butchery of the city. This bridge is intire, and very little different from that which is over the *Bacchiglione*, becaufe it is alfo divided into three arches, and has the arch in the middle greater than the other two. All thefe arches are of a fegment of a circle lefs than a femicircle, and without any ornament at all. The little ones are in height the third part of their breadth; that in the middle, is fomething lefs. The pilafters are in thicknefs the fifth part of the diameter of the leffer arches; and they have in their extremities, under the impoft of the arches, the ftones that project for the abovefaid reafons.

Both thefe bridges are made with ftone from *Coftoza*, which is a foft ftone, and is cut with a faw like wood. There are four bridges at *Padoua*, made after the fame proportions of thefe two at *Vicenza*; three of which have only three arches, and are the bridge of *Altina*, that of *San Lorenzo*, and that which is called *Ponte Corvo*; and one has five, and is, that which is called *Ponte Molino*. In all thefe bridges it is to be obferved, that the greateft care imaginable has been taken in joining the ftones together, which (as I have before obferved) is extremely requifite in all fabricks.

C H A P. XVI.

Of the Piazze, *and of the edifices that are made round them.*

BESIDES the ftreets, of which mention has been made above, it is neceffary that in cities, according to their bignefs, there fhould be more or fewer piazze comparted, in which people affemble to contract for things ufeful and neceffary for their wants: and as they are applied to different ufes, fo a proper and convenient place ought to be given to each. Thofe ample places are left in cities, befides the faid conveniency, that there the people affemble to walk, to difcourfe, and bargain in; they afford alfo a great ornament, when at the head of a ftreet, a beautiful and fpacious place is found, from which the profpect of fome beautiful fabrick is feen, and efpecially of fome temple. But as it is of advantage, that there be many piazze difperfed through the city, fo it is much more neceffary, magnificent, and honourable, that there be one principal, which truly may be called publick. Thefe principal piazze ought to be made of fuch bignefs, as the multitude of the citizens fhall require, that it may not be fmall for their conveniency and ufe, or that, through the fmall number of people, they may not feem uninhabited. In fea-port towns they muft be made near the port; and in inland cities they muft be made in the middle of them, that they may be convenient for every part of the city.

Portico's, fuch as the antients ufed, ought to be made round the piazze, as broad as their columns are high; the ufe of which is to avoid the rain, fnow, and every injury of the air and fun. But all the edifices that are made round a piazza, ought not to be (according to Alberti) higher than the third part of the breadth of the piazza, nor lower than the fixth. And to the portico's one is to afcend by fteps, which muft be made as high as the fifth part of the length of the columns.

Arches give a very great ornament to piazze that are made at the head of the ftreets, that is, in the entrance into the piazza; which, how they are to be made, and why they were antiently made, and from whence they were called triumphal, fhall be laid down at large, in my book of arches, and the defigns of many fhall be inferted. Hence great light will be given to thofe, that may be willing in our times, or hereafter, to erect arches to princes, to kings, and to emperors.

But, returning to the principal piazza, the palace of the prince, or of the fignory (as it happens either to be a principality or a republick) ought to be joined thereto, fo ought the mint the publick treafury, and the prifons.

Thesе

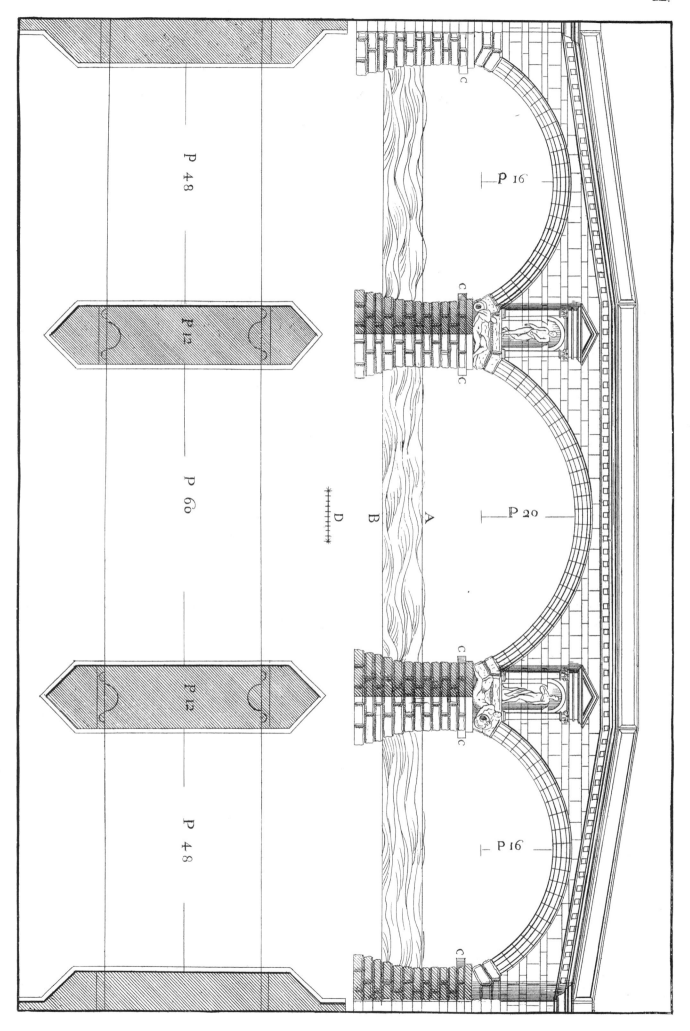

P 48

P 12

P 60

P 12

P 48

P 16

P 20

P 16

A

B

D

C

C

C

C

C

C

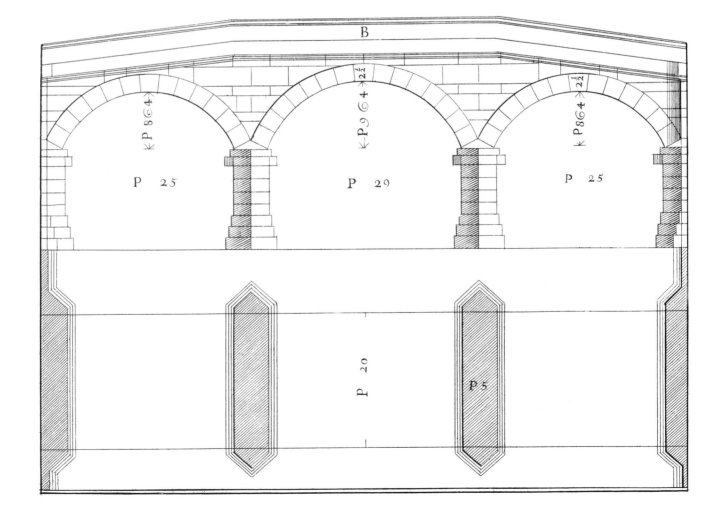

THESE laſt were antiently made of three ſorts; the one for thoſe that were debauched and leud, who were kept there in order to their reformation, which now are ordinarily aſſigned to mad-folks; the ſecond ſort was for debtors, and this is ſtill in uſe among us; the third is where the malefactors, either already condemned, or ſuch as are to be tried, are kept: which three ſorts are ſufficient, ſince the errors of men proceed either from im-modeſty, or from contempt, or from wickedneſs.

THE mint, and the priſons ought to be placed in very ſecure places, and be very ready at hand, encompaſſed with high walls, and well guarded againſt the violence and the treachery of the ſeditious citizens. The priſons may be made healthy and commodious, becauſe they have been inſtituted for the ſafe-keeping and not for the torment and pain of crimi-nals, or of other men; therefore their walls in the middle muſt be made of very large live ſtones, bound together with cramps, and with nails of iron or metal, and then coated on both ſides with bricks: becauſe, in ſo doing, the humidity of the live ſtones will not make them unhealthy, neither will they want for ſecurity. Paſſages muſt alſo be made round them; and the rooms for the keepers near, that they may eaſily hear if the priſoners ſhould con-trive any thing.

BESIDES the treaſury and the priſons, the curia ſhou'd be joined to the piazza, which is the place where the ſenate meets to conſult on affairs of ſtate. This muſt be made of ſuch bigneſs, as the dignity and number of the citizens ſhall ſeem to require; and if it be ſquare, whatever it ſhall be in breadth, adding one half more, that ſhall be its height. But if its form ſhall be longer than it is broad, the length and breadth muſt be added together, and the half of the whole ſum ſhall be taken for the height to the roof. In the middle of the height, large cor-nices ought to be made round the walls, which muſt project forward, that the voice of thoſe who diſpute, may not be loſt in the height of the curia, but reflected back, the better to come to the ears of the auditors.

ON the part facing the warmeſt region of the heaven, on one ſide of the piazza, the baſilica muſt be made, that is, the place where juſtice is adminiſtered, whither great part of the people and men of buſineſs reſort; of which I ſhall make particular mention, after I have ſhewn how the Greeks and Latins made their piazze, and have given the deſigns of them.

CHAP. XVII.

Of the PIAZZE *of the Greeks.*

THE Greeks, according to VITRUVIUS, in the firſt chapter of the fifth book, or-dered the piazze in their cities in a ſquare form, and made ample and dou-ble portico's round them, conſiſting of many columns, that is, one diameter and an half of a column diſtant the one from the other, or at moſt two diameters. Theſe porti-co's were as broad as the columns were long. Hence, as they were double, the place to walk in came to be as broad as twice the length of the column, and therefore very com-modious and ample. Upon the firſt columns, which (with regard to the place where they were) in my opinion, muſt have been of the Corinthian order, there were other columns, a fourth part leſs than the firſt: theſe had a poggio under them, as high as conveniency required; becauſe theſe upper portico's were alſo made to walk in, and to diſcourſe, and where people might conveniently be to ſee the ſpectacles that might be exhibited in the ſquare, either out of devotion or pleaſure. All theſe portico's ought to be adorned with niches and ſtatues, becauſe the Greeks took great delight in ſuch ornaments. Near to theſe piazze, although VITRUVIUS, when he teaches how they were ordered, does not make mention of thoſe places, there ought to be the baſilica, the curia, the priſons, and all the other places uſually joined to piazza's, of which mention has been made before. Beſides which (as he ſays in the ſeventh chapter of the firſt book) the antients uſed to make near the piazze, the temples conſecrated to MERCURY and ISIS, as to Gods preſiding over buſineſs and merchan-dize: and in *Pola*, a city of *Iſtria*, two are to be ſeen upon the piazze; the one like the other, for form, grandeur, and for ornaments. I have drawn them in the deſign of theſe piazze on one ſide of the baſilica. The plan and elevation of which, with all their par-ticular members, ſhall be ſeen more diſtinctly in my book of temples.

A, *The piazza.*
B, *The double portico's.*
C, *The baſilica where the judges had their tribunal.*

Plate 13.

U   D, *The*

D, *The temple of* Isis.
E, *The temple of* Mercury.
F, *The curia.*
G, *The portico, and the little court before the mint.*
H, *The portico, and the little court before the prifons.*
I, *The door of the atrio, from which one enters the curia.*
K, *The paffages round the curia, through which one comes to the portico's of the*
     piazza.
L, *The vault of the portico's of the piazza.*
M, *The vault of the portico's within.*
N, *The plan of the walls of the fmall courts, and of the temples.*
P, *The paffages round the mint and the prifons.*

Plate 14.   The elevation that follows the plan, is of one part of the piazza.

C H A P. XVIII.

Of the Piazze *of the Romans.*

THE Romans, and the Italians (as Vitruvius fays in the above-mentioned place) departing from the cuftom of the Greeks, made their piazze longer than they were broad ; fo that the length being divided into three parts, two were given to the breadth, becaufe of the gratuities in them made to the gladiators. This form was much more commodious for that purpofe than the fquare one ; and for this reafon alfo they made the intercolumniations of the portico's, that were round the piazze, of two diameters and a quarter of a column, or of three diameters, that the fight of the people might not be obftructed by the clofenefs of the columns. The portico's were as broad as the columns were long, and they had banker's fhops under them. The columns above were made one fourth part lefs than thofe below, becaufe the under parts, with refpect to the weight they bear, ought to be firmer than thofe above, as was faid in the firft book. In the part facing the hotteft region of the heaven they placed the bafilica, which I have marked in the defign of thefe piazze, two fquares in length ; and in the part within there are portico's round it, the third part of the fpace in the middle in breadth. Their columns are as long as the place is broad, and they may be made of the moft acceptable order.

In the part facing the north, I have placed there the curia, one fquare and an half in length ; its height is half the length and breadth put together. This was the place (as I have faid above) where the fenate met to confult about matters of ftate.

Plate 15.   A, *The winding ftairs, void in the middle, which lead to the places above.*
B, *The paffage through which one enters into the portico's of the piazza.*
C, *Portico's, and the little court on one fide of the bafilica.*
D, *}*
E, *} The places for the bankers, and for the moft honourable arts of the city.*
F, *Is the place for the fecretaries, whither the deliberations of the fenate were*
    remitted.
G, *The prifons.*
H, *Is the return of the portico's of the piazze.*
I, *The entrance into the bafilica, by one fide.*
K, *The return of the portico's that are in the fmall courts on one fide of the*
    bafilica.

All the faid parts are made by a larger fcale, and countermarked with the fame letters.

Plate 16.   The elevation that follows in a large form, is of one part of the portico's of the piazza.

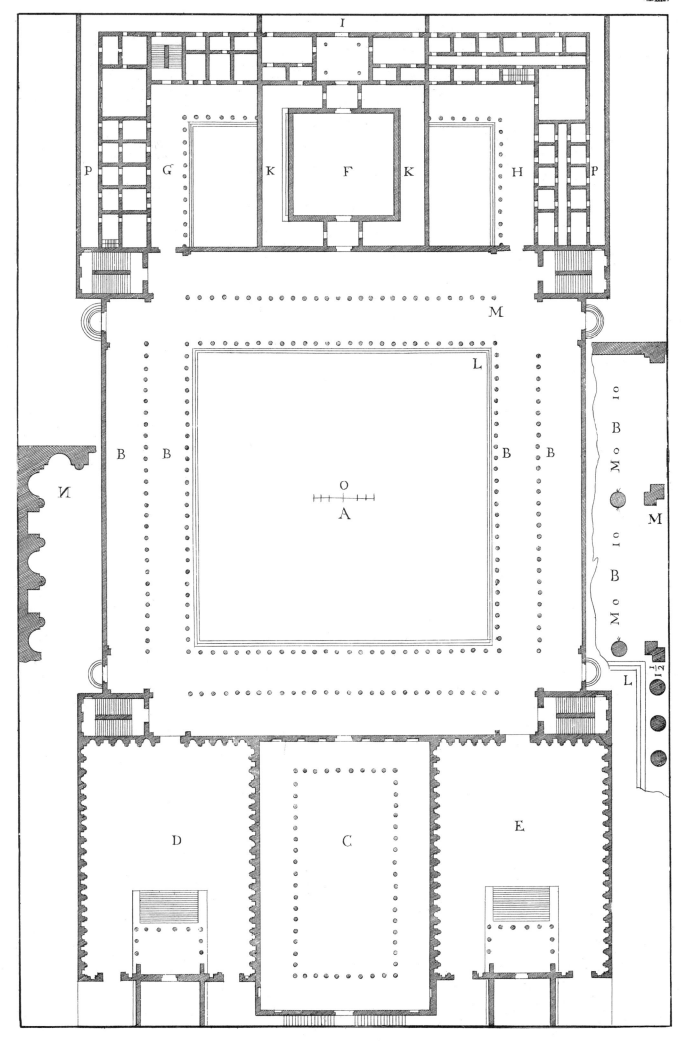

Mo 7½

Mo 10

M o   10   Mo 1½   Mo·1·

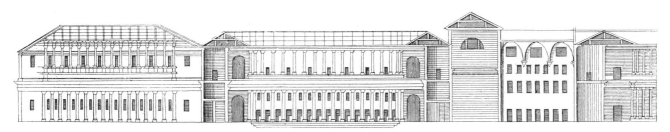

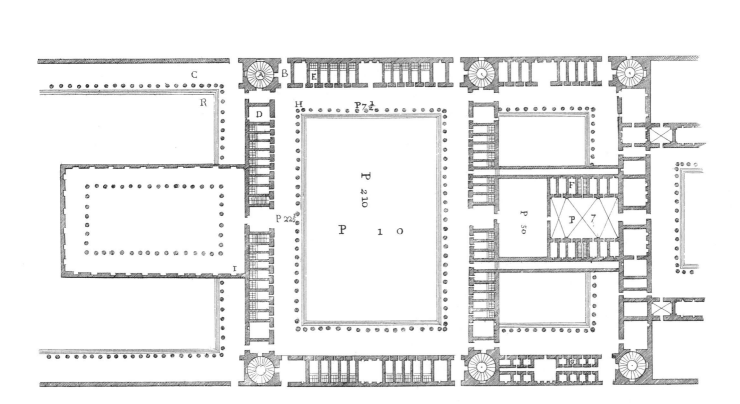

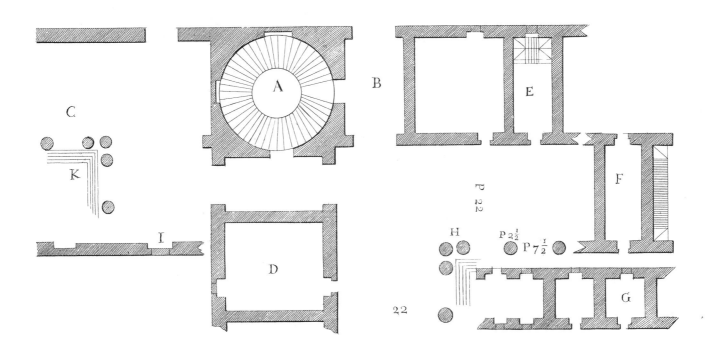

M o 6¾

M o — 9

M o ·I

M o 2 ¼

C H A P. XIX.

Of the antient B A S I L I C A's.

FORMERLY thofe places were called bafilica's, in which the judges fat under cover to adminifter juftice, and where fometimes great and important affairs were debated. Hence we read, that the tribunes of the people caufed a column to be taken away, which obftructed their feats, from the *Bafilica Portia* (in which juftice was adminifter'd) that ftood near the temple of ROMULUS and REMUS at *Rome*, and which now is the church of *San. Cofmo e Damiano*. Of all the antient bafilica's, that of PAULUS ÆMILIUS was very much celebrated, and reckoned among the marvels of the city. It ftood between the temple of SATURN and that of FAUSTINA, on which he fpent one thoufand five hundred talents, given him by CÆSAR, which amount, by computation, to about nine hundred thoufand crowns. They ought to be made adjoining to the piazze, as was obferved in the abovefaid, which were both in the *Forum Romanum* and facing the warmeft region of the heaven, that the merchants, and thofe that had law-fuits, might in wintertime, without being incommoded by the bad weather, go and remain there without inconvenience. They ought not to be made narrower than one third part, nor wider than the half of the length, if the nature of the place does not hinder it, or if one is not compelled to alter the meafure of this compartment.

OF this kind of edifice there is not the leaft antient veftigium remaining; wherefore, according to what VITRUVIUS mentions in the above-cited place, I have made the following defigns; in which the bafilica, in the fpace in the middle, that is, within the columns, is two fquares long.

THE portico's that are on the fides, and in the part where the entrance is, are in breadth the third part of the fpace in the middle. Their columns are as long as they are broad, and may be made of any order one pleafes. I have not made a portico in the part oppofite to the entrance, becaufe a large nich feems to me to fuit there very well, made of a fegment of a circle lefs than a femicircle, in which the tribunal of the prætor, or of the judges, may be, if they are many, to which there muft be an afcent by fteps, that it may have the greater majefty and grandeur. I do not deny, neverthelefs, but that portico's may alfo be made all round them, as I have done in the bafilica's reprefented in the defigns of the piazze. Through the portico's one goes to the ftairs that are on the fides of the faid nich, which lead to the upper portico's. Thefe upper portico's have their columns the fourth part lefs than thofe below. The poggio, or the pedeftal, that is between the upper and lower columns, ought to be made in height one fourth part lefs than the length of the columns above, that thofe that walk in the upper portico's, may not be feen by thofe that do bufinefs in the bafilica. A bafilica at *Fano*, was ordered by VITRUVIUS, with other compartments, which by the meafures which he gives the faid place, one may comprehend to have been an edifice of very great dignity and beauty. I would have inferted the defigns of it here, if they had not been done, with the utmoft diligence, by the moft reverend BARBARO in his *Vitruvius*.

OF the following defigns, the firft is the plan, the fecond is part of the elevation.

PARTS of the plan.

A, *The entrance into the bafilica*   Plate 17.
B, *Is the place for the tribunal oppofite to the entrance.*
C, *Are the portico's round it.*
D, *Are the ftairs that lead to the parts above.*
E, *Are the places for the filth.*

PARTS of the elevation.

F, *The profile of the place, made there to place the tribunal oppofite to the entrance.*   Plate 18.
G, *The columns of the portico's below.*
H, *Is the poggio, in height a fourth part lefs than the columns of the upper portico's.*
I, *The columns of the faid upper portico's.*

C H A P.

CHAP. XX.

Of the BASILICA's *of our times, and of the defigns of that of* Venice.

AS the antients made their bafilica's, that men in winter and fummer might have a place to affemble, and treat about their occafions and affairs; fo in our times in every city, both in *Italy* and out of it, fome publick halls are made, which may rightly be called bafilica's, becaufe, that near to them is the habitation of the fupreme magiftrate. Hence they come to be a part of it. [The word bafilica properly fignifies a royal houfe.] Here alfo the judges attended to adminifter juftice to the people.

THE bafilica's of our times differ in this from the antients, viz. the antient ones were upon, or even with the ground, and ours are raifed upon arches, in which are fhops for divers arts, and the merchandizes of the city. There the prifons are alfo made, and other places belonging to publick bufinefs. Befides which, the modern bafilica's have portico's in the part within, as has been feen in the above mentioned defigns; and the antient, on the contrary, either had no portico's, or had them in the part without upon the piazza.

OF thefe modern halls there is a very noble one at *Padoua*, a city illuftrious for its antiquity, and celebrated for learning throughout the world, in which the gentlemen every day affemble, and it ferves them as a covered piazza.

THE city of *Brefcia*, magnificent in all her actions, has lately made one which for its largenefs and ornaments is wonderful. And another is at *Vicenza*, of which only I have put the defigns, becaufe the portico's it has round it are of my invention; and becaufe I do not doubt but this fabrick may be compared with the antient edifices, and ranked among the moft noble, and moft beautiful fabricks, that have been made fince the antient times; not only for its grandeur, and its ornaments, but alfo for the materials, which is all very hard live ftone, and all the ftones have been joined and banded together, with the utmoft diligence. It would be unneceffary to put down the meafures of every part, becaufe they are all marked in their places, in the defigns.

Plate 19.   IN the firft plate, the plan and the elevation are defigned, with the plan of the pilafters in a large form.

Plate 20.   IN the fecond is defigned one part of the elevation in a larger form.

CHAP. XXI.

Of the PALESTRA's *and of the* XYSTI *of the Greeks.*

HAVING treated of ways, of bridges, and of piazza's, it remains that mention fhould now be made of thofe edifices made by the antient Greeks, into which men went to exercife themfelves; and it is very likely, that at the time the cities of Greece were governed as a republick, in every city there was one of thefe edifices; where the young men, befides the learning of fciences, by exercifing their bodies in the things belonging to the art of war, fuch as to know the orders, to throw the bar, to wreftle, to manage their arms, to fwim with a weight upon their fhoulders, they became fit for action, and for all the accidents of war. Hence they could afterwards, by their valour, and military difcipline, tho' but a few in number, overcome a very numerous army.

THE Romans, after their example, had the *Campus Martius*, in which the youth were publickly exercifed in the faid military actions, from which proceeded wonderful effects, and their notable victories in battle.

CÆSAR writes in his Commentaries, that being on a fudden attacked by the *Nervii*, and feeing that the feventh and twelfth legion were in a manner fo confined, that they could not fight,
commanded

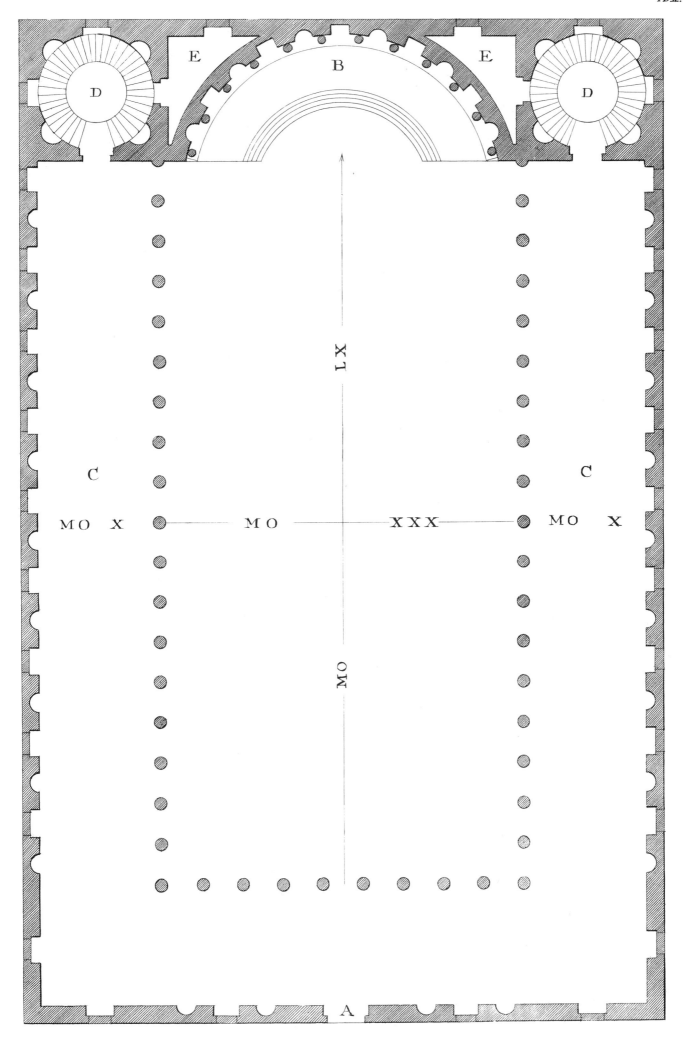

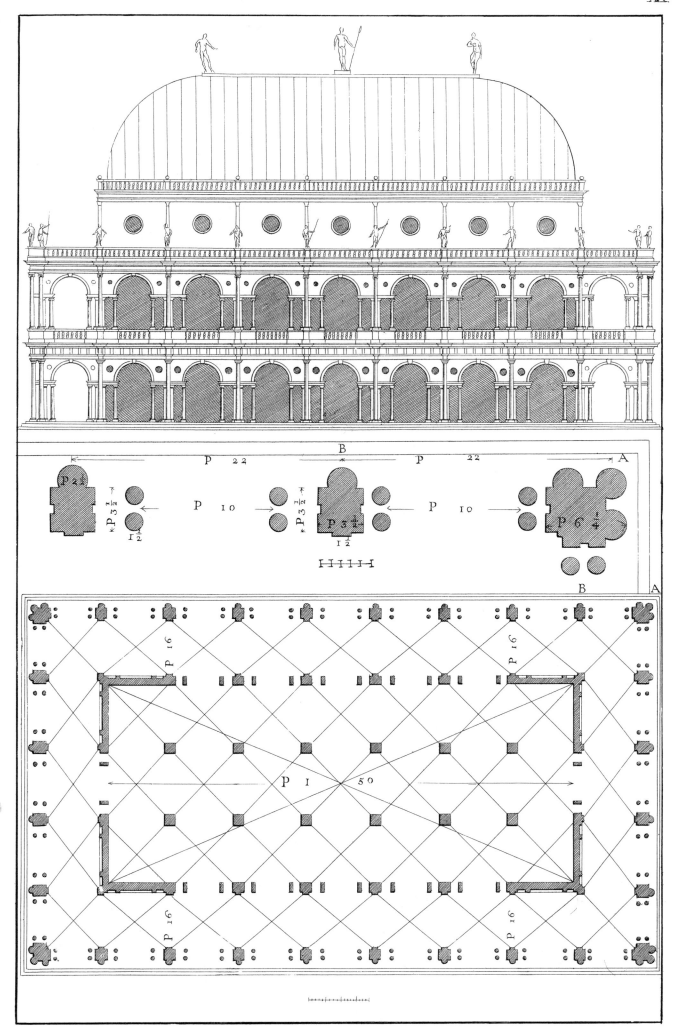

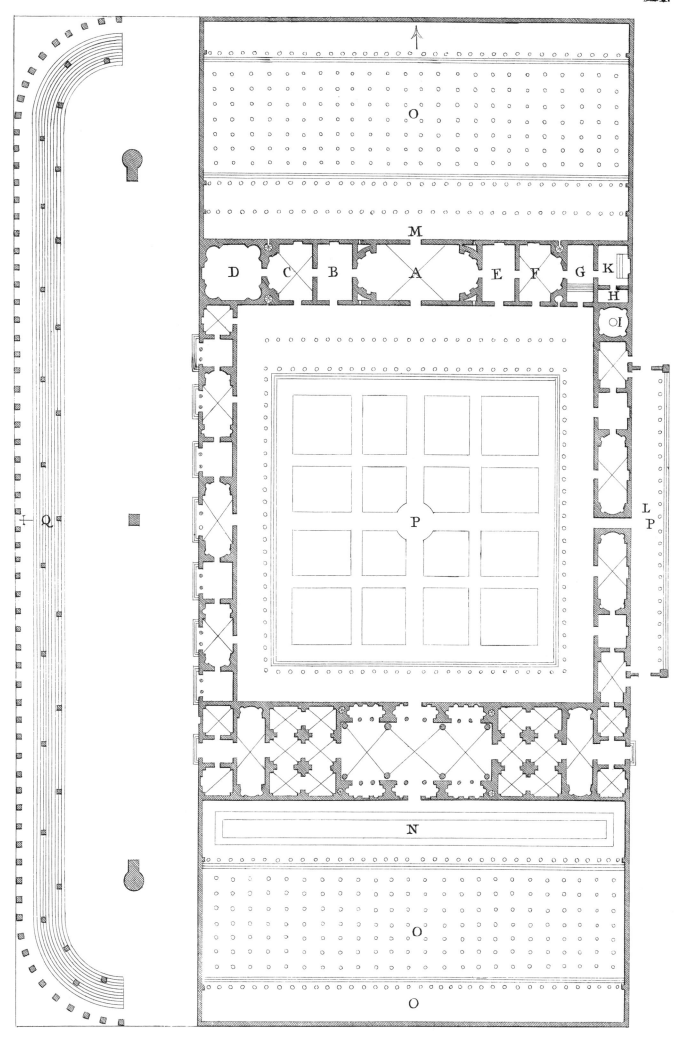

commanded that they fhould extend and place themfelves one on the flank of the other, that they might have an opportunity of handling their arms, and not be furrounded by the enemies; which being immediately done by the foldiers, he obtained the victory, and they the immortal name of being brave, and well difciplined: fince, in the very heat of battle, when things were full of danger and confufion, they performed that, which to many in our times would feem a thing very difficult to be done, even when the enemies are at a diftance, and when there is conveniency both of time and place. Of fuch like glorious actions the Greek and Latin hiftories are almoft all full; and there is no doubt but that it proceeded from their continual exercifing of the young men.

FROM this exercife, the faid places, which (as VITRUVIUS relates, in the eleventh chapter of his fifth book) the Greeks built, were by them called *Paleftra's* and *Xifti*, and their difpofition was this. In the firft place they defigned the fquare piazza, two ftadia in circumference; that is, of two hundred and fifty paces; and on three fides thereof they made fimple portico's, and under them ample halls, in which were the men of letters, fuch as philofophers, and the like, difputing and difcourfing. On the fourth fide, which was turned to the fouth, they made double portico's, that the rains driven by the winds, might not enter them far, in winter; and that the fun might be kept off in fummer. In the middle of this portico was a very great hall, one fquare and an half in length, where the young men were inftructed. On the left hand of which, was the place where the girls were inftructed; behind that, the place where the wreftlers powdered themfelves; and farther on, the rooms for cold wafhing, or what now we call cold bathing, which comes to be in the turning of the portico. On the left of the place for the young men, was the place where they anointed their bodies, in order to be the ftronger; and near to it the cold room, where they undrefs'd themfelves; and farther on, the warm room, where they made a fire, from whence one came into the hot room. This room had on one part of it the *laconicum*, which was the place where they fweated, and on the other the room for hot bathing; becaufe thefe prudent men were willing to imitate nature, which from an extream cold, leads gradually to an extream heat; and that one might not on a fudden, from the cold room, enter into the hot one, but intermediately thro' the warm one.

ON the outfide of the faid places there were three portico's, one on the fide where the entrance was, which might be made towards the eaft or weft; the other two were, one on the right, and the other on the left; one placed towards the north, and the other towards the fouth. That which faced the north, was double, and in breadth what the columns were long. The other, facing the fouth, was fimple, but much larger than either of the abovefaid, and was divided in this manner: the fpace of ten foot was left on the fide of the columns, and on that of the wall, which fpace is by VITRUVIUS called the margin; by two fteps fix foot broad, one defcended into a floor, not lefs than twelve foot in breadth, in which, during the winter feafon, the wreftlers might exercife themfelves under cover, without being interrupted by thofe that ftood under the portico to look on; who alfo, by reafon of the faid lownefs of the place where the wreftlers were, could fee better.

THIS portico was properly called *Xiftus*. The *Xifti* were fo made, that between two portico's there might be groves and plantations, and the ftreets between the trees paved with mofaic work.

NEAR the *Xiftus*, and the double portico, the covered places to walk in were defigned, by them called *Peridromis*; in which, in winter, when the fky was ferene, the wreftlers might exercife themfelves. The *ftadium* was on one fide of this edifice, and was the place where the multitude could ftand commodioufly to fee the wreftlers engage.

FROM this kind of edifices the Roman Emperors took example, who ordered the baths to delight and pleafe the people, as being places where men went to recreate and wafh themfelves; of which in the following book I fhall treat, God willing.

A, *The place where the boys were inftructed.*
B, *The place where the girls were inftructed.*
C, *The place where the wreftlers powdered themfelves.*

Plate 21.

X

D, *The*

D, *The cold bath.*
E, *The Place where the wreftlers anointed themfelves.*
F, *The cold room.*
G, *The warm room, through which one proceeds to the furnace.*
H, *The hot room, called the fweating room.*
I, *The laconicum.*
K, *The hot bath.*
L, *The outward portico before the entrance.*
M, *The outward portico towards the north.*
N, *The outward portico towards the fouth, where in the winter feafon the wreftlers exercifed themfelves, called Xiftus.*
O, *The groves between two portico's.*
P, *The uncovered places to walk in, called Peridromis.*
Q, *Stadium, where the multitude ftood to fee the wreftlers engage.*
+, *The eaft.*
O, *The fouth.*
P, *The weft.*
∴, *The north.*

THE other places made in the defign are efcdre and fchools.

The END of the THIRD BOOK.

THE

REGINA   VIRTUS

THE FOURTH BOOK OF
ARCHITECTURE
by
ANDREA PALLADIO

WHEREIN
the Antient Temples that are in ROME
are described and figured, & some
others that are in Italy and out of Italy.

LONDON,
Published by
ISAAC WARE,
Anno MDCCXXXXVIII.

THE FOURTH BOOK

O F

Andrea Palladio's

ARCHITECTURE.

The PREFACE *to the* READER.

IF upon any fabrick labour and induſtry may be beſtowed, that it may be comparted with beautiful meaſure and proportion; this, without any doubt, ought to be done in temples; in which the maker and giver of all things, the almighty and ſupream God, ought to be adored by us, and be praiſed, and thanked for his continual benefactions to us, in the beſt manner that our ſtrength will permit. If, therefore, men in building their own habitations, take very great care to find out excellent and expert architects, and able artificers, they are certainly obliged to make uſe of ſtill much greater care in the building of churches. And if in thoſe they attend chiefly to conveniency, in theſe they ought to have a regard to the dignity and grandeur of the Being there to be invoked and adored; who being the ſupream good, and higheſt perfection, it is very proper, that all things conſecrated to him, ſhould be brought to the greateſt perfection we are capable of. And indeed, if we conſider this beautiful machine of the world, with how many wonderful ornaments it is filled, and how the heavens, by their continual revolutions, change the ſeaſons according as nature requires, and their motion preſerves itſelf by the ſweeteſt harmony of temperature; we cannot doubt, but that the little temples we make, ought to reſemble this very great one, which, by his immenſe goodneſs, was perfectly compleated with one word of his; or imagine that we are not obliged to make in them all the ornaments we poſſibly can, and build them in ſuch a manner, and with ſuch proportions, that all the parts toge-ther may convey a ſweet harmony to the eyes of the beholders, and that each of them ſeparately may ſerve agreeably to the uſe for which it ſhall be appointed. For which reaſon, although they are worthy to be much commended, who being guided by an exceed-ing good ſpirit, have already built temples to the ſupream God, and ſtill build them; it does not ſeem, nevertheleſs, that they ought to remain without ſome little reprehenſion, if they have not alſo endeavoured to make them in the beſt and moſt noble form our condition will permit.

HENCE, becauſe the antient Greeks and Romans employed the utmoſt care in building the temples to their Gods, and compoſed them of the moſt beautiful architecture, that they might be made with ſo much greater ornaments, and in greater proportion, as that they might be ſuitable for the God to whom they were conſecrated; I ſhall ſhew in this book the form and the ornaments of many antient temples, of which the ruins are ſtill to be ſeen, and by me have been reduced into deſigns, that every one may know in what form, and with what ornaments churches ought to be built. And although there is but a ſmall part of ſome of them to be ſeen ſtanding above-ground, I nevertheleſs from that ſmall part, (the foundations that could be ſeen being alſo conſidered) have endeavoured, by conjecture, to ſhew what they muſt have been when they were entire. And in this VITRUVIUS has been a very great help to me; becauſe, what I ſaw, agreeing with what he teacheth us, it was not difficult for me to come at the knowledge of their aſpect, and of their form.

But to the ornaments, that is, the bafes, columns, capitals, cornices, and fuch like things, I have added nothing of my own; but they have been meafured by me with the utmoft attention, from different fragments, found in the places where thefe temples ftood. And I make no doubt, but that they, who fhall read this book, and fhall confider the defigns in it carefully, may be able to underftand many places, which in VITRUVIUS are reputed very difficult, and to direct their mind to the knowledge of the beautiful and proportionable forms of temples, and to draw from them various very noble inventions; making ufe of which in a proper time and place, they may fhew, in their works, how one may, and ought to vary, without departing from the precepts of the art, and how laudable and agreeable fuch variations are.

But before we come to the defigns, I fhall, as I ufually do, briefly mention thofe advertences, that in building of temples ought to be obferved; having alfo taken them from VITRUVIUS, and from other very excellent men, who have written of fo noble an art.

CHAPTER I.

Of the SITE that ought to be chofen for the building of temples.

TUSCANY was not only the firft to receive architecture into *Italy*, as a ftranger, from whence the order called Tufcan had its meafures; but alfo the things belonging to the Gods, which the greateft part of the world, led into blind error, adored. She was miftrefs of the neighbouring people, and fhewed what fort of temples, and in what place, and with what ornaments, refpecting the quality of the Gods, they ought to be built; which obfervations, although in many temples one may fee, they have not been confidered, I fhall briefly relate neverthelefs, how they have been left us by writers; that fuch as delight in antiquity, may remain in this part fatisfied, and that the mind of every one may be roufed and inflamed to employ all fuitable care in the building of churches; becaufe it would be a very unfeemly, and a blameable thing, that we, who have the true worfhip, fhould be out-done in this point, by thofe who had no light of truth.

AND, becaufe the places, in which facred temples are to be built, are the firft things that ought to be confidered, I fhall make mention of them in this chapter.

I SAY therefore, that the antient Tufcans directed that the temples dedicated to VENUS, to MARS, and to VULCAN, fhould be made without the city, as to thofe who incited men's minds to lafcivioufnefs, to wars, and to broils; and within the city to thofe that prefided over chaftity, over peace, and good arts; and that to fuch Gods, into whofe care particularly the city might be put; and thofe to JUPITER, JUNO, and to MINERVA, whom they alfo efteemed to be protectors of the city.

TEMPLES fhould be built upon very high places, in the middle of the country, and on a rock. And to PALLAS, to MERCURY, and to ISIS, becaufe they prefided over artificers and merchants, they ufually built temples near the piazza's, and fometimes over the very piazza; to APOLLO, and to BACCHUS near the theatre; to HERCULES near the circus, and the amphitheatre.

THOSE to ÆSCULAPIUS, to HEALTH, and to thofe Gods by whofe medicines they thought men recovered their health, they built in places extreamly healthy, and near wholefom waters; that by coming from a bad and a peftilential air, to a good wholefome one, and by drinking thofe waters, the infirm might the fooner, and with lefs difficulty, be cured, whereby a zeal for religion might be encreafed.

AND, to the reft of the other Gods, they likewife thought it neceffary to find places to build their temples, purfuant to the properties that they attributed to them, and to the manner of their facrifices. But we, who are by the fpecial grace of God freed from that darknefs, having departed from their vain, and falfe fuperftition, fhall chufe thofe fites

for

for temples, that fhall be in the moft noble, and moft celebrated part of the city, far from difhonoured places, and on beautiful and ornamented piazza's, in which many ftreets finifh, whereby every part of the temple may be feen with its dignity, and afford devotion and admiration to whomever fees and beholds it. And if in the city there be hills, the higheft part of them is to be chofen ; but in cafe there be no elevated places, the floor of the temple is to be raifed, as much as is convenient, above the reft of the city. One is befides to afcend to the temple by fteps; fince the afcent alone to a temple is what affords greater devotion and majefty.

THE fronts of temples muft be made to face the greateft part of the city, that religion may feem to be placed as the fafe-guard and protectrix of the citizens.

BUT if temples are built without the city, then their fronts muft be made to face the publick ftreets, or the rivers, if they are built near them; that paffengers may fee them, and make their falutations and reverences before the front of the temple.

C H A P. II.

Of the forms of TEMPLES, *and of the decorum to be obferved in them.*

TEMPLES are made round, quadrangular, of fix, eight, and more fides; all which terminate in the capacity of a circle, in the form of a crofs, and of many other forms and figures, according to the various inventions of men, which, when they are done with beautiful and fuitable proportions, and diftinguifhed by elegant and ornamented architecture, they deferve to be praifed. But the moft beautiful, and moft regular forms, and from which the others receive their meafures, are the round, and the quadrangular ; and therefore VITRUVIUS only mentions thefe two, and fhews us how they are to be comparted, as fhall be inferted when the compartment of temples comes to be treated of. In temples that are not round, one ought carefully to obferve, that all the angles be equal, let the temple be of four, of fix, or of more fides and angles.

THE antients had a regard to what was fuitable to every one of their gods ; not only in the choice of the places in which they were to build temples, as has been faid before ; but alfo in the choice of the form. Hence to the fun, and moon, becaufe they continually revolve round the world, and by their revolution produce effects manifeft to every body, they made temples of a round form, or at leaft fuch as came near to roundnefs; and thus alfo to VESTA, which they faid was goddefs of the earth, which we know is a round body.

To JUPITER, as patron of the air, and of the heavens, they made temples uncovered in the middle, with portico's round them, as I fhall hereafter obferve. In the ornaments alfo, they had very great confideration to what God they built : therefore to MINERVA, to MARS, and to HERCULES, they made the temples of Dorick work ; becaufe to the Gods of the foldiery, of which they were made prefidents, they faid fabricks without delicacy and neatnefs were moft fuitable.

To VENUS, to FLORA, to the Mufes, to the Nymphs, and to the more delicate goddeffes, they faid temples ought to be made that were fuitable to the blooming and tender virgin age : hence they gave the Corinthian work to them ; it appearing to them, that delicate and blooming works, ornamented with leaves, and with voluta's, were more fuitable to that age.

BUT to JUNO, to DIANA, to BACCHUS, and to other gods, whom neither the gravity of the firft, nor the delicacy of the fecond, feemed to fuit, they affigned Ionick works, which between the Dorick and Corinthian hold the middle place.

THUS we read, that the antients in building their temples endeavoured to obferve the decorum, in which confifts the moft beautiful part of architecture. And therefore we alfo, that have no falfe gods, in order to obferve the decorum concerning the form of temples, muft chufe the moft perfect, and moft excellent. And fince the round one is fuch, becaufe it is the only one amongft all the figures that is fimple, uniform, equal, ftrong, and capacious, let us make our temples round. For which purpofes this figure is particularly fit, becaufe it being inclofed by one termination only, in which is to be found neither beginning nor end, nor are they to be

Y   diftinguifhed

diftinguifhed one from the other; but having its parts fimilar one to another, and all participating of the figure of the whole; in a word the extream being found in all its parts, equally diftant from the middle, it is exceeding proper to demonftrate the infinite effence, the uniformity, and the juftice of God.

BESIDES which, it cannot be denied, but that ftrength and perpetuity, is more fought after in churches, than in all other fabricks; fince they are dedicated to the omnipotent and fupream God; and that in them are preferved the moft celebrated and moft memorable things of the city. Hence, and for this reafon alfo, it ought to be faid, that the round figure, in which there is never an angle, is particularly fuited to temples.

TEMPLES ought alfo to be very capacious, that many people may there be able to affift at divine fervice. And among all the figures that are terminated by an equal circumference, none is more capacious than the round. Thofe churches alfo are very laudable, that are made in the form of a crofs, which have their entrance in the part that reprefenting the foot of the crofs, and oppofite to which fhould be the principal altar, and the choir; and in the two branches, that are extended from either fide like arms, two other entrances, or two other altars; becaufe that being fafhioned in the form of the crofs, they reprefent to the eyes of the beholders that wood from which depended our falvation. And of this form, I have made the church of *San. Giorgio Maggiore* at *Venice*.

TEMPLES ought to have ample portico's, and with larger columns than other fabricks require; and it is proper that they fhould be great and magnificent (but yet not greater than the bignefs of the city requires) and built with large and beautiful proportions. Whereas, for divine worfhip, in which all magnificence and grandeur is required, they ought to be made with the moft beautiful orders of columns, and to each order ought to be given its proper and fuitable ornaments. They muft be made of the moft excellent, and of the moft precious matter; that the divinity may be honoured as much as poffible, both as well with the form, as matter: and if it were poffible, they ought to be fo made, that they might have fo much beauty, that nothing more beautiful could be imagined; and fo difpofed in each of their parts, that thofe who enter there, may be aftonifhed, and remain in a kind of extafy in admiring their grace and beauty.

OF all the colours, none is more proper for churches than white; fince the purity of colour, as of the life, is particularly grateful to God. But if they are painted, thofe pictures will not be proper, which by their fignification alienate the mind from the contemplation of divine things, becaufe we ought not in temples to depart from gravity, or thofe things, that being looked on render our minds more enflamed for divine fervice, and for good works.

C H A P. III.

Of the afpects of TEMPLES.

BY afpect is underftood the firft view which a temple exhibits to fuch as approach it. The moft regular and the beft underftood afpects of temples are feven, concerning which it feemed to me neceffary to infert here, what VITRUVIUS fays, in the firft chapter of the firft book, that this part, which, by reafon of the little attention paid to antiquity, has been by many reputed difficult, and by few hitherto well underftood, may be made eafy and clear by what I fhall mention of it, and by the defigns that are to follow, which may ferve as an example of what he teaches us. And I thought it proper to make ufe alfo of the names which he does, that they who fhall apply themfelves to the reading of VITRUVIUS, to which I exhort every one, may therein obferve the fame names, to the end that they may not feem to read of different things.

To come therefore to our purpofe, temples are either made with portico's or without: thofe that are made without portico's may have three afpects; the one is named *Antis*, that is, fronted with pilafters, becaufe the pilafters are called *Ante*, which are made in the angles or corners of the fabricks. Of the other two, the one is called *Proftilos*, that is, fronted with columns; and the other *Amphiproftilos*. That which is called in *Antis*, muft have two pilafters in the corners, that turn alfo on the fides of the temples, and in the middle of the front, between the faid pilafters, two columns, muft project forward, and fupport the frontifpiece that fhall be over the entrance. The other, which is called *Proftilos*, muft have more than the firft, alfo columns in the corners oppofite to the pilafters, and on the right and left in turning the corner, two other columns, that is, one on a fide. But if in the part backwards the fame difpofition of columns is obferved, and the frontifpiece, then the afpect muft be called *Amphiproftilos*.

Of the two firft afpects of temples there are not in our days any remains, and therefore there fhall be no examples of them in this book; neither did it feem to me neceffary to make defigns of them, the afpects of each of thefe being delineated in the plan, and the upright in the Commentary upon VITRUVIUS by Monfignor Reverendiffimo BARBARO.

But if portico's are made to temples, they are either to be made round the temple, or in the front only. Thofe that have portico's in the fore front only, it may be faid alfo that they have the afpect called *Proftilos*. Thofe that are made with portico's round tham, may be made with four afpects; becaufe they either may be made with fix columns in the front and in that backwards, and with eleven columns on each fide, computing thofe in the angles; and this afpect is called *Peripteros*, that is, winged round, and the portico's round the cell come to be as broad as an intercolumniation.

Antient temples are to be feen, that have fix columns in the front, and have no portico's round them notwithftanding; but in the walls of the cell, in the part without, there are half columns, which accompany thofe of the portico, and have the fame ornaments; as at *Nifmes* in *Provence*. Of this fort alfo it may be faid, that the temple of the Ionick order in *Rome* is, now the church of *Santa Maria Egittiaca*. Thefe thefe architects made to make the cell larger, and to avoid expence; the fame afpect of the alato round it remaining neverthelefs to thofe who faw the temple in flank. Or if to temples eight columns be put in the front, and fifteen on the fides, with the angular ones; thefe come to have double portico's round them, and therefore their afpect is called *Dipteros*, that is, double winged.

Temples may alfo be made, which have like the abovefaid, eight columns in front, and fifteen on the fides; but the portico's round them are not made double, becaufe one order of columns is taken away. Hence thefe portico's come to be as broad as two intercolumniations, and the thicknefs of a column, and their afpect is called *Pfeudodipteros*, that is, falfe winged round. This afpect was the invention of HERMOGENES, a very antient architect, who in this manner made the portico's round the temples broad and convenient, to take off the expence and labour, without taking any thing from the afpect. Or, finally, they are fo made, that in each front there be ten columns, and the portico's round them double, as in thofe that have the afpect *Dipteros*.

These temples had in the part within, other portico's with two orders of columns, one above the other, and thefe columns were lefs than thofe without. The roof came from the columns without to thofe within, and the whole fpace incompaffed by the columns within was uncovered. Hence the afpects of thefe temples was called *Hipethros*, that is, uncovered.

These temples were dedicated to JUPITER, as patron of heaven, and of the air. And in the middle of the court the altar was placed. Of this fort I believe the temple was, of which fome fmall veftigia are to be feen upon *Monte Cavallo* at *Rome*; and that it was dedicated to JUPITER QUIRINALIS, and built by the emperors: becaufe in VITRUVIUS's time (as he fays) there was none.

CHAP. IV.

Of the five kinds of TEMPLES.

THE antients ufed (as has been before faid) to make portico's to their temples, for the conveniency of the people, that they might have where to entertain one another, and to walk in without the cell, in which the facrifices were offered, and to give greater majefty and grandeur to thofe fabricks. Hence, becaufe the intervals that are between one column and the other, may be made of five fizes, according to thefe five kinds or manners of temples, that VITRUVIUS diftinguifhes: the names of which are *Picnoftilos*, that is, thick

with

with columns; *Siftilos*, wider; *Diaftilos*, ftill wider; *Areoftilos*, wider than is convenient; and *Euftilos*, which has reafonable and convenient intervals: of all which intercolumniations, how they be, and what proportions they ought to have, with the length of the columns, has been mentioned before in the firft book, and the defigns of them inferted.

It is not neceffary therefore to fay here any thing more, than that the four firft manners are defective. The two firft, becaufe the intercolumniations being but of one diameter and an half, or of two diameters of a column, are very little and narrow, (hence two perfons a breaft cannot enter into the portico's, but are obliged to go one behind the other,) and becaufe the doors and their ornaments cannot be feen at a diftance: and, finally, becaufe that by the ftraitnefs of the fpaces, walking round the temple is hindred. Thefe two manners are neverthelefs tolerable when the columns are made large, as may be feen in almoft all the antient temples.

The third, as three diameters of a column can be put between the columns, the intercolumniations come to be very wide: hence the architraves fplit, by reafon of the greatnefs of the fpaces. But one may provide againft this defect, by making over the architrave, in the height of the frize, arches, or *remenati*, that fupport the weight, and leave the architrave free.

The fourth manner, although not fubject to the defect of the abovementioned, becaufe architraves of ftone, or of marble, are not made ufe of, but that over the columns beams of timber are put; one may neverthelefs fay that it is alfo defective, becaufe it is low, and wide, and mean, and is properly of the Tufcan order; fo that the moft beautiful and the moft elegant manner of temples is that which is called Euftilos, which is when the intercolumniations are of two diameters and a quarter of a column; becaufe it ferves exceedingly well for ufe, beauty and ftrength.

I have called the manners of temples by the fame names that Vitruvius makes ufe of, as I have alfo the afpects, not only for the abovementioned reafon, but alfo becaufe thofe names have already been received in our language, and that they are underftood by every body, I fhall therefore make ufe of them in the defigns of the temples that fhall follow.

C H A P. V.

Of the Compartments of Temples.

ALTHOUGH in all fabricks it is requifite, that their parts fhould correfpond together, and have fuch proportions, that there may be none whereby the whole cannot be meafured, and likewife all the other parts; this however ought to be obferved in temples with the utmoft care, becaufe they are confecrated to divinity, for the honour and reverence whereof one ought to work as beautifully and exquifitely as is poffible. As therefore the round and quadrangular are the moft regular forms for temples, I fhall mention how each of thefe ought to be comparted; and fhall alfo infert fome things belonging to temples that we Chriftians make ufe of.

Round temples were antiently made, fometimes open, that is, without a cell, with columns that fupported the cupola, like thofe that were dedicated to Juno Lacinia; in the middle of which the altar was placed, and upon which the fire was never extinguifhed. Thefe are comparted in this manner: the diameter of the whole fpace is fo divided, that the temple is to take up three equal parts; one is given to the fteps, that is, to the afcent to the floor of the temple, and two remain to the temple and the columns, which are placed upon pedeftals, and are as high with the bafe and capital, as the diameter of the leffer courfe of fteps, and the tenth part of their height in thicknefs.

The architrave, the frize, and the other ornaments, are to be made as well in this, as in all the other temples, according to what was faid in the firft book. But thofe that are made clofe; that is, with a cell, are either made with wings round them, or with one portico only in the front. Of thofe that have wings round them, the rules are thefe; in the firft place, two fteps are to be made round them, and upon them the pedeftals are to be placed, on which the columns ftand; the wings are as broad as the fifth

I   part

part of the diameter of the temple, taking the diameter in the part within the pedeſtals. The columns are as long as the cell is broad, and are the tenth part of their length in thickneſs.

THE tribuna, or cupola, muſt be raiſed above the architrave, frize, and cornice of the wings, one half of the whole work. Thus VITRUVIUS comparts the round temples.

IN antient temples however there are no pedeſtals to be ſeen, but the columns begin from the floor of the temple: which pleaſes me much better, not only becauſe the pedeſtal ob-ſtructs the entrance very much; as alſo becauſe the columns, which begin from the ground, add more grandeur and magnificence. But if in round temples the portico is to be placed in the front only, then it muſt be made as long as the breadth of the cell, or an eighth part leſs, and may alſo be made ſhorter; but yet it muſt not be ſhorter than three quar-ters of the breadth of the temple, nor muſt it be made wider than the third part of its length.

IN quadrangular temples the portico's in the front muſt be made as long as the breadth of theſe temples. And if they are to be after the manner Euſtilos, which is both beautiful and elegant, then they are to be thus comparted. If the aſpect is to be made with four columns, all the front of the temple (excepting the projection of the baſes of the columns, which are in the angles) muſt be divided into eleven parts and an half, and one of theſe parts ſhall be called a module, that is, a meaſure, with which all the other parts muſt be meaſured; becauſe that by making the columns a module in thickneſs, four muſt be given to them, three to the intercolumniations in the middle, and four and a half to the other two intercolumniations, that is, two and a quarter each. If the front is to be of ſix co-lumns, then it muſt be divided into eighteen parts; if of eight, into twenty four and an half; and if of ten, into thirty one: always giving of theſe parts one to the thickneſs of the columns, three to the void in the middle, and two and a quarter to each of the other voids. The height of the columns muſt be according to what they ſhall be, whether Ionick or Corinthian.

How the aſpects of the other manners of temples ought to be regulated, that is, of Picnoſtilos, Siſtilos, Diaſtilos, and Arcoſtilos, has been fully ſet down in the firſt book, when we treated of intercolumniations.

BEYOND the portico one finds the anti-temple, and then the cell. The breadth is divided into four parts; eight of which are given to the length of the temple, and five of theſe eight are given to the length of the cell, including the walls, in which are the doors; and the other three remaining are for the anti-temple, which has on the ſides two wings of wall, con-tinued to the walls of the cell, in the ends of which are made two anti, that is, two pila-ſters as thick as the columns of the portico. And becauſe it may happen that between theſe wings there may be, either little or much ſpace, if the breadth be greater than twenty foot, between the ſaid pilaſters two columns may be put, and more alſo according as neceſſity ſhall require, directly oppoſite to the columns of the portico; the uſe of which will be to ſeparate the anti-temple from the portico; and thoſe three or more voids, which ſhall be be-tween the pilaſters, muſt be cloſed up with wood, or with marble parapets, leaving however the openings through which one may enter into the anti-temple. If the breadth be more than forty foot, other columns muſt be put in the part within, oppoſite to them, that ſhall have been put between the pilaſters, and muſt be made of the ſame height of thoſe with-out, but ſomewhat ſmaller, becauſe the open air will leſſen the thickneſs of thoſe without, and the incloſed will not permit the ſmallneſs to be diſcerned of thoſe within, and ſo they will appear equal.

AND altho' the ſaid compartment anſwers exactly in temples of four columns, the ſame proportion and manner neverthelefs do not ſuit the other aſpects; becauſe it is neceſſary that the walls of the cell ſhould meet with the columns without, and be in a line. Hence the cells of theſe temples will be ſomewhat larger than what has been mentioned.

THUS the antients comparted their temples, as VITRUVIUS teacheth us, and were willing that a portico ſhould be made, under which in bad weather men might avoid the ſun, the rain, the hail, and the ſnow; and on ſolemn days be amuſed until the hour of ſacrifice came on: but we, by omiting the portico's round the temples, build them very like baſi-lica's, in which, as it has been ſaid, portico's were made in the part within, as we now do in temples. Which happened, becauſe the firſt who, enlightned by truth, gave themſelves up to our religion, were accuſtomed, for fear of the Gentiles, to aſſemble in the baſilica's of

Z   private

private men: whence feeing that this form fucceeded very well, becaufe the altar was placed, with great dignity, in the place of the tribunal, and the choir ftood very conveniently round the altar, and the remaining part was free for the people, it has not been altered fince. And therefore in the compartment of the wings that we make in temples, what has been faid, when we treated of bafilica's, muft be obferved.

To our churches is joined a place feparate from the remainder of the temple, which we call the facrifty; where are kept the facerdotal veftments, the veffels, the facred books, and the other things neceffary for divine fervice, and here the priefts drefs themfelves. Near to it are towers built, in which bells are hung to call the people to the divine offices, which are not made ufe of by any but chriftians. Near the temple the habitations for the priefts are made; which ought to be commodious, with fpacious cloifters, and fine gardens; and particularly the places for the facred virgins ought to be fecure, high, remote from noife, and from the fight of the people.

It is fufficient to have faid thus much concerning the decorum, the afpects, the manners, and the compartments of temples, I fhall infert now the defigns of many ancient temples, in which I fhall obferve this order. Firft, I fhall put the defigns of the temples that are at *Rome*; afterwards thofe that are out of *Rome*, in other parts of *Italy*; laftly, thofe that are out of *Italy*. And for the fake of being better underftood, and to avoid being tedious, and fatiguing to the readers, was I minutely to mention the meafures of every part, I have marked them all with figures in the defigns.

The *Vicentine* foot, with which all the following temples have been meafured, is in the fecond book, Page 39.

The whole foot is divided into twelve inches, and each inch into four minutes.

C H A P. VI.

Of the defigns of fome ancient Temples *that are at* Rome; *and, firft, of that of* Peace.

WE fhall, for the fake of good omen, begin with the defigns of the temple formerly dedicated to Peace, of which the veftigia are to be feen near the church of *Santa Maria Nuova*, in the *Via Sacra*: and writers fay, that it is in the fame place where the *Curia* of Romulus, and *Hoftilia* was firft; then the houfe of Menius, the *Bafilica Portia*, and the houfe of Cæsar, and the portico that Augustus (after pulling down the faid houfe of Cæsar, which he thought too large and fumptuous an edifice) built, calling it after the name of Livia Drusilla his wife.

This temple was begun by the emperor Claudius, and finifhed by Vespasian after he returned victorious from *Judea*, in which he preferved all the veffels, and ornaments (which he carried in his triumph) of the temple of *Jerufalem*. One reads, that this temple was the greateft, the moft magnificent, and the richeft of the city; and certainly its veftigia, ruinous as they are, reprefent fo much grandeur, that one may very well judge what it was when whole.

Before the entrance there was a loggia of three fpaces, made of brick; and the remainder was a continued wall equal to the breadth of the front. In the pilafters of the arches of the loggia in the part without, there were columns placed for ornament, the order of which followed alfo in the wall continued. Over this firft loggia there was another uncovered, with its poggio; and directly over each column there muft have been a ftatue. In the part within the temple there were eight marble columns of the Corinthian order, five foot four inches thick, and fifty three foot long, with the bafe and capital. The architrave, the frize, and the cornice were ten foot and an half, and fupported the vault of the middle nave. The bafe of thefe columns was higher than half the diameter of the column, and had the orlo thicker than the third part of its height; which they perhaps thus made, fuppofing that it thus would fupport the weight that was put upon them the better. Its projection was the fixth part diameter of the column. The architrave, the frize, and the cornice, were carved with very beautiful inventions. The cimacium of the architrave is worthy of attention, being different from the others, and very gracefully made. The cornice has mogdilions inftead of a goccio-
latio.

latio. The cafes of the rofes that are between the mogdilions are fquare; and they ought fo to be made, as I have obferved they are in all the ancient edifices.

Writers fay that this temple was burnt in the time of the emperor Commodus; but I can't fee how that can be fo, there not being the leaft in it wood. But it might eafily happen that it has been ruined by earthquakes, or fome other fuch accident, and afterwards reftored at fome other time, when what related to architecture was not fo well underftood as it was in the time of Vespasian. What makes me believe this, is becaufe the fculptures are not fo well made, or worked with that diligence that one obferves in thofe which are in the arch of Titus, and of other edifices that were made in good times. The walls of this temple were adorned with ftatues, and with pictures, and all the vaults were made with a compartment of ftucco, neither was there any part but what was highly adorned. Of this temple I have made three draughts.

In the firft the plan is defigned. Plate 1.

In the fecond the upright of the outward part, of the part within, of the front, and of the inward part of the flank. Plate 2.

In the third are the particular members. Plate 3.

A, *the bafe*
B, *the capital*   } *of the columns that fupport the middle nave.*
C, *architrave, frize and cornice* }
D, *the compartment of ftucco made in the vaults.*

C H A P. VII.

Of the temple of Mars, *the* Avenger.

NEAR the tower of the *Conti's* the ruins are to be feen of the temple built formerly by Augustus to Mars the *Avenger*, to fulfil a vow he made, (when being together with Mark Antony at *Pharfalia*, againft Brutus and Cassius) to revenge the death of Cæsar, he engaged and overcame them.

By thofe parts that remain, one comprehends that this was a moft adorned and marvellous edifice; and the forum that was before it muft have made it much more admirable, into which, one reads, thofe that returned into the city, conquerors and triumphant, carried the enfigns of the triumph and victory; and that Augustus, in its moft beautiful part placed two pictures, in which were reprefented the manner of giving battle, and triumphing; and two other pictures done by the hand of Apelles, in one of which there were Castor and Pollux, the goddefs of Victory, and Alexander the great; in the other a reprefentation of a battle, and an Alexander. There were two portico's, in which Augustus dedicated the ftatues of all thofe who returned triumphant to *Rome*.

Of this forum there are not any veftiges to be feen, unlefs thofe wings of wall, which are on the fides of the temple, fhould perhaps be part of it; which is very likely, from the many places for ftatues that are therein.

The afpect of the temple is *alato a torno*, which we before have called, from Vitruvius, *peripteros*. And becaufe the breadth of the cell exceeds twenty foot, and there are columns placed between the two anti, or pilafters of the anti-temple oppofite to thofe of the portico, as has been before faid ought to be done in the like cafe, the portico is not continued round the temple: and alfo in the wings of the walls joined from one fide to the other, the fame order is not obferved in the part without, although all the parts correfpond within. Hence one comprehends, that behind, and on one fide, there muft have been the publick ftreet; and that Augustus was willing to accommodate himfelf to the fite, not to incommode, nor take away the neighbouring houfes from their owners.

The manner of this temple is the picnoftilos. The portico's are as large as the intercolumniations. In the part within, that is, in the cell, there is not the leaft mark or veftigium to be feen, neither is there any thing in the wall, whence it may pofitively be faid that there were either ornaments or tabernacles; however, as it is very likely that fome there were,

were, I have made them of my own invention.   The columns of the portico's are of Corinthian work.   The capitals are wrought in the manner of olive leaves.   They have the abaco much larger than what is ufually feen in others of the fame order, regarding the bignefs of the whole capital.   The firft leaves may be feen to fwell a little in the place where they come forth, which gives them a good grace.   Thefe have very beautiful foffits, or what we call cielings, therefore I have made their profile and their afpect in a plan.   Round this temple there were very high walls of peperino, which in the part without were of Ruftick work; and in that within, they had many tabernacles, and places to place ftatues in.

AND that the whole might be perfectly feen, I have made feven plates of it.

Plate 4.   IN the firft there is all the plan in a fmall form; and all the elevation of as much as is to be feen of this edifice, as well in the part without, as in that within.

Plate 5.   IN the fecond there is the upright of the flank of the portico, and of the cell.

Plate 7.   IN the third there is the upright of half the front, with part of the walls that are on the fides of the temple.

Plate 6.   IN the fourth there is the upright of the inward part of the portico, and of the cell, with the ornaments which I have added to it.

Plate 9.   IN the fifth are the ornaments of the portico.

G, *the capital.*
H, *the architrave, frize and cornice.*
I, *the cielings of the portico, that is, the foffits.*

Plate 8.   IN the fixth, is defigned the foffit of the portico, and how it turns in the anti, or pilafters of the anti-temple.

M, *the foffit of the architrave between the columns.*

Plate 10.   IN the feventh are the other members.

A, *the bafe of the columns of the portico, which alfo continues in the wall round the temple.*
B, *the cauriola, from which begin the divifions of the fquares made for an ornament in the wall under the portico's.*
C, *the plan of the columns placed for the ornament of the tabernacles in the cell.*
D, *the bafe.*
E, *is the capital.*

WHICH ornaments in the infide have been added by me, taken from fome antient fragments found near this temple.

F, *is the cornice that is feen in the wings of the walls, that form a piazza on the fides of the temple.*

CHAP. VIII.

Of the temple of NERVA TRAJANUS.

NEAR the faid temple built by AUGUSTUS, the veftigia are to be feen of the temple of NERVA TRAJANUS, the afpect of which is the proftilos; its manner is thick of columns.   The portico, together with the cell, is in length fomewhat lefs than two fquares.

THE floor of this temple is raifed from the ground with a bafement that goes round the whole fabrick, and forms the fides of the ftairs by which one afcends to the portico.   In

the

Plate I.

P 4 2

P 7 0 6 10

P 4 3 ¼

P 4 3 ¼

P 6 2 ½

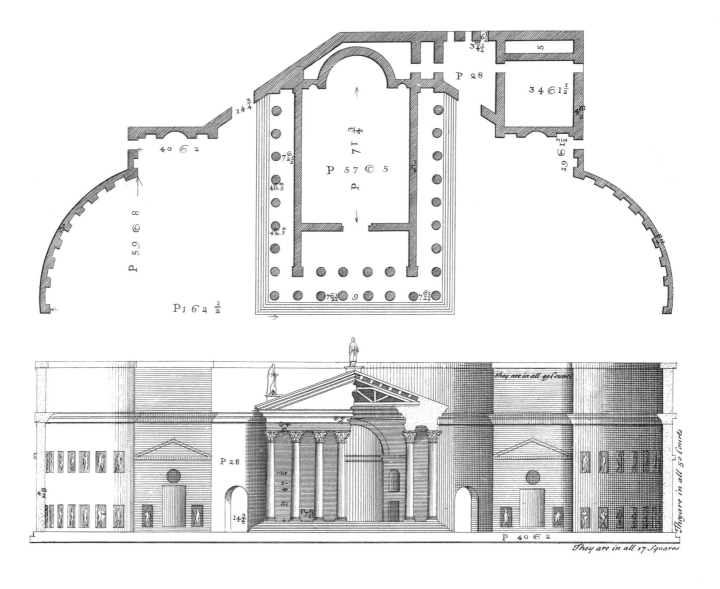

P 28

3 4 6 1¾

P 59 ⓒ 8

40 6 2

14¾

7 6¼

4 m 4 16 3

P 57 ⓒ 5

P 57 71¾

P 28

3 4 6 1¾

19 6 1½

P 1 6 2 ½

7 6¼ 9 7 2½

P 28

14¾

P 40 6 2

They are in all 17 Squares

Square in all 50 Courts

P4CII P 76 2½

P · 17 $\frac{3}{4}$

P 10

P 4 8

P · 8 4

$\frac{1}{2}$

P 6 $\frac{1}{2}$

P 16

P 7 $\frac{1}{2}$

M

P

N

$37\frac{1}{2}$

21

$37\frac{1}{2}$

P 4   6 3 $\frac{1}{4}$

IX.

L

I

P 3 ⊙ 5½ →
P 2 ⊙ 10 →

34 ↗
7
12
28
16
43

H

G

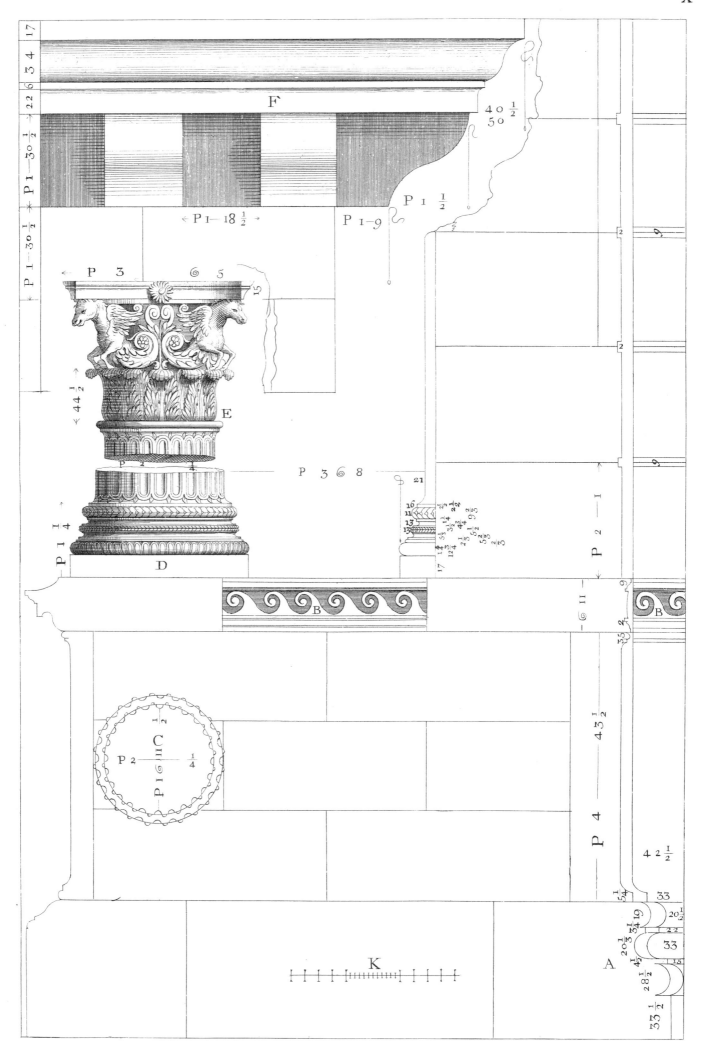

F

P 1 — 30 ½
P 1 — 30 ½
P 1 — 30 ½

17
3 4
2 2 6

P 1 — 18 ½

P 1 — 9

P 1   ½

4 0
5 0   ½

P   3   6   5

15

← 44 ½ →

E

P   2   4

P   3   6   8

D

P 1 ¼ →

P 1 ¼

21

16
11
13
13

14   3 ½   1 ½   2 ½
12 ½   3 ¼   2 ½
2 ½   1   4 ½
2 ½   5 ½   9 ½
5 ½   9 ½
5 ½
2 ½
3

17
12 ½
24

B

9

6 — II

35   2

B

P 2 — I

P 2 ┼ III ┼ ¼

C

P 1 6

P 4

43 ½

9

4 2 ½

5 ¼
5 ¼

33

20 ½
2 2

33

19
20 ⅓
3 ¼
4 ½

20 ⅓
4 ½

28 ½

15

33 ½

A

K

the extream parts of thofe fides there are two ftatues, that is, one on each head of the bafement.

THE bafe of the columns is Attick, different in this from what VITRUVIUS teaches, and from what I have faid in the firft book, that there are in it two tondino's more, the one under the cavetto, and the other under the cimbia.

THE tongues of the capital are carved in the form of olive leaves, and thofe leaves are difpofed by fives, as are the fingers in the hands of men. I have obferved, that all the antient capitals are made in this manner, and fucceed better, and have more grace than thofe in which the faid leaves are made by fours.

IN the architrave are very beautiful carved works, intaglio's, that divide one fafcia from the other; and thefe intaglio's, and thefe divifions are on the fides of the temple only, becaufe the architrave in the front, and the frize were made all even, that the infcription might conveniently be put there; of which thefe few letters are ftill to be feen, although jagged and fpoilt by time.

IMPE ATOR NERVA CAESAR AVG. PONT. MAX.

TRIB. POT. II. IMPERATOR II. PROCOS.

THE cornice is very well carved, and has very beautiful, and very convenient projections. The architrave, the frize, and the cornice are, all together, the fourth part of the length of the columns. The walls are made of peperino, and were coated with marble. In the cell along the wall I have put tabernacles with ftatues, as by the ruins it fhould feem there have been.

BEFORE this temple there was a piazza, in the middle of which the ftatue of the faid emperor was placed: And writers fay, that fo many and fo wonderful were its ornaments, that they aftonifhed thofe that beheld them, as not thinking them the work of men, but of giants.

HENCE the emperor CONSTANTIUS when he came firft to *Rome*, was ftruck with the rare ftructure of this edifice; then turning to his architect, faid, that he would in *Conftantinople* make a horfe like that of NERVA, to his own memory. To whom ORMISIDA anfwered (fo was that architect's name) that it was firft neceffary to make him fuch another ftable, fhewing him this piazza.

THE columns that are round it have no pedeftals, but rife from the ground; and it was very reafonable, that the temple fhould be more eminent than the other parts. Thefe are alfo of Corinthian work. And upon the cornice directly over them there were fmall pilafters, upon which ftatues muft have been placed. Nor muft any body wonder, that I have put fuch a number of ftatues in thefe edifices, becaufe one reads that there were in *Rome* fo many, that they feemed there a fecond people.

OF this edifice I have made fix plates.

IN the firft is half the front of the temple.   Plate 12.

      T, *the entrance that is on the flank of it.*

IN the fecond is the elevation of the part within, and near it is the plan of the temple, Plate 11. and of the piazza together.

      S, *is the place where the ftatue of* TRAJAN *was.*

IN the third is the upright of the flank of the portico; and by the intercolumniations Plate 13. may be feen the orders of the columns that were round the piazza.

IN the fourth there is the half front of the piazza oppofite to the temple.   Plate 14.

IN the fifth are the ornaments of the portico of the temple,   Plate 15.

A a   A, *the*

A, *the bafement of the whole fabrick.*
B, *the bafe.*
C, *the architrave.*
D, *the frize.*

E, *the cornice.*
F, *the foffit of the architrave between the columns.*

Plate 16.   In the fixth are the ornaments that were round the piazza.

G, *the bafe.*
H, *the architrave.*
I, *the frize, which was carved with figures in baffo relievo.*
K, *the cornice.*

L, *the fmall pilafters, upon which ftatues were placed.*
M, *the ornaments of the fquare doors, that were in the front of the piazza, oppofite to the portico of the temple.*

C H A P.   IX.

Of the temple of ANTONINUS *and of* FAUSTINA.

NEAR to the abovementioned temple of PEACE, is to be feen the temple of ANTO-NINUS, and of FAUSTINA. Hence it is the opinion of fome, that ANTONINUS was by the antients placed in the number of their gods, fince he had a temple, and had Salian priefts, and Antonine priefts.

THE front of this temple is made with columns. Its manner is the picnoftilos. The floor or pavement of the temple is raifed from the ground the third part of the height of the columns of the portico; and to that one afcends by fteps, to which the two bafe-ments that continue with their order round the whole temple, make the fides. The bafe of thefe bafements is thicker than half of the cimacia, and is made more plain, and thus I have obferved the antients made all fuch bafements, and alfo in the pedeftals that are placed un-der the columns, with much reafon, fince, all the parts of fabricks the nearer they are to the ground, fo much the more folid they ought to be. In the extream part of thefe, directly over the angular columns of the portico, there were two ftatues, that is, upon each head of the bafement one. The bafe of the columns is Attick. The capital is carved in the man-ner of olive leaves. The architrave, the frize, and the cornice, are the fourth and one third of the faid fourth part of the height of the columns.

IN the architrave are alfo read thefe words:

DIVO ANTONINO ET

DIVAE FAVSTINAE EXS. C.

IN the frize there are grifons carved, which face each other, and put their fore-feet upon candlefticks, after the fame form, as thofe made ufe of in facrifices. The cornice has not a hollow dentello, and is without modiglions; but it has between the dentello, and the gocceiolatio a very large ovolo.

ONE cannot difcover that, in the infide of the temple, there were any ornaments; but I am apt to believe, the magnificence of thofe emperors being confidered, that there muft have been fome, and therefore I have put ftatues.

THIS temple had a court before it, which was made of peperino. In its entrance op-pofite to the portico of the temple, there were very beautiful arches, and every where round it there were columns, and a great many ornaments, of which the leaft veftigium is not at prefent to be feen. Being in *Rome*, I faw a part of it demolifhed, that was then ftanding.

ON the fides of the temple there are two other open entrances, which were without arches. In the middle of this court there was the ftatue of ANTONINUS on horfeback, of bronzo, which is now in the piazza of *Campidoglio*.

I HAVE

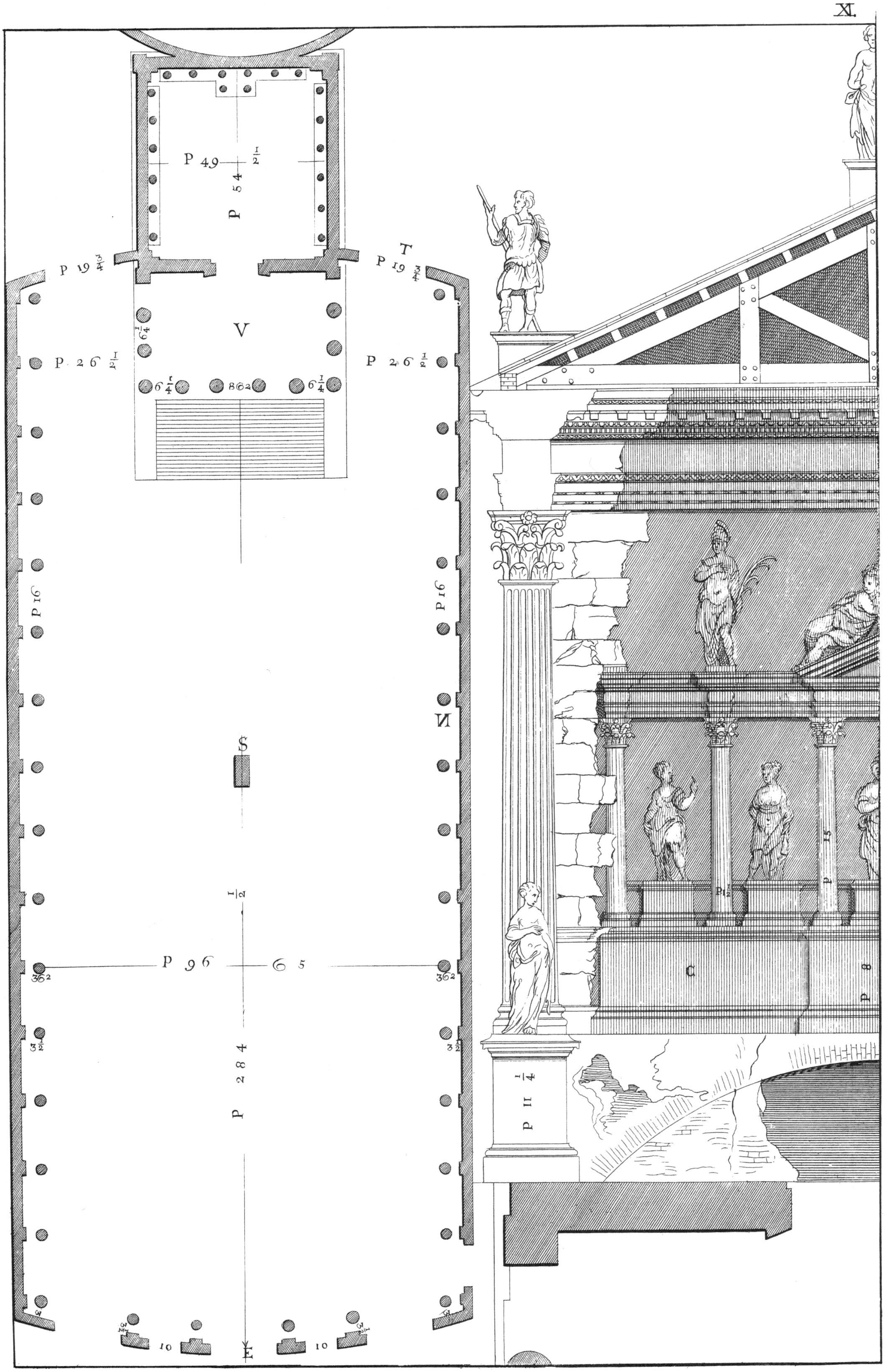

P 49 $\frac{1}{2}$
P 54
P

P 19 $\frac{3}{4}$ T   P 19 $\frac{3}{4}$

P 26 $\frac{1}{2}$ V   P 26 $\frac{1}{2}$

6 $\frac{1}{4}$

6 $\frac{1}{4}$ 862   6 $\frac{1}{4}$

P 16   P 16

N

S

$\frac{1}{2}$

P 96   6 5   36 2

36 2

3 $\frac{1}{2}$ 3 2

P 2 8 4

P 11 $\frac{1}{4}$

C

P 8

P 1$\frac{1}{2}$ P 15

3 $\frac{1}{2}$ 3 $\frac{1}{2}$

10   10

A

P 9 6 4 $\frac{1}{2}$

B P 26 4 $\frac{1}{4}$

P 7 6 6 $\frac{1}{2}$

C P 26 $\frac{1}{2}$

D P 24 $\frac{3}{4}$

P 4 6 3 $\frac{1}{2}$

P 4 9

P 4 6 1   P 6 - 6 $\frac{1}{4}$

$\frac{1}{4}$

P II

P 14

P 29 $\frac{1}{2}$

P 19 $\frac{3}{4}$

T

P 3 2

P 3 $\frac{1}{2}$

P 3 $\frac{1}{4}$

P 3 6 2

P 3 $\frac{1}{4}$

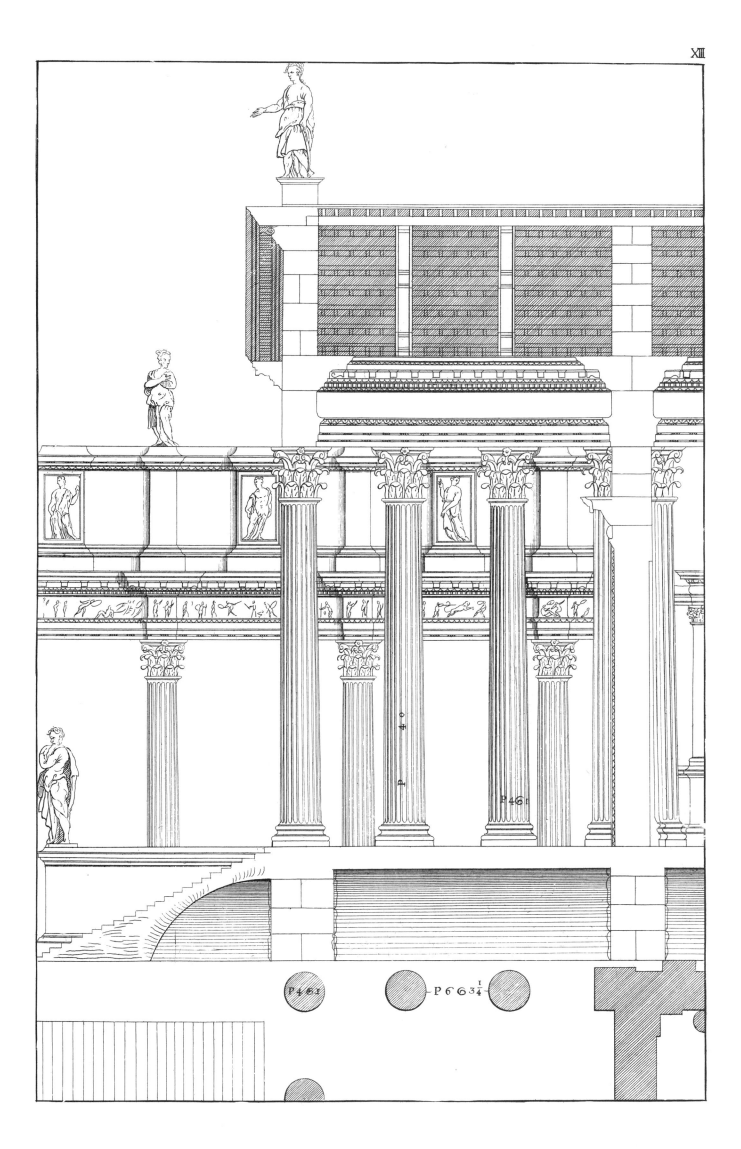

P 46 r

P 46 r   P 6 6 3¼

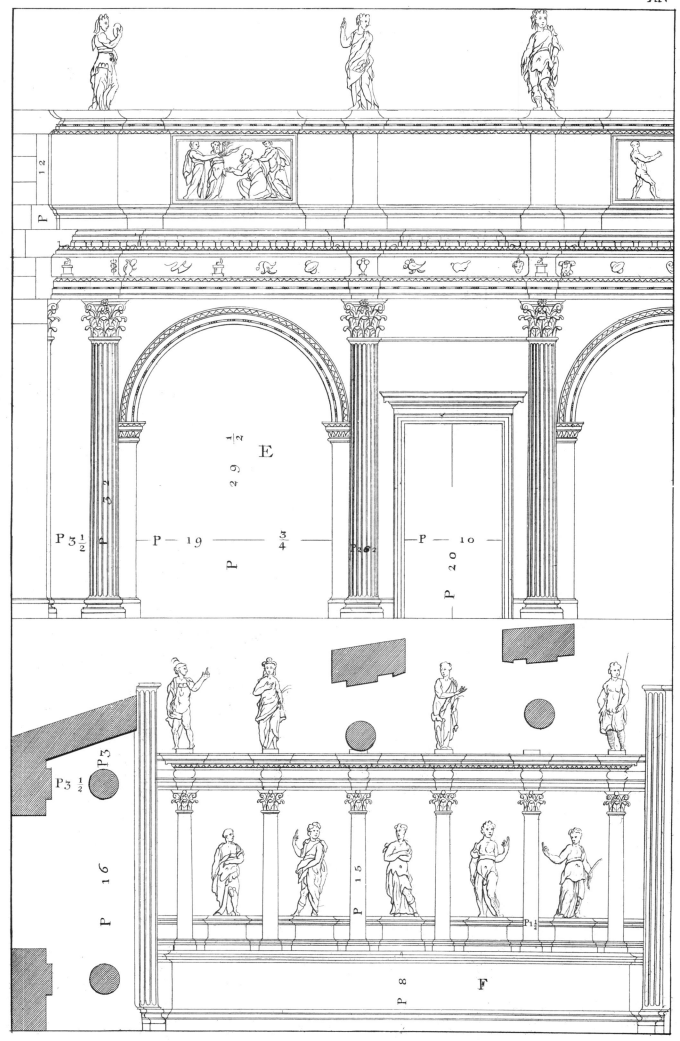

P 1 2

P

$29\frac{1}{2}$

E

P $3\frac{1}{2}$

P 32

P — 19 —

$\frac{3}{4}$

P

P 26 2

P — 10 —

P 20

P 3

P $3\frac{1}{2}$

P 16

P 3

P 15

P $1\frac{1}{2}$

P 8

F

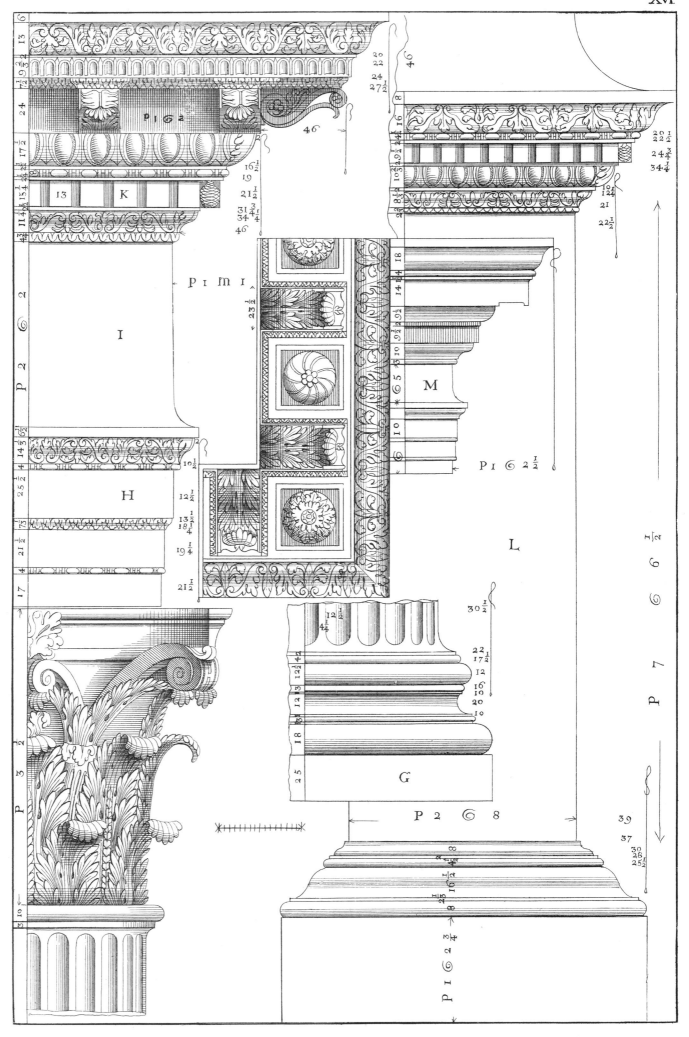

I HAVE made five plates of this temple.

IN the firſt is the elevation of the flank of the outſide. By the intercolumniations Plate 17. of the portico may be ſeen the order of the columns, and the ornaments that were round the court.

IN the ſecond is the upright of half the front of the temple, and of the return of the Plate 19. court.

IN the third is the elevation of the portico, and of the inward part of the cell. Plate 18.

    B, *the wall that divides the portico from the cell.*

ON one ſide of it is deſigned the plan of the temple, and of the court. Plate 20.

    A, *the place where the ſtatue of* ANTONINUS *was*
    Q, *the entrance on the flank of the temple.*
    R, *the entrance oppoſite to the portico of the temple.*

IN the fourth is the elevation of half the entrance that was in the front of the temple. Plate 21.

IN the fifth are the ornaments of the portico of the temple.

A, *the baſement.*	E, *the frize.*
B, *the baſe.*	F, *the dentello, not hollowed.*
C, *the capital.*	G, *a little cornice placed between in the*
D, *the architrave, where the inſcrip-*	*ſides of the temple in the part without.*
tion is.	

CHAP. X.

Of the temple of the SUN *and of the* MOON.

NEAR the arch of TITUS, in the garden of *Santa Maria Nova*, there are two temples to be ſeen, of the ſame form, and with the ſame ornaments; one of which, becauſe it is placed in the eaſt, is thought to have been the temple of the SUN; the other, becauſe it looks towards the weſt, to be that of the MOON.

THESE temples were built, and dedicated by TITUS TATIUS, king of the Romans. They come very near a round form, becauſe they are as broad as they are long; which was done in reſpect of the courſe of the ſaid planets, which is circular round the heavens.

THE loggia's that were before the entrance of theſe temples are all ruined; neither are there any other ornaments to be ſeen, but thoſe that are in the vaults, which have compartments of ſtucco moſt exquiſitely wrought, and of a beautiful invention.

THE walls of theſe temples are very thick, and between one temple and the other on the flank of the great chapels, which are oppoſite to the entrance, the veſtigia are to be ſeen of ſome ſtairs, which muſt have led up to the roof.

I HAVE made the loggia's forwards, and the ornaments within as I have imagined they muſt have been, conſideration being had to that which is ſeen above ground, and that little that it has been poſſible to ſee of the foundations.

I HAVE made two tables of this temple.

IN the firſt are the plans of both, as they are joined together; and one may ſee where the Plate 22. ſtairs were, as was ſaid led up to the roof. Near theſe plans are the elevation of the outward part, and of that within.

IN

Plate 23. IN the fecond are the ornaments, that is, thofe of the vaults, the others being ruined, no veftigia of them are to be feen; and the elevations on the flank.

    A, *the compartments of the chapels that are oppofite to the doors, and are each of them twelve fquares.*
    C, *the profile and facoma of the faid fquares.*
    B, *the compartments of the great nave; it is divided into nine fquares.*
    D, *the profile and modeno of the faid fquares.*

C H A P. XI.

Of the temple vulgarly called the GALLUCE.

NEAR the trophies of MARIUS the following edifice is to be feen, in a round form, which, next to the *Pantheon*, is the greateft round fabrick in *Rome*. They vulgarly call this place the *Galluce*; hence fome have faid, that in that place was the bafilica of CAIUS and of LUCIUS, together with a beautiful portico AUGUSTUS caufed to be made in honour of CAIUS and of LUCIUS his nephews; which I do not believe, becaufe this edifice has not any of thofe parts that are required in bafilica's. How fuch were made, I have mentioned before in the third book, when, according to VITRUVIUS, I divided the places of the piazza's; and therefore I believe that it was a temple.

THIS edifice is all of brick, and muft have been coated with marble; but now it is entirely ftripped. The cell in the middle, which is perfectly round, is divided into ten faces, and in each face it has a chapel hidden in the thicknefs of the walls, excepting in the face where the entrance is. The two cells that are on the fides muft have been very much adorned, becaufe there are many niches to be feen; and it is very likely that there were columns, and other ornaments which accompanying the faid niches, muft have made a very beautiful effect. Thofe who directed the emperor's chapel at *San Pietro*, and of the king of *France*, which have fince been ruined, took example from this edifice; which having members on all its parts, inftead of abutments, is exceeding ftrong, and after fo long a time is ftill ftanding. Of this temple, becaufe (as I have faid) there are not any ornaments to be feen, I have Plate 24. made only one table, in which is the plan and the elevation of the infide.

C H A P. XII.

Of the temple of JUPITER.

UPON *Monte Quirinale*, now called *Monte Cavallo*, behind the houfes of Signori COLONNA, the veftigia are to be feen of the following edifice, which is called the frontifpiece of NERO. Some would have it that there ftood the tower of MÆCENAS, and that from this place NERO, with great delight, faw the city of *Rome* burnt: In which they are very much deceived, becaufe the tower of MÆCENAS was upon *Monte Efquilino*, not very far from the baths of DIOCLESIAN. There have been fome others that have faid, that the houfes of the CORNELII were in this place.

FOR my part, I believe that this was a temple dedicated to JUPITER; becaufe that when I was in *Rome*, I faw them dig where the body of the temple was, and fome Ionick capitals were found, which ferved for the inward part of the temple, and were thofe of the angles of the loggia's; becaufe the part in the middle, in my opinion, was uncovered.

THE afpect of this temple was the falfe-wing'd, called by VITRUVIUS pfeudodipteros. The manner was thick of columns. The columns of the outward portico's were of the Corinthian order. The architrave, the frize, and the cornice, were the fourth part of the height of the columns. The architrave had its cimacium of a very beautiful invention. The frize in the fides was carved with flowered work; but in the front, which is ruined, there muft
have

P 11 9 $\frac{1}{2}$

P

P 6 $\frac{3}{4}$

P 6 6 4

P 4 — 8 ½

P 67

↓

I

664 P 7 664

A

P I — 2 5

R

Q

P

B

P 6 ¾

P 4 ¾

A

P 9 @ 3½

P 10 ¾

P 6 ¼

Q

P 39

P 4 @ 1

P 30

B

P 11 @ 9½

P 5 @ 6½ C

P 8

P 13½

P 3¾

P 20

P 3 ¼

P 5 ¾

P 7 ¾

P 3¼

P — — 27 ¼

P — 1 5

R

P — 3 °

P 6

3

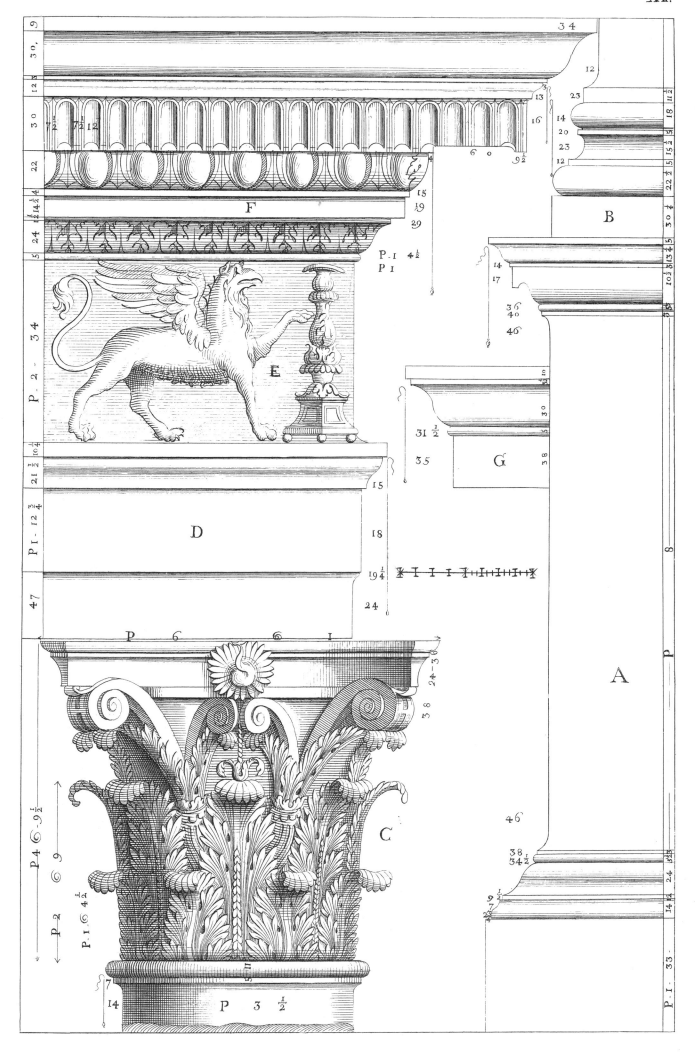

D

B

C

A

A

B

O

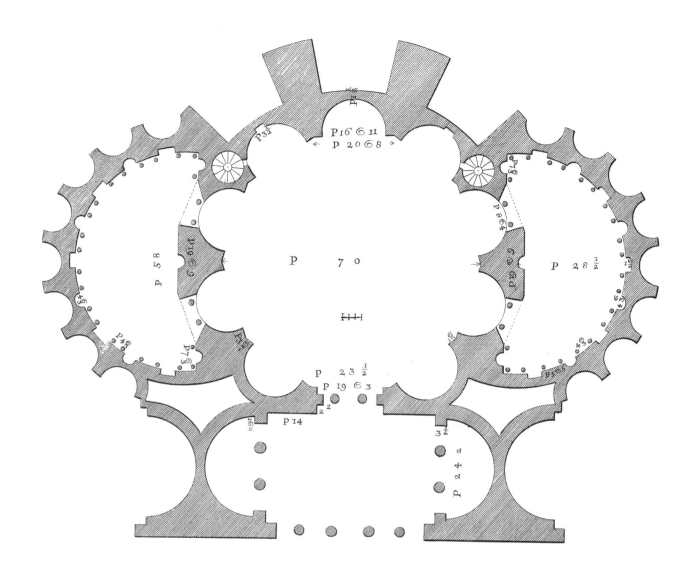

have been the letters of the infcription. The cornice has the modiglions fquared, and one of thefe comes directly over the middle of the column. The modiglions that are in the cornice of the frontifpiece are directly plumb; and fo they ought to be made. In the inward part of the temple there muft have been portico's, as I have defign'd them. Round this temple there was a court, adorned with columns and ftatues; and forwards there were two horfes, which are to be feen in the publick way; from which this mount has taken the name of *Monte Cavallo.* The one of them was made by PRAXITELES, and the other by PHIDIAS. There were very commodious ftairs, that afcended to the temple, and in my opinion this muft have been the greateft and moft adorned temple that was in *Rome.*

I HAVE made fix plates of it.

IN the firft is the plan of the whole edifice, with the back part where the ftairs were, Plate 25. which, afcending one over the other, led to the courts that were on the fides of the temple. The elevation of this manner of ftairs, with the plan, in a large form, has been fet down before in the firft book, where I have treated of the different manners of ftairs.

IN the fecond is the flank of the temple outwardly. Plate 26.

IN the third is half of the outward front of the temple. Plate 28.

IN the fourth is the inward part; and in both thefe plates a fmall part of the ornaments of Plate 27. the courts may be feen.

IN the fifth is the flank of the inward part. Plate 29.

IN the fixth are the ornaments. Plate 30.

A, *The architrave, the frize and the cornice.*
C, *the bafe.*
E, *the capital of the columns of the portico.*

D, *the bafe of the pilafters that anfwer to the columns.*
B, *the cornice that is round the courts.*
F, *the acroteria.*

C H A P. XIII.

Of the temple of FORTUNA VIRILIS.

NEAR the *Pons Senatorius,* now called that of *Santa Maria,* is to be feen, almoft intire, the following temple, and is the church of *Santa Maria Egittiaca.* It is not known for certain how it was called by the ancients. Some fay that it was the temple of *Fortuna Virilis;* of which one reads, as a wonderful thing, that when it was burnt with all that was in it, only the gilded wooden ftatue, that was there, of SERVIUS TULLIUS was found fafe, and in no part damaged by the fire.

BUT becaufe regularly the temples to FORTUNE were made round, fome others have faid, that it was no temple, but the bafilica of C. LUCIUS; grounding this their opinion upon fome letters that have been found there. Which in my judgment cannot be; not only becaufe this edifice is little, and the bafilica's were neceffarily large edifices, by reafon of the great number of people who did bufinefs there; as alfo, becaufe in bafilica's portico's were made in the part within, and in this temple there are not any veftigia of a portico; I therefore believe certainly that it was a temple.

ITS afpect is the proftilos, and has half columns in the walls of the cell in the part without, that accompany thofe of the portico, and have the fame ornaments. Hence to thofe that view it in flank, it affords the afpect of the *alato a torno.* The intercolumniations are of two diameters and a quarter, fo that its manner is the fiftilos. The pavement of the temple is raifed from the ground fix foot and an half, and one afcends to it by fteps, to which the bafements which fupport the whole fabrick form a poggio. The columns are of the Ionick order. The bafe is Attick, although it feems that it ought to have been Ionick, as well as

B b
the

the capital. It is not, however, found in any edifice, that the ancients made ufe of the Ionick, defcribed by VITRUVIUS. The columns are fluted, and have twenty four channels. The voluta's of the capital are oval ; and the capitals that are in the angles of the portico, and of the temple, make a front two ways : which I do not remember to have feen any where elfe. But becaufe it has appeared to me a beautiful and graceful invention, I have made ufe of it in many fabrick's ; and how it is made, will appear in the defign. The ornaments of the door of the temple are very beautiful, and in beautiful proportion. All this temple is made of peperino, and is covered with ftucco.

I HAVE made three plates of it.

Plate 31.   IN the firft is the plan with fome ornaments.

H, *the bafe* 　　　　⎫
I, *the dado* 　　　　⎬ *of the bafements that fupport the whole fabrick.*
K, *the cimacium* 　⎭
L, *the bafe of the columns upon the bafement.*
F, *the ornaments of the door.*
G, *the fcroll of the faid door in front.*

Plate 32.   IN the fecond is the front of the temple.

M, *the architrave, the frize, and the cornice.*
O, *the front* 　　　　　　　⎫
P, *the plan* 　　　　　　　　⎬ *of the capital.*
Q, *the flank* 　　　　　　　⎪
R, *the fhaft without the voluta* ⎭

Plate 33.   IN the third is the flank of the temple.

M, *part of the frize, that goes with thofe carvings round the whole temple.*
S, *the plan of the angular capitals, by which it may eafily be known how they are to be made.*

C H A P. XIV.

Of the temple of V E S T A.

FOLLOWING the bank along the *Tyber*, near the faid temple is found another round temple, which is at prefent called *St. Stefano*. They fay that it was built by NUMA POMPILIUS, and dedicated to the goddefs VESTA ; and he would have it of a round form, in refemblance of the element of the earth, by which human generation is fubfifted, and of which they fay that VESTA was the goddefs.

THIS temple is of the Corinthian order. The intercolumniations are of one diameter and an half. The columns with the bafe and capital, are eleven tefte in length. (By a tefte is underftood the diameter of the foot of the column, as has been faid elfewhere.) The bafes are without zoccolo or dado ; but the ftep whereon they reft, ferves for it, which was done by the architect who ordered it, that the entrance into the portico might be lefs incumbered, the manner being thick of columns.

THE cella, computing alfo the thicknefs of the walls, has as much in diameter as the columns are long.

THE capitals are carved in the manner of olive leaves. The cornice is not to be feen, but it has been added by me in the defign. Under the foffit of the portico there are very beautiful compartments. The door and the windows have very beautiful and plain ornaments. Under the portico, and in the inward part of the temple, there are cimacia's that fupport the windows, and go quite round, affording the afpect of a bafement, upon which the wall is founded, and upon which refts the tribuna. This wall in the outward part,

I   that

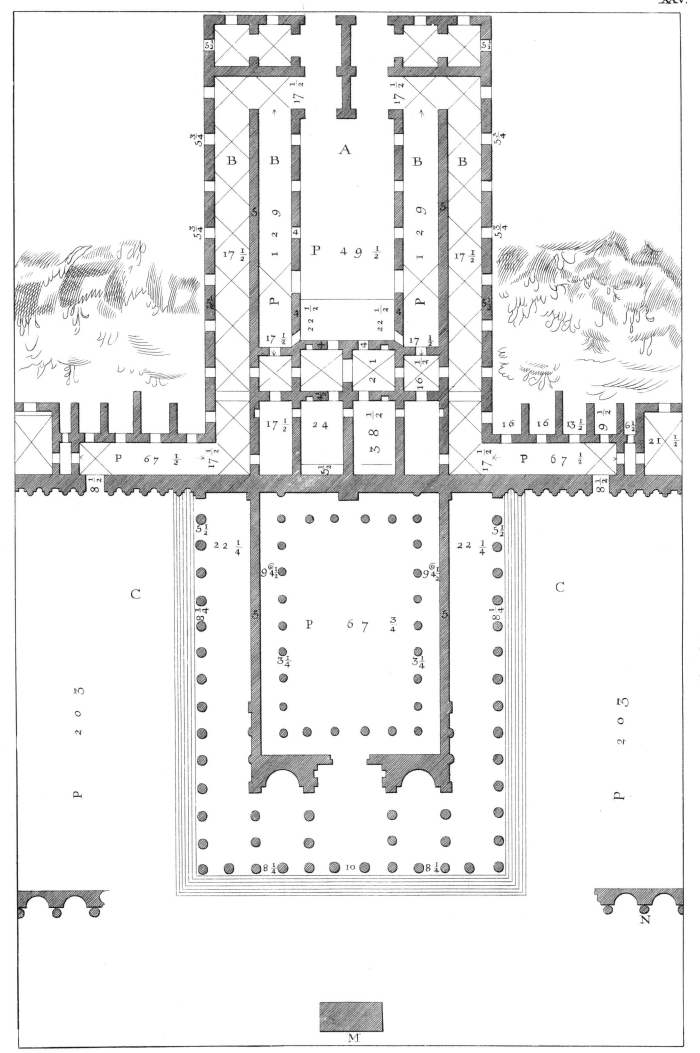

A

B

P 8¼   P 5½

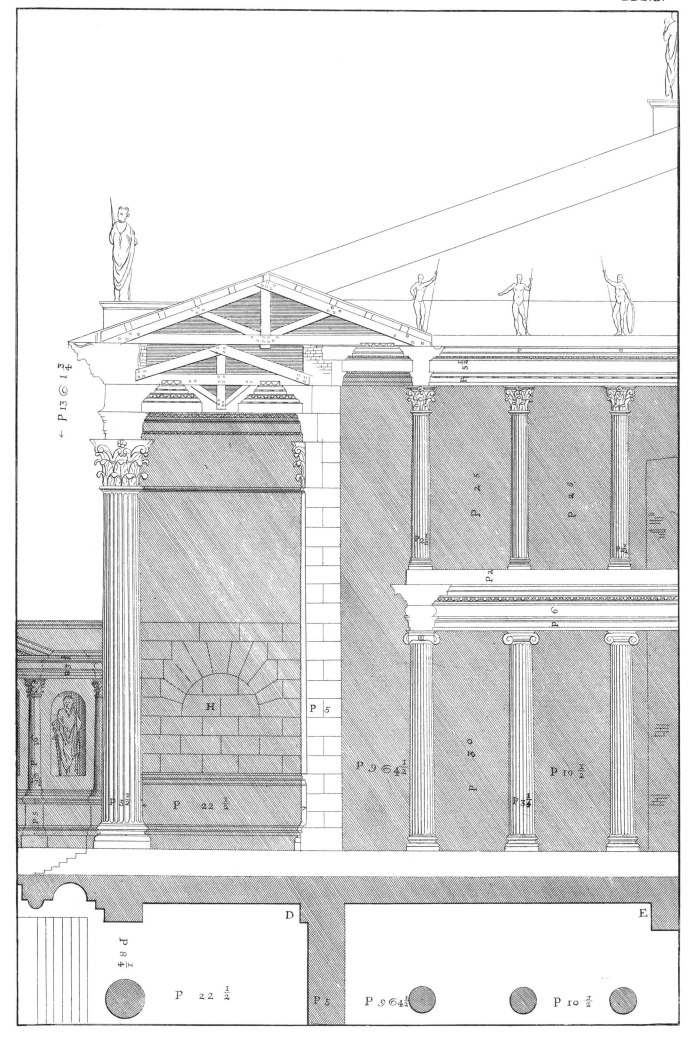

P 13 ☉ 1 3/4

P 5 1/2

P 22 1/2

H

P 5

P 8 1/4

P 9 64 1/2

P 2 5

P 4 5

P 2

6

P

P 5

P 9 64 1/2

P 10 1/2

P 3 1/4

D

E

P 8 1/4

P 22 1/2

P 5

P 9 64 1/2

P 10 1/2

XXX.

A

F

B

E

C

D

G

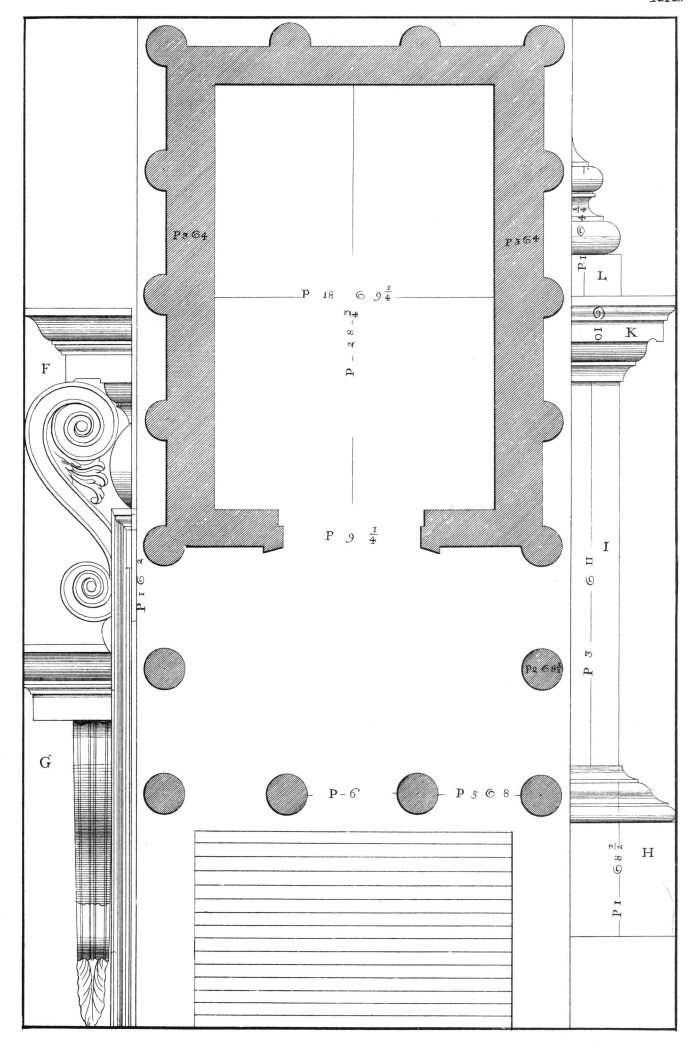

P 8 6 4

P 5 6 4

P 18 6 9 $\frac{1}{4}$

P — 28 — $\frac{3}{4}$

F

P 9 $\frac{1}{4}$

P 16 2

P 4 6 8 $\frac{1}{2}$

G

P — 6

P 5 6 8

P 1 $\frac{1}{4}$ 4

L

P 9 6

10

K

P 3 — 6 11

I

H

P 1 — 6 8 $\frac{1}{2}$

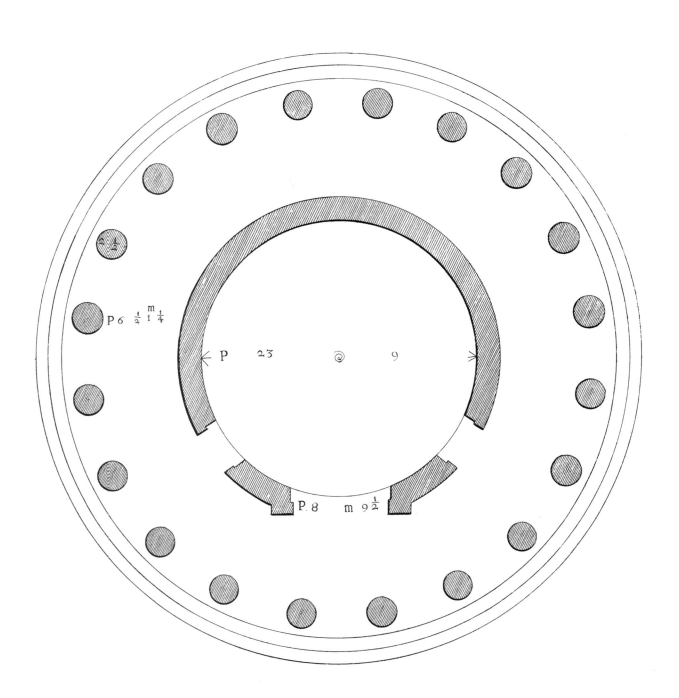

that is, under the portico, is diſtinguiſhed from the cornice by ſquares up to the ſoffit ; and in the inward part it is poliſhed, and has a cornice even with that of the portico's, which ſupport the tribuna.

OF this temple I have made three plates.

IN the firſt is deſigned the plan.   Plate 34.

IN the ſecond the elevation, as well of the part without, as of that within.   Plate 35.

IN the third are the particular members.   Plate 36.

A, *is the baſe of the columns.*
B, *is the capital.*
C, *the architrave, the frize, and the cornice.*
D, *the ornaments of the door.*
E, *the ornaments of the windows.*

F, *the outſide little cornice round the cella, from which the ſquares begin.*
G, *the inward little cornice, upon which is the ſoglio's of the windows.*
H, *the ſoffit of the portico.*

CHAP. XV.

Of the temple of MARS.

AT the *Piazza* vulgarly called *de i Preti,* which is found in going from the *Rotonda* to the column of ANTONINUS, the remains of the following temple are to be ſeen ; which, according to ſome, was built by the Emperor ANTONINUS, and dedicated to the God MARS.

ITS aſpect is the *alato a torno.* The manner is thick of columns.. The intercolumniations are one diameter and an half. The portico's round it are ſo much broader than an intercolumniation, as the projections of the anti project from the remainder of the walls. The columns are of the Corinthian order. The baſe is Attick, and has a baſtoncino under the cimbia of the column. The cimbia, or liſtello, is very ſmall, and ſucceeds thus very graceful. It is made ſo ſmall always when it is joined with a baſtoncino over the torus of the baſe. It is alſo called a baſtone, becauſe there is no danger of its breaking.

THE capital is carved after the manner of olive leaves, and is very well contrived. The architrave, inſtead of an intavolato, has an half ovolo, and over it a cavetto ; and the cavetto has very beautiful intaglio's, and are different from thoſe of the temple of PEACE, and of the temple which we have ſaid was on *Monte Quirinale,* dedicated to JUPITER.

THE frize projects out one eighth part of its height, and is ſwelled in the middle. The cornice has its modiglion ſquare, and over that the gocciolatoio, and has no dentello, which VITRUVIUS ſays ought to be made as often as modiglions are uſed ; that rule, however, is to be ſeen obſerved in very few antient edifices.

OVER the cornice in the ſides of the temple, there is a ſmall cornice, perpendicular to the front of the modiglions, and was made to place ſtatues on, that they might all be entirely ſeen, and that their legs and feet might not be hid by the projection of the cornice.

IN the inward part of the portico there is an architrave of the ſame height of that without, but is different in this, that it has three faſcia's. The members that divide one faſcia from the other are ſmall intavolato's, carved in the manner of ſmall leaves, and archetti, and the leſſer faſcia is alſo carved with leaves. Beſides this, inſtead of an intavolato, it has a fuſaiolo over a gola diritta, worked very delicately in foliage. This architrave ſupports the vaults of the portico's. The architrave, frize, and the cornice, are one of the five parts, and an half, or two elevenths of the length of the columns ; and although they are leſs than a fifth part, they nevertheleſs admirably ſucceed, and with much grace.

THE walls in the outward part are of peperino, and within the temple there are other walls of baked ſtone, that they might be the better able to ſupport the vault, which was made with beautiful ſquares wrought with ſtucco.

THESE walls are coated with marble, and there were niches and columns round them for ornament.

ALMOST a whole flank of this temple is to be ſeen; I have however endeavoured to repreſent it whole, by means of what I could collect from its ruins, and from the doctrine of VITRUVIUS: and therefore have made five plates of it.

Plate 37.   IN the firſt I have deſigned the plan.

Plate 38.   IN the ſecond the elevation of the front forwards.

Plate 39.   IN the third one part of the ſide without.

Plate 40.   IN the fourth one part of the ſide of the portico, and of the temple within.

Plate 41.   IN the fifth are the ornaments of the portico.

A, *the baſe.*
B, *the capital.*
C, *the architrave.*
D, *the frize.*
E, *the cornice.*
F, *the ſmall cornice, upon which the ſta-*
tues were placed.
G, *the ſoffit of the architrave between the columns.*
H, *the architrave in the inward part of the portico, which ſupports the vault.*

C H A P.   XVI.

Of the Baptiſterium of CONSTANTINE.

THE deſigns that follow are of the *Baptiſterium* of CONSTANTINE, which is at *St. Giovanni Laterano.* This temple, in my opinion, is modern work, made of the ruins of antient edifices; but becauſe it is a beautiful invention, and has the ornaments well carv'd, and with various manners of intaglia's, of which an architect may upon ſeveral occaſions make uſe; it appeared to me fit to be placed among the antient, and the rather, becauſe it is by every body eſteemed to be ſo.

THE columns are of porphyry, and of the Compoſite order. The baſe is compoſed of Attick and of the Ionick; having two baſtones of Attick, and the two cavettoes of the Ionick. But inſtead of two aſtragals or tondino's, which are made between the cavetto's in the Ionick, this has only one, which occupies that ſpace which the two ſhould take up.

ALL theſe members are beautifully wrought, and have moſt beautiful intaglia's. Upon the baſes of the loggia there are foliages, that ſupport the ſhafts of the columns; which are worthy of notice. And the judgment of that architect is to be praiſed, who underſtood ſo well to accommodate them (the ſhafts of the columns not having as much length as was requiſite) without taking from the work any part of its beauty and majeſty.

I HAVE alſo made uſe of this invention in the columns that I have put for an ornament to the door of the church of *S. Giorgio Maggiore* in *Venice,* which did not hold out in length as far as was requiſite; and are of ſo beautiful marble, that they could not well be left out of the work. The capital, are compoſed of the Ionick and Corinthian, the method of which has been mentioned in the firſt book, and they have acanthus' leaves.

THE architrave is beautifully carved. Its cimacium has, inſtead of the gola reverſa, a fuſaiolo, and over it a half ovolo.

THE frize is plain. The cornice has two gola diritta's, the one upon the other, a thing very ſeldom ſeen, that is, that two members of the ſame ſort ſhould be placed the one upon
the

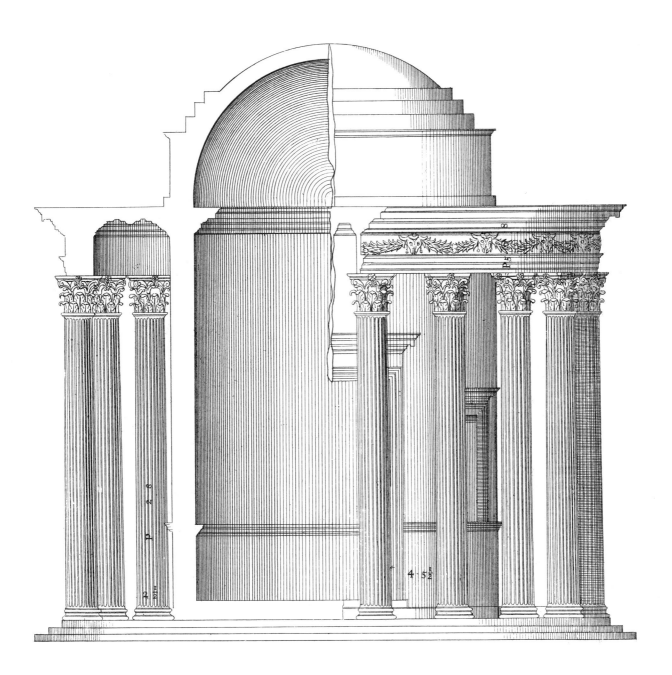

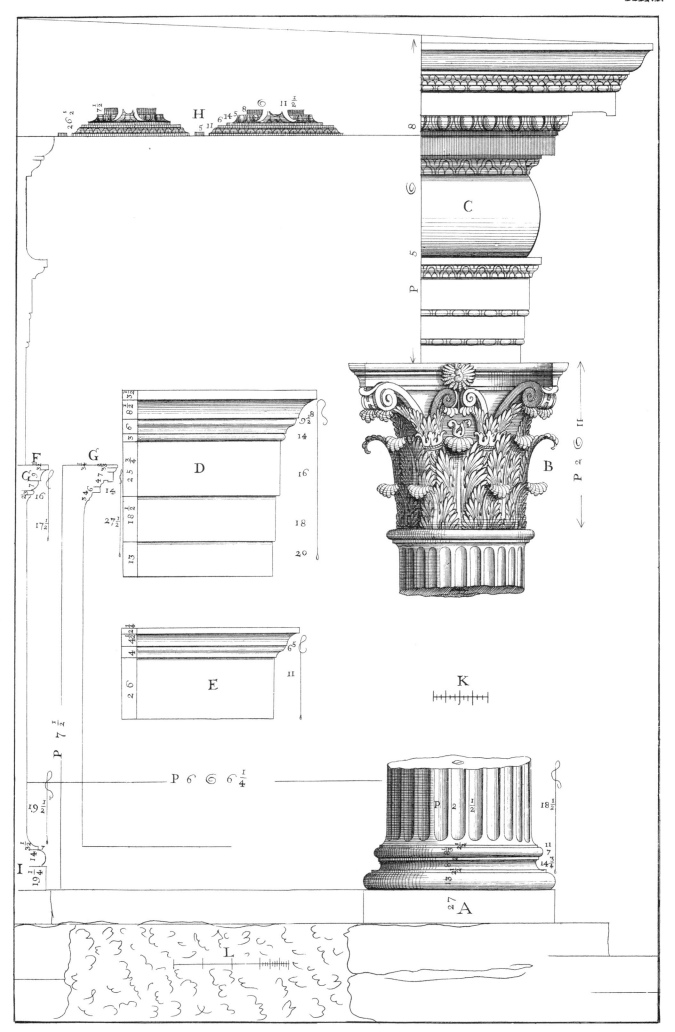

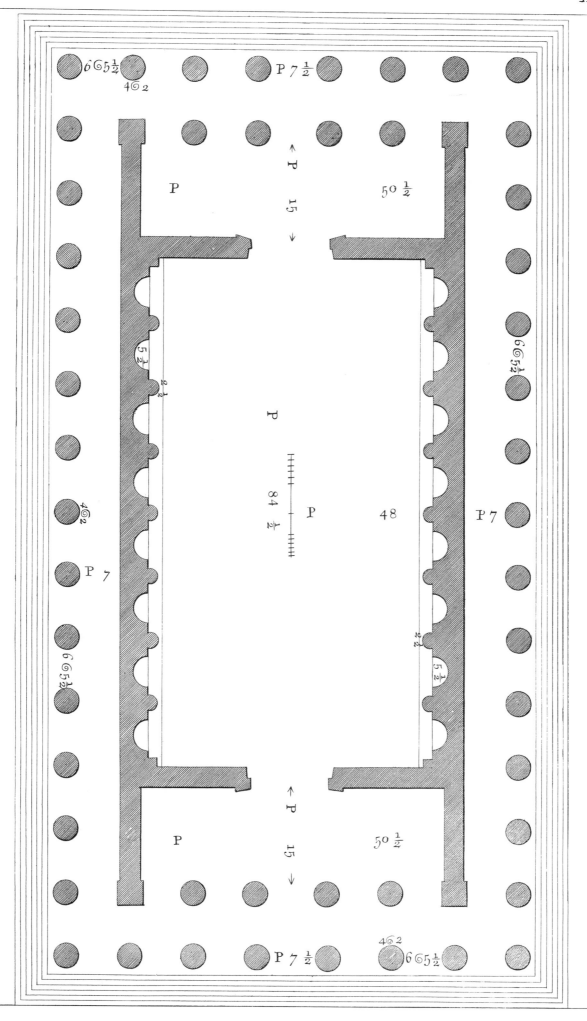

P 6 6 5½

P 4 6¼

P 4 0

P 7 6 4 ½

P 4 1

P 4 1

p 6 6 5 ½

P 4 6 2

P 6 6 5 ½

P 6 6 5 ½

P 6 6 5 ½

P 4 6 ½

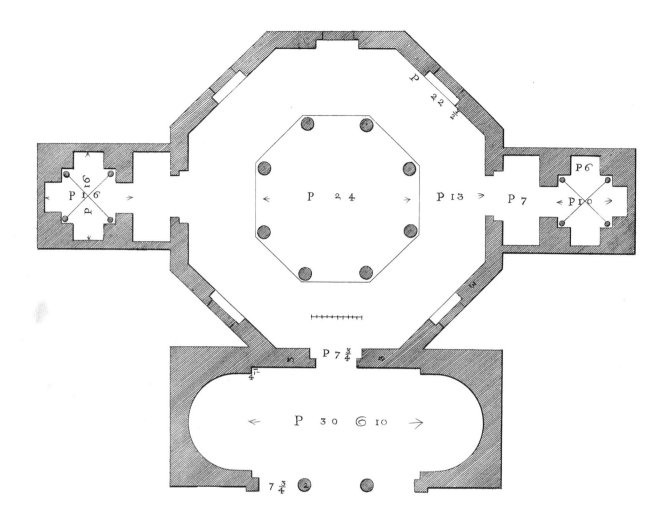

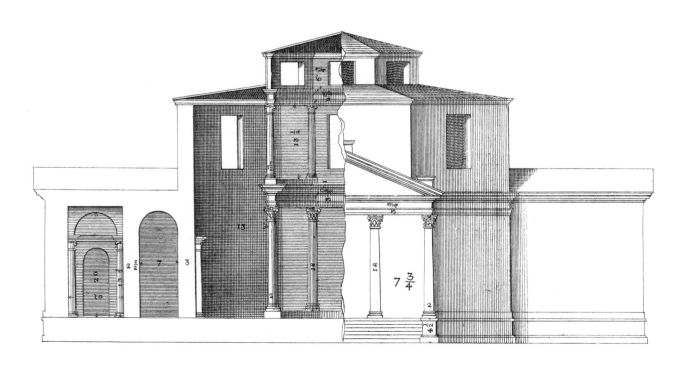

the other, without any other member between except the liftello or gradetto. Over thefe gola's there is a dentello, and then the gocciolatoio with the intavolato; and laft of all, the gola diritta: fo that in this cornice the architect obferved not to make modiglions, by making dentels in it.

Of this temple I have made two plates.

In the firft is defigned the plan and the elevation, as well of the part without, as that within. Plate 42.

In the fecond are the particular members. Plate 43.

A, *the bafe.*
B, *the capital.*
C, *the architrave, frize, and the cornice.*
D, *the foffit of the architrave between one column and the other.*
E, *the foot divided into twelve inches.*

C H A P. XVII.

Of the temple of BRAMANTE.

AFTER the grandeur of the Roman empire began to decline, through the continual inundations of the Barbarians, architecture, as well as all the other arts and fciences, left its firft beauty and elequence, and grew gradually worfe, till there fcarce remained any memory of beautiful proportions, and of the ornamented manner of building, and it was reduced to the loweft pitch that could be.

But, becaufe (all human things being in a perpetual motion) it happens that they at one time rife to the fummit of their perfection, and at another fall to the extremity of imperfection; architecture in the times of our fathers and grandfathers, breaking out of the darknefs in which it had been for a long time as it were buried, began to fhew itfelf once more to the world.

Therefore under the pontificate of pope Julius, Bramante, a moft excellent man, and an obferver of antient edifices, made moft beautiful fabricks in *Rome*; and after him followed Michel' Angelo Buonaroti, Jacobi Sansovino, Baldassar da Siena, Antonio da San Gallo, Michel da San Michele, Sebastian Serlio, Georgio Vasari, Iacobo Barozzio da Vignola, and the Cavalier Lione; of whom wonderful fabricks are to be feen in *Rome*, in *Florence*, in *Venice*, in *Milan*, and in other cities of *Italy*.

Besides which, moft of them have been at the fame time excellent painters and fculptors, as well as writers; and fome of thefe are ftill living, together with fome others whom I do not name, to avoid being tedious. But to return to our fubject.

Since Bramante was the firft who brought good, and beautiful architecture to light, which from the time of the antients had been hid; for feveral reafons it feemed to me fit, that his works fhould have a place among the antients: I have therefore placed the following temple, directed by him, upon the *Monte Janiculo*, in this book. And becaufe it was made in commemoration of St. Peter the Apoftle, who they fay was crucified there, it is called *St. Pietro Montorio*.

This temple is of Dorick work, both within and without. The columns are of granate, the bafes and the capitals of marble, the remainder is all of pietra tiburtina.

I have made two plates of it.

In the firft is the plan. Plate 44.

In the fecond is the elevation of both the outfide and in. Plate 45.

C c CHAP.

C H A P. XVIII.

Of the temple of Jupiter Stator.

BETWEEN the *Campidoglio* and the *Palatino*, near the *Foro Romano*, three columns are to be seen of the Corinthian order, which were, according to some, on the flank of the temple of VULCAN, and, according to others, of the temple of ROMULUS. There are not wanting some who say they were of the temple of JUPITER STATOR. And I am of opinion that this temple was vowed by ROMULUS when the Sabines, having by treachery taken the *Campidoglio*, and the *Rocca*, were going towards the palace in a victorious manner.

THERE have been others who have asserted that these columns, together with those that are under the *Campidoglio*, were part of a bridge, that CALIGULA made to pass from the *Palatino* to the *Campidoglio*: which opinion is known to be far from truth, because, by the ornaments, one sees that these columns were of two different edifices, and because the bridge that CALIGULA made was of wood, and passed across the *Forum Romanum*.

BUT to return to our purpose, whatever temple these columns belonged to, I have not seen any better work, or more delicately wrought. All the members have a most beautiful form, and are very well understood. I believe that the aspect of this temple was the peripteros, that is, winged round, and the manner of the picnostilos. It had eight columns in the fronts, and fifteen in the sides, reckoning those of the angles. The bases are composed of the Attick, and of the Ionick. The capitals are worthy of consideration for the beautiful invention of the intaglio's made in the abaco. The architrave, the frize, and the cornice are the fourth part of the length of the columns. The cornice alone is somewhat less in height than the architrave and frize together, which is what I have not seen in other temples.

OF this temple I have made three plates.

Plate 46.   IN the first is the elevation of the front.

Plate 47.   IN the second is designed the plan.

Plate 48.   IN the third the particular members.

> A, *the base.*
> B, *the capital.*
> C, *the architrave, the frize, and the cornice.*
> D, *is part of the soffit of the architrave between the columns.*

C H A P. XIX.

Of the temple of Jupiter, *the* Thunderer.

AT the foot of the *Campidoglio* some vestigia of the following temple are to be seen, which some say was that of JUPITER the Thunderer, and that it was built by AUGUSTUS, for the danger that he escaped when, in the Cantabrian war, in a voyage that he made by night, the litter wherein he was, was struck with lightning, by which a servant who was before was killed, without doing the least hurt to the person of AUGUSTUS. Of which I a little doubt, because the ornaments there to be seen, are wrought most delicately with most beautiful intaglio's. And it is manifest, that in the time of AUGUSTUS the works were made more solid; as may be seen in the portico of *Santa Maria Ritonda*, built by M. AGRIPPA, which is very simple, and also in other edifices. Some would have it, that the columns that are there, were of the bridge which CALIGULA made; which opinion I have just now shewn to be entirely false.

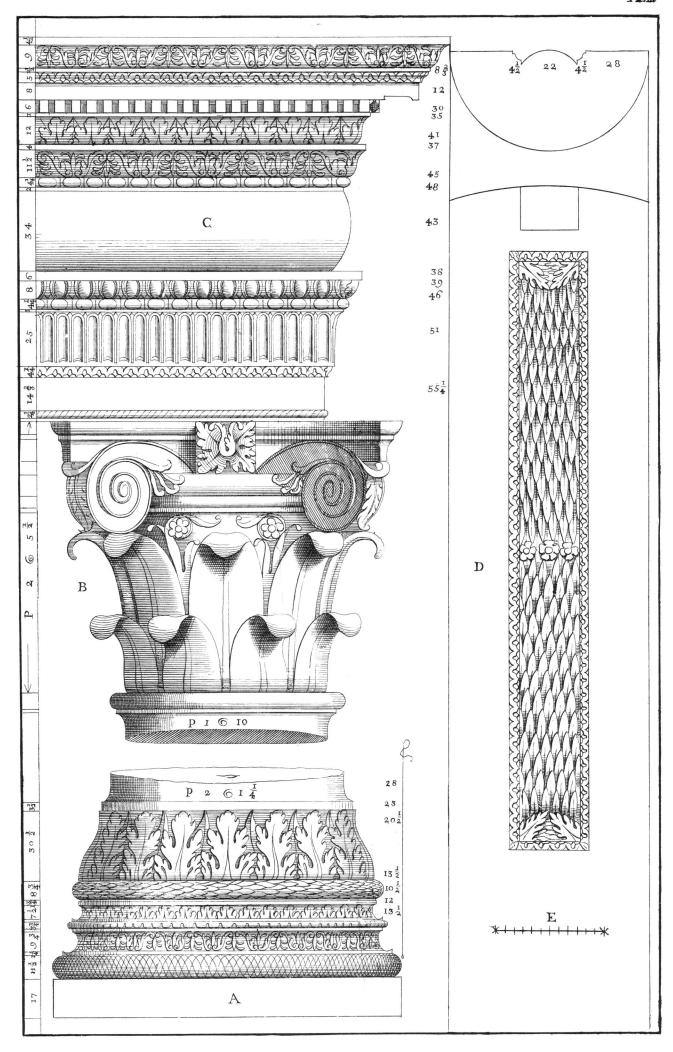

C

B

P 1 6 10

P 2 6 1¼

A

D

E

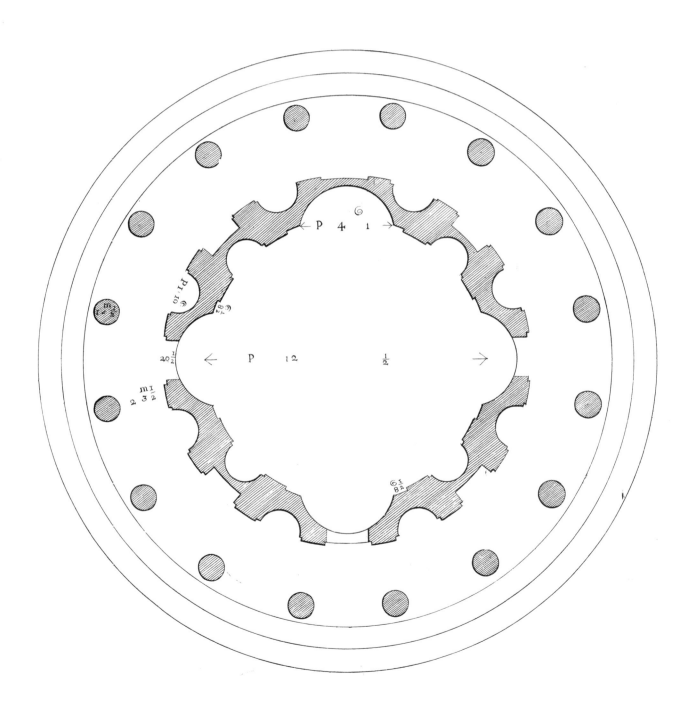

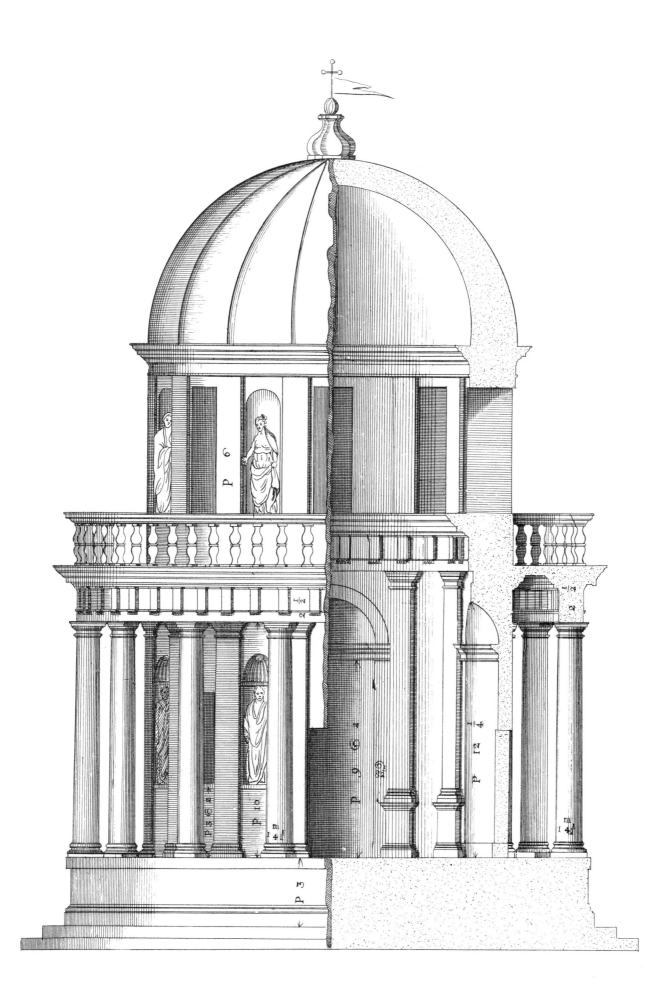

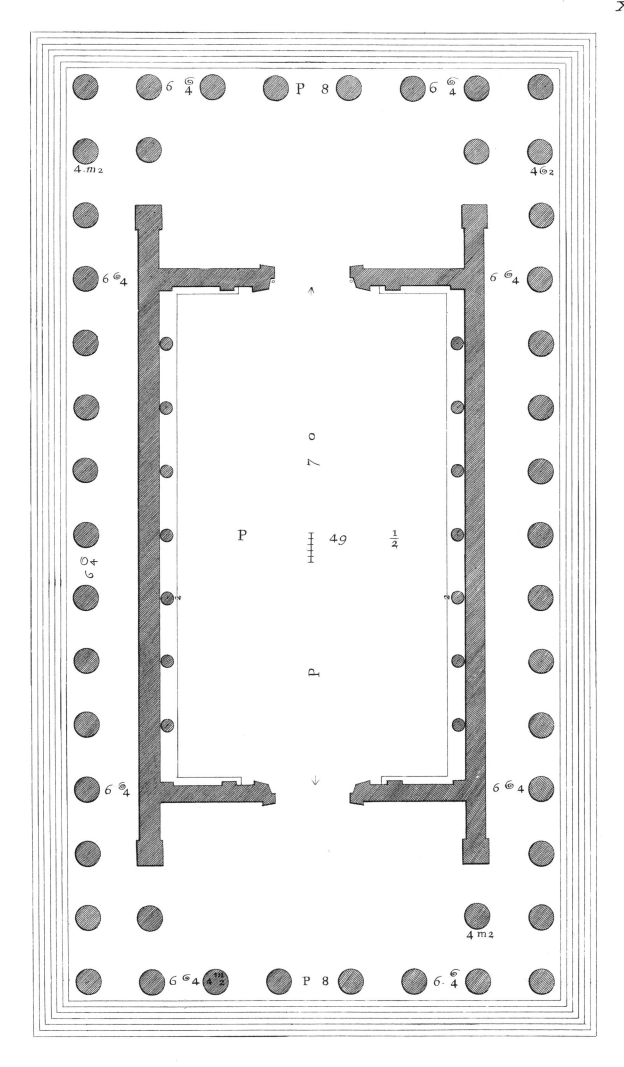

7

29

15½ 15

41

7¾

31 ¾

15 ⅓
23

39 ¾

14 ¾
25

P 2 6 9½

6
4½ 18
4 ⅔
41
3 ¾
30 ¼
4 ⅓
24 4 ¼

C

B

P 3 1½

II

4

13

37½
39½

P 1 — 1

P 1 — 7

E

P 1 — 31
P 1 — 34

15

17

20 ¼

33 ½

41

15½

19

27

30 ⅓

P 4 6 7½

39

P 1 38

15 ½
25 ½

6 4½

D 10

P

20 ⅓
5

P 4 m 2

15⅔ 4 6

3 8 17 8 2

20

33

39½

28
24
16
23 ¾
30
19
21
14

A

THE aſpect of this temple was that which was called dipteros, that is, double winged. It is very true, that in the part towards the *Campidoglio* there was no portico. But by what I have obſerved in other edifices built near hills, I am apt to believe, that it was in this part made as the plan ſhews; that is, that it had a very thick wall, which incloſed the cella, and the portico's, and then leaving a little ſpace, there was another wall, with abutments that went into the hill. Becauſe in ſuch caſes the ancients made the firſt wall very thick, that the damp might not penetrate into the inward part of the edifice; and they made the other wall with abutments, that it might be the better able to ſupport the weight of the hill; and they left the ſaid ſpace between the one and the other of the ſaid walls, that the water which fell from the hill might there have a free courſe, and do no damage to the fabrick. The manner of this temple was the picnoſtilos. The architrave, and the frize in the front were in a line, that they might contain the carving of the inſcription, and ſome of the letters are ſtill there to be ſeen. The ovolo of the cornice over the frize is different from any I have yet ſeen, with this variety, that there is in this cornice two ſorts of ovolo's, very judiciouſly made. The modiglions of this cornice are ſo diſpoſed, that directly over the columns comes a plain ſpace, and not a modiglion, as in ſome other cornices; although they regularly ought to be made ſo, that directly over the middle of the columns there ſhould come a modiglion. And becauſe by the deſigns of the temples already mentioned, the reaſons for this are alſo comprehended, I have made only two plates of it.

In the firſt is the plan.   Plate 49.

    A, *is the ſpace between the two walls.*
    B, *are the abutments that go into the hill.*
    C, *are the ſpaces between the abutments.*

In the ſecond are the particular members of the portico.   Plate 50.

    A, *the baſe.*
    B, *the capital.*
    C, *the architrave, the frize, and the cornice.*
    D, *the ſoffit of the architrave between the columns.*

CHAP. XX.

Of the PANTHEON, *now called the* Ritonda.

AMONG all the temples that are to be ſeen in *Rome*, none is more celebrated than the *Pantheon*, now called the *Ritonda*, nor that remains more entire; ſince it is to be ſeen almoſt in its firſt ſtate as to the fabric, but ſtript of the ſtatues, and other ornaments.

IT was built, according to the opinion of ſome, by M. AGRIPPA about the year of CHRIST 14. but I believe that the body of the temple was made at the time of the Republick, and that M. AGRIPPA added to it only the portico; which may be apprehended from the two frontiſpieces that are in the front.

THIS temple was called the *Pantheon*, becauſe after JUPITER, it was conſecrated to all the gods; or perhaps (as others will have it) becauſe it is of the figure of the world, that is, round; being as much in height from the pavement up to the opening, where it receives light, as it is in breadth from one wall to the other. As one deſcends now to the floor, or pavement, ſo one formerly aſcended by ſteps.

AMONG the moſt celebrated things one reads that were in the temple, there was an ivory ſtatue of MINERVA, made by PHIDIAS; and another of VENUS, who had for a pendent in her ear the half of that pearl which CLEOPATRA drank after ſupper to ſurpaſs M. ANTONY's liberality. This part only of this pearl they ſay was eſteemed to be worth 250,000 gold ducats.

ALL this temple is of the Corinthian order, both without, and within. The baſes are compoſed of the Attick, and of the Ionick. The capitals are carved in the manner of olive

I   leaves;

the architraves, the frizes, and the cornices have moſt beautiful ſacoma's, or modeno's, and are with few intaglio's.

In the thickneſs of the wall that incompaſſes the temple, there are ſome voids made, that the earth-quakes may the leſs injure the fabrick, and to ſave both materials and expence.

This temple has in the fore part a moſt beautiful portico, in the frize of which theſe words are to be read :

M. AGRIPPA L. F. COS. III FECIT.

Underneath which, that is, in the faſcia's of the architraves, in ſmaller letters, theſe other words are, which ſhew that the emperors Septimius Severus, and M. Aurelius reſtored it, after it had been conſumed by time.

IMP. CAES. SEPTIMIVS SEVERVS PIVS PERTINAX
ARABICVS PARTHICVS PONTIF. MAX. TRIB. POT.
XI. COS. III. P. P. PROCOS. ET IMP. CAES. MARCVS.
AVRELIVS ANTONINVS PIVS FELIX AVG. TRIB.
POT. V. COS. PROCOS. PANTHEVM VETVSTATE
CVM OMNI CVLTV RESTITVERVNT.

In the inward part of the temple there are, in the thickneſs of the wall, ſeven chapels with niches, in which there muſt have been ſtatues ; and between one chapel and the other there is a tabernacle, ſo that there are eight tabernacles.

It is the opinion of many, that the middle chapel, which is oppoſite to the entrance, is not antient, becauſe the arch of it breaks ſome columns of the ſecond order ; but that in the chriſtian time, after pope Boniface, who firſt dedicated this temple to divine wor-ſhip, it was enlarged ; as it was proper in chriſtian times to have a principal altar greater than the others.

But, as I obſerve that it accompanies all the reſt of the work very well, and that it has all its members exceedingly well wrought, I look upon it as certain, that it was alſo made at the time when the remainder of this edifice was erected.

This chapel has two columns, that is, one on each ſide, which project and are fluted ; and the ſpace that is between one flute and the other, is carved very neatly with an aſtragal. And becauſe all the parts of this temple are very remarkable, and that the whole may be ſeen, I have made ten plates of it.

Plate 51.   In the firſt is the plan. The ſtairs that are ſeen on each ſide of the entrance lead over the chapel to a ſecret way, which goes quite round the temple, through which one goes out to the ſteps, in order to aſcend up to the top of the edifice by ſome ſtairs that are round it.

That part of the edifice that is ſeen behind the temple, and is marked M, is part of the baths of Agrippa.

Plate 52.   In the ſecond is half of the front forwards.

Plate 53.   In the third is half of the front under the portico.

This temple has, as may be ſeen in theſe two plates, two frontiſpieces ; the one of the portico, the other in the wall of the temple.

Where thé letter T is, are ſome ſtones that come out a little : of what uſe theſe were I cannot imagine.

The beams of the portico are all made of bronzo.

Plate 54.   In the fourth plate is the elevation of the flank of the part without.

X is

XL IX.

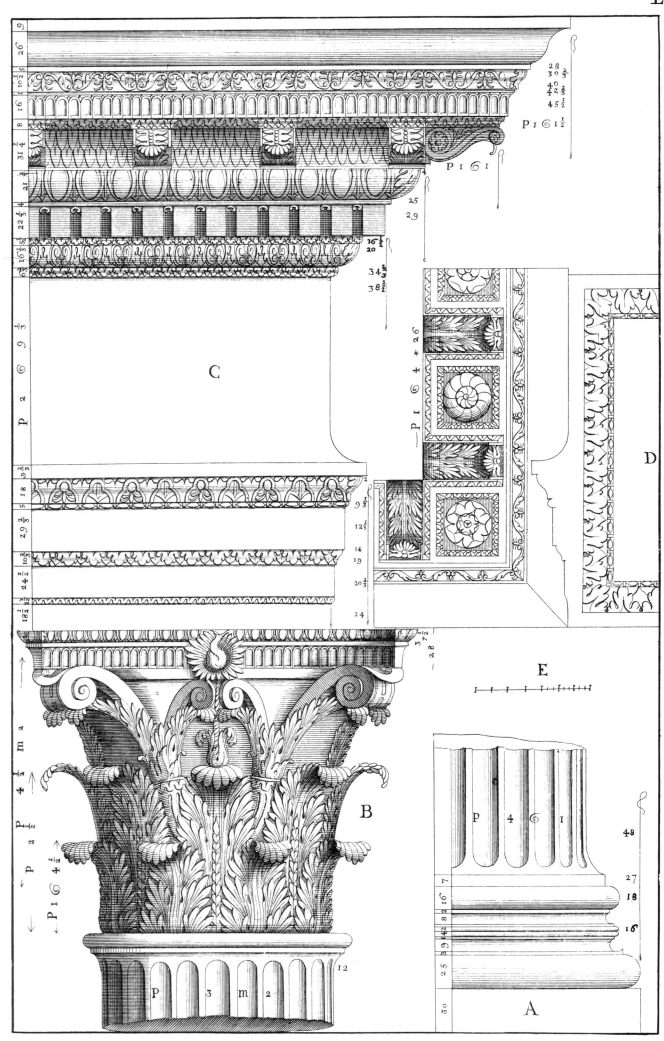

L.

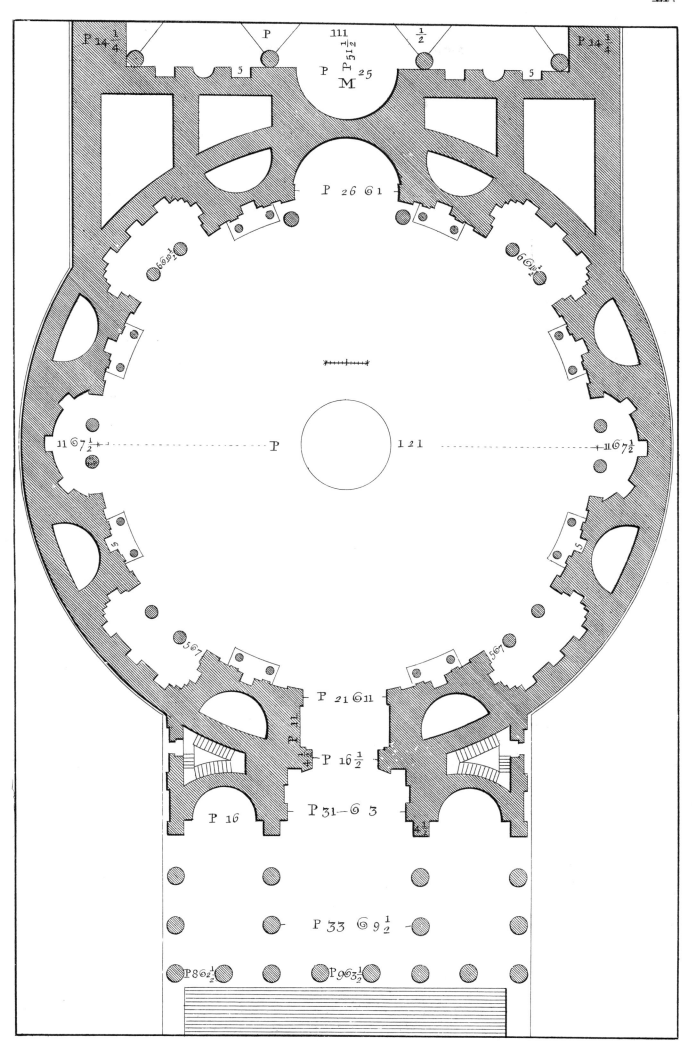

LII.

4 ¼

2 ½

4 ¼

←P.8.½

P.6.10

P.2 ½

P.2 ½

P.3.32

X

T P.2.32

P.3.42   P.5.10   P.1 ¼

V

P.5.2

22   P.10

D

E

H.5.15

P.10

P.1.29

P   36

P   16

LIII.

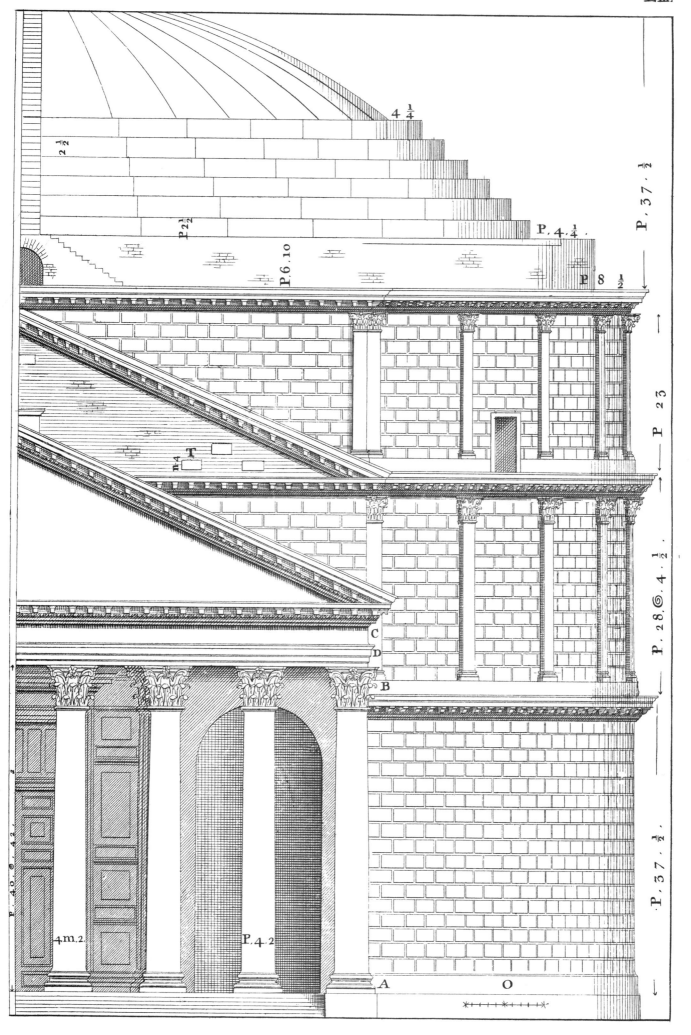

$4\frac{1}{4}$

$2\frac{1}{2}$

P.$2\frac{1}{2}$

P.6.10

P.$4\frac{1}{4}$

P.$37.\frac{1}{2}$

P.8.$\frac{1}{2}$

P.23

P

m.4. T

C
D
B

P.28.6.4.$\frac{1}{2}$

4.m.2.

P.4.2

A   O

P.40.4.2.

P.37.$\frac{1}{2}$

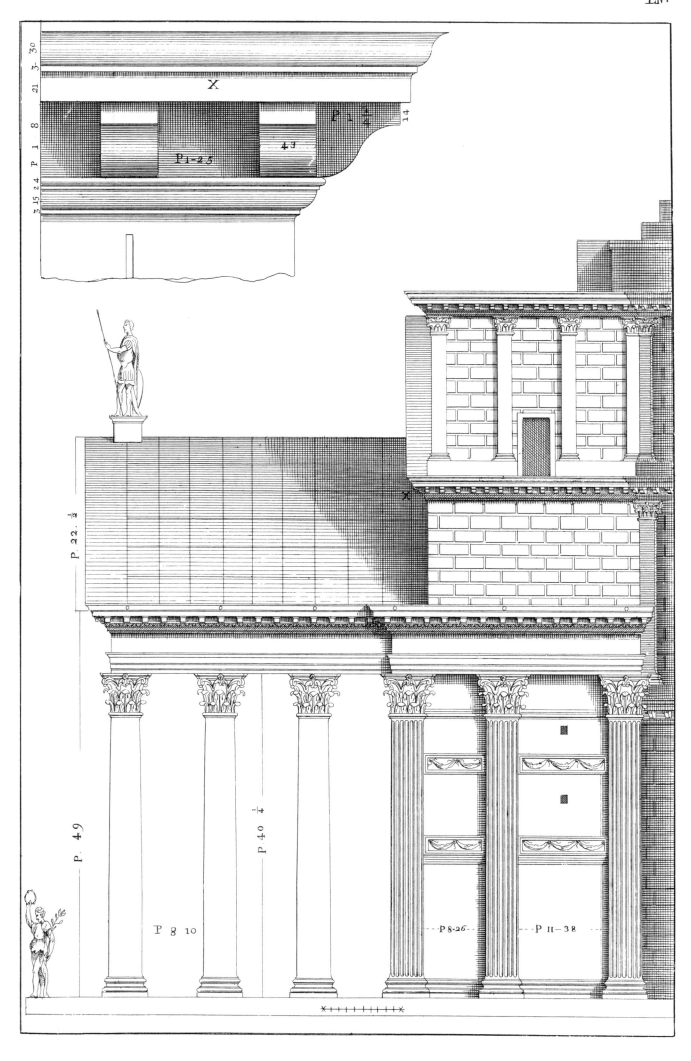

LIV

X, *is the fecond cornice that goes quite round the temple.*

IN the fifth is the elevation of the flank in the part within. Plate 55.

IN the fixth are the ornaments of the portico. Plate 56.

 A, *the bafe.*
 B, *the capital.*
 C, *the architrave, the frize and the cornice.*
 D, *is the facoma of the ornaments made over the columns, and the pilafters in the*
   inward part of the portico.
 T, *the pilafters of the portico, which anfwer to the columns.*
 V, *the windings of the caulicoli of the capitals.*
 X, *the foffit of the architrave between each column.*

IN the feventh is part of the elevation of the inward part oppofite to the entrance, where Plate 57. is to be feen how and with what ornaments, the chapels, and the tabernacles are difpofed, and how the fquares are comparted in the vault; which probably (by fome veftigia that are there) were ornamented with filver plates. Becaufe, if there had been any fuch ornaments of bronzo, there is no doubt but thofe of the like fort, which (as I have faid) are in the portico, would alfo have been taken away.

IN the eighth, in a form fomewhat larger, is defigned one of the tabernacles in front, Plate 58. with part of the chapels that are on the fides of it.

IN the ninth are the ornaments of the columns, and of the pilafters of the inward part. Plate 59.

 L, *the bafe.*
 M, *the capital.*
 N, *the architrave, the frize and the cornice.*
 O, *the windings of the caulicoli of the capitals.*
 P, *the fluting of the pilafters.*

IN the tenth are the ornaments of the tabernacles that are between the chapels; in which Plate 60. the fine judgment of the architect is to be obferved; who, to bind the architrave, the frize and the cornice of thefe tabernacles, (the pilafters of the chapels not being as much out from the wall as was neceffary to contain the projection of that cornice) he only made the gola diritta, and the remainder of the members he converted into a fafcia.

 E, *is the facoma of the ornaments of the door.*
 F, *the defign of the feftoons that are on each fide of the faid door.*

AND with this temple let an end be put to the defigns of the temples that are in *Rome.*

C H A P. XX.

Of the DESIGNS *of fome temples that are out of* Rome, *in* Italy; *and, in the firft place, of the temple of* BACCHUS.

WITHOUT the gate, as it is now called, of *Santa Agnefa,* and by the antients *Viminalis,* from the name of the hill where it is placed, the following temple is to be feen pretty intire, which is dedicated to Santa AGNESA.

I BELIEVE that it was a fepulchre, becaufe there was a very large cafe of porphry found in it, very beautifully carved with vines, and little children gathering grapes; which has made fome believe that it was the temple of BACCHUS. And becaufe it is the common opinion, and now ferves for a church, I have placed it among the temples.

BEFORE its portico the veſtigia of a court are to be ſeen, of an oval form, which I be-lieve was adorned with columns, and niches in the intercolumniations, which muſt have been for its ſtatues.

THE loggia of the temple, by what is to be ſeen of it, was made of pilaſters, and had three openings. In the inward part of the temple there were columns placed two and two, which ſupported the cuba.

ALL theſe columns are of granate ; and the baſes, the capitals, and the cornice of marble. The baſes are in the Attick manner. The capitals are of the Compoſite order, very beau-tiful, and have ſome leaves which project from the roſa, from which the voluta's ſeem to ſpring very gracefully. The architrave, the frize, and the cornice are not very well wrought ; which makes me believe that this temple was not made in good times, but in thoſe of the latter emperors. It is very rich with works, and with various compartments ; part of them of beautiful ſtones, and part of Moſaick work, as well in the pavement, as in the walls, and in the vaults.

OF this temple I have made three plates.

Plate 61.   IN the firſt is the plan.

Plate 62.   IN the ſecond the elevation.

Plate 63.   IN the third is to be ſeen how the columns were ordered that ſupport the arches upon which the tribuna reſts.

> A, *the baſe.*
> B, *the capital.*
> C, *the architrave, the frize, and the cornice.*
> D, *the beginning of the arches.*
> E, *the foot with which the ſaid members were meaſured.*

C H A P. XXII.

Of the TEMPLE *whoſe veſtigia are to be ſeen near the church of* Santo SEBASTIANO, *upon the* Via Appia.

WITHOUT the gate of *St. Sebaſtiano*, which formerly was called the *Appian* gate, from the moſt famous way (which was with wonderful art and expence made by APPIUS CLAUDIUS) are to be ſeen the veſtigia of the following edifice, near to the ſaid church of *St. Sebaſtiano*. By what can be comprehended of it, it was all of baked ſtone.

OF the loggia's that are round it there is ſtill a part ſtanding. The entrance into the ſaid cortile had double loggia's ; and on each ſide of the ſaid entrance there were rooms, that muſt have ſerved for the uſe of the prieſts.

THE temple was in the middle of the cortile. The part that is to be ſeen, and is raiſed from the ground, upon which was the floor of the temple, is moſt ſolid work, and receives light only from the doors, and from ſix ſmall windows that are in the niches, and therefore it is ſomewhat dark, as all the antient temples are. In the fore part of this temple, oppoſite to the entrance into the cortile, there are the foundations of the portico ; but the columns have been taken away. I have neverthelefs placed them of the bignefs, and diſtance, that by the ſaid foundations may be known they were of. And becauſe none of the ornaments of this temple are to be ſeen, I have made one plate only of it, in which the plan is deſigned.

Plate 64.   A, *is the floor of the temple, and of the portico from which the columns muſt have begun to riſe.*

D, *the*

22.½

40.¼

4—2

P. 8—10

P. 3

R

S

P. 4.20

P 33.¼

P. 10——44

P. 5—18

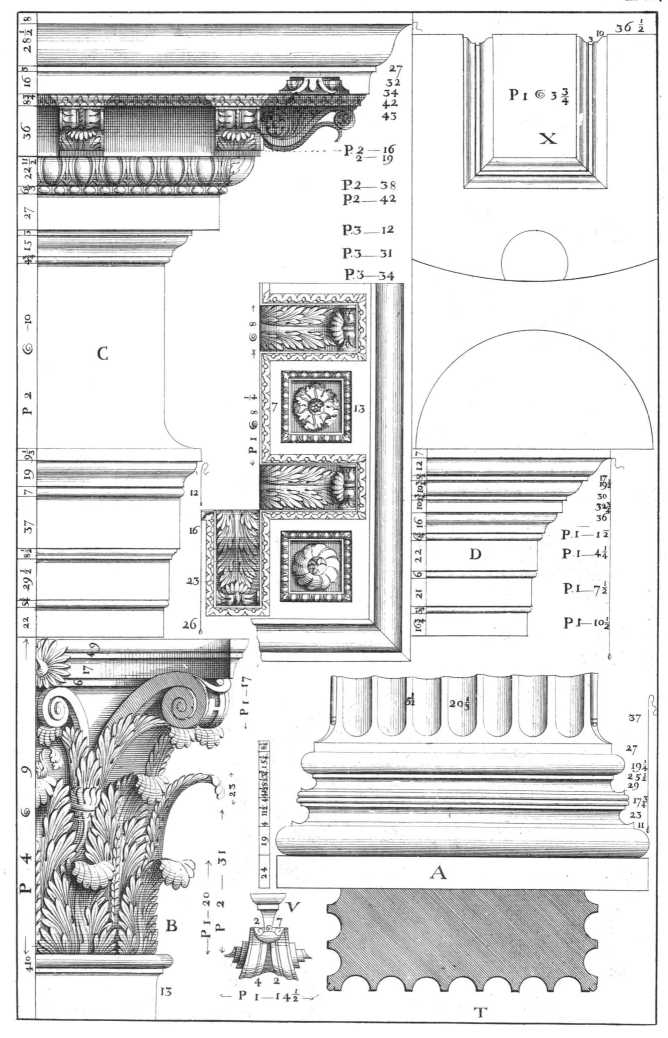

P.2 — 16
P.2 — 19

P.2 — 38
P.2 — 42

P.3 — 12

P.3 — 31

P.3 — 34

P I – 11

K

P 1½

I

P I – 2½

P 2 6 9

P I ¼   13

P I 6 9½

29

15¼

14½

P 3 – 15

H

G

19 ¾

44

E

P I

21
7
P I ——— 22
P I ——— 26
P I ——— 39
P I ——— 40½
P 2 —— 5 ⅔
P 2 —— 8 – ½

13

13⅓
15⅔

18

20

P 2 6 4

P 5 6 4

F

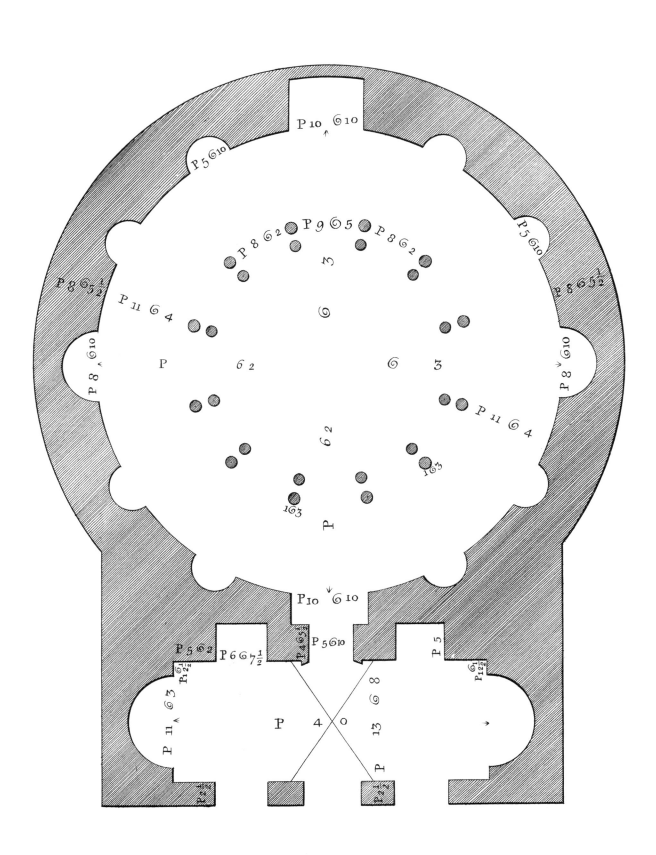

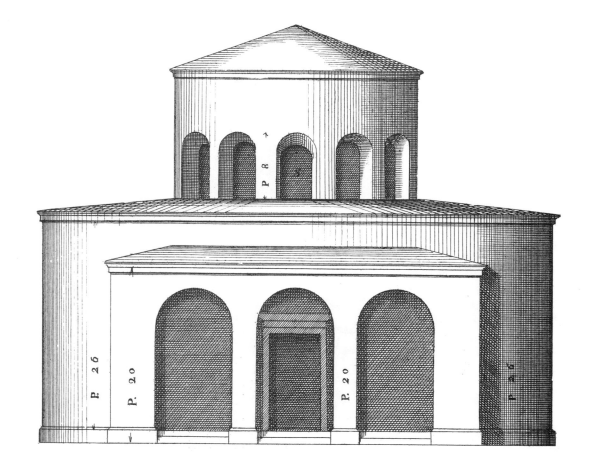

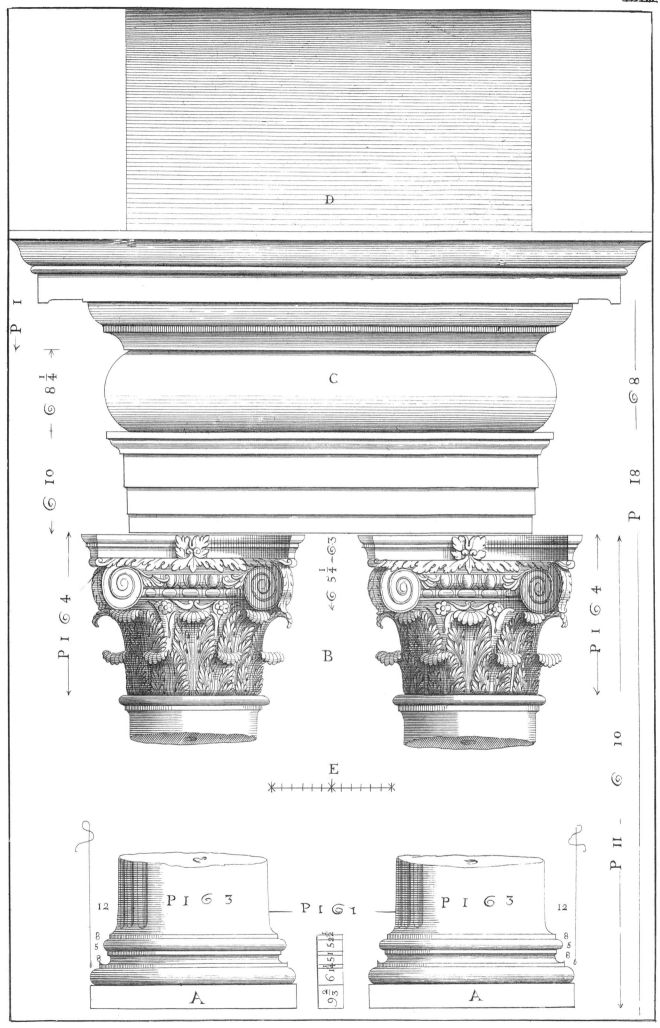

D

P I

6 10 ← 6 8 1/4 →

C

P 18 — 6 8

P I 6 4 ← 6 5 4 1/4 — 6 3 → P I 6 4

B

P I 6 4

E

P II — 6 10

12   P I 6 3 — P I 6 1 — P I 6 3   12

8   9 2/3 6 1/45 1 5 2/2   8
5   5
6   6

A   A

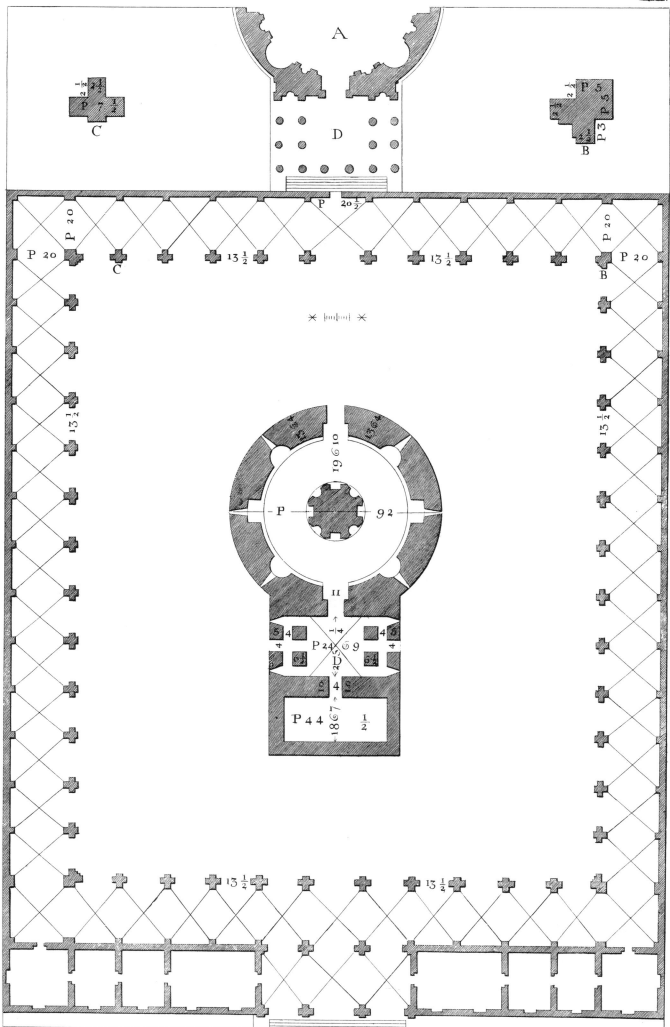

D, *the plan of the temple, and of the portico in the part under the said floor.*
B, *the angular pilasters of the cortile.*
C, *are the other pilasters, that form the loggia's round it.*

C H A P. XXIII.

Of the temple of V E S T A.

A T *Tivoli,* sixteen miles distant from *Rome,* upon the fall of the river *Aniene,* now called *Teverone,* the following round temple is to be seen, which the inhabitants of these places say was the room of the *Sibilla* T I B U R T I N A : which opinion is without any foundation. However I believe (for the reasons beforementioned) that it was a temple dedicated to the goddess V E S T A.

T H I S temple is of the Corinthian order. The intercolumniations are of two diameters. Its pavement is raised from the ground the third part of the length of the columns. The bases have no plinth, that the place to walk in under the portico might be more free and ample. The columns are as long exactly as the cell is broad, and they incline inwardly towards the wall of the cell; so that the shaft of the column above falls perpendicularly upon the shaft of the column below in the inward part.

T H E capitals are exceedingly well made, and are wrought in the manner of olive leaves; I therefore believe that it was built in good times. Its door, and the windows, are narrower in the upper part than in the lower, as V I T R U V I U S teacheth they ought to be made, in the sixth chapter of the fourth book.

A L L this temple is of pietra tiburtina covered with a very light stucco, hence it appears to be made of marble.

I H A V E made four plates of this temple.

I N the first the plan is designed.   Plate 65.

I N the second the elevation.   Plate 66.

I N the third are the members of the portico.   Plate 67.

     A, *is the basement that goes round the temple.*
     B, *the base of the columns.*
     C, *the capital.*
     D, *the architrave, the frize, and the cornice.*

I N the fourth are designed the ornaments of the door and of the windows.   Plate 68.

     A, *are the ornaments of the door.*
     B, *the ornaments of the windows in the part without.*
     C, *the ornaments of the windows in the inward part.*

T H E fascia's of the ornaments of the door, and of the windows, are different from the others that are usually made.

T H E astragals, that are under the cimacia's, project beyond the said cimacia's; a thing I have never seen in other ornaments.

                                C H A P.

C H A P. XXIV.

Of the temple of Castor and Pollux.

AT *Naples*, in a moſt beautiful part of the city, below the piazza *del Caſtello* and the *Vicaria*, the portico of a temple is to be ſeen, built and conſecrated to Castor and Pollux by Tiberius Julius Tarsus, and by Pelagon, a freedman of Augustus; as it appears by its inſcription made with theſe Greek letters:

ΤΙΒΕΡΙΟΣ ΙΟΥΛΙΟΣ ΤΑΡΣΟΣ ΔΙΟΣ ΚΟΥΡΟΙΣ ΚΑΙ ΤΗΙ ΠΟΛΕΙ ΤΟΝ ΝΑΟΝ ΚΑΙ ΤΑ ΕΝ ΤΩΙ ΝΑΩΙ.
ΠΕΛΑΓΩΝ ΣΕΒΑΣΤΟΥ ΑΠΕΛΕΥΘΕΡΟΣ ΚΑΙ ΕΠΙΤΡΟΠΟΣ ΣΥΝΤΕΛΕΣΑΣ ΕΚ ΤΩΝ ΙΔΙΩΝ ΚΑΘΙΕΡΟΣΕΝ.

That is,

TIBERIVS IVLIVS TARSVS JOVIS FILIIS, ET VRBI, TEMPLVM, ET QVAE IN TEMPLO.
PELAGON AVGVSTI LIBERTVS ET PROCVRATOR PERFICIENS EX PROPRIIS CONSECRAVIT.

Which ſignify, that Tiberius Julius Tarsus began to build this temple, and thoſe things that are within it, to the ſons of Jupiter, (that is, to Castor and Pollux) and to the city; and that Pelagon, the freedman, and commiſſary of Augustus, finiſhed it with his own money, and conſecrated it.

This portico is of the Corinthian order. The intercolumniations are more than a diameter and an half, but do not reach to two diameters. The baſes are made in the Attick manner. The capitals are carved in the manner of olive leaves, and are moſt carefully wrought. The invention of the caulicoli is very beautiful, that are under the roſa, which bind one another together, and ſeem to ſpring out of the leaves which adorn the other caulicoli in the upper part, which ſupport the horn of the capital. Hence, as well by this, as by many other examples ſcattered throughout this book, it is evident that an architect is not reſtrained from departing ſometimes from the common cuſtom, provided ſuch a variation be graceful and natural. In the frontiſpiece is carved a ſacrifice in baſſo relievo, by the hand of an excellent ſculptor.

Some ſay that in this place there were two temples, one round, and the other quadrangular. No veſtigia are to be ſeen of the round one, and the quadrangular is, in my opinion, modern; and therefore, leaving the body of the temple, I have only put the elevation of the Plate 69 front of the portico in the firſt plate, and in the ſecond its members.
and 70.

A, *the baſe.*
B, *the capital.*
C, *the architrave, the frize and the cornice.*
D, *the foot divided into twelve inches, with which the ſaid members are meaſured.*

C H A P. XXV.

Of the temple that is below Trevi.

BETWEEN *Fuligno*, and *Spoleti*, below *Trevi*, is found the little temple, of which are the deſigns that follow. The baſement which ſupports it is eight foot and an half high. To this height one aſcends by the ſteps placed on the ſides of the portico, which lead to two little portico's, that project from the remainder of the temple.

The aſpect of this temple is proſtilos. Its manner is thick of columns. The chapel that is oppoſite to the entrance into the cella has very beautiful ornaments, and the columns have wreathed flutings; and ſo theſe, as well as thoſe of the portico's, are of the Corinthian order, delicately wrought, and with beautiful variety of intaglia's. Hence, as well in this, as in all the other temples, it evidently appears, that what I have ſaid in the firſt book is true; that is, that the antients in ſuch kinds of edifices, and particularly in the ſmall ones, applied very great diligence in poliſhing each part, and in making all poſſible ornaments for
I   them,

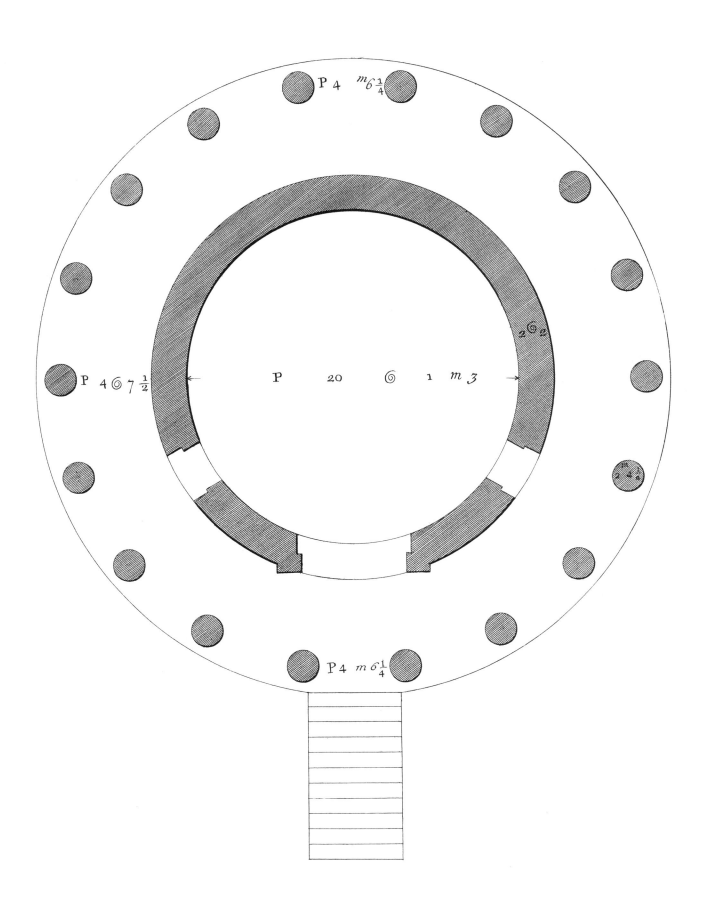

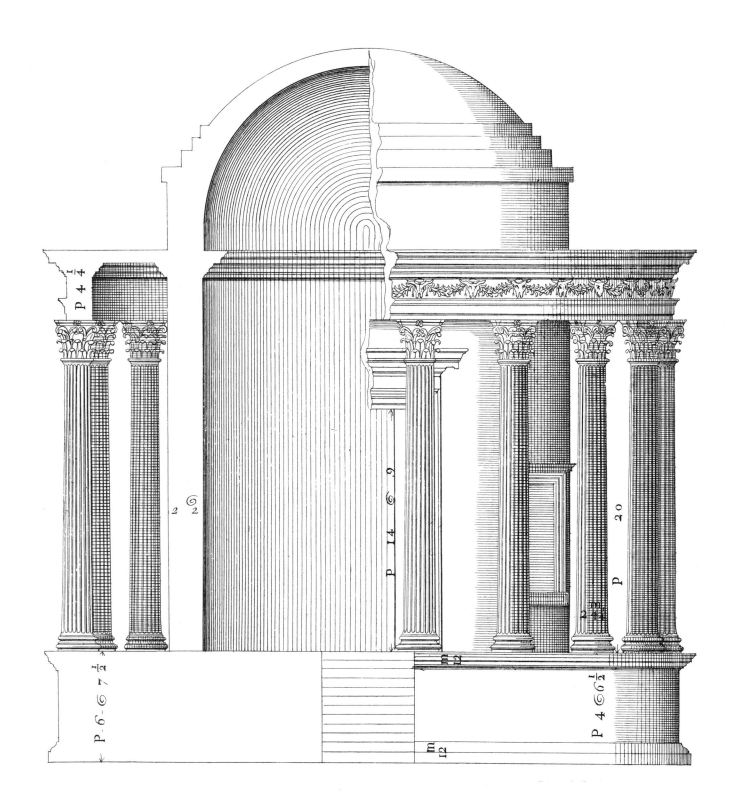

27

P.1,36.

P.2,10.

C

B

A

D

them, that they might be well : but in large fabricks, or amphitheatres, and such like, they polished some small part only, leaving the remainder rough, to save expence, and the time that would have been wasted in polishing the whole; as shall be seen in the book of the amphitheatres, which I hope soon to put out.

I HAVE made four plates of this small temple.

IN the first is the plan, where the floor of the temple is marked, A.   Plate 71.

  B, *is the plan of the portico under the said floor.*
  C, *the base*
  D, *the cimacia* } *of the basement which encompasses and supports the whole temple.*
  E, *the base of the columns of the fore front.*
  F, *the base* } *of the columns and pilasters of the little portico's, to*
  G, *the capital and cornice* } *which the steps lead.*

IN the second is the elevation of half the front on the outside.   Plate 73.

  H, *the architrave, the frize, and the cornice.*

IN the third is the elevation of half the part within.   Plate 72.

  L, *the capital of the portico.*

IN the fourth is the elevation of the flank.   Plate 74.

C H A P. XXVI.

Of the temple of S C I S I.

THE following temple is upon the piazza of *Scisi*, a city of *Umbria*, and is of the Corinthian order. The pedestals placed under the columns of the portico are well worthy notice; because, as I have said before, in all the other antient temples, the columns of the portico's are seen to come down to the ground; neither have I seen any other that had pedestals. Beneath one pedestal and the other are the steps that ascend from the piazza to the portico. The pedestals are as high as the middle intercolumniation is broad, which is two inches broader than the others. The manner of this temple is that which VITRUVIUS calls sistilos, that is, of two diameters.

THE architrave, the frize and cornice together are the fifth part and a little more of the height of the columns. The cornice, which makes the frontispiece instead of modiglions, has some leaves, and in the remainder it is entirely like that which goes directly over the columns. The cella of the temple is in length the fourth part more than its breadth.

I HAVE made three plates of it.

IN the first is the plan.   Plate 75.

IN the second is the elevation of the front forward.   Plate 76.

IN the third are the ornaments.   Plate 77.

  A, *the capital, the architrave, the frize, and the cornice.*
  B, *the pedestal, and the base of the columns.*
  C, *the cornice which forms the frontispiece.*
  D, *the foot divided into twelve inches.*

C H A P. XXVII.

Of the defigns of fome temples that are out of Italy; *and, firft, of the two temples of* POLA.

IN *Pola,* a city of *Iftria,* befides the theatre, amphitheatre, and an arch, moft beautiful edifices, of each of which mention fhall be made, and their defigns put in their places, there are upon the piazza, on the fame part, two temples of the fame bignefs, and with the fame ornaments, diftant the one from the other fifty eight feet and four inches; the defigns of which follow.

THEIR afpect is the proftilos. The manner is that, which, according to VITRUVIUS, I have before called fiftilos, that has the intercolumniations of two diameters; and the intercolumniation in the middle is of two diameters and a quarter. Round thefe temples there goes a bafement, at the height of which they have their floor, or pavement; and the afcent to it is by fteps placed in the front forwards, as has been feen in many other temples. The bafes of the columns are in the Attick manner, and have the orlo as thick as all the reft of the bafe. The capitals are in the manner of olive leaves, very neatly wrought. The caulicoli are dreffed with oak leaves; which variety is feen but in few others, and is worthy of notice. The architrave is alfo different from the greater part of the others; becaufe its firft fafcia is large, the fecond lefs, and the third under the cimacium is alfo lefs. Thefe fafcia's project forward in the lower part; which was done that the architrave might have but little projection, and thus might not obftruct the letters which are in the frize in the front, which are thefe:

ROMAE ET AVGVSTO CAESARIS INVI. F. PAT. PATRIAE.

THE foliage made in the faid frize goes round the other parts of the temple. The cornice has but few members, and is wrought with the ufual intaglia's. The ornaments of the door are not to be feen; I have, neverthelefs, inferted them in the manner I think they muft have been. The cella is in length one fourth part more than its breadth. The whole temple, including the portico, is above two fquares in length.

I HAVE made three plates of thefe temples.

Plate 78.   IN the firft is defigned the plan.

B, *is the pedeftal, upon which is the bafe of the columns.*

Plate 79.   IN the fecond is the elevation of the front forwards.

E, *the architrave, the frize and the cornice over the columns.*
P, *the ornaments of the door, made according to my invention.*

Plate 80.   IN the third is the elevation of the flank.

D, *the campana of the capital.*
F, *the plan of the faid capital.*

C H A P. XXVIII.

Of two temples of NISMES; *and, firft, of that which is called* La Maifon Quaree.

IN *Nifmes,* a city of *Provence,* which was the native country of ANTONINUS PIUS the emperor, among many other beautiful antiquities, the two following temples are to be feen. This firft is by the inhabitants of that city called *La Maifon Quaree,* becaufe it is of a quadrangular form, and they fay it was a bafilica. (What bafilica's were, their ufe, and
how

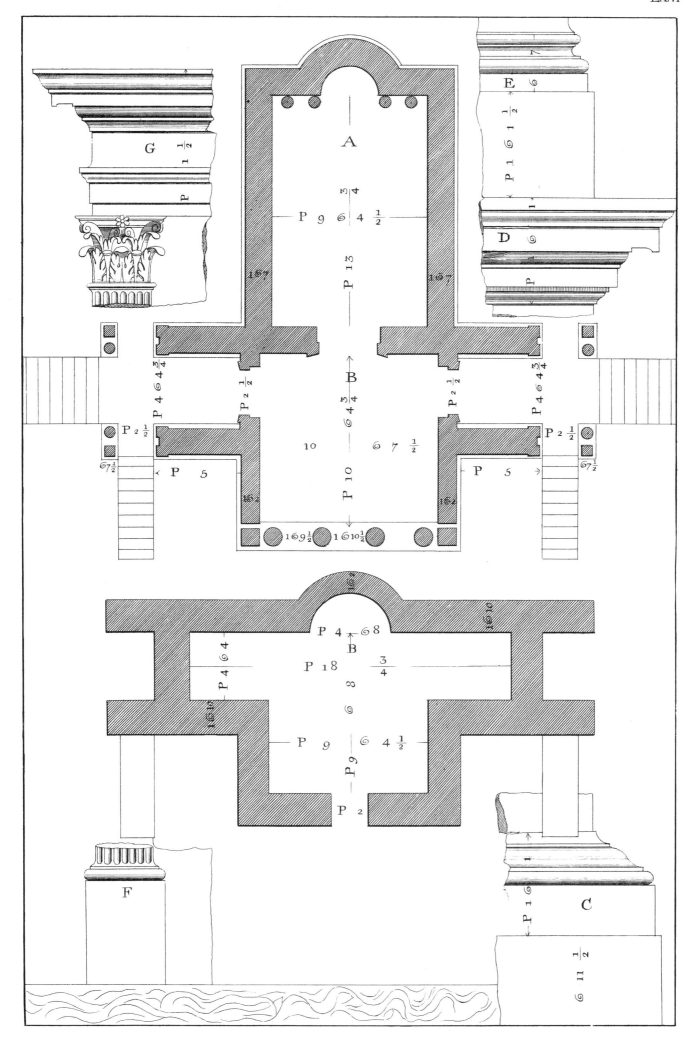

L

P 1 6 4 ½

M

P 1½

G

P 6

P 7½   P 2   ½   P   5

P 1 6 1½

L

P 11

P 3½

7 ½

P 2   3   6 8

P 2 3

P 5 6 5 ½

P 5

P 1 6 1

H

H

H

G

P 1½

P 16 2¼

6

E

P 5

P 2 ½ 7½

P 6

F

N

D

P 5 6 5 ½

C

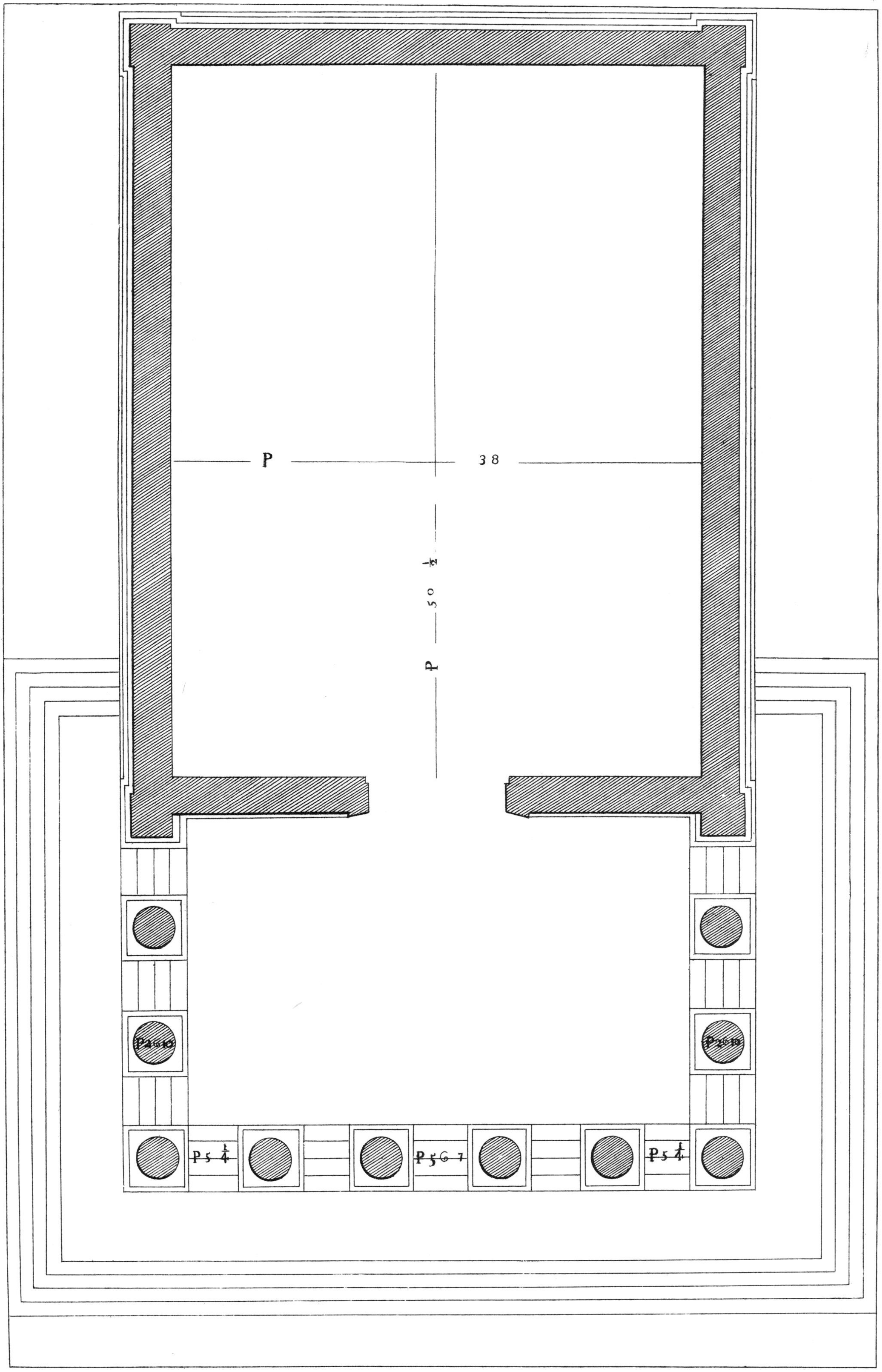

P   3 8

P   5 0 ½

P4 9 10

P 28 19

P5 ¼   P 5 6 7   P5 ¼

P 8

P 5 ½

A

P 2 7 ¼

P 6

B

P 2 6 ½

P 5 ¼

A

B

C

D

P 1-2

P 1-8

28

25

28

28

16

67

P 3 6 11 ½

P 2 6 3

P 1 6 4 ½

P 1 6 10

P 1 6 10

P — 3 — 6 2

P 2 6 5 ½

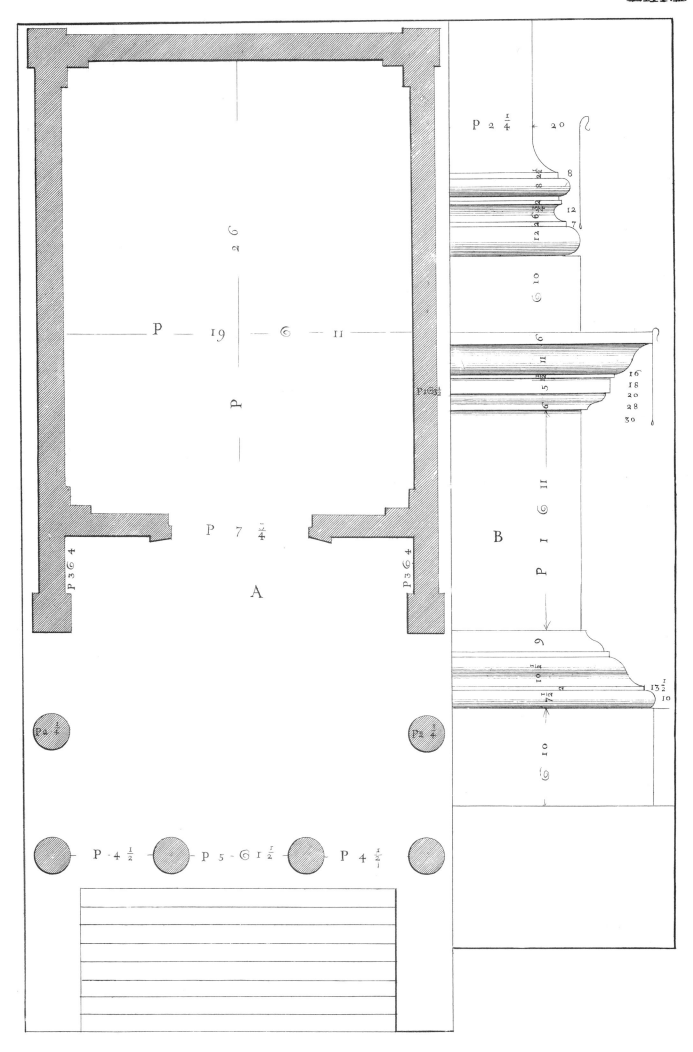

E

D

F

16

36

$6 \cdot 10\frac{1}{2}$

$5\frac{1}{4}$
$6\frac{1}{2}$

$\frac{1}{4}$

$6 \cdot 10\frac{1}{2}$

P

P I 6 I 2

P I 4

P 4 6 I

$P 4 6 7\frac{3}{4}$

$P \ 2 \ 2 \frac{1}{2}$

F

D

P 2 6 7

P 1 6 4 $\frac{1}{4}$

6 9

6 11

2 3 4 $\frac{1}{4}$ P 3 6 5

5 0 4

6 9 6

$\frac{1}{4}$
7 $\frac{1}{4}$

P 1 6 11 $\frac{1}{2}$

P 2 $\frac{1}{4}$

P 4 $\frac{1}{2}$

P 4 6 9 $\frac{1}{2}$

how they were made, has been mentioned in the third book, according to what Vitruvius says of them.) As they were of a form different from this, I believe certainly that it
was a temple. What its aspect is, and its manner, by what has been said in so many other
temples, is sufficiently manifest.

The floor of the temple is raised from the ground ten foot five inches. A pedestal
forms a basement round it, upon whose cimacia are two steps which support the base of the
columns. And it might very easily be, that it was such steps Vitruvius means,
when at the end of the third chapter of the third book he says, that in making a poggio
round a temple, the scamili impari should be made under the bases of the columns, which
are to answer directly to the body of the pedestal, which is, under the columns, and be level
under the base of the column, and above the cimacium of the pedestal; which place has
perplexed many. The base of this basement has fewer members, and is thicker than the
cimacium, which, as has been elsewhere observed, ought to be done in pedestals. The base of the
columns is Attick, but it has some bastoncini more; hence it may be called Composite, and is
suitable to the Corinthian order.

The capitals are wrought in the manner of olive leaves, and the abaco carved. The
flower placed in the middle of the front of the capital takes up the height of the abaco,
and the orlo of the campana, which I have remarked was observed in all the ancient capitals
of this kind. The architrave, the frize and the cornice, are the fourth part of the length of
the columns, and all their members are carved with most beautiful inventions. The modiglions are different from any I have seen; and this their difference from the ordinary is very
graceful. And although the capitals are in the manner of olive leaves, they are nevertheless
carved in the manner of oak leaves.

Over the gola diritta, instead of an orlo, there is an ovolo carved; which is seen but in
few cornices. The frontispiece is directly made as Vitruvius teacheth in the before mentioned place.

As there are nine parts in the length of the cornice, one is given to the height of the
frontispiece under the cornice. The erte, or pilasters of the door, are as thick in the front
as the sixth part of the breadth of the openings. This door has very beautiful ornaments,
and is very well carved. Over its cornice, and even with the pilasters, there are two pieces of
stone wrought in the manner of architraves, which project forward from the said cornice, and in
each of them there is a square hole ten inches and an half broad every way, in which I believe
beams have been put, which reached to the ground, and where an additional door might
have been made to put on and take off: which must have been made with latices, that
the people standing without might see what was doing in the temple, without hindering the
priests.

There are six plates of this temple.

In the first, which is this, is designed the plan.

Plate 81,

In the second the elevation of the front forwards.

Plate 82,

In the third the elevation of the flank.

Plate 83,

In the fourth is part of the members.

Plate 84,

A, *the base of the columns.*
B, *the cimacia* ⎫ *of the pedestal.*
C, *the base* ⎭

And afterwards there is the designs of the fourth part of the upright, and of the plan
of the capital.

In the fifth are the architrave, the frize, and the cornice.

Plate 85,

In the sixth are the ornaments of the door.

Plate 86,

E, *the perforated piece of stone placed over the cornice of the door, even with the pilasters, and projecting from them.*

The foliages which are over it, are those of the frize that goes quite round the temple over
the columns.

CHAP.

C H A P.   XXIX.

Of the other temple of NISMES.

THE following defigns are, of the other temple of *Nifmes*, which the people of the city fay was the temple of VESTA; which in my opinion cannot be, as well becaufe to VESTA the temples were made round, in refemblance of the element of the earth, of which they faid fhe was the goddefs; as alfo becaufe this temple had paffages round it, clofed by continued walls, in which were the doors on the fides of the cella, and the door of the cella was in the front, fo that it could not receive light from any part: neither can any reafon be given why temples to VESTA fhould be made obfcure; I rather therefore believe that it was dedicated to fome of their infernal gods.

IN the inward part of this temple there are tabernacles, in which ftatues muft have been. The inward front, oppofite to the door, is divided into three parts. The floor, or pavement, of the middle part, is level with the remainder of the temple. The two other parts have their floor raifed to the height of the pedeftals; and to it one afcends by two pair of ftairs, which begin in the paffages, which, as I have faid, are round this temple. The pedeftals are a little higher than the third part of the length of the columns. The bafes of the columns are compofed of the Attick, and of the Ionick, and have a moft beautiful facoma. The capitals are are alfo compofed, and very neatly wrought. The architrave, the frize, and the cornice are without intaglia's, and the ornaments placed in the tabernacles that are round the cella are alfo plain.

BEHIND the columns that are oppofite to the entrance, and which make, in our way of fpeaking, the great chapel, there are fquare pilafters, which alfo have compofed capitals, but different from thofe of the columns; and they differ alfo the one from the other, becaufe the capitals of the pilafters that are immediately near the columns, have intaglia's different from the other two; but all of them have fo beautiful and graceful a form, and are of fo beautiful an invention, that I don't remember to have ever feen capitals of that fort better and more judicioufly made.

THESE pilafters fupport the architraves of the chapels on the fides, to which one afcends, as I have faid, by the ftairs in the paffages, and therefore are by this means wider than the columns are thick; which is worthy obfervation.

THE columns that are round the cella fupport fome arches made of fquared ftones; and from one of thefe arches to the other the ftones are placed, which form the greater vault of the temple.

ALL this edifice is made of fquared ftones, and covered with flat ftones, placed in fuch a manner that the one goes over the other; that fo the rain might not penetrate.

I HAVE made ufe of the greateft diligence in thefe two temples, becaufe they feemed to me edifices worthy of great confideration; and by which it may be known that it was in a manner peculiar to that age, that in every place the good way of building was underftood. I have made five plates of this temple.

Plate 87.   IN the firft the plan is defigned.

Plate 89.   IN the fecond is half of the front oppofite to the door in the inward part.

Plate 88.   IN the third is the elevation of part of the flank.

Plate 90 *and* 91.   IN the fourth and fifth are the ornaments of the tabernacles, of the columns, and of the foffits, which are all marked with letters.

A, *the architrave, the frize, and the cornice over the columns.*

B, *the capital of the columns.*

P, *the plan.*

D, *the capital of the pilafters behind the columns.*

E, *the capital of the other pilafters.*

Plate 90.   F, *bafe of the columns and pilafters.*

G, *the pedeftal.*

H, *are the ornaments of the tabernacles, which are round the temple.*

S, *are the ornaments that belong to the tabernacle of the great chapel.*

M, R, *and* O, *are the compartments of the foffit of the faid chapel.*

THE

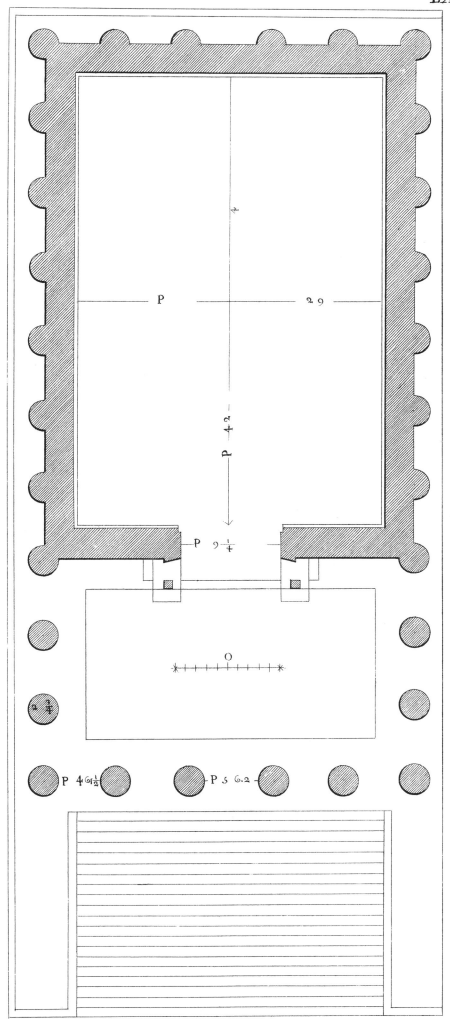

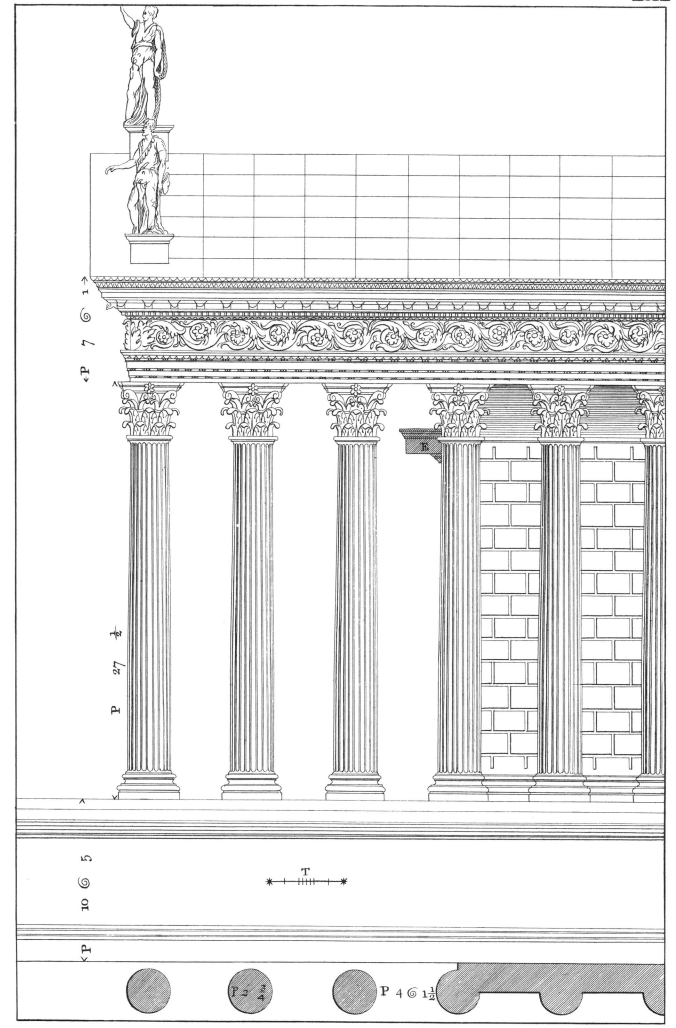

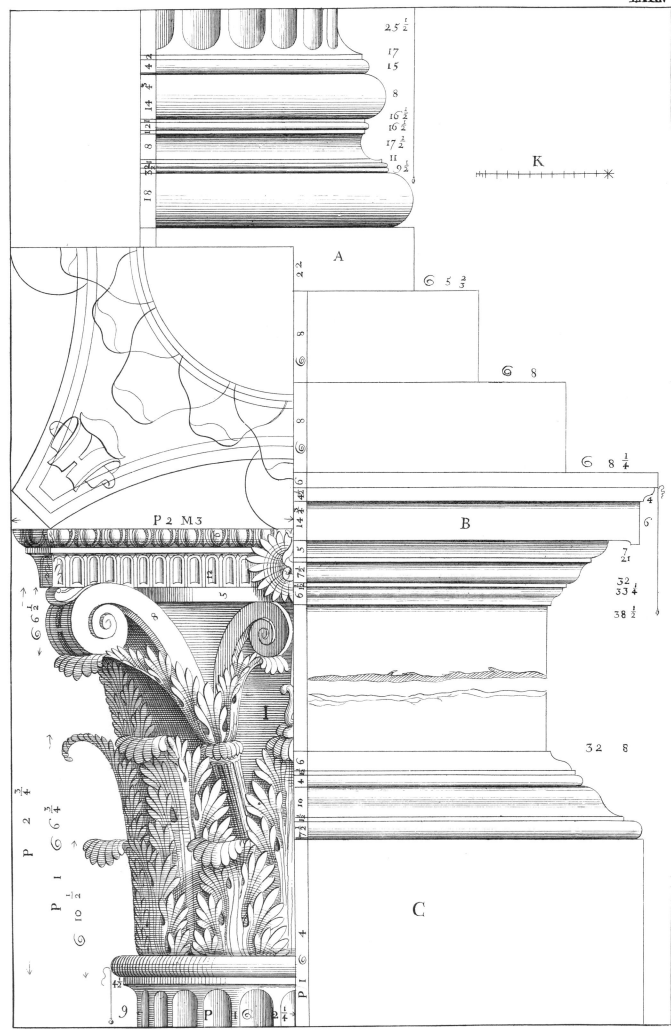

A

B

C

K

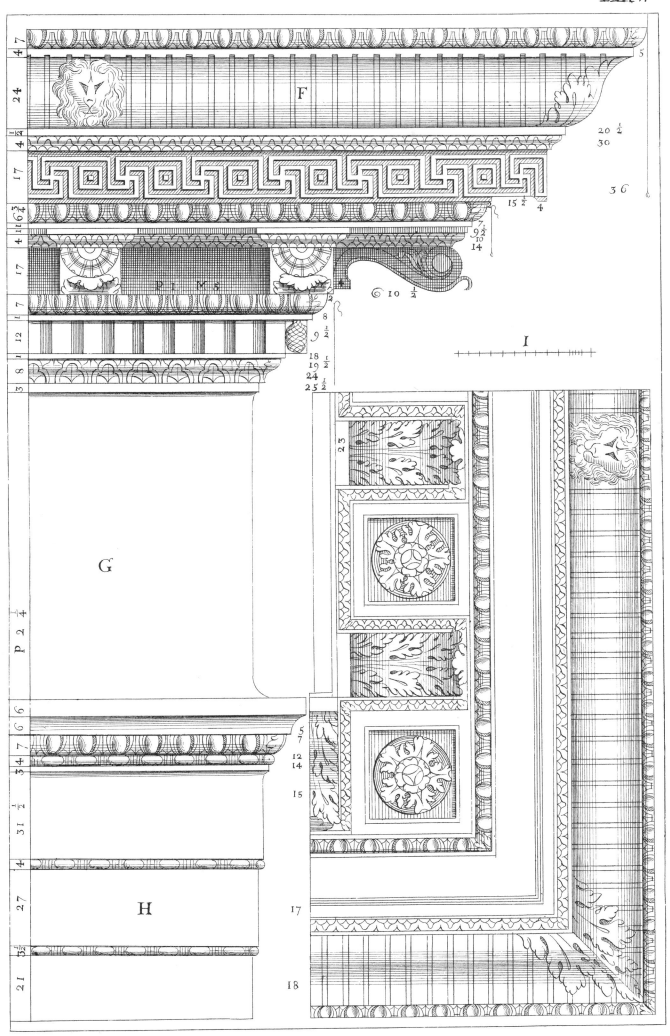

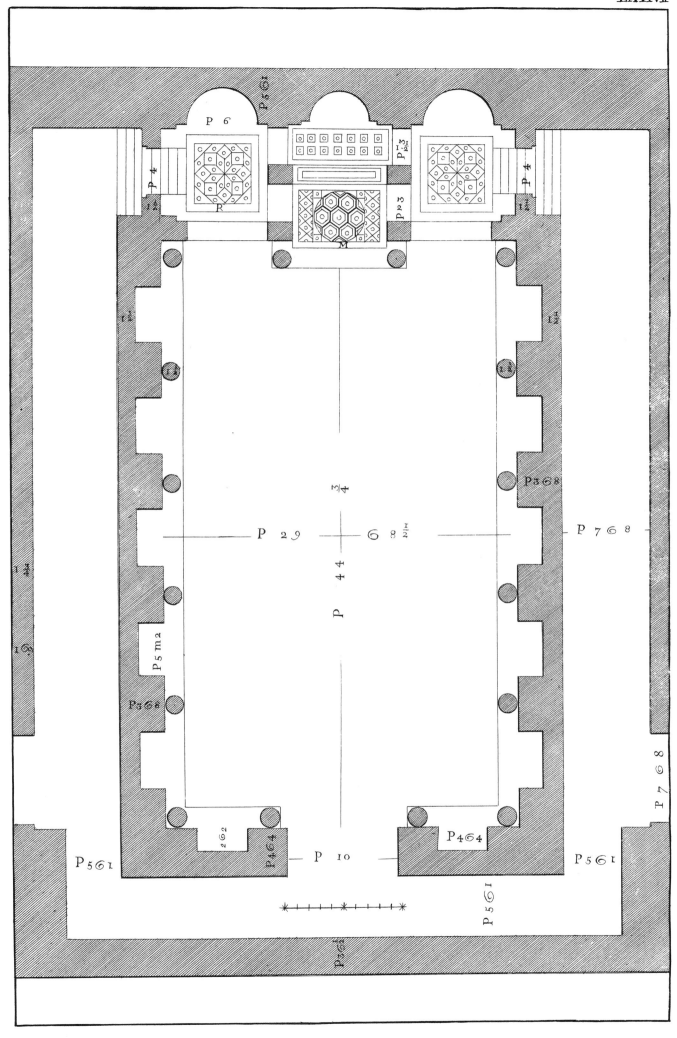

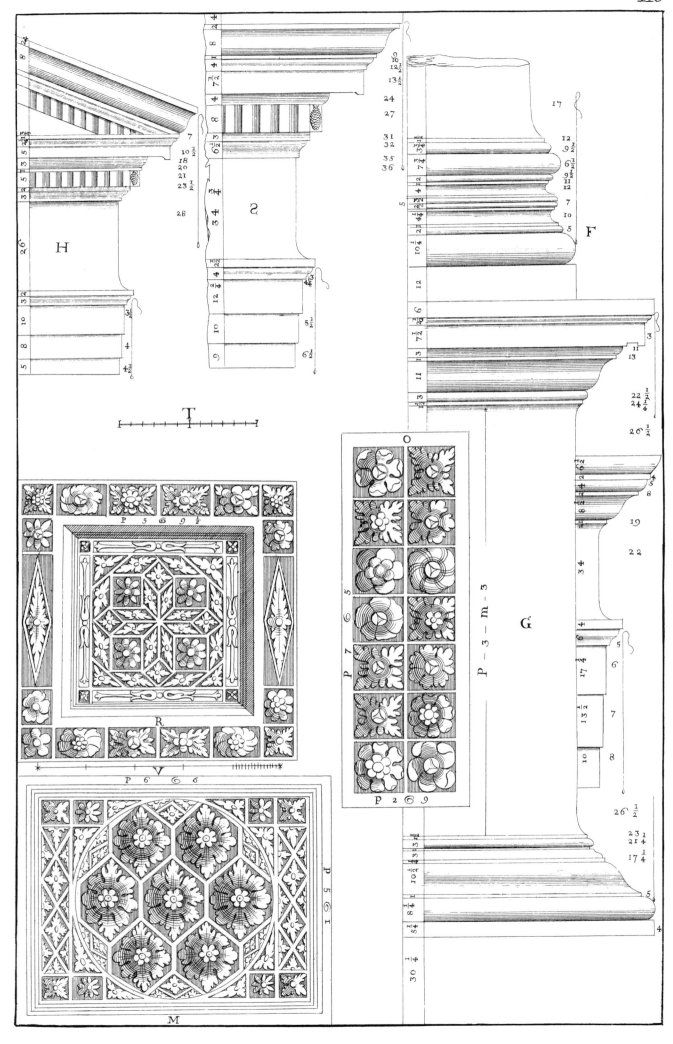

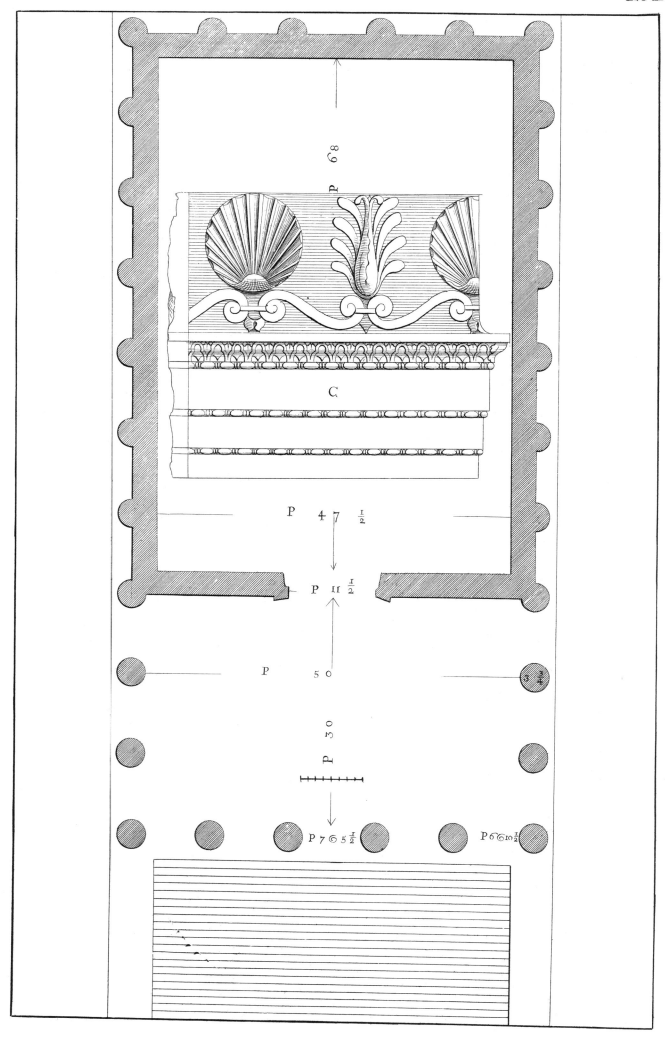

F   S. P. Q. R.   F
INCENDIO CONSVMPTVM. RESTITVIT.

C   C

P 3 3/4

P3 3/4   P3 3/4   B

A   A

3 5/4

G

P 7 6 5 1/2   P 6 6 10 1/2

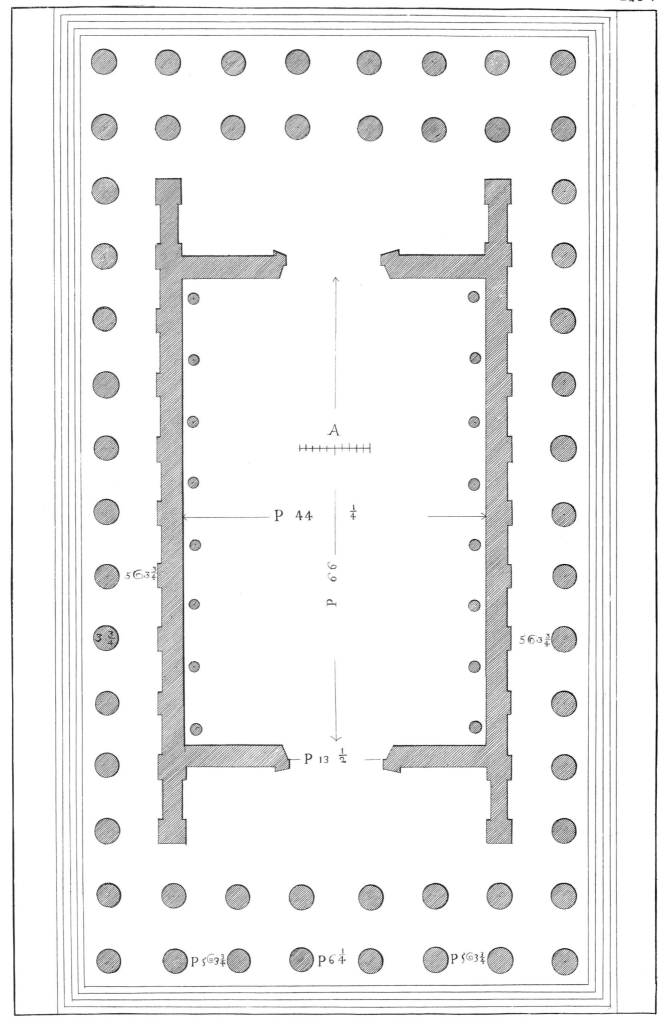

P 5

E

610

P 8½

P 38

B

F

E

A

37

6

25

7½ 3 14

16

23

25

10

44

15

1 3 4

21

17½

10

21½

A

P 563¾

P 563¾

P ¾

672½

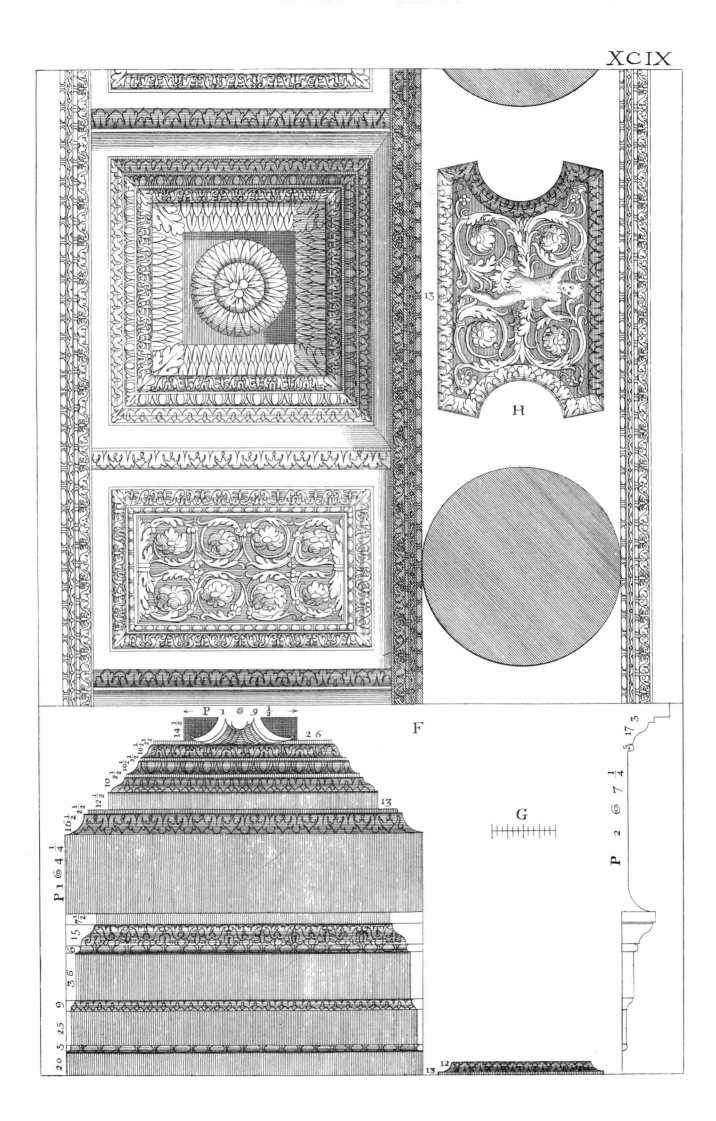

H

13

F

G

P 1 6 9 ½

14 ½
2 6

10½
2½
10½
2½
10
2½
12½
2½
16½
2½

P 1 6 4 ¼

7½
6 15
3 6
9
20 5 25

13

13 12

P 2 6 7 ¼

5 17 3

THE facoma or profile drawn near the dado of the pedeftal is of the architrave of the frize, and of the fmall cornice, which are over the pilafters, and is that which is marked C in the defign of the flank.

C H A P. XXX.

Of two other temples in Rome; *and, firft, of that of* CONCORD.

BESIDES the temples before mentioned, when thofe in *Rome* were treated of, the columns of the portico of the following temple are to be feen at the foot of the *Campidoglio*, near the arch of SEPTIMIUS, where formerly was the beginning of the *Forum Romanum*, which, in confequence of a vow, was built by F. CAMILLUS, and, according to fome, dedicated to CONCORD.

IN this temple publick affairs were very often debated; by which it may be comprehended that it was confecrated, becaufe it was in confecrated temples only, that the priefts permitted the fenate to affemble to tranfact publick affairs; and thofe only were confecrated which were built by the Augurs; hence thefe temples were alfo called curia's.

AMONG the ftatues with which it was adorned, writers make mention of that of LATONA, who had in her arms APOLLO and DIANA, her children; of that of ÆSCULAPIUS, and of HYGEIA his daughter; of that of MARS, of MINERVA, of MERCURY, and of that of VICTORIA, was in the frontifpiece of the portico, which, during the confulate of M. MARCELLUS, and of M. VALERIUS, was demolifhed by lightning.

FROM what by the infcription, which is ftill to be feen in the frize, appears, this temple was confumed by fire, and afterwards rebuilt by order of the fenate, and of the people of *Rome*. Hence I believe that it was not reftored to the beauty and perfection it had at firft. Its infcription is this:

S. P. Q. R. INCENDIO CONSUMPTUM RESTITUIT.

THAT is, the fenate and the Roman people rebuilt this temple, after it had been confumed by fire.

THE intercolumniations are lefs than two diameters. The bafes of the columns are compofed of the Attick and of the Ionick, and are fomething different from thofe which are commonly made, but are neverthelefs made in a beautiful manner. The capitals may be faid to be a mixture of the Dorick and Ionick: they are very well wrought. The architrave, and the frize in the outward part of the front are level, neither is there any diftinction between them; which was done, that an infcription might be put there. But in the part within, that is, under the portico, they are divided, and have the intaglia's, which are to be feen in the defign. The cornice is plain, that is, without intaglia's. Of the walls of the cella not the leaft part antient is to be feen; but have been fince rebuilt not very well; one may neverthelefs know how it muft have been. I have made three plates of this temple.

IN the firft the plan is defigned. Plate 92.

  G, *the architrave and the frize, which are under the portico.*

IN the fecond is the elevation of the front of the temple. Plate 93

IN the third are the members. Plate 94.

A, *the bafement which went quite round the temple.*
B, *the bafe of the columns.*
C, *the front of the capital.*

D, *the plan*
E, *the facoma without the voluta* } *of the capital.*
F, *the architrave, the frize and the cornice.*

C H A P. XXXI.

Of the temple of NEPTUNE.

OPPOSITE to the temple of MARS the *Avenger*, of which the defigns have been already given, in the place that is called *in Pantano*, which is behind *Morforio*, was antiently the following temple, the foundations of which were difcovered in digging to build a houfe; and there was alfo found a very great quantity of marbles, all of them moft excellently wrought.

It is not known by whom it was built, nor to what god it had been confecrated. But becaufe in the fragments of the gola diritta of its cornice, one fees dolphins carved, and in fome places between each dolphin there are tridents, I believe that it was dedicated to Neptune. The afpect of it is winged round. Its manner thick of columns. The intercolumniations were one twelfth part of the diameter of the columns lefs than a diameter and an half, which I judge worthy to be obferved, as I have never feen intercolumniations fo fmall in any other antient edifice. Of this temple not the leaft part is to be feen ftanding; but from its remains, which are many, it is that one has come to the knowledge of the whole, that is, of the plan, and of the elevation, and of its particular members, which are all wrought with wonderful artifice. I have made five plates of it.

Plate 95.   In the firft is the plan.

Plate 96.   In the fecond is the elevation of half the front without the portico.

D, *is the modeno of the door.*

Plate 97.   In the third is the elevation of half the front, under the portico, that is, the firft columns being taken away.

A, *the profile of the pilafters that are round the cella of the temple, oppofite to the columns of the portico.*
E, *the profile of the wall of the cella in the part without.*

Plate 98.   In the fourth are the particular members, that is, the ornaments.

A, *the bafe.*
B, *the capital; over which are the architrave, the frize, and the cornice.*

Plate 99.   In the fifth are the compartments, and the intaglia's of the foffits of the portico's which were round the cella.

F, *the proffile of the foffits.*   H, *the foffit of the architrave between one*
G, *the foot divided into twelve inches.*   *capital and another.*

W. Kent Invt.   I. Wart Sculpt.

FINIS.